EATING,
BODY WEIGHT, and
PERFORMANCE in
ATHLETES

Disorders of Modern Society

KELLY D. BROWNELL, PhD

Professor of Psychology
Professor of Epidemiology and Public Health
Yale University
New Haven, Connecticut

JUDITH RODIN, PhD

Philip R. Allen Professor of Psychology
Professor of Medicine and Psychiatry
Dean of the Graduate School of Arts and Sciences
Yale University
New Haven, Connecticut

JACK H. WILMORE, PhD

Margie Gurley Seay Centennial Professor of Kinesiology
University of Texas at Austin
Austin, Texas

EATING,
BODY WEIGHT, and
PERFORMANCE IN
ATHLETES

Disorders of Modern Society

| LEA & FEBIGER | 1992 | Philadelphia ▪ London |

Lea & Febiger
200 Chester Field Parkway
Malvern, Pennsylvania 19355
U.S.A.
(215) 251-2230

Executive Editor—George Mundorff
Developmental Editor—Tanya Lazar
Project Editor—David Amundson
Production Manager—Samuel A. Rondinelli

Library of Congress Cataloging-in-Publication Data

Eating, body weight, and performance in athletes : disorders of modern
  society / Kelly D. Brownell, Judith Rodin, Jack H. Wilmore.
      p.   cm.
  Includes index.
  ISBN 0-8121-1474-4
    1. Athletes—Nutrition.   2. Physical education and training.
I. Brownell, Kelly D.   II. Rodin, Judith.   III. Wilmore, Jack H.,
1938–
TX361.A8E38   1992
613.2'024796—dc20   91-4939
                                                                    CIP

Reprints of chapters may be purchased from Lea & Febiger in quantities of 100 or more.

PRINTED IN THE UNITED STATES OF AMERICA

Print number: 5   4   3   2   1

For life's greatest gifts, my children, Matthew, Kevin, and Kristy Brownell

—Kelly D. Brownell

For my son, Alex, who makes life so unendingly special

—Judith Rodin

For my wife, Dottie, and my daughters, Wendy, Kristi, and Melissa

—Jack H. Wilmore

CONTRIBUTORS

ARNOLD E. ANDERSEN, M.D.
Associate Professor of Psychiatry and Behavioral Sciences
Director, Eating and Weight Disorders Clinic
Johns Hopkins Hospital
Baltimore, Maryland

JACQUELINE R. BERNING, M.S., R.D.
Nutrition Consultant
U.S. Swimming
Nutrition Consultant
University of Colorado Athletic Department
Fort Collins, Colorado

KELLY D. BROWNELL, Ph.D.
Professor of Psychology
Professor of Epidemiology and Public Health
Yale University
New Haven, Connecticut

DAVID L. COSTILL, Ph.D.
Director, Human Performance Laboratory
Ball State University
Muncie, Indiana

ROD K. DISHMAN, Ph.D.
Professor and Director, Behavioral Fitness Laboratory
University of Georgia
Athens, Georgia

BARBARA L. DRINKWATER, Ph.D.
Research Physiologist
Pacific Medical Center
Seattle, Washington

E. RANDY EICHNER, M.D.
Professor of Medicine
Chief of Hematology
University of Oklahoma Health Sciences Center
Oklahoma City, Oklahoma

KATHLEEN L. ELDREDGE, M.S.
Psychology Intern
Palo Alto Department of Veterans Affairs
Palo Alto, California

KEVIN FRANKE, Ph.D.
Assistant Clinical Professor
Department of Psychiatry
Northwestern University Medical School
Chicago, Illinois

EDWARD S. HORTON, M.D.
Professor and Chairman, Department of Medicine
University of Vermont College of Medicine
Burlington, Vermont

CRAIG L. JOHNSON, Ph.D.
Executive Director, Department of Psychology
Laureate Psychiatric Clinic and Hospital
Tulsa, Oklahoma

LYNN LARSON, M.Phil.
Department of Psychology
Yale University
New Haven, Connecticut

DONNA A. LOPIANO, Ph.D.
Director, Intercollegiate Athletics for Women
University of Texas at Austin
Austin, Texas

ROBERT M. MALINA, Ph.D.
Professor of Kinesiology and Health Education
College of Health Education
University of Texas at Austin
Austin, Texas

CAROL N. MEREDITH, Ph.D.
Assistant Professor of Internal Medicine
School of Medicine
University of California
Davis, California

JAMES E. MITCHELL, M.D.
Professor of Psychiatry
University of Minnesota Medical School
Minneapolis, Minnesota

ERIC T. POEHLMAN, Ph.D.
Assistant Professor of Medicine
University of Vermont
Burlington, Vermont

CLAIRE POMEROY, M.D.
Assistant Professor of Medicine
University of Minnesota Medical School
Minneapolis, Minnesota

JUDITH RODIN, Ph.D.
Philip R. Allen Professor of Psychology
Professor of Medicine and Psychiatry
Dean of the Graduate School of Arts and Sciences
Yale University
New Haven, Connecticut

RANDA RYAN, M.S.
Performance Team Director
Intercollegiate Athletics for Women
University of Texas at Austin
Austin, Texas

SUZANNE N. STEEN, M.S., R.D.
Sports Nutritionist, Scientific Director of Clinical Trials
Center for the Study of Nutrition and Medicine
New England Deaconess Hospital
Boston, Massachusetts

JUDITH S. STERN, Sc.D.
Professor and Director, Food Intake Laboratory
Department of Nutrition and
Division of Clinical Nutrition and Metabolism
University of California
Davis, California

DAVID L. TOBIN, Ph.D.
Director, Eating Disorders Program
Assistant Director of Psychiatry
Department of Psychiatry
University of Chicago
Chicago, Illinois

MICHELLE P. WARREN, M.D.
Associate Professor of Clinical Obstetrics and
Gynecology and Clinical Medicine
Head, Reproductive Endocrinology
St. Luke's-Roosevelt Hospital
New York, New York

HARVEY P. WEINGARTEN, Ph.D.
Professor and Chair, Department of Psychology
Associate Member, Department of Medicine
McMaster University Medical Center
Hamilton, Ontario
Canada

JACK H. WILMORE, Ph.D.
Margie Gurley Seay Centennial Professor of Kinesiology
University of Texas at Austin
Austin, Texas

G. TERENCE WILSON, Ph.D.
Oscar K. Buros Professor of Psychology
Rutgers University
Piscataway, New Jersey

CONNEE ZOTOS, Ph.D.
Lecturer in Kinesiology
University of Texas at Austin
Austin, Texas

CONTENTS

IV. EFFECTS OF EATING AND WEIGHT PROBLEMS ON THE ATHLETE

V. APPLIED ISSUES

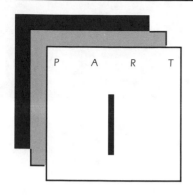

P A R T

I

INTRODUCTION

EATING, BODY WEIGHT, AND PERFORMANCE IN ATHLETES: AN INTRODUCTION

Kelly D. Brownell, Judith Rodin, and Jack H. Wilmore

Eating disturbances, weight preoccupation, and frank eating disorders among athletes are being recognized as important issues. Increasing numbers of studies on these topics are being published in the scientific literature. Articles in magazines and newspapers paint a picture of secrecy and torment among the sufferers. Coaches, parents, athletic administrators, and the athletes themselves ask for information on diagnosis and management. A few athletic departments have established programs and have staff members identified to deal with these issues.

This growing recognition notwithstanding, the response to the problem lags far behind its importance. Athletes are being hospitalized, even attempting suicide, because of psychological problems related to eating and weight. Many with eating problems feel shame and embarrassment and keep the problem hidden. Parents are concerned, but they do not know how to respond. Coaches have many reactions, ranging from fear, guilt, and anger to genuine concern. Some ignore the problem, others refuse to accept responsibility, and still others cooperate with efforts to intervene. Athletic administrators are concerned about the welfare of their athletes, and they are aware of the adverse publicity created when highly visible athletes have their athletic careers threatened by eating disorders. Teammates often realize that a problem exists but are reluctant to speak with the coach or the afflicted athlete.

The purpose of this book is to integrate, evaluate, and synthesize information on eating and weight problems in athletes. Information is available from many sources, but it has not been assembled into a coherent picture or systematically evaluated. Studies are scattered among the literatures of many disciplines. Practical experience with these problems exists among countless athletes, coaches, and administrators, but it has not been put to paper. Our objective is to collect and integrate this information to identify: (1) the scope of the problem; (2) the genesis of the problem; (3) the effects on health, psychological well-being, and performance, and (4) appropriate methods for prevention and management of the problem.

To lay the foundation for this book, this chapter gives an overview of the field, beginning with examples of how eating and weight issues have drawn increasing attention at many levels. Then we discuss the factors that place athletes at risk for these problems, why the problems are so often hidden, and how the organization of the book is designed to accomplish our objectives.

☐ CASE EXAMPLES

Liz Natale, a former Division I All-American in track, while recovering from anorexia nervosa, participated in a conference on eating disorders in athletes.[1] The report from the conference represents an interesting case history:

Liz brought the audience to tears as she explained the psychological pressure that contributed to her eating disorder. She explained that her coach felt she would never be successful if she didn't lose weight. Liz also felt threatened that she could lose her grant-in-aid. She told of the physical and emotional strain of starving during the season and "blimping out" during the off season. Today, she said, she still suffers from the medical and psychological consequences of her disordered eating behavior.

When Liz first played organized soccer as a youngster, she was the fastest player on the team. Her teammates and coaches were impressed that she would always be the first one to the ball. She said she internalized the message that people would like her only if she was fast.

With this thinking as a foundation, she entered college. She weighed 132 pounds, with 10% body fat. She was told that this was way too much weight for a runner. Nobody ever had told her to lose weight or even commented about her body. It was at this point that she became self-conscious of her diet, and her problems began.

At the end of her freshman year, Liz qualified for the Division I outdoor track championships and advanced to the semifinals, an outstanding accomplishment for a first year runner. But she did not make the finals. As the runners were lining up for the final, her coach told her she was not running because she was not as skinny as the finalists.

When she returned home for the summer, her mother was moved to tears because some of Liz's hair had fallen out, a direct result of her eating disorder. While at home that summer, Liz ate normally and gained weight. But when she began school in the fall, she stopped eating again.

Liz noticed that her personality began to change, and she didn't socialize at all. All she cared about was how much she weighed and how she trained.[1]

This example shows how preoccupation with eating and weight can affect the health, psychological functioning, and performance of the athlete. It also highlights how a problem can be caused, or at least supported, by demands of the coach, the intense competition of modern athletics, and the personality of the athlete.

These issues are also highlighted in the second case example, this time with a swimmer. One of us (KDB) interviewed an Olympic swimmer and found that weight was a major issue for her and her coach. She was a muscular college senior favored to win her event in the 1988 Olympics in Seoul, South Korea. She competed for a college team with a coach notorious for a hard-line stance on weight. Knowing that she was so successful, I predicted that her coach would not be concerned with her weight. Quite the contrary occurred. The interview went something like this:

KDB: You must feel good about your body and your weight, considering how well you have done athletically.

Athlete: I do feel good, and at my current weight, I feel I have never trained better.

KDB: What do you weigh?

Athlete: 162 pounds, but my coach wants me to weigh 154.

KDB: I thought you had never trained better. Why the 154 pounds?

Athlete: Because that's what I weighed last year when I set the world record.

KDB: What does the coach do?

Athlete: He reminds me of my weight a lot, and I have to train differently than I would like.

KDB: How so?

Athlete: After our afternoon workout, which lasts about 2 hours, most people on the team work out in the weight room. This is what I feel I need. Instead, I have to run to lose the weight.

KDB: How hard is it to lose the weight?

Athlete: It's very hard. No matter how hard I train and how much I run, my body stays at a higher weight.

These case examples cannot be used to define the nature and extent of these problems with athletes in general. They do show the pressure some athletes feel and how this can be manifested in concerns with eating and weight. In some cases, these concerns translate into healthy habits that improve performance and the general well-being of the athlete. In other cases, behaviors and attitudes are not healthy, and major problems develop.

☐ PRESS ACCOUNTS

On August 3, 1989, the Associated Press carried a story about eating disorders among female athletes at the University of Texas in Austin and the pressure exerted by coaches to reduce weight. The release stated that "an alarming number of women athletes at the University of Texas in Austin have eating disorders" and that the problem had been particularly severe among members of swimming teams produced by one former coach.

According to the AP release, the *Austin American-Statesman* had reported that in the previous 18 months one of every 10 female athletes—a total of 12—at UT had been diagnosed as having a serious eating disorder. In a series of stories compiled from university records and interviews, the *American Statesman* said that virtually all the cases had been traced to the pressure and training methods of their coaches. Another 20 to 30% of the UT women athletes had shown symptoms of an eating disorder, and 50 to 60% had expressed "tremendous concern" about their weight, according to a survey of female athletes at UT.

The release stated that, according to the *American-Statesman*, the eating disorders had been most prevalent among members of one coach's nationally ranked swimming teams. The coach, who led the swimming team "to five NCAA championships in 6 years, emphasized weight in training and competition and insisted that swimmers remain under maximum weight limits. Those who failed to do so were required to participate in special workouts."

Current and former members of the swimming team said the pressure to meet the coach's guidelines was "so intense that many routinely fasted, induced vomiting, used laxatives and diuretics, or exercised in addition to workouts. They did not want to be relegated to a group they called 'the fat club.' " One two-time Olympic medal swimmer said her fear of reporting to workouts while over the weight guidelines led her into a bulimic cycle of binges and purges that finally made it necessary for her to be hospitalized for 9 weeks. The former coach, according to the release, said he didn't recall when he first learned of the swimmer's problem and that he wasn't aware of it "until toward the end."

This account is interesting for several reasons. First, it shows the tendency to blame athletic programs for fostering and then hiding these serious problems. This is justified in some cases but not in others. The University of Texas, for example, was one of the first to establish a program to deal with eating problems (see Chapter 22). This open attitude might have made the problems of their athletes more visible to the press. Second, it highlights the perceived pressure exerted by some coaches to control the weights of their athletes. Again, this might be justified in some cases, but it points to the need for involvement of coaches in any program designed to identify and remedy eating problems in athletes.

☐ ATTENTION AT THE NATIONAL LEVEL

The National Collegiate Athletic Association (NCAA) launched an educational program on eating disorders in 1989 entitled "Nutrition and Eating Disorders in College Athletics." The program included a series of videotapes on eating and its disorders for athletes, coaches, trainers, and others involved in collegiate sports. Accompanying these tapes were written materials, articles, and posters (Fig. 1–1).

We believe the NCAA effort is both justified and necessary. Such a group has credibility and can assemble the expertise needed to recommend a comprehensive program. Even at the college level, many schools are not likely to have the necessary expertise or resources to mount a program. Even less is available at the junior high and high school levels. Having national organizations take the lead should generate considerable visibility and sensitivity to the problems, and we hope lead to the development of concrete programs for dealing with athletes.

☐ FACTORS THAT MAY PREDISPOSE ATHLETES TO EATING DISORDERS

If athletes are at increased risk for eating and weight problems, it is important to identify the factors that place them at risk. The development of eating and weight problems in athletes has cultural, psychological, and physiological bases. These issues are covered in detail in Chapters 8 through 12 and in Chapter 18, but we would like to provide some background information in this chapter.

CULTURAL FACTORS

Young people, especially women, are faced with enormous pressure to be thin and to have an aesthetically pleasing body shape (see Chapter 10). Having the perfect body symbolizes self-control, mastery, acceptance, and other factors our society values.[2,3] The ideal has become increasingly lean and physically fit, since the 1950s, so athletes face the pressure that exists in society in general to conform to the esthetic ideal. The underlying concept is that the body is infinitely malleable—that with the right diet and exercise, it can be shaped and molded as one

Fig. 1–1. Poster distributed to member colleges by the National Collegiate Athletic Association. The poster portrays how the athlete's life can be controlled by weight concerns and lists the warning signs for anorexia and bulimia.

wishes.[2,4] This ignores, of course, the considerable literature suggesting that there are biological limits to how much the body can change (see Chapters 2, 3, and 6).

PSYCHOLOGICAL FACTORS

A number of the psychological risk factors for eating disorders are common in athletes. Examples are a compulsive, driven quality about exercise and weight control, perfectionistic attitudes, competitiveness, and intense concern with performance. These qualities might lead to excellence in athletic performance, but they also place an individual at risk for eating disorders. Distinguishing the beneficial from the pathologic can be difficult.

One can see some qualities of athletes even in the descriptions of the psychological aspects of severe eating disorders. In a review of psychological aspects of anorexia nervosa, Strober noted that different diagnostic criteria have been used over time but that several discriminating features emerge consistently:[5]

1. Self-inflicted weight loss accompanied thereafter by a sustained avoidance of mature body shape, which cannot be directly ascribed to other identifiable causes
2. A morbid and persistent dread of fat
3. The manipulation of body weight through dietary restraint, self-induced vomiting, abuse or purgatives, or excessive exercise
4. Disturbances in body image, manifest in misrepresentation of actual body dimensions or extreme loathing of bodily functions
5. Amenorrhea and the development of other behavioral-physiological sequelae of starvation

Overlap exists in both the behavior and the attitudes of people with eating disorders and some athletes. The issue of cause and effect, however, as well as merely coincidental overlap in character types, needs to be considered. It is possible that individuals with personality and behaviors characteristic of the eating disorders gravitate toward athletics. The competitiveness, perfectionism, intensive exercise, and ability to restrict food intake might predispose a person to success in athletics.

The reverse side of the cause and effect picture suggests that some individuals at risk enter sports and that the training, pressure, and demands of the sport create eating and weight problems. Finally, it is possible that there are merely surface similarities between the eating and weight concerns of athletes and of people with eating disorders, and that these similar profiles are created by different underlying causes. Each of these hypotheses is considered in detail in this book. We believe that participation in modern athletics increases risk for eating and weight problems, including clinical eating disorders. Whether this occurs only in individuals who are susceptible when they enter sports is less clear.

BIOLOGICAL FACTORS

Another issue that must be considered is developmental biology. In young women particularly, with training and competition occurring at younger ages, the fight to control eating and weight occurs at a time when important biological changes can be exerting pressure in the opposite direction. During adolescence, body fat increases dramatically in females, presumably in preparation for reproduction. The athlete who challenges the body by restricting food intake and lowering weight confronts a natural biological process. We can only speculate at this point about the psychological and physiological effects created when the body fights back.

Menstrual function is an example of where sports and biology collide. Some athletes consider menstrual cycles a nuisance, or even a major barrier to performance. The cessation of menses, or in younger athletes, the delay of menarche, is frequently considered a blessing. Amenorrhea is a significant problem in some sports (see Chapter 15 by Warren), and too little is known about its psychosocial and health effects or about its long-term effects on fertility.

If the body responds to dieting and weight loss as a threat, lowering energy requirements can be a natural response. In fact, a number of studies point to surprisingly low calorie intakes in highly-trained female athletes in particular.[6-12] In three such studies, for example, the average daily intake for female runners was 1,759 calories, but the mean intake was 1,541 calories for amenorrheic runners and 1977 calories for eumenorrheic runners.[7-9] This suggests that there is a relationship between menstrual function and low energy intake.

The data indicate that many athletes exist on low levels of calories. Given their low body fat and high levels of exercise, one would expect that they might need and be able to support a much higher intake. Yet many athletes claim they cannot eat more without gaining weight. Without prospective studies, it is not possible to determine whether the exercise and restricted weight cause low calorie needs or whether the finding is merely correlational. However, the fact that calorie requirements are low in many athletes creates what we believe is a biological risk factor for eating disorders. An individual who must exist on so few calories must greatly increase the degree of dietary restraint necessary to control intake. This sets the stage for the attitudes (e.g., preoccupation with eating and weight) and behaviors (e.g., binge eating) that predispose an individual to eating disorders. The use of dangerous dieting practices such as fasting, vomiting, diuretics, and fluid restriction is the likely consequence.

FACTORS SPECIFIC TO ATHLETICS

The pressure to perform and the level of competition in modern athletics have never been greater. With more television exposure and the large amounts of money involved in professional sports, athletes are eager to attempt any measure to give them an advantage. In sports in which winners are distinguished from losers by hundredths of a second or by small differences in judges' ratings, it is easy to see how losing an extra few pounds or eating in the proper manner might be thought to provide a competitive edge.

The intense competition among today's athletes places an enormous burden on the individual athlete. Many athletes train or compete year-round, so few have the opportunity to pursue other interests. It is common to hear of athletes who have been groomed by parents and coaches from an early age to be elite performers; by the time such athletes reach their peak, they essentially have no life outside the sport. Given the pivotal role their sport plays in their life, it is not surprising that the pressure to gain any competitive edge is intense. Weight and eating patterns can often become the lightning rod for this pressure.

Athletes have many roles to fulfill (see Chapter 18). The days are numbered for the student-athletes who are students in name only. Colleges are under increasing scrutiny with respect to admissions standards, required curriculum, and graduation rates for athletes. Athletes, therefore, must function as students in addition to excelling at their sports.

ARE ATHLETES AT HIGH RISK?

The definitive answer to this question can only come from longitudinal studies in which athletes and nonathletes are followed for considerable periods of time. Such studies do not exist, as discussed in the chapter on the prevalence of eating disorders (Chapter 9). Therefore we must use other, less direct methods of answering this question.

Evidence from three sources converges to indicate that athletes are at increased risk for eating disturbances. First, given the known risk factors for eating disorders (as discussed above), athletes should be at increased risk. They exist in a highly competitive culture in which the manipulation of eating and weight is thought to be essential for both performance and appearance. The psychological characteristics associated with eating disorders, including perfectionistic standards, might be the very factors that drive some athletes to be as good as they are. Biological changes resulting from weight restriction can also interact with eating behavior to place a person at risk.

Existing studies on eating problems in athletes comprise the second source of information on this topic. These studies are discussed in detail in Chapter 9. Some studies show fewer problems or the same number of problems among athletes as in control groups, but more evidence shows significant problems. The precise prevalence of eating disturbances in athletes in various sports cannot be determined from existing data. The general picture one develops from reviewing the literature is that a problem does exist.

The third source of information is from the world of athletics. There is a growing consensus among those involved with athletics that there is a problem. College athletics departments have begun establishing programs to identify and aid athletes with these problems. As mentioned above, the NCAA has launched an educational program on the eating disorders aimed at coaches, athletes, and athletic administrators.

For these reasons, it appears that athletes *are* at high risk. The chapters in this book discuss the sources of this risk, how risk becomes reality in specific individuals, the effects of these problems on behavior, health, and performance, and how the problems can be managed.

☐ THE HIDDEN NATURE OF THE PROBLEM

Chapter 9 in this book integrates the literature on the prevalence of eating disturbances in athletes. The chapter shows that estimates of prevalence vary widely and that much of the necessary research has not been done. We would like briefly to present two of our own research experiences that illustrate how secret these problems can be.

In a study of female athletes, we administered a questionnaire to 110 elite athletes representing 7 different sports. Of the 87 respondents, none scored in the disordered eating range with a standardized questionnaire measure. Within 2 years following the study, 18 of the athletes had to receive either inpatient or outpatient treatment for eating disorders.

In the course of a similar study, this time with 9 amenorrheic and 5 eumenorrheic nationally ranked distance runners, 3 were identified with a standardized, validated questionnaire to have "possible" problems but did not have clearly diagnosable eating disorders based on their responses to the questions. Four of the 9 amenorrheic runners were subsequently diagnosed with anorexia nervosa, 2 with bulimia nervosa, and 1 with both. None of the 5 eumenorrheic runners was later diagnosed with eating disorders.

These experiences, although admittedly anecdotal, point to one of the central features of eating disturbances. All people who suffer from disordered eating are secretive. Athletes in particular might be reluctant to admit problems and might not respond truthfully to questionnaires. They carry the shame, guilt, and embarrassment of anyone with an eating disorder, but they are also extremely concerned that they will be discovered by coaches and teammates. They fear that discovery will lead to recrimination, troubled relationships with others, and even removal from competition. With increasing attention to, and concern about eating disorders among athletes, this secrecy could escalate.

A concerted effort is necessary to discover who has eating problems and how the problems affect the emotional and physical life of the athlete. Establishing an environment where athletes perceive a sensitivity to these secrecy issues and where they feel safe discussing their problems is one key to identification. Chapter 22 presents a series of methods to help athletes be open and to share their difficulties in a supportive context.

◻ ORGANIZATION OF THIS BOOK

After this introductory chapter, which is Section I, the book is divided into four main sections. We have organized the discussion to progress from basic to applied issues and to cover the information necessary to understand fundamental issues regarding eating and weight regulation, the causes and pathology of eating problems in athletes, the effects of these problems on the athlete, and finally, methods for preventing and treating eating and weight problems in the athletic population.

Section II, **Basic Issues**, provides essential, basic information on appetite, satiety, nutrient intake, body build, and body composition. These affect the behavior and performance of the athlete. Disturbed eating patterns occur against a background in which physiology, culture, and psychology interact. To form a comprehensive picture of eating problems in athletes, it is important to be aware of the basic physiological processes that govern energy intake, energy expenditure, and weight regulation.

Section III, **Causes, Pathology, and Prevalence of Eating and Weight Problems in Athletes**, reviews information on prevalence, social factors and the ideal body shape, athletes who lose and regain weight repeatedly, pathology and development of eating disorders, and the special case of eating disorders in males. These provide a perspective on the magnitude of the problem and help us understand the genesis of eating disturbances in athletes. Collectively, these chapters show how various factors converge to place athletes at risk for eating problems.

The chapters in Section IV, **Effects of Eating and Weight Problems on the Athlete**, underscore the serious nature of the eating disorders and how they can affect the health, psychological well-being, and performance of the athlete. General medical issues related to low body weight and undereating and to eating disorders in general are covered, as are several issues such as menstrual dysfunction and osteoporosis that are particularly relevant to athletes. The last chapter in this section discusses the effects of overtraining, an issue of increasing importance.

In Section V, **Applied Issues**, the information in the previous chapters is integrated into a comprehensive picture on how to prevent and manage eating disturbances in athletes. The section begins with a chapter on the culture of modern athletics. It highlights the level of training and the extraordinary commitment required of today's athletes and how these translate into pressure that can make an athlete susceptible to many problems, including eating disorders. Chapters then follow on providing a sound nutrition plan for the athlete, setting reasonable body weight and body composition standards, clinical treatment options for athletes, and a detailed plan for managing eating disorders in athletic settings. These chapters show that the problems need not be hidden and mysterious and that specific efforts can be undertaken to identify and manage eating disturbances in athletes.

□ SUMMARY

Some people in the world of athletics believe that much is being made of a trivial matter; others feel too little is being done too late. It is our intent in this book to bring some clarity to this important and now highly publicized issue. We discuss whether athletes have such problems, what puts them at risk, and what can be done. Our hope is to review and integrate the science in the area, propose innovative methods for management, and point to unresolved clinical and research issues that need further study.

□ REFERENCES

1. Molloy, J.: Colloquium addresses athletes and eating disorders. NCAA Sports Sci. 1:3, 1990.
2. Rodin, J.: Body Traps. New York: William Morrow, 1991.
3. Brownell, K.D.: Personal responsibility and control over our bodies: When expectation exceeds reality. Health Psychol., in press.
4. Brownell, K.D.: Dieting and the search for the perfect body: Where physiology and culture collide. Behav. Ther., 22:1, 1991.
5. Strober, M.: Anorexia nervosa: History and psychological concepts. In Handbook of Eating Disorders: Physiology, Psychology, and Treatment of Obesity, Anorexia, and Bulimia. Edited by K.D. Brownell and J.P. Foreyt. New York: Basic Books, 1986, pp. 231–246.
6. Brownell, K.D., Steen, S.N., and Wilmore, J.H.: Weight regulation practices in athletes: Analysis of metabolic and health effects. Med. Sci. Sports Exerc., 19:546, 1987.
7. Drinkwater, B.L., et al.: Bone mineral content of amenorrheic and eumenorrheic athletes. N. Engl. J. Med., 311:277, 1984.
8. Marcus, R., et al.: Menstrual function and bone mass in elite women distance runners. Ann. Int. Med., 102:158, 1983.
9. Nelson, M.E., et al.: Diet and bone status in amenorrheic runners. Am. J. Clin. Nutr., 43:910, 1986.
10. Short, S.H., and Short, W.R.: Four-year study of university athletes' dietary intake. J. Am. Dietet. Assoc., 82:632, 1983.
11. Benson, J., Gillien, D.M., Bourdet, K., and Loosli, A.: Inadequate nutrition and chronic calorie restriction in adolescent ballerinas. Physician Sportsmed., 13:79, 1985.
12. Druss, R.G.: Body image and perfection on ballerinas: Comparison and contrast with anorexia nervosa. Gen. Hosp. Psychiatry, 2:115, 1979.

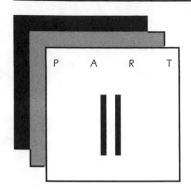

P A R T

II

BASIC ISSUES

CHAPTER

2

DETERMINANTS OF FOOD INTAKE: HUNGER AND SATIETY

Harvey P. Weingarten

As the title of this book suggests, the issues of eating and weight are primary concerns of modern Western society. For the athlete, concerns about eating and weight usually center on the question of optimal eating habits and body weight (or body composition) in relation to athletic performance. The worry of the eating disorder clinician frequently gravitates toward the real possibility that eating styles or practices prevalent among athletes predispose or precipitate eating disorder such as binging and bulimia.

Concerns about eating and weight are not limited to the world of athletics. We are experiencing an alarming rate of increase of eating disorders in the general population, especially among women. Although one might argue about the exact prevalence of disorders such as bulimia nervosa and anorexia nervosa, one cannot dispute either the inordinate societal concern with eating and weight or the high prevalence of dieting.

How are the scientific and clinical communities to respond to these issues? What advice should be given to athletes in regard to eating and weight as they prepare for competition? What are the dangers of binge eating or even frequent purging? Is dieting dangerous? What therapeutic maneuvers are likely to be effective in the treatment of eating disorder?

The answers to these questions are likely to be provided or guided by data from laboratories examining basic biological and behavioral mechanisms controlling food intake. Many noteworthy conferences examining the clinical issues surrounding eating and weight incorporate sessions on basic determinants of feeding behavior. This arrangement is not fortuitous or coincidental. Rather, it acknowledges the contributions of the basic mechanism laboratory to the understanding of eating and weight problems and to the design of rational and effective therapies designed to ameliorate these problems.

The present chapter, which reviews the current understanding of the biological and behavioral determinants of food intake, is presented in the same spirit. It is hoped that the review provides a context for understanding eating pathology and points to possible fruitful areas of further study and clinical intervention.

Research on the determinants of food intake attempts to identify the psychological and biological mechanisms that control eating. This research is motivated to a large extent by the desire to develop techniques to control caloric intake in individuals for whom, for either therapeutic or cosmetic reasons, a reduction of food intake and body weight is desirable. Implicit in this enterprise are the assumptions that (1) the level of caloric intake is a major determinant of body weight and that (2) a reduction of caloric intake, i.e., dieting, is an effective procedure for a long-term reduction of body weight. Although both of these assumptions can be questioned (see Chapters 3 and 4),[1-3] their existence continues to motivate much of the empirical work on the determinants of eating.

Research on eating typically adopts one of two strategies. The first emphasizes *meals* and attempts to identify the mechanisms involved in the initiation (e.g., hunger and appetite) and termination (e.g., satiety) of meals. This perspective acknowledges that in most animals, including man, eating is organized into periodic bouts of behavior called meals and that meals represent, therefore, a behavioral reality and a basic unit of eating. A second strategy adopts daily (i.e., 24-hour) caloric intake as the unit of analysis. This perspective affiliates with the view that the sequencing of meals is of less consequence than the total number of calories consumed in a daily period. The mechanisms controlling individual meals and overall daily intake might be related. In fact, some prominent theories of eating suggest an intimate relationship between the two.[4] A review of the literature on determinants of food intake, however, is accomplished best by discussing each of these approaches independently.

☐ CONTROL OF THE MEAL

Meals comprise a complex cascade of behaviors; at least four components can be identified. First, there is meal initiation, which represents the transition from noneating to eating. This phase includes food-seeking and sensations (e.g., cravings, hunger) that are related to eating but occur prior to contact with food. Second, there is the period of contact with food during which eating is maintained. The major variable of this phase is the amount eaten at the meal, or meal size. Third, eating terminates, an event typically associated with feelings of satiety (fullness) and satisfaction. Finally, after meal termination, the organism is refractory to eating for some period of time—an event known as the intermeal interval. It is likely that separate mechanisms underlie these different phases of the meal.[5,6]

MEAL INITIATION: HUNGER

Anticipating contact with food, humans experience the sensations of hunger and cravings, which promote eating. The biological mechanisms underlying these states are not well understood. Some early research suggested that gastrointestinal (especially stomach) motility[7] or low plasma glucose[8] produces the experience of hunger. At the psychological level, intense desires for specific foods (food cravings) are probably some of the most intense and ubiquitous experiences with food. In survey studies, 97% of women and 67% of men report experiencing intense desires for specific foods.[9] It is often assumed that cravings originate from some body deficit and that cravings serve to identify the substance(s) that would correct the deficiency. Cravings might also represent the desire for specific tastes and smells, however, not the need for some pharmacological or nutritional effects of food.[9] The simple presence of palatable (good tasting) food, even in sated (full) humans, also activates a strong desire to eat.[10]

Meal initiation is controlled by either internal (biological signals such as glucose and insulin) or external (e.g., learning, habits, social influences) factors. The distinction between internal and external controls of meal initiation is maintained in this chapter although it is recognized that, ultimately, external influences on food intake must be manifested through internal physiological systems.[11]

Internal Controls

Many empirical studies have attempted to identify the specific physiological signals that stimulate eating. Most of this research emanates from the perspective that meals are a response to an internal stimulus signaling energy depletion. These depletion models stress that the body strives to maintain a constant energy state (homeostasis) with eating, because hunger is presumed to be activated by low energy levels and, as a result of the ensuing eating, nutrients are absorbed and redress the energy depletion state.

Jean Mayer's "glucostatic hypothesis"[4] guided the search for the meal initiation signal for several decades. This hypothesis suggested that a decrease of glucose utilization promoted meal initiation. It was speculated, further, that glucoreceptors in the brain, especially in the hypo-thalamus, detected the level of glucose utilization and, in response to this signal, turned hunger on or off.[12] Considerable evidence indicates that reductions of glucose utilization, produced by substances such as 2-deoxy-glucose (2DG) or insulin, result in meal initiation and induce hunger in humans.[8] Although these findings demonstrate the *capacity* of glucoprivation to induce eating, it is doubtful that low glucose controls naturally-occurring eating because the level of glucoprivation necessary to activate eating is considerably greater than that experienced nor-mally.[13] One possibility, however, is that sufficiently intense levels of energy depletion are attained in prolonged and intense exercise, exer-tion, or energy expenditure. Other candidates for a depletion-related meal initiation signal have been proposed. A prominent hypothesis sug-gests that decreased oxidative metabolism in the liver initiates eating, regardless of whether it results from decreased availability of glucose or other fuels.[14]

Convincing evidence for a meal initiation signal not related to deple-tion comes from Campfield and colleagues.[15,16] They describe a glucose transient in blood, termed the premeal glucose decline, which is causally related to the initiation of spontaneous meals in the free-feeding rat. The premeal glucose decline is small but reliable. It consists of a drop of blood glucose, no more than a 10% decline, commencing approxi-mately 20 minutes prior to meal onset (see Fig. 2–1). Meal initiation occurs typically as blood glucose returns to baseline. The evidence that the glucose decline *causes* meal initiation is impressive. The decline cor-relates highly with initiation of spontaneous meals. More important, blocking the glucose decline prevents meal initiation, and inducing the decline results in meal initiation.[16] Meals can appear in the absence of premeal declines; in the rat, ingestion of novel foods is not associated with glucose declines. The range of circumstances for which the premeal glucose decline is necessary or sufficient for meal initiation remains to be determined.

The ability of energy depletion to explain meal initiation is limited. First, depletion models imply that organisms ride a roller coaster of energy balance from the heights of repletion to the depths of depletion. Intuitively, this seems a poor design for a biological machine. Second, organisms rarely approach the levels of energy depletion necessary to activate depletion-induced controls of meal initiation. Depletion controls appear to represent emergency meal-initiation responses to situations rarely experienced. In fact, regulation of energy stores, at both the met-abolic and behavioral levels, is designed to prevent emergency situations from arising.

External Controls

Partially because of disillusionment with internal depletion models, oth-ers have investigated the ability of external factors, such as learning, habits, social, and cognitive factors, to control eating.

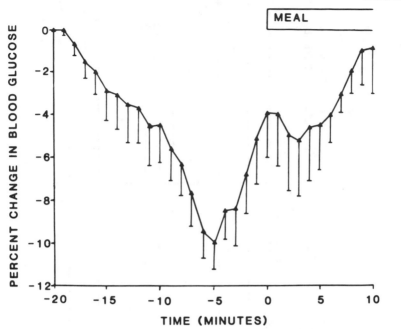

Fig. 2–1. Average time course of premeal decline in blood glucose concentration. Meal onset was taken as the time-zero reference. Data points were selected each minute from this reference point in each of 9 experiments, expressed as percent change from baseline, and the means and standard errors of the mean were plotted. Note that meal initiation occurs while the glucose concentration is returning to base-line. The average baseline glucose concentration was 103.6 + 4.5 mg/dL. From Camp-field, L.A., Brandon, P., and Smith, F.J.: On-line continuous measurement of blood glucose and meal pattern in free-feeding rats: The role of glucose in meal initiation. Brain Res. Bull., 14:611, 1985.

In the short term, external factors reliably promote meal initiation.[17–19] Mere exposure to palatable food, even to sated humans, is sufficient to motivate considerable caloric intake.[10] Animal studies provide dramatic examples of the ability of external cues to promote eating even in the absence of any energy depletion. For example, my colleagues and I[19–21] taught rats, using standard classical conditioning procedures, to associate an arbitrary external stimulus and food. After rats had learned to associate the external cue with eating, the cue was presented to the rats when they were sated. They responded rapidly to the external cue by initiating a large meal, approximately 20% of their total 24-hour food intake (see Fig. 2–2). The size of meals initiated by sated rats in response to external cues is often greater than that motivated by potent pharmacological agents or direct application of neurotransmitters to the brain.[21]

Food-associated external cues also motivate eating in humans. In-

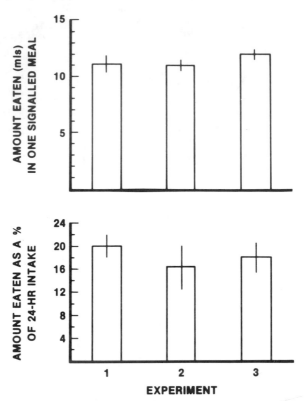

Fig. 2–2. Size of conditioned meals. Top panel: size of conditioned meals (in mL) eaten by sated rats in response to a food-associated external cue. Data represent three replications of the experiment in three separate groups of rats (N = 8). Protocol for conditioning described in reference 20. Bottom panel: size of the conditioned meal as a percent of total food intake eaten in the 24-hour period. Conditioned meals can be as large as 16 to 20% of total daily (24-hour) caloric intake.

numerable everyday anecdotes suggest that humans initiate meals in response to external cues—temporal cues (e.g., a traditional meal time) being perhaps the most notable. Formal research reinforces the capacity of learned external cues to initiate eating in humans. Birch et al.[22] paired specific visual, auditory, or location cues with the presence or absence of food. Preschool children, tested under conditions of satiety, ate more in the presence of food-associated cues than in the presence of cues that had not been paired with food.

Learning and conditioning also contribute to the defense of body weight. In the face of reduced opportunity for eating, rats that have learned to anticipate the arrival of food lose less weight than those that receive unexpected eating opportunities, a phenomenon dependent on a learned adaptive increase in eating when food is available.[19,23]

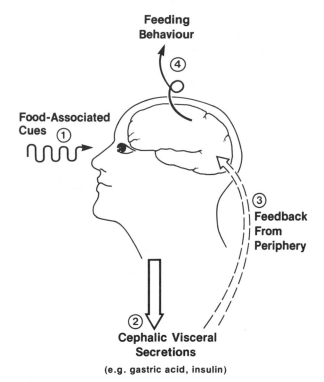

Fig. 2–3. Schematic representation outlining the way in which cephalic phase visceral secretions might mediate externally-controlled feeding. Circled numbers detail the proposed sequence of events. From Weingarten, H.P., and Watson, S.D.: Sham feeding as a procedure for assessing the influence of diet palatability on food intake. Physiol. Behav., *28*:403, 1982.

The prime physiological candidates believed to underlie externally controlled meal initiation are the cephalic phase digestive responses. Cephalic phase responses are secretory-motor events (e.g., insulin secretion and motility changes) involved with digestion that are activated by either the expectation of food or nutrient stimulation of the oral cavity. It is suggested that when external cues become associated with food, cephalic responses are brought under control of the external stimulus. Subsequent exposure to these stimuli activates cephalic secretion, and in response to activation of these peripheral events, the brain initiates eating (see Fig. 2–3).

Cephalic responses are elaborated in situations in which food is expected; one pairing of an external cue with food can give a stimulus the ability to induce cephalic release.[24] The magnitude of cephalic release correlates with meal size[25] and also predicts the amount of weight rats gain when maintained with chronic exposure to palatable foods.[26]

In sum, there are many demonstrations of the ability of learned, social,

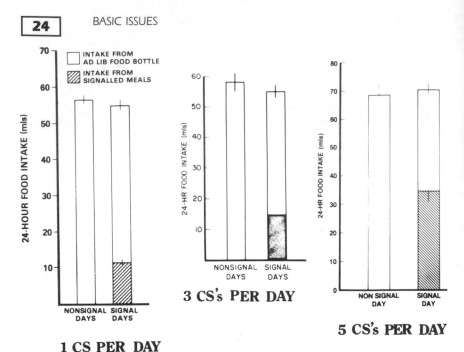

Fig. 2–4. Compensation data. Compensation of 24-hour food intake to signaled (conditioned) meals. Data shown are average (± 1 SEM) food intake on signal and nonsignal days. On nonsignal days, intake represents expected 24-hour intake. On signal days, total intake is cumulative amount eaten in response to signaled meals and intake from ad libitum food source. Left panel: Rats take one signaled meal. Middle panel: rats take three signaled meals, each 5 mL in size. Right panel: rats exposed to five external cues, presented once per hour. In all cases, on signal days, rats decrease ad libitum intake subsequent to the signaled meal to maintain constant 24-hour intake.

or environmental factors to activate a meal. It is important to recognize, however, that repeated exposure to external cues might not result in long-term increases of food intake and body weight. For example, in a conditioned-eating study, rats exposed repeatedly to food-associated external cues did not increase 24-hour caloric intake even though all rats ate robustly in response to initial presentations of the cues (Fig. 2–4).[20]

PALATABILITY

Once the meal is initiated and contact with food is made, the palatability of the diet exerts a predominant influence on meal size. "Palatability" refers to the organism's evaluation of the stimulus properties of the food (e.g., taste, texture). Loosely, the term refers to the degree to which the food is liked, although how palatability should be measured is controversial.[27] Three classes of events determine a food's palatability: the

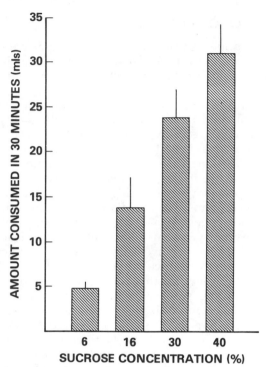

Fig. 2–5. With sham feeding, meal size increases with increasing sucrose concentration. From Weingarten, H.P., and Watson, S.D.: Sham feeding as a procedure for assessing the influence of diet palatability on food intake. Physiol. Behav., *28:*401, 1982.

stimulus properties of the food, the physiological state of the organism, and learned anticipated consequences of the food.[28]

Sweet is a potent stimulant of food intake.[29] The clearest ability of sweet to drive eating is seen with sham feeding, in which the oropharynx is surgically disconnected from the remainder of the digestive tract. When the oral cavity is stimulated with sweet and (because of the use of sham feeding) nutrient does not accumulate in the stomach, meal size rises directly with the sweetness of the food (Fig. 2–5).[30] The mechanisms by which sweet stimulates appetite are not clearly established, but positive feedback from the periphery[31] and brain dopamine systems[32] have been implicated.

The hedonic response to food, i.e., whether it is liked or disliked, is modulated by the internal state of the organism—a phenomenon termed alliesthesia.[33] Hunger (food deprivation) and energy depletion increase palatability. Satiety, nutrient loads in the gastrointestinal tract, and energy repletion decrease palatability. The alteration of a food's palatability by energy state changes during eating might be one of the mechanisms controlling meal size.[34]

LEARNED CONTROL OF MEAL SIZE

Meal size is also influenced by the organism's expectation of the meal's eventual postingestive effects. When an organism eats, it associates the taste of the food and its subsequent postingestive consequences.[35] When the postingestive consequence is aversive, e.g., sickness or malaise, the food is subsequently avoided or rejected—a phenomenon termed conditioned taste aversion. In contrast, foods resulting in positive, postingestive consequences, such as energy repletion, become preferred—a phenomenon known as taste-to-postingestive-consequence, or caloric-based, learning. Although these two complementary phenomena of learning about food are robust, it remains unclear exactly which postingestive events produce this learning. In the case of aversion, lower gastrointestinal symptoms, such as diarrhea or pain, lead to avoidance of food but do not engender a dislike of the food itself. In contrast, upper gastrointestinal symptoms, especially nausea, lead to a true dislike of the food.[36] At the positive end, nutrients that increase fuel oxidation in the liver lead to the development of a preference for that food.[37] It is unclear whether other postingestive events are necessary or sufficient for taste-to-postingestive-consequences learning.

Organisms modulate meal size in response not only to anticipated beneficial or aversive consequences but also to the expected caloric value of a meal. In a prototype experiment, Birch and Deysher[38] allowed preschool children to eat, on separate occasions, a high or low calorie snack. The high and low calorie snacks were distinctively flavored to allow for an association between the flavor and the caloric value of the snack. Children learned to anticipate the caloric consequences of the snacks, and they modulated meal size on the basis of these expectations. The animal literature is replete with similar demonstrations.[35]

MEAL TERMINATION: SATIETY

Accumulation of food in the digestive tract activates satiety factors that produce meal termination. Two classes of satiety signals are distinguished: *preabsorptive* signals, activated prior to the absorption of nutrients and arising from mechanical and chemical stimulation of gastrointestinal tissues, and *postabsorptive* signals, initiated after the absorption of food in the intestines.

The postabsorptive signal with greatest historical impact was blood glucose. Mayer's glucostatic hypothesis[4] suggested that increased glucose utilization, characteristic of the period after the meal when nutrient from the meal is being absorbed, signaled satiety. It is difficult to conceive that plasma glucose, because of its dominant role as an energy source and its privileged use as a fuel by the brain, is unrelated to satiety. It has been difficult, however, to demonstrate that blood glucose controls meal termination per se.[39] Postabsorptive glucose might modulate other satiety systems[34] or participate in determining the length of the inter-meal interval during which the organism is refractory to eating.[5]

The search for meal termination signals has focused more recently on preabsorptive signals. It is clear that the entire proximal gastrointestinal tract (including mouth, stomach, and small intestine) elaborates signals relevant to meal termination.[40]

Oropharyngeal stimulation, isolated in the sham feeding preparation, activates oral satiety signals that can terminate a meal and result in a discrete intermeal interval. In isolation, however, the contribution of oral satiety is small and might be evident under defined experimental circumstances only. Oral stimulation, though, potentiates satiety signals emanating from other regions of the gastrointestinal tract.[41]

The stomach sends potent satiety signals that, in isolation, can terminate eating.[42,43] One component of gastric satiety results from distension, or stretching, of the stomach. Other humoral or hormonal signals, however, resulting from chemical stimulation of the gastric mucosa, also contribute to the overall satiety signal produced by the stomach.

An important development in the understanding of satiety was appreciation of the importance of intestinal signals. The small intestine is a warehouse of peptides that are released by nutrient stimulation of the intestinal mucosa. The gut peptide for which a role in meal termination has been best established is cholecystokinin (CCK). The evidence that CCK is part of the satiety mechanism leading to the termination of meals is impressive.[40,44,45] First, exogenous administration of CCK accelerates meal termination, without overt signs of malaise, in a host of animal species including man. Second, blocking the physiological effects of CCK with receptor antagonists delays the onset of satiety[46] and results in the experience of hunger in man.[47] Although other gut peptides (e.g., bombesin and glucagon) have been implicated in meal termination, the evidence that any of these represents true postprandial satiety factors is less compelling than the case for CCK.[48]

At the psychological level, another important development was the understanding that satiety does not indicate a generalized unwillingness to eat. Rather, during a meal, the accruing satiety is focused primarily on the food being eaten and on other foods with similar sensory properties.[49] The recognition of "sensory-specific satiety" suggests that, even after meal termination and the experience of satiety, humans can rapidly initiate further eating if foods with different sensory properties are offered (e.g., dessert after a main course). A corollary to this observation is that exposure to a variety of foods leads typically to higher levels of daily caloric intake. In the extreme, chronic exposure to palatable foods can result in the development of obesity.[50,51]

☐ CONTROL OF DAILY (24-HOUR) FOOD INTAKE

A second major factor determining hunger and satiety acts in concert with mechanisms controlling the meal. In rats, monkeys, and probably man, mechanisms also exist to regulate the total number of calories eaten in a daily (24-hour) period. In humans, largely for methodological reasons, controls of daily caloric intake are studied less often than meals. Measurements of meal size and of other meal-related parameters are easily adapted to short laboratory experiments. In contrast, accurate assessment of 24-hour intake in humans requires confinement to hospital or specialized laboratories or the use of indirect measures such as food recalls or diaries, the validity of which are often questioned.

The idea that the number of calories eaten in a 24-hour period is regulated was promoted enthusiastically by Adolph,[52] who suggested that animals eat for calories and, within limits, maintain a relatively constant daily caloric intake. Daily caloric intake can be exquisitely regulated. For example, in response to substantial infusion of nutrients into the stomach, rats reduce voluntary food intake on almost a calorie-for-calorie basis in such a way as to keep 24-hour caloric intake constant.[53] Similarly, rats induced to eat conditioned meals in response to presentation of food-associated external stimuli reduce intake later in the day to maintain a constant daily caloric intake (Fig. 2–4).[20] Finally, in an impressive series of experiments, McHugh and Moran[54] demonstrated that, in response to either calorie infusions or deprivation, monkeys adjust subsequent energy intake precisely to maintain a constant daily caloric intake (see Fig. 2–6).

There is some controversy whether humans also demonstrate the capacity to regulate 24-hour caloric intake. Some studies suggest that, in response to a reduction of caloric density, humans show little compensation for 3 days and, even once some compensation is observed, humans compensate for no more than 40% of the calories reduced in the diet.[55] In contrast, other studies demonstrate an almost immediate and complete compensation by humans for covert caloric dilution.[56] Humans also compensate almost perfectly for calories introduced covertly by intravenous glucose by reducing oral intake to a degree equivalent to the number of calories infused.[57] In general, mechanisms controlling daily food intake in humans are more accurate when calories are reduced than when calories are increased.[56,58] An important unresolved issue is whether chronic exercise affects the level at which 24-hour caloric intake is maintained—or, more generally, the degree to which repeated exercise modulates energy balance.

☐ SUMMARY

Studies of the determinants of food intake classify conveniently into those that emphasize control of the meal and those that focus on 24-hour caloric intake. In terms of the meal, it has become clear that a plethora of controls exist. Some are linked to controls of hunger and others to satiety. Some determinants are linked directly to the energy needs of the body, whereas others are more closely associated with the psychological needs of the individual. The possibility that the number

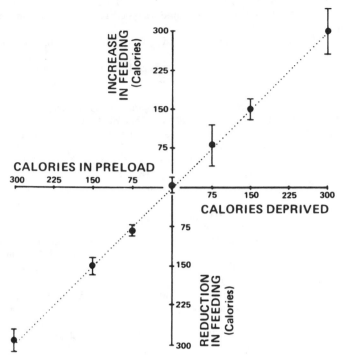

Fig. 2–6. Composite representation of behavioral responses expressed in kcal to challenges of gastric loads and deprivations. From McHugh, P.R., and Moran, T.H.: Accuracy of the regulation of caloric ingestion in the rhesus monkey. Am. J. Physiol., *235*:R29–R34, 1978.

of calories humans ingest in 24 hours is also regulated is a critical finding in considering the structure of the system that controls food intake.

The recognition that multiple systems exist to control food intake has been, perhaps, the major conceptual advance in the understanding of the determinants of food intake. A prime challenge is to articulate the relationships between these various controls and to identify how they act harmoniously to ensure energy balance. Further study of the ways in which these controls are altered in acute or chronic elevations of energy expenditure, characteristic of the athlete, might prove instructive in this enterprise.

☐ REFERENCES

1. Spitzer, L., and Rodin, J.: Human eating behavior: A critical review of studies in normal weight and overweight individuals. Appetite, 2:293, 1981.
2. Polivy, J., and Herman, C.P.: Diagnosis and treatment of normal eating. J. Consult. Clin. Psychol., 55:635, 1987.

3. Stunkard, A.J.: The Salmon Lecture. Some perspectives on human obesity. Bull. N.Y. Acad. Med., *64*:902, 1988.
4. Mayer, J.: Regulation of energy intake and body weight: The glucostatic and lipostatic hypotheses. Ann. N.Y. Acad. Sci., *63*:15, 1955.
5. LeMagnen, J.: Hunger. Cambridge, Cambridge University Press, 1985.
6. Weingarten, H.P., and Martin, G.M.: Mechanisms of conditioned meal initiation. Physiol. Behav., *45*:735, 1989.
7. Rosenzweig, M.R.: The mechanisms of hunger and thirst. *In* Psychology in the Making. Edited by Leo Postman. New York, Alfred A. Knopf, 1962.
8. Epstein, A.N., Nicolaidis, S., and Miselis, R.: The glucoprivic control of food intake and the glucostatic theory of feeding behavior. *In* Neural Integration of Physiological Mechanisms and Behavior. Edited by G.J. Mogenson and F.R. Calareso. Toronto, University of Toronto Press, 1975, pp. 148–168.
9. Weingarten, H.P., and Elston, D.: The phenomenology of food cravings. Appetite, *15*:231, 1990.
10. Cornell, C.E., Rodin, J., and Weingarten, H.P.: Stimulus-induced eating when satiated. Physiol. Behav., *45*:695, 1989.
11. Rodin, J.: Has the distinction between internal versus external control of feeding outlived its usefulness? *In* Recent Advances in Obesity Research, Vol. 2. Edited by G.A. Bray. London, Newman, 1978.
12. Stellar, E.: The physiology of motivation. Psychol. Rev., *61*:5, 1954.
13. Smith, G.P., Gibbs, J., Strohmayer, A., and Stokes, P.E.: Threshold doses of 2-deoxy-D-glucose for hyperglycemia and feeding in rats and monkeys. Am. J. Physiol., *222*:77, 1972.
14. Friedman, M.J., and Stricker, E.M.: The physiological psychology of hunger: A physiological perspective. Psychol. Rev., *83*:409, 1976.
15. Campfield, L.A., Brandon, P., and Smith, F.J.: On-line continuous measurement of blood glucose and meal pattern in free-feeding rats: The role of glucose in meal initiation. Br. Res. Bull., *14*:605, 1985.
16. Campfield, L.A., and Smith, F.J.: Systemic factors in the control of food intake. *In* Handbook of Behavioral Neurobiology, Vol. 10. Edited by E.M. Stricker. New York, Plenum Press, 1990.
17. Rodin, J.: Social and environmental determinants of eating behavior. *In* Body weight Regulatory System: Normal and Disturbed Mechanisms. Edited by R. Cioffi. New York, Raven Press, 1981, pp. 323–335.
18. Galef, B.F., Jr.: Communication of information concerning distant diets in a social, central-place foraging species, *Rattus norvegicus. In* Social Learning: Psychological and Biological Perspectives. Edited by J.R. Zentall and B.G. Galef, Jr. Hillsdale, NJ: Lawrence Erlbaum, 1988.
19. Weingarten, H.P.: Stimulus control of eating: Implications for a two factor theory of hunger. Appetite, *6*:387, 1985.
20. Weingarten, H.P.: Meal initiation controlled by learned cues: Basic behavioral properties. Appetite, *5*:147, 1984.
21. Weingarten, H.P.: Learning, homeostasis, and the control of feeding behavior. *In* Taste, Experience, and Feeding. Edited by E.D. Capaldi and T.L. Powley. Washington, American Psychological Association, 1990, pp. 14–28.
22. Birch, L.L., McPhee, L., Sullivan, S., and Johnson, S.: Conditioned meal initiation in young children. Appetite, *13*:105, 1989.
23. Valle, F.P.: Effect of exposure to feeding-related stimuli on food consumption in rats. J. Comp. Physiol. Psychol., *66*:773, 1968.
24. Weingarten, H.P., and Powley, T.L.: Pavlovian conditioning of the cephalic phase of gastric acid secretion in the rat. Physiol. Behav., *27*:217, 1981.

25. Powley, T.L.: The ventromedial hypothalamic syndrome, satiety, and a cephalic phase hypothesis. Psychol. Rev., 84:89, 1977.
26. Berthoud, H.R.: Cephalic phase insulin response as a predictor of body weight gain and obesity induced by a palatable cafeteria diet. J. Obesity Weight Regulation, 4:120, 1985.
27. Weingarten, H.P., and Bédard, M.: Diet palatability: Its definition, measurement, and experimental analyses. In Neuropharmacology of Appetite. Edited by S. Cooper and J. Liebman. New York, Oxford Press, in press.
28. Grill, H.J., and Berridge, K.C.: Taste reactivity as a measure of the neural control of palatability. In Progress in Psychobiology and Physiological Psychology, Vol. 2. Edited by J.M. Sprague and A.N. Epstein. New York, Academic Press, 1985, pp. 1–61.
29. Sclafani, A.: Carbohydrate taste, appetite, and obesity: An overview. Neurosci. Biobehav. Rev., 11:131, 1987.
30. Weingarten, H.P., and Watson, S.D.: Sham feeding as a procedure for assessing the influence of diet palatability on food intake. Physiol. Behav., 28:401, 1982.
31. Geiselman, P.J.: Carbohydrates do not always produce satiety: An explanation of the appetite- and hunger-stimulating effects of hexoses. In Progress in Psychobiology and Physiological Psychology, Vol. 12. Edited by A.N. Epstein and A.R. Morrison. New York, Academic Press, 1987, pp. 211–241.
32. Davis, J.D.: The microstructure of ingestive behavior. Ann. N.Y. Acad. Sci., 575:106, 1989.
33. Cabanac, M.: Sensory pleasure. Q. Rev. Biol. 54:1, 1979.
34. Bédard, M., and Weingarten, H.P.: Postabsorptive glucose decreases excitatory effects of taste on ingestion. Am. J. Physiol., 256:R1142, 1989.
35. Booth, D.A.: Food-conditioned eating preferences and aversions with interoceptive elements: Conditioned appetites and satieties. Ann. N.Y. Acad. Sci., 443:22, 1985.
36. Rozin, P., and Vollmecke, T.A.: Food likes and dislikes. Ann. Rev. Nutr., 6:433, 1986.
37. Tordoff, M., Tepper, B., and Friedman, M.I.: Food flavor preferences produced by drinking glucose and oil in normal and diabetic rats: Evidence for conditioning based on fuel oxidation. Physiol. Behav., 41:481, 1987.
38. Birch, L.L., and Deysher, M.: Conditioned and unconditioned caloric compensation: Evidence for self-regulation of food intake in young children. Learn. Motiv., 16:341, 1985.
39. Gowans, S.P., and Weingarten, H.P.: Plasma glucose does not participate in taste-to-postingestive consequence conditioning. Am. J. Physiol, in press.
40. Smith, G.P., and Gibbs, J.: Postprandial satiety. In Progress in Psychobiology and Physiological Psychology, Vol. 8. Edited by J. Sprague and A.N. Epstein. New York, Academic Press, 1979, pp. 178–242.
41. Kraly, F.S., Carty, W.J., and Smith, G.I.: Effect of pregastric food stimuli on meal size and intermeal interval in the rat. Physiol. Behav., 20:779, 1978.
42. Deutsch, J.A.: The role of the stomach in eating. Am. J. Clin. Nutr., 42:1040, 1985.
43. Robinson, P.H., McHugh, P.R., Moran, T.H., and Stephenson, J.D.: Gastric control of food intake. J. Psychosom. Res., 32:593, 1988.
44. Collins, S.M., and Weingarten, H.P.: The role of gastrointestinal peptides in the regulation of food intake. In Surgery for the Morbidly Obese Patient. Edited by M. Dietel. Philadelphia, Lea & Febiger, 1989, pp. 39–48.
45. Smith, G.P.: Gut hormone hypothesis of postprandial satiety. In Eating and its Disorders. Edited by A.J. Stunkard and E. Stellar. New York, Raven Press, 1984.
46. Dourish, C.T., Rycroft, W., and Iversen, S.D.: Postponement of satiety by blockade of brain cholecystokinin (CCK) receptors. Science, 245:1509, 1990.
47. Wolkowitz, O.M., Gertz, B., Weingartner, H., Beccoria, L., et al.: Hunger in humans induced by MK-329, a specific peripheral-type cholecystokinin receptor antagonist. Biol. Psychiatry 28:169, 1990.

48. Moran, T.H., and McHugh, P.R.: Gastric and non-gastric mechanisms for satiety action of cholecystokinin. Am. J. Physiol., *254*:R628, 1988.
49. Rolls, B.J.: Sensory-specific satiety. Nutr. Rev., *44*:93, 1986.
50. Ramirez, I., Tordoff, M.G., and Friedman, M.I.: Dietary hyperphagia and obesity: What causes them? Physiol. Behav., *45*:163, 1989.
51. Sclafani, A.: Dietary-induced overeating. Ann. N.Y. Acad. Sci., *576*:281, 1989.
52. Adolph, E.F.: Urges to eat and drink in rats. Am. J. Physiol., *151*:110, 1941.
53. Rothwell, N.J., and Stock, M.J.: Regulation of energy balance. Ann. Rev. Nutr., *1*:235, 1981.
54. McHugh, P.R., and Moran, T.H.: Accuracy of the regulation of caloric ingestion in the rhesus monkey. Am. J. Physiol., *235*:R29, 1978.
55. Porikos, K.P., Hesser, M.F., and van Itallie, B.: Calorie regulation in normal-weight men maintained on a palatable diet of conventional foods. Physiol. Behav., *29*:293, 1982.
56. Foltin, R.W., Fishman, M.W., Emurian, C.S., and Rachlinski, J.J.: Compensation for caloric dilution in humans given unrestricted access to food in a residential laboratory. Appetite, *10*:13, 1988.
57. Gil, K.M., Skeie, B., Kvetan, V., Askanazi, J., and Friedman, M.I.: Parental nutrition and oral intake: Effect of glucose and fat infusions. J. Parenter. Enteral Nutr., in press.
58. Mattes, R.D., Pierce, C.B., and Friedman, M.I.: Daily caloric intake of normal-weight adults: Responses to changes in dietary energy density of a luncheon meal. Am. J. Clin. Nutr., *48*:214, 1988.

3

DETERMINANTS OF BODY WEIGHT REGULATION

Eric T. Poehlman and Edward S. Horton

Regulation of body energy reserves occurs through changes in the energy content of food consumed or energy lost through total daily energy expenditure. Energy balance is the net result of energy input minus energy output. Fluctuations in energy balance have important nutritional and performance implications for athletes as well as for humans in general. The imbalance between intake and expenditure contributes to the pathogenesis of many lifestyle-related diseases (e.g., obesity, diabetes mellitus, and hypertension) and to the difficulty some athletes have in controlling body weight.

At one end of the energy expenditure spectrum is the endurance-trained athlete. This individual typifies a human model of energy balance in which a high level of expenditure is exquisitely balanced against a high level of food intake to maintain stable body weight and provide necessary fuel reserves. This observation itself suggests that energy expenditure determines energy requirements and subsequently input and

Acknowledgments: Dr. Poehlman is supported by the National Institute of Aging (AG-07857) and the American Association of Retired Persons Andrus Foundation. Dr. Horton is supported by the National Institute of Diabetes and Digestive and Kidney Disease (DK 26317). Research presented in this chapter was supported in part by the General Clinical Research Center (National Institutes of Health, Division of Research Resources Grant RR-109).

that physical activity is involved in regulating energy intake. At the other end of the spectrum is the obese individual in whom, during weight gain, a state of energy imbalance results from mismatched energy intake and energy expenditure. It is important to note, however, that the obese individual might have achieved a state of energy balance (but at a higher level of body fat) if body weight and body composition are stable. It is our primary purpose in this chapter to provide the coach, athlete, and health professional with an appreciation of the factors regulating energy balance and the influence exercise has in the regulation of both energy intake and expenditure. In this chapter, we briefly discuss: (1) the components of energy expenditure; (2) methods of measurement; (3) the influence of physical activity on energy intake, resting metabolic rate (RMR), and thermic effect of feeding (TEF); and (4) possible mechanisms involved in the regulation of energy expenditure. The rationale for the selection of these topics is to highlight the importance of considering both intake and expenditure, as well as their interaction in the regulation of body weight and composition.

☐ DEFINITIONS OF THE COMPONENTS OF ENERGY EXPENDITURE

As shown in Figure 3-1, energy expenditure can be divided into three components: RMR, TEF, and the thermic effect of activity (TEA). Whereas food intake is episodic in nature (see Chapter 2), energy expenditure is continuous.

Resting metabolic rate, the largest portion of total energy expenditure, constitutes 60 to 75% of total daily energy expenditure in sedentary humans. It is influenced by such factors as age, sex, body size and composition, body temperature, thermogenic hormones, and prior exercise. It includes the energy expended in maintaining the integrated systems of the body and body temperature at rest, and it includes the energy required to maintain electrolyte gradients, to sustain cardiovascular and pulmonary work at rest, and to provide energy used by the central nervous system and other chemical reactions. Thyroid hormones are believed to play a major role in the regulation of RMR. Hypothyroidism is associated with a low RMR and hyperthyroidism with an increased RMR. It is difficult, however, to demonstrate a correlation between circulating concentrations of thyroid hormones and RMR in euthyroid individuals.

The thermic effect of a feeding (TEF) is the increased energy expenditure above the RMR after meal ingestion. The increase in energy expenditure is due to the energy required to digest, absorb, and metabolize nutrients. Following meal ingestion a measurable TEF lasts 4 to 8 h, depending on the quantity and type of macronutrient ingested (i.e., protein, fat, or carbohydrate). TEF constitutes approximately 10% of daily energy expenditure. TEF has been divided into two subcomponents: obligatory and facultative thermogenesis. The obligatory com-

Fig. 3–1. The three major components of daily energy expenditure: RMR, resting metabolic rate; TEF, thermic effect of feeding; and TEA, thermic effect of activity. From Poehlman, E.T.: A review: Exercise and its influence on resting energy metabolism in man. Med. Sci. Sports Exerc., *21*:515–525, 1989.

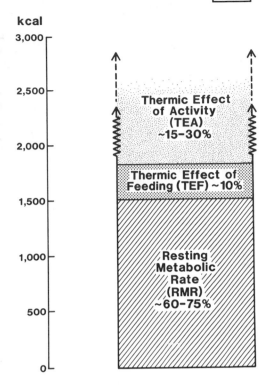

ponent of TEF is the energy cost associated with absorption and transport of nutrients and the synthesis of protein, fat, and carbohydrate. Several investigators have shown that the energy cost of storing and digesting macronutrients is higher than the theoretical values of obligatory nutrient disposal and storage.[1,2] This excess energy expended above the obligatory thermogenesis has been termed "facultative thermogenesis" and is thought to be partially mediated by sympathetic nervous system activity.

The thermic effect of activity (TEA) is the most variable component of energy expenditure in humans. This includes the additional energy expended above RMR and TEF due to muscular activity, including shivering and fidgeting, as well as purposeful physical exercise. In sedentary humans, TEA constitutes approximately 15% of total daily energy expenditure; athletes training 5 to 6 h/day, it can constitute 50% of total daily energy expenditure. From a practical standpoint, the energy expenditure associated with physical activity is usually under 100 kcal/day in very sedentary individuals and can exceed 3000 kcal/day in individuals participating in endurance events. Thus physical activity represents the most significant factor governing 24-hour energy expenditure in humans. RMR, TEF, and TEA represent only partially distinct entities be-

TABLE 3–1. PREFERRED METHODS FOR ESTIMATING THE COMPONENTS OF TOTAL DAILY ENERGY EXPENDITURE

COMPONENT OF ENERGY EXPENDITURE	PREFERRED LABORATORY METHOD	COMMENT
Total daily energy expenditure	Doubly labeled water	Expensive but not invasive
Resting metabolic rate (RMR)	Indirect calorimetry using ventilated hood or tent	Fasted volunteer sleeps overnight in room where RMR is measured
Thermic effect of feeding (TEF)	Prolonged measurement of metabolic rate with hood or tent	Metabolic rate measured until it returns to baseline
Thermic effect of physical activity (TEA)	Indirect calorimetry	Direct energy cost of activity measured with mouthpiece, nose clips, or face mask
Fidgeting and nonexercise expenditure	Use of indirect calorimetry, doubly labeled water	Nonexercise expenditure = 24-h EE − RMR + TEF + TEA; or % time active quantified by radar using Doppler technique

cause they often overlap during the course of a normal day. Although daily variations in energy balance exist in which individuals are in slight energy deficit or surplus, it is clear that maintenance of stable body weight depends on tight coupling of energy intake and energy output over long periods of time.

☐ METHODS OF MEASUREMENT

Many methods of measurement of energy expenditure have become available over the years that vary in complexity and accuracy. Various studies use different methods of measurement, and the method of measurement can influence the outcome. It is important to gain an understanding of the differences in methods used to assess energy expenditure and their possible applications to laboratory research as well as their application in other settings.

DIRECT CALORIMETRY

The most accurate but not usually the most convenient method of measuring energy expenditure is direct calorimetry. This method yields errors of only 1 to 2% in long-term measurements. With direct calorimetry, one obtains a measure of the amount of heat generated by the body within an insulated environment.

Despite its accuracy, direct calorimetry has several disadvantages and is not widely used to study energy balance. Traditional total-body calorimeters are expensive to construct and operate and require an individual to remain confined for extended periods of time. Thus these conditions do not provide information on "free living" energy expenditure.

To circumvent some of these problems a "mobile space suit" has been developed that works on the principle of gradient layer calorimetry and permits the determination of energy expenditure during various physical activities.[3] With these suits, heat production is measured by tightly wrapping a substance of known thermal conductivity around the body and recording changes in temperature between outer and inner layers.

INDIRECT CALORIMETRY

The most widely used methods for measuring energy expenditure involve indirect calorimetry. These techniques have become the method of choice for the nutritionist or physiologist for exploring energy expenditure and the fuel source (protein, fats, and carbohydrates) used to provide energy in humans. The term "indirect" signifies that energy production is estimated by measuring oxygen consumption and carbon dioxide production rather than directly measuring heat transfer. This method requires that a steady state of CO_2 production and respiratory exchange be reached and that subjects have normal acid-base balance. For resting measurements, the volunteer is usually measured after a 10- to 12-hour fast in a supine or semireclined position. Depending on the equipment, the subject typically breathes through a mouthpiece, facemask, or ventilated hood or resides in a room calorimeter in which expired gases are collected. The room where the measurements are conducted is usually darkened and quiet, and the volunteer remains undisturbed during the measurement process. The measurements typically last 30 min to 1 h. Valuable information has been gained regarding the regulation of energy expenditure in humans using indirect calorimetry. Bogardus et al.[4] have shown that individual rates of energy expenditure tend to aggregate in families, suggesting that genetics plays a role in determining one's predisposition to be a "high burner" or "low burner" of calories. This group has further suggested that a reduced rate of energy expenditure is a familial trait and can predispose an individual to gain body weight.[5] Typical RMR values range from 0.7 kcal/min to 1.6 kcal/min depending on body size and gender.

Several methods have been used to measure O_2 consumption and CO_2 production, either at rest or during exercise. They vary in complexity, versatility, availability, and cost, but most provide fairly accurate data when used properly. Generally, an "open circuit" method is used in which both ends of the system are open to atmospheric pressure. The subject's inspired and expired air are kept separate by means of a 3-way respiratory valve or nonrebreathing mask. The expired gases are usually collected in a Douglas bag or Tissot respirometer for measurement of volume and analysis of O_2 and CO_2 content. This technique has been used to measure energy expenditure at rest and during exercise.

This approach has several disadvantages. These include hyperventilation in subjects who are not well-adapted to a mouthpiece, which yields inappropriately high rates of O_2 consumption and CO_2 production. It is frequently difficult to obtain an airtight seal around the subject's nose and mouth with a mask. Last, neither the mask nor the mouthpiece is suitable for prolonged measurements (i.e., energy expenditure after food consumption). When mouthpieces and face masks are used to measured O_2 consumption over prolonged periods, measurements are periodic and frequently uncomfortable for the volunteer.

To circumvent these problems, a ventilated hood system has been valuable for making relatively long-term (several hours) measurements of energy expenditure. Instead of collecting expired gases with a mouthpiece or face mask, a transparent hood with a snugly fitting collar is used. Air is drawn through the system by an adjustable-speed fan. The flow rate is measured by a pneumotachograph, and samples of the outflowing air are analyzed for O_2 and CO_2 content after adjusting for temperature and water vapor content. Oxygen consumption and CO_2 production are calculated from the differences in their concentrations in the inflowing and outflowing air and the flow rate.

Several indirect noncalorimetric methods for estimating energy expenditure have been used, but in general the errors are too great for research purposes. These include measurements of pulmonary ventilation volume, heart rate recording, activity recording, and use of mechanical meters (pedometers). Some of these methods are calibrated for individual subjects by indirect calorimetry in the laboratory and then used for estimates of energy expenditure under field conditions.

The use of doubly labeled water has now made it possible to measure total daily energy expenditure in free-living subjects over extended periods (typically 2 weeks). This is a major advance because of its noninvasive nature and apparently accurate assessment of total energy expenditure. The basis of this technique is that after a bolus dose of two stable isotopes of water (^2H_2O and $H_2^{18}O$), ^2H_2O is lost from the body in water alone, whereas $H_2^{18}O$ is lost not only in water but also as CO_2 via the carbonic anhydrase system.[6] The difference in the two turnover rates is therefore related to the CO_2 production rate, and with a knowledge of the fuel mixture oxidized (from the composition of the diet), energy expenditure can be calculated. The technique is simple to perform and involves (1) collection of baseline urine (or plasma) samples, (2) oral administration of the isotopes, (3) collection of urine (or plasma) to determine total body water, and (4) collection of daily urine (or plasma) samples for the period of study (usually 2 weeks in adults). The technique has been rigorously examined in humans and has an estimated error of 3 to 5%.[7]

With this array of techniques it is now possible to more fully dissect the components of energy expenditure in free-living humans. Daily energy expenditure, and thus daily energy requirements, can be derived using (1) doubly labeled water for measuring total daily expenditure, (2) respiratory gas analysis and indirect calorimetry for measuring RMR, (3) respiratory gas analysis for measuring the energy expenditure of given physical activities, and (4) the estimated thermic effect of feeding. With these techniques it is also possible to examine the effects of exercise on nonexercising energy expenditure. This component refers to the energy cost of daily activities such as fidgeting and nonpurposeful movement. This remains an unexplored area of research and significantly contributes to daily energy expenditure. With the use of doubly labeled water, one can estimate the energy cost of nonexercising energy expenditure by subtracting from daily energy expenditure the energy cost of RMR, TEF, and exercise. It is presently unclear whether exercise causes individuals to be more active or less active during nonexercising time. From a practical perspective, one could hope that participation in various types of exercise actually stimulate energy expenditure during nonexercising time. One could equally hypothesize, however, that an individual would be more sedentary during nonexercising time because of fatigue and thereby partially negate the enhancing effects of exercise on total energy expenditure. Is there an ideal exercise prescription that will not only directly increase energy expenditure but possibly enhance physical activity during nonexercising time? Variations in nonexercising energy expenditure in response to an exercise program could partially contribute to the large variation in weight loss and changes in body composition among individuals despite similar exercise prescriptions.

☐ INFLUENCE OF PHYSICAL ACTIVITY ON FOOD INTAKE

Exercise plays a central role in influencing food intake. One research question of interest is whether the increased energy expenditure caused by physical activity is matched by corresponding increases in caloric intake, in order to maintain energy balance. Of equal importance is the source (carbohydrates, protein, and fat) of the calories consumed in response to increased physical activity. This question is of particular interest to individuals participating in prolonged or vigorous exercise in which adequate food and nutrient intake is required to sustain the physical activity and replete energy stores. Methodological limitations, however, frequently hamper understanding of the relation between spontaneous food intake and energy expenditure. Self-recording of food intake is frequently unreliable and demonstrates large interindividual variation. The simple fact that volunteers are aware that food intake is being measured makes it impossible to assess changes in spontaneous food intake in response to an environmental stressor such as exercise. Self-recording of food intake, however, can be useful in the understanding of nutritional trends in a group of individuals. To critically examine the interaction of food intake and physical exercise, surreptitious monitoring of food intake is preferred.

The effects of short-term and long-term exercise on food intake have been examined in some detail. The effects of one bout of exercise on appetite have been recently examined by Thompson et al.[8] They compared the short-term effects of low- and high-intensity steady-state cycling exercise of similar caloric output on test meal intake (in terms of liquid and solid-source kilocalories, carbohydrate, fat, and protein) in young males. Brief suppression of perceived hunger was observed immediately after high-intensity exercise but not after low-intensity exercise. This suggests that exercise intensity is a determinant of appetite. Appetite suppression was of short duration, however, and it did not affect total caloric intake in a meal 1 hour after exercise. On the basis of these results, it is unlikely that transient suppression of appetite by physical exercise would contribute to loss of body weight.

Kissileff et al.[9] examined the short-term effects of 40 minutes of strenuous and moderate exercise on food intake in obese and nonobese women. Nonobese women reduced their food intake after strenuous exercise as compared to moderate exercise, whereas obese women showed no adaptive response to the exercise stimuli. Future studies should try to identify possible mechanisms for the disparate responses between obese and lean individuals and between athletic and nonathletic individuals in response to short-term exercise.

The long-term effects of exercise on food intake have also been examined, but study results have been inconsistent. In a classic study, Mayer et al.[10] described physical activity levels in which different food intake responses were provoked. Rats were exercised for a minimum of 14 days. Exercise durations less than 60 min were not followed by increased food intake; in fact, small decreases in food intake were observed. At 2 to 6 h of exercise, food intake was tightly matched to exercise energy expenditure. This finding suggests that exercise is a strong modulator of food intake and that various levels of exercise modify food intake in different ways. Widdowson et al.[11] measured daily energy intake and energy output of 12 cadets leading a rigorously controlled life at a military academy. When individual daily intake and expenditure were compared over the short term (1 to 2 days), no relation was found between the two variables. The means of the individual intakes and expenditures over 14 days, however, were well matched. Short-term matching of food intake to increased physical activity in humans is probably imprecise, whereas extended exercise might be more precisely coupled to food intake.

McGowan et al.[12] explored the effects of no exercise, regular exercise, and double exercise on self-reported caloric intake. Caloric intake did not differ significantly between the exercise conditions, suggesting that short-term fluctuations in physical activity were not accompanied by corresponding changes in caloric intake. The study data were subject to bias, however, because the subjects recorded their own food intakes and were aware of the study's hypothesis.

In our opinion, the most impressive work examining the response of food intake to energy expenditure in humans has been performed by

Woo and colleagues.[13,14] Of particular note are the duration of their studies and the controlled environment that permitted spontaneous assessment of food intake behavior. In the first study,[13] they examined the effects of increased activity on the caloric intake in 6 obese women during 3 19-day sessions: 1 sedentary session and 2 sessions with treadmill exercise that increased daily energy expenditure by 100% (mild) and 125% (moderate) of sedentary levels. Daily energy expenditure and ad libitum intakes were determined by physical activity diaries and covert monitoring of food intake. Negative energy balances were observed with mild and moderate exercise, because subjects did not increase their food intakes to compensate for the increased activity. In obese women, moderate levels of physical activity do not appear to influence food intake.

In a follow-up study, Woo and Pi-Sunyer[14] engaged five nonobese women in sedentary, mild, and moderate levels of physical activity. The women matched food intake with energy expenditure during a sedentary period, with compensatory increases in food intake in response to both physical activity regimens. The authors speculated that high levels of body fat contribute to the unresponsiveness of food intake to physical activity.

Although there is substantial evidence that exercise influences food intake (at least in normal-weight individuals), specific metabolic signals have not been identified. In general, signaling mechanisms have been thought to be related to glucose and fat metabolism. A "glucostatic" signal, generated by changes in intracellular glucose utilization, might operate in the short term to control food intake after a bout of exercise.[15] The influence of long-term exercise on food intake might be governed by a "lipostatic" signal that is generated by body fat reserves.[16] Tremblay et al.[17] showed that runners who were formerly obese resist losing fat despite an increase in exercise. Their plateau in weight loss was coincident with their inability to increase in vitro adipocyte-stimulated lipolysis over the level measured in control subjects.

Tremblay et al.[18] recently suggested that acute exercise influences caloric intake by its influence on the fuel source oxidized during and after exercise. That is, depending on the magnitude of the exercise-induced increase in fat oxidation, individuals can either overeat or undereat in response to exercise. They proposed that exercise exerts control over food intake either by its influence on body fat reserves or by altering the source of fuel oxidation.

The goal for athletes who consider their weight to be optimal should be to maintain energy balance by matching caloric intake to energy expenditure. Ensuring adequate energy intake to meet the metabolic demands of increased physical activity might not be a simple task. Because the level of energy expenditure ultimately determines the level of caloric intake, it is important to appreciate the biological and behavioral contributions to the matching (or mismatching) of intake to expenditure and their influence on energy balance.

☐ PHYSICAL TRAINING AND RESTING METABOLIC RATE

Although exercise training and RMR are frequently considered independent components of energy expenditure, recent studies have shown that exercise training enhances RMR when subjects are maintained in energy balance. This finding suggests that in addition to the direct energy cost of exercise training, exercise training also influences resting energy expenditure.[19,20]

The fact that RMR is closely correlated with body size has led to the view that basal energy requirements are constant for a given body size, body composition, age, and sex.[21] Nevertheless, RMR has been shown to vary widely among individuals independent of these determinants. Another factor that might influence individual variation in RMR is level of physical activity. Both cross-sectional and exercise intervention studies have examined the effects of physical activity on RMR.

Tremblay et al.[22] measured RMR in 8 trained and 8 lean untrained males. RMR was similar in these 2 groups of men (~1.37 kcal/min). In a later study, however, Tremblay et al.[23] noted a higher RMR in 20 physically trained men (1.17 ± 0.03 kcal/min) compared to 39 untrained men (1.05 ± 0.02). In the same study, 8 moderately obese women participated in an 11-week program of physical training and an 8% increase in RMR (per kilogram of fat-free weight) was found.

Our own work has also supported a higher RMR in highly trained men.[24,25] We found a 10% higher RMR in a group of trained men after comparing them to an untrained group matched for fat-free weight and body fat. This finding suggests that differences in body composition cannot solely account for the differences in RMR in trained and untrained men. Although thyroid hormones play a major role in regulating RMR, no differences in plasma levels of triiodothyronine or thyroxine were noted. The additional energy expenditure associated with a higher RMR can be extrapolated to an increase in daily energy expenditure of ~170 kcal per day and would result in a loss of approximately 8 kg over 1 year if caloric intake was not increased accordingly. Thus, high levels of food intake are a prerequisite for active individuals to maintain energy balance. This finding of increased RMR was later confirmed in older endurance-trained men (>60 years) who were found to have a higher RMR (~7%) than age-matched inactive men (Fig. 3-2).[26] These findings suggest that, regardless of age, males appear to have the capacity to increase RMR in response to exercise training.

Fewer studies have examined the effects of exercise training on RMR in females. The studies by Lawson et al.[27] and Lennon et al.[28] support increased RMR after exercise training in young females. In the study by Lawson et al., the RMR of 6 obese females was increased after a 10-week program of jogging. No alteration in body weight or body composition was observed. This result suggests that the women increased their caloric intake to match an increase in energy expenditure by exercise to maintain energy balance. In the study of Lennon et al.,[28] a high-intensity exercise group had an elevated RMR, whereas a low-intensity exercise

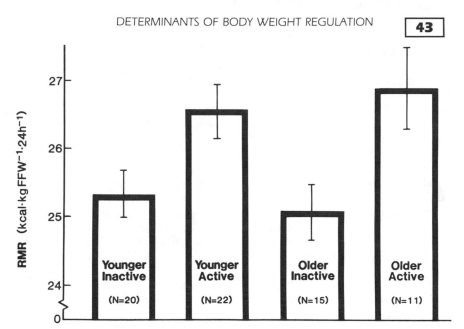

Fig. 3–2. Effects of age and level of endurance training on the ratio of RMR to fat-free weight. A significant main effect of endurance training, but not age, was found, indicating that younger and older endurance-trained (active) had a higher RMR (~6%) relative to untrained (inactive) younger and older men. From Poehlman, E.T., McAuliffe, T.L., VanHouten, D.R., and Danforth, E., Jr.: Influence of age and endurance training on metabolic rate and hormones in healthy men. Am. J. Physiol., *259:E66*, 1990.

group failed to show any significant change in RMR. This suggests that a threshold of exercise intensity of at least 50% VO_{2max} in a physical conditioning program is necessary to increase RMR. Other studies do not support a "training effect" on RMR in females, however. LeBlanc et al.[29] measured resting oxygen consumption in 30 females separated into untrained, moderately trained, and highly trained females. The authors reported no statistical difference in fasting oxygen consumption among the 3 groups. Similar results were reported by Owen et al.[30] who found no difference between trained and untrained women in RMR normalized per kilogram of body weight.

Discrepant results among investigators might be partially due to differences in the definition of a highly trained individual and small sample sizes that lack the statistical power to detect significant differences between active and inactive individuals. Another possible reason for the discrepant results might be the failure to account for dietary practices that could influence resting metabolic rate and body composition. This deficiency in experimental design is surprising because "normal" eating behavior of many young women in affluent societies is characterized by restriction of food intake in order to comply with social pressures to be lean. In a recent study from our laboratory,[31] we measured the influence of exercise training and dietary restraint on RMR in nonobese females. We noted a significant relation between RMR and VO_{2max} ($r = 0.54$; $P < 0.01$) in this population that was independent of differences in fat-free weight. Furthermore, higher levels of dietary restraint were associated with higher levels of percent body fat ($r = 0.31$; $P < 0.05$) and a tendency to have a lower RMR ($r = -0.29$; $P < 0.07$) after controlling for differences in body composition. Collectively, these findings suggest that resting energy requirements are higher in endurance-trained females. Second, restrained eating might lower the resting energy requirements by its influence on RMR and might contribute to the propensity to gain body fat. It is also reasonable to speculate that the absence of a relation between RMR and VO_{2max} in other studies of young females might have been partially due to the inclusion of restrained eaters in the sample populations.

PHYSICAL TRAINING AND THE THERMIC EFFECT OF FEEDING

The thermic effect of feeding (TEF), as stated previously, makes up approximately 10% of 24-h energy expenditure and is thought to be quantitatively important in the long-term regulation of body weight. The TEF is proportional in magnitude and duration to the size of the ingested meal.[32]

Several studies have examined the effect of "training status" on TEF. Tremblay et al.[22] examined TEF after consumption of a 1600-kcal meal in 8 trained and 8 untrained males. TEF was higher in untrained (~50 kcal) compared to trained individuals (~26 kcal). They concluded that exercise training exerted a sparing effect on energy expenditure after meal ingestion. LeBlanc et al.[33] and Poehlman et al.[24] confirmed these results by reporting a lower TEF in trained men as compared with sedentary subjects after ingestion of a meal. Furthermore, plasma norepinephrine, which increased in sedentary subjects after meal consumption, was not altered in trained men.[33] These findings suggest that reduced TEF associated with exercise training was related to diminished activity of the sympathetic nervous system.

The findings from studies using female volunteers yield different results with respect to the relation between training status and TEF. LeBlanc et al.[29] found a reduced TEF in the first 60 min after meal ingestion in exercise-trained female subjects when compared with untrained females. No differences in TEF, however, were found between groups for the integrated increase in oxygen consumption over the total 2-hour period after meal ingestion. The authors speculated that trained females, at least during the first 60 min after meal consumption, shunted more of the nutrients to replete glycogen reserves, a less costly metabolic pathway than storage of carbohydrates in the form of fat. Owen et al.[30] measured TEF for 4 h after consumption of a meal and found no difference between athletic and nonathletic women. TEF was directly related to the burning of carbohydrate, but no association was noted between TEF and utilization of fat or protein. Thus, at present, there is no convincing evidence that exercise training alters the magnitude of TEF in females.

It could be hypothesized that in males, high levels of endurance training result in a greater efficiency (i.e., lower TEF) of nutrient utilization after meal consumption. This improved efficiency could represent an adaptive mechanism in the highly trained individual who seeks to preserve energy in the face of high levels of energy output generated by exercise training. It is possible that the absence of differences in TEF between trained and untrained females is related to the lower level of endurance fitness achieved in female athletes relative to their male counterparts and/or higher levels of body fat. A lower TEF might only be observed in highly trained individuals with very low levels of body fat.

☐ POSSIBLE MECHANISMS FOR THE HIGHER RESTING METABOLIC RATE IN TRAINED INDIVIDUALS

The mechanism(s) for the high RMR in highly trained men and women remain to be established. An increase in substrate cycling in response to exercise might contribute to the higher metabolic rate in trained individuals. A substrate cycle is said to exist when two opposing, nonequilibrium reactions catalyzed by different enzymes are operating simultaneously. At least one of the reactions must involve the hydrolysis of adenosine triphosphate (ATP). Thus the substrate cycle is the liberation of heat and consumption of energy, yet there is no net conversion of substrate to product. In a recent study, Bahr et al.[34] found that in young males the triglyceride/fatty acid substrate cycle (as determined by infusion of glycerol) was three times higher in the immediate postexercise state and that the energy cost associated with this cycle can account for a significant part (50%) of postexercise oxygen consumption.

The energy cost of protein and amino acid metabolism might contribute to the higher RMR. Lamont et al.[35] compared whole-body leucine kinetics in endurance-trained and sedentary control subjects. Trained subjects had a higher resting metabolic rate relative to untrained volunteers, and the correlation between protein turnover and resting metabolic rate reached $r = 0.61$; $P < 0.05$.

The endurance-trained individual is in energy balance, but in a "high caloric flux." Frequently these individuals expend in excess of 1500 kcal/day in their training but consume a large number of calories to satisfy energy needs and to replete glycogen stores. In previous studies, VO_{2max} has been found to correlate positively with RMR.[25] The metabolic link between VO_{2max} and resting metabolic rate, however, remains unclear. A plausible hypothesis is that the high VO_{2max} is a biological marker for the high-flux state of the endurance-trained athlete. That is, the higher state of caloric flux in the trained individual could be associated with the higher RMR. Preliminary evidence that the level of caloric flux influences metabolic rate is provided by Woo et al.[36] A high-flux state was created by overfeeding 6 men whose energy expenditure was increased proportionally by participation in long-duration aerobic exercise to maintain energy balance. RMR was found to be higher after a high level of energy intake was matched to a high level of exercise training. Future research examining the effects of energy flux on energy expenditure would enhance our understanding of environmental factors regulating body composition when individuals are in energy balance.

☐ SUMMARY

This chapter has focused on the interrelationships of food intake, physical activity, RMR, and TEF. Energy expenditure determines energy needs, but research examining the interaction of food intake with energy expenditure has been hampered by methodological limitations. Important questions regarding the influence of various levels of physical activity on the regulation of food and macronutrient intake in different populations remain unanswered and represent interesting areas for future research. RMR represents the largest component of daily energy expenditure and responds to periods of energy imbalance and possibly periods of high-energy flux when individuals achieve energy balance. Physical activity represents the most variable component of energy expenditure and thus offers the most attractive therapeutic modality to control body weight and lose body fat. TEF represents a smaller component of total energy expenditure and has been shown to be influenced by physical activity. An understanding of those factors influencing energy intake and energy expenditure will advance our knowledge of energy metabolism and will help develop strategies designed to plan for nutritional and energy requirements in exercising and nonexercising individuals.

☐ REFERENCES

1. Acheson, K.J., Ravussin, E., Wahren, J., and Jéquier, E.: Thermic effect of glucose in man: Obligatory and facultative thermogenesis. J. Clin. Invest., 74:1572, 1984.
2. Thiebaud, D., et al.: Energy cost of glucose storage in human subjects during glucose-infusions. Am. J. Physiol., 244:E216, 1983.
3. Webb, P., Annis, J.F., and Troutman, S.J., Jr.: Energy balance in man measured by direct and indirect calorimetry. Am. J. Clin. Nutr., 33:1287, 1980.
4. Bogardus, C., et al.: Familial dependence of resting metabolic rate. N. Engl. J. Med., 315:96, 1986.
5. Ravussin, E., et al.: Reduced rate of energy expenditure as a risk factor for body-weight gain. N. Engl. J. Med., 318:467, 1988.
6. Lifson, N., Gordon, G.B., and McClintock, R.: Measurement of total carbon dioxide production by means of $D_2{}^{18}O$. J. Appl. Physiol., 7:704, 1955.
7. Schoeller, D.A., et al.: Energy expenditure by doubly labeled water: Validation in humans and proposed calculation. Am. J. Physiol., 250:R823, 1986.

8. Thompson, D.A., Wolfe, L.A., and Eikelboom, R.: Acute effects of exercise intensity on appetite in young men. Med. Sci. Sports Exerc., *20*:222, 1988.
9. Kissileff, H.R., et al.: Acute effects of exercise on food intake in obese and nonobese women. Am. J. Clin. Nutr., *52*:240, 1990.
10. Mayer, J., et al.: Exercise, food intake and body weight in normal rats and genetically obese adult mice. Am. J. Physiol., *177*:544, 1954.
11. Widdowson, E.M., Edholm, O.G., and McCance, R.A.: Food intake and energy expenditure of cadets in training. Br. J. Nutr., *8*:147, 1954.
12. McGowan, C.R., et al.: The effect of exercise on non-restricted caloric intake in male joggers. Appetite, *7*:97, 1986.
13. Woo, R., Garrow, J.S., and Pi-Sunyer, F.X.: Effect of exercise on spontaneous calorie intake in obesity. Am. J. Clin. Nutr., *36*:470, 1982.
14. Woo, R., and Pi-Sunyer, F.X.: Effect of increased physical activity on voluntary intake in lean women. Metabolism, *34*:836, 1985.
15. Mayer, J., and Thomas, D. W.: Regulation of food intake and obesity. Science, *156*:328, 1967.
16. Friedman, M.I., and Ramirez, I.: Relationship of fat metabolism to food intake. Am. J. Clin. Nutr., *42*:1093, 1985.
17. Tremblay, A., Després, J.P., and Bouchard, C.: Adipose tissue characteristics of ex-obese long distance runners. Int. J. Obesity, *8*:641, 1984.
18. Tremblay, A., Plourde,. G., Després, J.P., and Bouchard, C.: Impact of dietary fat content and fat oxidation on energy intake in humans. Am. J. Clin. Nutr., *49*:799, 1989.
19. Poehlman, E.T., and Horton, E.S.: The impact of food intake and exercise on energy expenditure. Nutr. Rev., *48*:129, 1989.
20. Poehlman, E.T.: A review: Exercise and its influence on resting energy metabolism in man. Med. Sci. Sports Exerc., *21*:515, 1989.
21. Ravussin, E., et al.: Determinants of 24-h energy expenditure in man. J. Clin. Invest., *78*:1568, 1986.
22. Tremblay, A., Côte, J., and LeBlanc, J.: Diminished dietary thermogenesis in exercise-trained human subjects. Eur. J. Appl. Physiol., *52*:1, 1983.
23. Tremblay, A., et al.: The effect of exercise-training on resting metabolic rate in lean and moderately obese individuals. Int. J. Obesity, *10*:511, 1986.
24. Poehlman, E.T., Melby, C.L., and Badylak, S.F.: Resting metabolic rate and postprandial thermogenesis in highly trained and untrained males. Am. J. Clin. Nutr., *47*:793, 1988.
25. Poehlman, E.T., Melby, C.L., Badylak, S.F., and Calles, J.: Aerobic fitness and resting energy expenditure in young adult males. Metabolism, *38*:85, 1989.
26. Poehlman, E.T., McAuliffe, T.L., Van Houten, D.R., and Danforth, E., Jr.: Influence of age and endurance training on metabolic rate and hormones in healthy men. Am. J. Physiol., *259*:E66, 1990.
27. Lawson, S., Webster, J.D., Pacy, P.J., and Garrow, J.S.: Effect of a 10 week aerobic programme on metabolic rate, body composition in lean and sedentary females. Br. J. Clin. Prac., *41*:684, 1987.
28. Lennon, D.F., et al.: Diet and exercise training effects on resting metabolic rate. Int. J. Obesity, *9*:39, 1984.
29. LeBlanc, J., Mercier, P., and Samson, P.: Diet-induced thermogenesis with relation to training state in female subjects. Can. J. Physiol. Pharmacol., *62*:334, 1984.
30. Owen, O.E., et al.: A reappraisal of caloric requirements in healthy women. Am. J. Clin. Nutr., *44*:1, 1986.
31. Poehlman, E.T., Viers, H.F., and Detzer, M.: Influence of physical activity and dietary restraint on resting energy expenditure in young nonobese females. Can. J. Physiol. Pharmacol., *69*:320–326, 1991.

32. Hill, J.O., Heymsfield, S.B., and McMannus, C.B. III: Meal size and the thermic response to food in male subjects as a function of maximal aerobic capacity. Metabolism, 33:743, 1984.
33. LeBlanc, J., Diamond, J., Côté, J., and Labrie, A.: Hormonal factors in reduced postprandial heat production of exercise trained subjects. J. Appl. Physiol., 56:772, 1984.
34. Bahr, R., Hansson, P., and Sejersted, O.M.: Triglyceride/fatty acid cycling is increased after exercise. Metabolism, 39:993, 1990.
35. Lamont, L.S., Patel, D.G., and Kalhan, S.C.: Leucine kinetics in endurance-trained humans. J. Appl. Physiol., 69:1, 1990.
36. Woo, R., O'Connell, M., Horton, E.S., and Danforth, E., Jr.: Changes in resting energy metabolism with increased intake and exercise (abstract). Clin. Res., 33:712A, 1985.

C H A P T E R

4

NUTRIENT INTAKE AND THE REGULATION OF BODY WEIGHT AND BODY COMPOSITION

Carol N. Meredith and Judith S. Stern

According to a 1989 survey sent out to the National Governing Bodies of the U.S. Olympic Committee, the aspects of nutrition that coaches and trainers considered most important for athletes were adequate diet, supplements, fluid balance, weight loss, and weight gain. Athletes, coaches, and trainers are acutely conscious of body size, shape, and composition as they relate to performance and the weight requirements of their sport. They are constantly seeking the best dietary strategies to attain an ideal body.

Research has identified the best combination of nutrients to enhance performance in competitions involving endurance exercise (see Chapter 5). Long-term regulation of body weight and body composition by diet and exercise, however, is more complex. Studies in humans and experimental animals show that a restriction of food intake affects basal metabolic rate, thermic effect of meals, fat stores, lean tissue stores, voluntary activity, and probably food choice. In addition, once the diet-restricted individual starts to eat freely again, there may be changes in the amount and type of food chosen, rate of weight gain, fat stores, and fat distribution. Studies in experimental animals have shown that these adaptations can be modulated by the composition of the diet and by exercise. The proportions of carbohydrate, protein, fat, and fiber in the diet modulate the response during weight loss and during weight gain. Exercise training during weight loss and weight gain can modulate effects on metabolism and body composition in different ways, depending on its type, intensity, and frequency.

This chapter describes how changes in dietary quality and quantity affect body composition in sedentary and active persons. This information is fundamental for athletes and their coaches, to understand the dietary strategies that will allow athletes to attain good performance, develop an esthetically pleasing body shape, qualify in an appropriate weight class, ensure adequate growth and development, and protect their long-term health.

☐ WEIGHT LOSS IN ATHLETES

In contrast to most people, athletes have a high energy expenditure and can maintain a lean body while consuming substantial amounts of food. To become even leaner, they can increase exercise duration or intensity or cut back on food intake.

The ideal body for most athletes is muscular and low in fat. For athletes whose sport involves defying the pull of gravity as they run or jump, carrying around less weight will improve performance. Among the leanest athletes are distance runners and triathletes. It is easiest for them to maintain low body weight because of the high energy cost of their sports. Many athletes who compete in defined weight categories seek an exceptionally low body weight relative to height or body frame, as has been noted in wrestlers and rowers. Finally, there are sports and activities where points are awarded for esthetic appeal, such as gymnastics, ice-skating, dancing, or diving. The efforts of these athletes to reduce body fat are hampered by the comparatively low energy cost of their physical training.

The athlete can attempt to lose body weight by producing an imbalance in the amount of food energy consumed and the amount of energy expended in training, or, as a short-term strategy, by dehydration; however, a negative energy balance produces rapid metabolic adaptations, which tend to slow the rate of weight loss. Added exercise can decrease energy conservation during dieting and alter the composition of weight loss by preserving lean tissue.

Energy expenditure at rest decreases if energy intake is not sufficient for daily needs. Energy conservation is influenced by thyroid hormones and dietary carbohydrate intake.[1] Dietary carbohydrate, as opposed to dietary fat, enhances energy metabolism, mediated in part by thyroid hormone.[1] Exercise training superimposed on negative energy balance has been reported by a number of investigators to suppress the reduction in resting metabolic rate (RMR).[2-4] Other scientists, however, have found that this is associated with a further reduction in RMR[5,6] or no effect.[7,8] Discrepancies could be due to different states of training, different levels of energy deficit, variations in the duration, type and intensity of exercise, and individual variability.[9] Highly trained athletes consuming an adequate diet have a higher RMR than sedentary persons, due to a higher proportion of lean tissue[10] and possibly to a mild "acute phase reaction" produced by regular vigorous exercise[11] or to changes in the metabolism of catecholamines.[12] An energy deficit lowers the metabolic rate, whereas vigorous training slightly increases metabolic rate. A dieting athlete combines these two competing stimuli.

Some 10% of the energy in food is expended as the cost of its digestion and metabolism (thermic effect of food, or TEF). Athletes consuming very little food proportionately lower the metabolic cost of diet consumption. But athletic training can also modify the thermic effect of food. In lean young persons who start training, there is a direct relationship between the improvement in aerobic capacity and the increase in the thermic effect of food.[13] The effect of a single bout of exercise on the increased thermic effect of food varies with the time elapsed since exercise. It is greatest near the exercise bout, and by 16 h after exercise it is usually back to normal.[10,14,15] In highly trained men, the thermic effects of a single meal are about 36% higher than for sedentary men.[16] The exercise-related increases in TEF are probably related to the energy cost of resynthesizing muscle glycogen[17] and to an enhanced sensitivity to catecholamines.[16] Again, the athlete who goes on a hypocaloric diet and continues to train vigorously provides divergent signals for the regulation of the thermic effect of food. For the athlete who wants to lose weight, however, it is useful to know that the body's attempt to conserve energy appears to become less effective if training continues, making weight loss easier.

When food is restricted, the body uses its own reserves to provide energy for exercise and other activities. Tissues mainly oxidize a combination of fat and glucose for energy, but some tissues, such as the brain and red blood cells, use only glucose as fuel. When dietary intake is very low, the body uses its small reserves of liver glycogen to provide glucose to other tissues, but mainly it draws on the large reserve of gluconeogenic amino acids maintained in its proteins, especially in muscle, to make glucose in the liver. The constant need for a supply of glucose gradually diminishes the body's protein and lean tissue, unless the low-energy diet is very rich in dietary protein. Inevitably, most low-energy diets lead to a gradual loss of protein and lean tissue from the body at the same time that they produce a loss of body fat. Exercise, however, can alter the rate of protein loss in different tissues, with a conservation of protein in exercised tissues even during starvation.[18]

Other adaptations to an energy deficit are too numerous to detail here. There are hormonal changes mediated by the hypothalamus. In addition to lower levels of thyroid hormones and increased corticosteroids, the reproductive hormones tend to decline. Undernutrition is associated with a decline in voluntary physical activity,[19] and dieting can have a similar effect. Sedentary free-living subjects who have lost 23% of their body weight during dietary treatment for obesity show a 25% decline in nonresting energy expenditure per unit of body weight,[20] which is apparently due to increased efficiency of movement and a curtailment of voluntary activity.[21] Everyday movements such as walking at different speeds and random movements while standing or sitting (fidgeting) account for some of the differences in daily energy expenditure between different persons of similar age and body composition.[22] The effect of low food intake on trivial movements and the desire to exercise has not been examined in athletes.

RAPID WEIGHT LOSS

Athletes competing in specific weight categories use dietary and other means to lose weight fast. If the composition of weight loss is not important, the quickest way to lose weight is by losing body water.

Dehydration can be accomplished by sweating in a sauna or a rubberized suit, by using diuretics, and by low water intake. The amount of water lost by wrestlers a day before competing can be 5% of body weight.[23] Water is essential for regulating body temperature, and a dehydrated athlete becomes overheated and fatigued more easily. In a hot environment, the dehydrated athlete can feel nauseous and confused even before heat exhaustion occurs. Loss of endurance and coordination due to dehydration can impair exercise performance.[23] In the extreme, dehydration can lead to death.[24]

Fasting has been used to produce rapid weight loss. The decline in body weight is due to water and protein loss in addition to loss of fat tissue. In the absence of food, a person loses body water through greater urine output, even if water intake is adequate, to help excrete some of the metabolites produced by the breakdown of fat and protein. Glycogen stores in the liver are gradually depleted, but muscle glycogen remains almost normal if the person is at rest.

Fasting can be detrimental to athletic performance. Low-intensity endurance exercise performed at 45% of maximal aerobic capacity (VO_{2max}) is not impaired.[25] Intense aerobic exercise performance, however, measured as time to exhaustion, declines in cyclists[26] and runners[27] following as little as 24 h of fasting. This decline is probably linked to depletion of muscle glycogen, which is less critical for low-intensity exercise than for exercise performed at intensities greater than about 60% VO_{2max}.

In sedentary men, a 3-day fast leads to accelerated muscle protein breakdown, as shown by an increase in the excretion of 3-methylhistidine.[28] If exercise is performed in the glycogen-depleted state, which can be the case during a fast, there is a greater breakdown of body proteins, indicated by greater urea excretion[29] and by an increase in leucine oxidation.[30] It is likely that exercise combined with fasting accelerates the loss of lean tissue.

Very-low-calorie diets providing less than 800 kcal/day have an effect that is intermediate between fasting and a restricted diet. Body builders who are preparing for competition by trying to lose subcutaneous fat in order to enhance the "cut" of their muscles consume such diets in the days before the event but should be aware of a possible decline in exercise capacity and in muscle mass.

PROLONGED DIETARY RESTRICTION

Some athletes who need to stay light to improve performance consume surprisingly low amounts of food. For example, the energy intake of female distance runners determined by diet records is usually similar to the average intake of sedentary women, even though they run 70 miles per week.[31,32] Forty-eight percent of young dancers consume less than 1900 Kcal/day.[33] The proportion of protein, carbohydrate, and fat in a restricted diet can modulate the effects of an energy deficit on body composition.

The Recommended Dietary Allowance for protein (0.8 g/kg per day) is inadequate for endurance athletes[34] and for sedentary persons on a low-energy diet.[35] Endurance athletes need at least 1.2 g protein/kg per day,[34] and protein intake should be even higher when they restrict energy intake. The loss of lean body mass that accompanies weight loss in sedentary persons can be reduced by increasing the amount of protein in the diet, as shown by a more rapid return to nitrogen balance.[35] A high protein intake in untrained obese subjects during very-low-calorie diets appears to protect their capacity for endurance exercise and anaerobic exercise.[36] In athletes consuming a normal diet, a bout of endurance exercise has a catabolic effect on the body's proteins[37] followed by a marked increase in muscle protein synthesis.[38] Over the long term, the net effect of exercise on body proteins is anabolic, as shown by the large lean mass of many athletes and the improved retention of dietary nitrogen when an energy deficit is caused by endurance exercise rather than by dietary restriction.[39,40] The effects of low energy intake on exercise-induced catabolic and anabolic phases of muscle protein metabolism have not been studied in detail. Before supplementing their diet with protein, athletes should keep dietary records to analyze their protein intake. The typical American diet is rich in protein. A very large protein intake could, in the long term, damage kidney health in susceptible persons.

Athletes can adapt to a high-fat diet without impairing their capacity for endurance exercise at low to moderate intensities.[41] In previously sedentary persons, a low-energy diet providing most of the energy as carbohydrate or as fat does not decrease the capacity for participating in an endurance exercise program.[42] However, athletes are encouraged to eat a low-fat diet. In the short term, a high-fat diet is detrimental to performance, and its long-term effects include an increased risk of cardiovascular disease and some types of cancer.[43] Fat is the most concentrated form of fuel a person can consume and metabolically the easiest to store.[44] Favorite snack foods in our society, such as doughnuts, chocolate, ice cream, and desserts, are sugary and rich in fat. In experimental animals, this combination of easily absorbed carbohydrate and high fat

TABLE 4–1. THE 1990 DIETARY GUIDELINE FOR AMERICANS, APPROPRIATE FOR ATHLETES AS WELL

Maintain healthy weight*
Choose a diet low in fat, saturated fat, and cholesterol
Choose a diet with plenty of vegetables, fruits, and grain products
Use sugars in moderation
Use salt and sodium in moderation

* Athletes might want to attain a lower weight, appropriate for their sport.

produces a release of insulin and an increase in lipoprotein lipase activity in adipose tissue, favoring accelerated storage of dietary fat.[45] Rats fed a high-fat diet acquire a "high-fat" body. When treadmill exercise is combined with a high-fat diet, accumulation of body fat is tempered.[46]

The high-carbohydrate diet recommended for the days before a competition is the best for maintaining low fat stores and high muscle glycogen levels. A diet providing about 70% of energy as carbohydrates is less fattening than a high-fat diet supplying the same amount of calories.[47] A survey of various types of endurance athletes, such as cyclists, runners, and swimmers, showed that at higher energy intakes the proportion of carbohydrate in the diet increased; even in athletes with a relatively low energy intake, dietary carbohydrate was greater than for the population in general.[48]

Some athletes, especially in sports demanding skill and strength rather than endurance, tend to eat a high-fat diet. Because the average American diet is so rich in fat, athletes must make a conscious effort to reduce their fat intake. Even very active men with a daily energy expenditure of 4000 kcal should consume no more than 134 g of fat per day, to comply with dietary guidelines that restrict fat to 30% of total calories (Table 4-1). This amount of fat would be provided by 2 glasses of whole milk, 2 strips of bacon, 1 ounce of butter, 3 cookies, 1 ounce of cheese, a club steak, plus 1 scoop of ice cream, which might not seem like a large amount of food to a highly trained athlete.

During recovery from a bout of endurance or resistance exercise, glucose utilization is enhanced, with rapid resynthesis of muscle glycogen (see Chapter 5). The intake of high-carbohydrate drinks and foods after exercise favors glycogen storage, which enhances exercise performance.

Some athletes choose a vegetarian diet, supplying foods that are rich in fiber and, usually, low in fat. The fiber affects the rate of nutrient absorption and alters the insulin response to a meal. A high-fiber, low-fat diet affects the excretion pattern of estrogens and other steroid hormones.[49] Women consuming a low-calorie vegetarian diet are more likely to have anovulatory cycles and lowered reproductive hormone levels in the luteal phase than women consuming the same amount of calories in an omnivorous diet.[50] In athletic women, a high-fiber, very-low-fat vegetarian diet might be inadvisable because of the risk of amenorrhea and impaired bone health that can lead to stress fractures and, in the long term, predispose them to osteoporosis in old age. Finally, because meat is the best source of readily absorbable iron, vegetarians should choose foods high in iron. Iron deficiency impairs health and performance and is more prevalent in female athletes.[51]

In experimental animals, treadmill exercise along with food restriction increases the amount of weight lost and fat lost.[52] In humans, when weight loss programs combine exercise with a low-energy diet, the additional effect on weight loss may be slight, but the composition of the body changes. Obese women combining a low-energy diet with a heavy resistance training program gain lean mass while losing fat mass, whereas sedentary controls lose both fat and lean tissue. The effects of exercise on body weight are not significant.[53] Combined aerobic and strength training of sedentary middle-aged men during a hypocaloric diet has a similar effect, increasing muscle mass and decreasing fat mass, with little effect on total weight.[54] In obese sedentary women assigned to a low-energy diet and a walking program or a low-energy diet alone, however, the loss of body protein and lean tissue is similar in both groups.[5] These data suggest that during low-calorie diets in previously sedentary subjects, resistance training can have a greater effect on protein conservation than endurance training.

Losing body fat is more difficult for lean persons than for obese persons. An analysis of body composition changes in sedentary persons consuming low-energy diets shows a direct relationship between initial body fat and the proportion of total weight that is lost as fat.[55] Persons who are already lean, such as most athletes, find it difficult to conserve lean tissue as they lose weight unless they promote muscle hypertrophy by vigorous resistance exercise.

In active men eating their usual diet, body fat is lower in proportion to weekly hours spent running, cycling, or rowing.[56] In previously sedentary subjects, however, exercise alone without restriction of energy intake has a limited effect on fat loss, that only becomes apparent after many months of training. Among persons who are highly trained, changes in energy balance due to lower food intake or greater physical activity produce different effects. Exercise has a lesser effect than food restriction on body weight loss and nitrogen loss.[40]

☐ RETURN TO UNRESTRICTED DIETARY INTAKE

Even professional athletes do not maintain top physical condition throughout the year. During the training season, they are usually very careful with the amount and quality of their diet, but away from the training camp or the vigilant eye of the coach they are likely to consume the food they enjoy. If this is the typical American diet, it contains foods that are rich in fat and drinks that are sweet, with adequate to high amounts of protein. The athlete who has been eating a carefully restricted diet for a number of months is likely to desire precisely that type of diet.

Studies in rats that are allowed to choose their food freely after an episode of food restriction show that they increase their selection of dietary fat and rapidly regain weight. Treadmill exercise prevents this increase in fat selection and reduces body fat regain.[52] Athletes who gain and lose weight repeatedly during training and competition can show alterations in energy metabolism.[57] College wrestlers who repeatedly go through weight cycles have a significantly lower resting metabolic rate compared to noncyclers of similar weight, height, and body fat content.[57] It is not known whether the repeated weight gains and losses result in a lower RMR or if there is a subgroup of wrestlers with a low RMR prior to their history of weight cycling.

When an athlete starts to eat freely but continues to train, the effects on metabolism and body weight are different. At the end of a weight-reduction program involving diet and exercise, obese subjects almost invariably gain weight. In men who maintain regular exercise, however, the rate of weight regain is slower than in those who revert to sedentary habits over the subsequent 18 months.[58] Weight fluctuation in formerly obese subjects studied for 2 years is lower if they exercise.[59] In a survey of formerly obese women, 90% of those who could maintain a reduced weight, exercised regularly. Among the women who regained weight, 66% did not exercise.[60]

◻ WEIGHT GAIN IN ATHLETES

Sumo wrestlers are the most extreme example of athletes competing at high body weights. Their sport is a combination of skill and strength, and a large lower body mass makes them more difficult to topple. In most sports in which a large mass is important, strength and endurance are also necessary, as in football, weight-lifting, rugby, boxing, and rowing. Many athletes in these sports must struggle to increase their weight, especially if they are adolescents who have not completed their linear growth.

Resting energy expenditure and the thermic response to meals increase in sedentary subjects given diets providing excess energy.[61] A meta-analysis of several overfeeding studies shows linear relationships between total excess kilocalories and the gain in total weight and the gain in lean body mass (measured by densitometry, nitrogen balance, or potassium-40).[62] About 44% of weight gain is lean tissue. As shown in elegant studies of identical twins, however, genotype has a marked effect on the amount and distribution of fat and lean tissue gain during overfeeding.[63] In sedentary subjects, overfeeding has no effect on submaximal exercise capacity.[64]

Athletes who wish to increase muscle mass have been an easy prey for sellers of vitamins, minerals, protein supplements, and amino acid supplements, although none of these expensive products has been found to be effective.[65] It is likely that an increase in total food intake while maintaining vigorous training affects lean tissue mass. In a study of older men who underwent 12 weeks of heavy resistance training, the group that received a complete supplement providing an additional 560 kcal/day showed a greater increase in subcutaneous fat and in the size of the trained muscles.[66]

☐ CONCLUSION

Regulation of body weight and body composition by diet appears to be different in athletes compared to sedentary subjects. During low energy intake, the loss of lean tissue and the reduction in resting energy expenditure are less pronounced in athletes who continue to exercise. When athletes consume excess calories while training, their accumulation of fat is lower than for sedentary persons.

Maintaining lean tissue while decreasing body fat is easier if the athlete consumes a diet low in fat, adequate in protein, and high in complex carbohydrates. Such a diet, which is currently recommended for the good health of all Americans (Table 4-1), is especially appropriate for athletes of all types. It provides not only essential vitamins and minerals but also a proportion of macronutrients that is healthy and favors athletic performance. Athletes who want to maintain weight while training vigorously might have to increase the total amount of calories in their diets. These calories should come from cereals, whole grains, vegetables, and fruits, and not from foods that are high in fat or sugar. Athletes who want to lose fat should restrict fat in their diets but avoid extreme fad diets or fasting, which can be harmful to performance and health.

☐ REFERENCES

1. Hendler, R.G., Walesky, M., and Sherwin, R.S.: Sucrose substitution in prevention and reversal of the fall in metabolic rate accompanying hypocaloric diets. Am. J. Med., *81*:280, 1986.
2. Molé, P.A., et al.: Exercise reverses depressed metabolic rate produced by severe caloric restriction. Med. Sci. Sports Exerc., *21*:29, 1989.
3. Lawson, S., Webster, P.J., Pacy, P.J., and Garrow, J.S. Effect of a 10-week aerobic training program on metabolic rate, body composition, and fitness in lean sedentary females. Br. J. Clin. Practice, *41*:684, 1987.
4. Lennon, D., et al.: Diet and exercise effects on resting metabolic rate. Int. J. Obesity, *9*:39, 1985.
5. Heymsfield, S.B., Casper, K., Hearn, J., and Guy, D.; Rate of weight loss during underfeeding: Relation to level of physical activity. Metabolism, *38*:215, 1989.
6. Warwick, M., and Garrow, J.S.: The effect of addition of exercise to a regime of dietary restriction on weight loss, nitrogen balance, resting metabolic rate and spontaneous physical activity in three obese women in a metabolic ward. J. Obes., *5*:25, 1981.
7. Phinney, S.D., LaGrange, B.M., O'Connell, M., and Danforth, E.: Effects of aerobic

exercise on energy expenditure and nitrogen balance during very low calorie dieting. Metabolism, 37:758, 1988.

8. Van Dale, D., Saris, W. H., Shoffelen, P.F., and Tenttoor, F.: Does exercise give an additional effect in weight reduction regimens? Int. J. Obesity, 11:367, 1987.

9. Gore, C.J., and Withers, R.T.: Effect of exercise intensity and duration on postexercise metabolism. J. Appl. Physiol., 68:2362, 1990.

10. Segal, K., Gutin, B., Nyman, A.M., and Pi-Sunyer, F.X.: Thermic effect of food at rest, during exercise, and after exercise in lean and obese men of similar body weight. J. Clin. Invest., 76:1107, 1985.

11. Haralambie, G., and Keul, J.: Serum glycoprotein levels of athletes in training. Experientia, 26:959, 1970.

12. Herring, J.L., Molé, P.A., Meredith, C.N., and Stern, J.S.: Effect of a three-day suspension of exercise training on resting metabolic rate in women runners. Med. Sci. Sports Exerc., in press.

13. Davis, J.R., et al.: Variations in dietary induced thermogenesis and body fatness with aerobic capacity. Eur. J. Appl. Physiol., 50:319, 1983.

14. Young, J.C., et al.: Prior exercise potentiates the thermic effect of a carbohydrate load. Metabolism, 35:1048, 1986.

15. Tremblay, A.E., et al.: The effect of exercise-training on resting metabolic rate in lean and moderately obese individuals. Int. J. Obesity, 10:511, 1986.

16. Lundholm, K., et al.: Thermogenic effect of food in physically well-trained elderly men. Eur. J. Appl. Physiol., 55:486, 1986.

17. Devlin, J.T., and Horton, E.S.: Potentiation of the thermic effect of insulin by exercise: Differences between lean, obese, and non-insulin dependent diabetic men. Am. J. Clin. Nutr., 43:884, 1986.

18. Goldberg, A., Etlinger, J.D., Goldspink, D.F., and Jablecki, C.: Mechanism of work-induced hypertrophy in skeletal muscle. Med. Sci. Sports Exerc., 7:248, 1975.

19. Spurr, G.B.: Physical activity, nutritional status, and physical work in relation to agricultural productivity. *In* Energy Intake and Activity. Edited by E. Pollitt and P. Amante. New York, Alan R. Liss, 1984, pp. 207–261.

20. Weigle, D.S., et al.: Weight loss leads to a marked decrease in nonresting energy expenditure in ambulatory human subjects. Metabolism, 37:930, 1988.

21. Weigle, D.S.: Contribution of decreased body mass to diminished thermic effect of exercise in reduced-obese men. Int. J. Obesity, 12:567, 1988.

22. Ravussin, E., et al.: Reduced rate of energy expenditure as a risk factor for body weight gain. N. Engl. J. Med., 318:467, 1988.

23. Webster, S., Rutt, R., and Weltman, A.: Physiological effects of a weight loss regimen practiced by college wrestlers. Med. Sci. Sports Exerc., 22:229, 1990.

24. Barcenas, C., Hoeffler, H., and Lie, J.T. Obesity, football, dog days and siriasis: A deadly combination. Am. Heart J., 92:237, 1976.

25. Knapik, J.J., Jones, B.H., Meredith, C.N., and Evans, W.J.: Influence of a 3.5 day fast on physical performance. Eur. J. Appl. Physiol., 56:428, 1987.

26. Loy, S.F., et al.: Effects of 24-hour fast on cycling endurance time at two different intensities. J. Appl. Physiol., 61:654, 1986.

27. Nieman, C., et al.: Running endurance in 27-h fasted humans. J. Appl. Physiol., 63:2502, 1987.

28. Giesecke, K., et al.: Protein and amino acid metabolism during early starvation as reflected by excretion of urea and methylhistidines. Metabolism, 38:1196, 1989.

29. Lemon, P.W.R., and Mullin, J.P.: Effect of initial muscle glycogen levels on protein catabolism during exercise. J. Appl. Physiol., 48:624, 1980.

30. Knapik, J.J., et al.: Leucine metabolism during fasting and exercise. J. Appl. Physiol., 70:43, 1991.

31. Schweiger, U., et al.: Diet-induced menstrual irregularities: Effects of age and weight loss. Fertil. Steril., 48:746, 1987.
32. Nelson, M.E., et al.: Diet and bone status in amenorrheic runners. Am. J. Clin. Nutr., 43:910, 1986.
33. Benson, J., Gillien, D.M., Bourdet, K., and Loosli, A.R.: Inadequate nutrition and chronic calorie restriction in adolescent ballerinas. Physician Sports Med., 13:79, 1985.
34. Meredith, C.N., Zackin, M.J., Frontera, W.R., and Evans, W.J.: Dietary protein requirements and body protein metabolism in endurance-trained men. J. Appl. Physiol., 66:2850, 1989.
35. Hoffer, L.J., et al.: Metabolic effects of very low calorie weight reduction diets. J. Clin. Invest., 73:750, 1984.
36. Davis, P.G., and Phinney, S.D.: Differential effects of two very low calorie diets on aerobic and anaerobic performance. Int. J. Obesity, 14:779, 1990.
37. Haralambie, G., and Berg, A.: Serum urea and amino nitrogen changes with exercise duration. Eur. J. Appl. Physiol., 36:39, 1976.
38. Carraro, F., et al.: Effect of exercise and recovery on muscle protein synthesis in human subjects. Am. J. Physiol., 259:E470, 1990.
39. Todd, K.S., Butterfield, G.E., and Calloway, D.H.: Nitrogen balance in men with adequate and deficient energy intake at three levels of work. J. Nutr., 114:2107, 1984.
40. McMurray, R.G., Ben-Ezra, V., Forsythe, W.A., and Smith, A.T.: Responses of endurance-trained subjects to caloric deficits induced by diet or exercise. Med. Sci. Sports Exerc., 17:574, 1985.
41. Phinney, S.D., et al.: Capacity for moderate exercise in obese subjects after adaptation to a hypocaloric, ketogenic diet. J. Clin. Invest., 66:1152–1161, 1980.
42. Walberg, J.L., et al.: Exercise capacity and nitrogen loss during a high or low carbohydrate diet. Med. Sci. Sports Exerc., 20:34, 1988.
43. National Research Council: Diet and Health: Implications for Reducing Chronic Disease Risk. Report of the Committee on Diet and Health, Food and Nutrition Board. Washington, DC, National Academy Press, 1989.
44. Sims, E., and Danforth, E.: Expenditure and storage of energy in man. J. Clin. Invest., 79:1019, 1987.
45. Suzuki, M., and Tamura, T.: Intake timing of fat and insulinogenic accumulation. In Diet and Obesity. Edited by G.A. Bray et al. Japan Scientific Society Press, 1988, p. 248.
46. Applegate, E.A., Upton, D.E., and Stern, J.S.: Exercise and detraining effects on food intake, adiposity, and in vivo lipogenesis in Osborne-Mendel rats made obese on high fat diets. J. Nutr., 114:447, 1984.
47. Flatt, J.P.: Energetics of intermediary metabolism. In Substrate and Energy Metabolism. Edited by J.S. Garrow and D. Halliday. London, John Libbey, 1985, pp. 58–69.
48. Saris, W.M.H.: Physiologic aspects of exercise in weight cycling. Am. J. Clin. Nutr., 49:1099, 1989.
49. Gorbach, S.L., and Goldin, B.R.: Diet and the excretion and enterohepatic cycling of estrogen. Prev. Med., 1:525, 1987.
50. Pirke, K.M., et al.: Dieting influences the menstrual cycle: Vegetarian versus non-vegetarian diet. Fertil. Steril., 46:1083, 1986.
51. Nickerson, H.J., et al.: Causes of iron deficiency in adolescent athletes. J. Pediatr., 114:657, 1989.
52. Gerardo-Gettens, T., et al.: Exercise decreases fat selection in female rats during weight cycling. Am. J. Physiol., 260:R518, 1991.
53. Ballor, D.L., Katch, V.L., Becque, M.D., and Marks, C.R.: Resistance weight training during calorie restriction enhances lean body weight maintenance. Am. J. Clin. Nutr., 47:19, 1988.

54. Pavlou, K.N., Steffee, W.P., Lerman, R.H., and Burrows, G.A.: Effects of dieting and exercise on lean body mass, oxygen uptake, and strength. Med Sci. Sports Exerc., 17:466, 1985.

55. Henry, C.J.K., Rivers, J.P., and Payne, P.R.: Protein and energy metabolism in starvation reconsidered. Eur. J. Clin. Nutr., 42:543, 1988.

56. Meredith, C.N., Zackin, M.J., Frontera, W.R., and Evans, W.J.: Body composition and aerobic capacity in young and middle-aged endurance-trained men. Med. Sci. Sports Exerc., 19:557, 1987.

57. Steen, S.N., Oppliger, R.A., and Brownell, K.D.: Metabolic effects of repeated weight loss and regain in adolescent wrestlers. JAMA, 260:47, 1988.

58. Pavlou, K.N., Krey, S., and Steffee, W.P.: Exercise as an adjunct to weight loss and maintenance in moderately obese subjects. Am. J. Clin. Nutr., 49:115, 1989.

59. King, A.C., Frey-Hewitt, B., Dreon, D.M., and Wood, P.D.: The effects of minimal intervention strategies on long-term outcomes in men. Arch. Intern. Med., 149:2741, 1989.

60. Kayman, S., Bruvold, W., and Stern, J.S.: Maintenance and relapse after weight loss in women: Behavioral aspects. Am. J. Clin. Nutr., 52:800, 1990.

61. Bandini, L.G., et al.: Energy expenditure during carbohydrate overfeeding in obese and nonobese adolescents. Am. J. Physiol., 257:E357, 1989.

62. Forbes, G.B.: Human Body Composition: Growth, Aging, Nutrition, and Activity. New York, Springer-Verlag, 1987.

63. Poehlman, E.T., et al.: Genotype-controlled changes in body composition and fat morphology following overfeeding in twins. Am. J. Clin. Nutr., 43:723, 1986.

64. Tremblay, A.E., et al.: Heredity and overfeeding-induced changes in submaximal exercise VO_2. J. Appl. Physiol., 62:539, 1987.

65. Barnett, D.W., and Conlee, R.K.: The effects of a commercial dietary supplement on human performance: Am. J. Clin. Nutr., 40:586, 1984.

66. Meredith, C.N., Frontera, W.R., O'Reilly, K.P., and Evans, W.J.: Body composition in elderly men: Effect of dietary modification during strength training. J. Am. Geriatr. Soc., in press.

C H A P T E R

5

NUTRITION AND HUMAN PERFORMANCE

Jack H. Wilmore and David L. Costill

Athletes are constantly searching for the perfect diet, one that will help them attain their optional, or "personal best," performance during high-level competition. An intense desire to be successful leads athletes to become both experimenter and subject, hoping to identify, largely by trial and error, that one factor or combination of factors that will give them the winning edge. Consequently, athletic or sports nutrition has evolved over centuries largely through tradition and self-experimentation. During the second half of this century, a research focus was established that has been directed toward better defining optimal athletic nutrition. This chapter provides an overview of the research delineating the role of protein, fats, carbohydrates, vitamins, and minerals in the optimal preparation of athletes for competition.

☐ COMPOSITION AND ENERGY LEVEL OF THE DIET

There is general agreement on the relative nutrient demands of the athlete concerning the percentage of energy to be derived from protein, fats and carbohydrates.[1-5] Proteins should constitute 10 to 15% of the

Adapted from Wilmore, J.H., and Freund, B.J.: Nutritional enhancement of athletic performance. Rev. Clin. Nutr., 54:1, 1984.

total energy intake. Fats should be limited to 30% or less of the total energy intake, with saturated fats constituting less than 10% of the total. Carbohydrates would constitute the remaining 55 to 60%, or more. For athletes who have extraordinary energy demands, e.g., expending an additional 8.38 MJ (2000 kcal) to 16.76 MJ (4000 kcal) per day in practice or in competition, the relative contribution can change, with carbohydrates providing up to 70% of the total energy consumed. Costill and his associates[6-8] demonstrated that subjects who trained heavily and were maintained on a relatively low carbohydrate diet, i.e., approximately 40% of total energy, had a steady decline in muscle glycogen levels with successive days of training. When these same subjects were fed a diet high in carbohydrate, i.e., approximately 70% of total energy, but of equal energy content, muscle glycogen levels remained relatively stable. The importance of maintaining high muscle glycogen levels and normal blood glucose levels in athletes who are training at high intensities and for long durations is discussed in a subsequent section of this review.

Consideration must also be given to the total number of calories consumed. Although this is highly variable dependent on the size, sex, and the sport of the athlete, values as high as 50.3 MJ (12,000 kcal) per day have been reported.[9] At the other extreme, athletes in certain sports, such as wrestling, boxing, and horse racing, need to monitor their weight carefully in order to meet established standards for competition. This focus on weight has led to nutritional abuses, dehydration, and increased risk of heat stress and renal ischemia.[10] In addition, there is increasing concern regarding the nutritional behaviors used to achieve excessive weight losses in athletes and their potential association with eating disorders such as anorexia nervosa and bulimia nervosa.[11-14]

Some athletes in sports such as swimming and distance running have difficulty in maintaining their desired weight, i.e., they experience a gradual weight loss over the course of a season. These athletes appear to have difficulty consuming sufficient energy to maintain body weight. As an example, a male world-class swimmer 16 years of age and 65 kg body weight might have a normal energy expenditure of 12.8 MJ (3070 kcal) per day.[15] With 4 h of swim training in the pool, and 1 h of dry land drills, an additional 3.35 MJ (800 kcal) per h would be spent, amounting to 16.75 MJ (4000 kcal) in 5 h, or a total of 29.55 MJ (7070 kcal) in 24 h. With such high rates of energy expenditure, the need for sleep increases, with 12 h per night or more being quite common. With 12 h of sleep and 5 h of exercise, the athlete is left with 7 h in which to ingest over 29 MJ. This might be why many of these young athletes consume a large number of calories in the form of high-caloric-density foods. In this case, if all nutrient requirements have been met, high-caloric-density foods might be acceptable to provide the needed calories.

◻ PROTEIN NEEDS

For a number of years it was assumed that athletes should consume rather large quantities of protein, either through high-protein foods or through protein supplements. This assumption possibly evolved from early beliefs that the muscle consumed itself as fuel for its contractions and that supplementation of protein was essential to prevent general muscle atrophy from chronic exercise.[16] More recently, attention has focused on the protein needs of those athletes involved in sports that require training to increase either strength or muscle mass, or both, in which actual increases in contractile proteins are known to occur.[17,18]

There are two possible pathways by which increased protein intake could influence performance: more efficient use of protein as a major substrate for muscle contraction, and enhanced synthesis of protein in response to strength-type exercise training. Each of these is briefly discussed, followed by a brief review of studies in which protein supplementation has been experimentally evaluated.

It is generally recognized that exercising muscles can use muscle glycogen, plasma glucose, plasma free fatty acids, and plasma and muscle triglycerides as energy sources.[19] More recently, it has been found that with dynamic exercise of an acute nature, there is a reduction in the rate of muscle protein synthesis, while muscle proteolysis may be increased.[19–21] Further, research indicates that amino acids can account for between 5 and 15% of the oxidative metabolism of the working muscle.[19,22,23] This contribution will vary, depending on the type of exercise, its duration and intensity, and the individual's previous diet.[19] Lemon and Nagle[24] concluded that the branched-chain amino acids (glucose-alanine cycle) are the most important amino acids contributing to exercise energy needs. They further state that, although protein (amino acids) is clearly not as important as either carbohydrates or free fatty acids, under some conditions protein can contribute significantly to the total exercise calories. Thus protein does appear to be an important energy source during exercise, but there is no evidence at this time that increasing protein intake will enhance metabolic efficiency.

The second pathway by which protein supplementation might increase athletic performance is through its potential enhancement of protein synthesis. Strength-type exercise training is used not only to increase muscle strength, but also muscle mass. For certain types of athletes, an increase in muscle bulk is considered a desirable outcome of training to facilitate peak performance (e.g., American football and throwing events in track and field). In a review article, Booth et al.[17] noted that during the first 2 h of exercise, both rates of protein synthesis and protein degradation are decreased in working skeletal muscle. After 4 to 12 h of continuous work, protein synthesis and degradation are both increased. This response, however, would appear to depend on the type of exercise, because there is a high degree of specificity of response to different types of exercise.[25] Booth et al.[17] concluded that a change in muscle protein synthesis is more important than a change in degradation for causing adaptive alterations in the level of protein subsequent to muscular exercise. Further, Goldberg et al.[26] proposed that both an increased rate of synthesis and a decreased rate of degradation are responsible for the increase in muscle mass consequent to strength training. The additional influence of protein supplementation on these adaptive responses of protein synthesis and degradation to exercise training has not been adequately studied, although supplementation could conceivably enhance protein synthesis.[18]

Does protein supplementation enhance athletic or work performance? Horstman[27] concluded that the average diet in the Western culture provides adequately for the protein needs of the athlete. Even with heavy physical training or work, in which energy expenditure can exceed 20.9 MJ (5000 kcal), the diet consumed should provide adequate total protein if the proportion of protein in the total energy consumed is maintained. Although this would appear to be theoretically sound, studies are equivocal relative to the appropriate protein intake levels for athletes.

Yoshimura et al.,[28] in a summary of their previous work, demonstrated a close association between the anemia identified during hard physical training, which they have referred to as sports anemia, and protein intake levels. They reported a decrease in hemoglobin and plasma protein over the course of strenuous training while consuming a diet containing 1.3 g of protein/kg/day. They found that by taking more than 2.0 g protein/kg/day they could prevent this sports anemia. It could also be prevented by changing the protein source from approximately 30% fish protein and 70% vegetable protein to 57% animal protein, maintaining the protein intake at 1.2 to 1.3 g/kg/day. They concluded that sports anemia is the result of an osmotic fragility caused by chemical hemolysis. Miller et al.[29] confirmed that mechanical trauma to red blood cells at footstrike is a major cause of hemolysis during running.

Studies examining nitrogen balance in elite athletes found that a protein intake of 0.8 g/kg/day (U.S. RDA) might not be adequate. Tarnopolsky et. al.[30] studied the effects of training status on nitrogen balance, body composition, and urea excretion during periods of habitual and altered protein intakes. Extensive experiments were performed on elite body builders and elite endurance athletes (runners and nordic skiers). Compared to a group of sedentary controls, the body builders required 1.12 times greater daily protein intake, whereas the endurance athletes required 1.67 times greater protein intake. The higher intake requirements for the endurance athletes resulted from a much higher daily excretion of urea reflecting increased protein catabolism during exercise.

What is the recommended level of protein intake for athletes in training? In recent review articles, Lemon[23] and Butterfield[31] suggest that a specific recommendation will depend on a number of factors. Certainly the type, intensity, and duration of training sessions are important considerations, as is the energy balance state of the individual. It is possible that some athletes need 2.0 g/kg per day or more. The reader is referred to reviews by Butterfield,[31] Haymes,[18] Lemon,[23] and Viru[21] for additional and more detailed information in this area.

☐ FAT AND CARBOHYDRATE NEEDS

As mentioned in the previous section, carbohydrates were at one time considered to be the only fuel source for working muscles. Since that time, fat and protein have been identified as major sources of energy,

TABLE 5–1. THE SOURCES OF STORED ENERGY IN A 70-KG MAN

BODY FUELS	kg	kcal
Fat, adipose triglyceride	12.00	110,000
Muscle protein	6.00	24,000
Glycogen from liver	0.07	280
Glycogen from muscle	0.40	1,600
Glucose from body fluids	0.02	80
Free fatty acids from body fluids	0.004	4
	Total	135,964

Data from Goodman, M.N., and Ruderman, N.B.: Influence of muscle use on amino acid metabolism. Exerc. Sports Sci. Rev., *10*:1, 1982.

fat serving as a primary energy source during exercise, providing 25 to 90% of the total energy depending on the intensity of exercise and metabolic state of the muscle.[32–34] Does fat have special ergogenic properties, and if it does, should fat be supplemented in the diet? First, the body has an ample amount of fat in storage as adipose tissue. A very lean male distance runner who is 5% body fat at 60 kg will have 3 kg of fat, or the energy equivalent of over 96.4 MJ (23,000 kcal). This would be sufficient fuel to run over eight marathons (26.2 miles or 42 km per marathon). Most athletes have relative body fats considerably above 5% of their total weight. Fat is important as an energy source because it represents a considerable reservoir of stored energy and it is relatively easily mobilized. Conversely, carbohydrates have a finite storage capacity, as illustrated in Table 5–1 for a normal 70-kg man in the postabsorptive state.[19]

The importance of fat as a substrate is recognized primarily through its role in sparing the use of carbohydrates, which have a finite and a relatively small energy reserve. The more the body can use fat as the primary substrate, the more it can protect its limited carbohydrate supply.[5,6]

How can the athlete adapt to rely more on the use of free fatty acids? First, the rate of glycogen use is directly related to the intensity of exercise.[35–37] The greater the intensity, the greater the rate of use. In addition, the greater the intensity of exercise, the greater the proportional contribution of carbohydrates to the total energy demands.[7,8]

Second, as athletes become better conditioned aerobically through cardiorespiratory endurance training, they develop an increased capacity to oxidize fatty acids, which results in a greater reliance on fat oxidation for energy during work at the same absolute intensity in the trained state.[33,38] This is the result of an enhanced activity of the enzymes for fat degradation.[39,40] Costill and Miller[7] reported that highly trained marathon runners running at 70% of their aerobic capacity for 60 min derived over 75% of their energy from fat metabolism.

Third, it has been demonstrated that free fatty acid use is a direct function of plasma free fatty acid concentrations, i.e., the higher the plasma levels, the greater the use.[41] Rennie and Holloszy[42] have shown that availability of free fatty acids has a direct inhibitory effect on glucose uptake and glycogen use in well-oxygenated perfused skeletal muscle. Thus, factors that enhance free fatty acid mobilization and oxidation will result in the sparing of glycogen and generally improve endurance performance. Two factors to enhance mobilization that have been investigated experimentally are heparin and caffeine. Van Handel[43] conducted a comprehensive review of the literature on caffeine as an ergogenic aid and concluded that caffeine administration does enhance endurance performance, due primarily to alterations in the mobilization and use of carbohydrate and fat. He also suggested that there might be increases in neuronal excitability, possibly reducing the threshold of motor neurons, thereby altering either fiber recruitment patterns or the perception of work, or both.

A major breakthrough in athletic nutrition came in the 1960s, when a group of Scandinavian researchers initiated experimental observations of carbohydrate storage and use with prolonged, endurance-type exercise.[44] The early studies of Christensen and Hansen[45] had shown that as the intensity of exercise increased, the relative contribution of carbohydrate as the fuel source increased. Following 3 days on a diet low in carbohydrate, exercise time to exhaustion was significantly reduced. Conversely, following 3 days on a diet high in carbohydrate, exercise time to exhaustion was substantially increased (210 min vs 80 min). Also in the 1960s, Bergstrom[46] introduced the needle biopsy technique into the field of exercise physiology and athletic nutrition. This allowed investigators to determine actual alterations in muscle glycogen with varying diets and the influence of differences in muscle glycogen levels on endurance performance.

In a classic study, Bergstrom et al.[47] provided their subjects with three different diets, each for a prescribed period of time. One diet was high in carbohydrates, the second high in fat and protein (low in carbohydrates), and the third was a normal mixed diet; each diet containing the same number of calories. Before starting the diet, the subject depleted his muscle glycogen stores by riding a cycle ergometer to exhaustion at approximately 75% of his maximal aerobic capacity. This was followed by 3 days on the prescribed diet and then a second ride to exhaustion. Prior to the second ride, a muscle biopsy was obtained to determine glycogen content. The total length of time the subject could ride before reaching exhaustion and the initial glycogen content were as shown in Table 5–2. These results and those of other investigators underline the important fact that endurance performance is directly related to the muscle glycogen content at the start of the exercise bout.[48–53] Although it is generally agreed that glycogen loading is of little benefit for endurance events shorter than 60 minutes,[8] Maughan and Poole[54] demonstrated a substantial improvement in the performance of an anaerobic exercise

TABLE 5-2. GLYCOGEN CONTENT AND TIME TO EXHAUSTION ON A CYCLE ERGOMETER FOLLOWING THREE DIFFERENT DIETARY REGIMES

DIET	GLYCOGEN CONTENT (g/100 g Wet Tissue)	TIME TO EXHAUSTION (Min)
Mixed	1.75	113.6
High fat and protein	0.63	56.9
High carbohydrate	3.31	166.5

Data from Bergstrom J., Hermansen, L., Hultman, E., and Saltin, B.: Diet, muscle glycogen and physical performance. Acta Physiol. Scand., 71:140, 1967.

bout, i.e., cycling to exhaustion at 104% of the subject's aerobic capacity, following a glycogen loading regimen.

Costill and Miller[7] have discussed the importance of liver as well as muscle glycogen stores relative to exercise performance. Blood-borne glucose serves as a major contributor to the metabolic pool, representing less than 10% of the total muscle oxygen consumption at rest, but increasing to levels approaching 75 to 90% of the muscle's carbohydrate metabolism during extended periods of endurance exercise. With the liver serving as the major contributor of glucose in the blood, liver glycogen stores become important when considering the total energy pool. It has also become apparent that maintaining normal blood glucose levels during prolonged endurance exercise is critical to completing that bout of exercise. The studies of Coyle and his associates[55,56] pointed out the importance of carbohydrate feedings during exercise to maintain blood glucose at normal or near-normal levels. They demonstrated that a decline in blood glucose contributes to fatigue during prolonged exercise and that carbohydrate feedings during exercise can reverse this decline. The issue of fluid replacement beverages, their carbohydrate and electrolyte composition, and their use during exercise is important but is not discussed in this chapter (see reviews of Brouns,[57] Costill,[6] Lamb and Brodowicz,[58] and Murray[59]).

To provide the optimal levels for peak athletic performance, glycogen stores must be elevated. Sherman[8] described the resynthesis process as biphasic, with a rapid initial response to pre-exercise levels and a slower secondary phase to above-normal levels. Piehl[60] demonstrated that there is a marked storage of glycogen in the muscle during the first 5 h following a glycogen-depleting exercise bout that is closely related to the carbohydrate intake. Pre-exercise values were not reached until 46 hours following the exercise bout, however. The amount of carbohydrate consumed following the exercise bout is directly related to the subsequent resynthesis, i.e., the more carbohydrate consumed, the greater the resulting muscle glycogen level. There does appear to be an upper limit, however, with carbohydrate intake in excess of 600 g/day resulting in little further increase in muscle glycogen resynthesis.[61] It has also been shown that the use of complex carbohydrate diets, after the initial 24-h period following exercise, should result in relatively larger amounts of muscle glycogen synthesis compared to equivalent glucose-based diets.[8] Finally, Ivy et al.[62] found that the timing of when the carbohydrate is ingested after exercise is important, glycogen resynthesis being enhanced during the initial 2 h after exercise.

The pattern of exercise and diet to ensure optimal muscle glycogen loading prior to athletic competition has received considerable attention. Åstrand[63] initially proposed the following routine. Approximately 1 week prior to competition the athlete performs an exhaustive training bout in an attempt to deplete muscle glycogen stores. This is followed by 3 days of light to moderate activity with a diet low in carbohydrate and high in protein and fat. Finally, 3 days prior to competition, the athlete minimizes activity and consumes a diet high in carbohydrate. Several variations on this pattern have been shown to be successful in maximally elevating muscle glycogen levels.[8] Sherman,[8] however, in his critical review of existing dietary/exercise protocols to optimize muscle glycogen storage, concluded that the best method involves a gradual tapering of activity during the 6 days preceding competition, combined with a diet that is high in carbohydrate (525 g/day) during the final 3 days to competition. This eliminates the need for the depletion and the low-carbohydrate phases used in previous protocols. He also emphasized that enhanced muscle glycogen stores will allow an athlete to maintain a high work intensity longer during prolonged aerobic exercise but will not allow the athlete to work at a faster rate.[8]

☐ VITAMIN AND MINERAL NEEDS

Historically, some athletes have taken massive doses of various vitamins in hopes of improving athletic performance.[64] Mineral supplementation has occurred to a much lesser extent. The problems and diseases associated with vitamin deficiencies are well documented, but do athletes have vitamin or mineral deficiencies? In the absence of deficiencies, will supplementation of vitamins or minerals above the RDA result in enhanced athletic performance? This section reviews the available literature regarding vitamin and mineral supplementation and their effects on athletic performance.

VITAMINS

Of the 13 substances classified as vitamins, only C, E, and the B-complex vitamins have been extensively investigated relative to their potential for facilitating athletic performance. B-complex vitamins are involved in coenzyme activity with the metabolism of fats and carbohydrates, and in the formation of erythrocytes.[18] Although several studies have shown that the supplementation of one or a combination of the B-complex vitamins facilitates performance, there is consensus that supplementation is of no measurable value relative to the athlete's performance providing there is not a pre-existing deficiency.[18,64-66] In studies in which the investigators created a deficiency in one or more of the B-complex vitamins, there is typically a decrement in performance, which is reversed with supplementation to the deficient vitamins.[18] When there is no deficiency, there is no compelling evidence to advocate the use of supplements. In fact, Weight et. al.,[67] in a double-blind, cross over, placebo-controlled study, demonstrated no measurable effect of a vitamin and mineral supplement that contained from 100% to over 4000% of the RDA.

Vitamin C plays an important role in the formation of collagen, a critical protein in connective tissue, and assists in the absorption of iron. It also functions in the metabolic reactions of amino acids and in the synthesis of catecholamines and the anti-inflammatory corticoids of the adrenal gland.[64] Supplementation of vitamin C has produced equivocal findings in research studies. It is the consensus of those who have reviewed this area, however, that even with increased requirements with training, supplementation of vitamin C, in the absence of deficiency, has no ergogenic properties.[18,64-66]

Vitamin E has received a great deal of attention over the years, being the focus of numerous newspaper and magazine articles that have suggested a number of medical conditions that might be alleviated by this miracle vitamin.[68] Further, there is good reason to believe that a large segment of the athletic population is consuming large supplementary doses of vitamin E.[68] Vitamin E is a fat-soluble vitamin that derives most of its activity from alpha-tocopherol. Although it is postulated to have an important ergogenic effect through its relationship with oxygen use and energy supply, reviews have generally concluded that supplementation of vitamin E does not improve athletic performance.[18,64-66]

In the absence of a specific vitamin deficiency, it appears that supplementation with vitamins has little or no benefit relative to enhanced athletic performance. However, many of the studies lacked adequate controls, did not have proper experimental designs, and used questionable performance parameters. More rigorous studies using proper controls and experimental designs and more relevant criteria of athletic performance will be necessary before final conclusions can be drawn regarding vitamin supplementation and athletic performance. It must be remembered that the difference between first and second place in r ost elite athletic performances is determined by fractions of a second. At present, our experimental designs do not allow us to discriminate at this level of performance.

MINERALS

Minerals, unlike vitamins, are much less likely to be supplemented by the athletic population. Athletes have shown far less concern for their mineral status, possibly because far fewer ergogenic qualities have been ascribed to specific minerals. Of the minerals, iron and calcium have been most frequently investigated. Unfortunately, only a few studies have been conducted on calcium supplementation, but these would suggest that supplementation is of no value in the presence of a normal dietary calcium intake. Iron, however, has received a great deal of attention in the research literature. First, it has been estimated that 22% of females in the United States, 17 to 44 years of age, with hemoglobin levels above 10g/100 mL, are iron-deficient.[69] Further, in a study of male and female middle- and long-distance runners, Clement and Asmundson[70] reported that 29% of the men and 82% of the women had plasma ferritin concentrations at risk for iron deficiency. Ehn et al.,[71] in their study of 8 male long-distance runners, found normal hemoglobin and serum iron levels, but bone marrow studies showed either an absence or only traces of iron, indicating latent iron deficiency. They attributed this deficiency to low absorption and increased elimination of iron. Hunding et al.[72] identified iron deficiency in 63 of 113 joggers and competitive runners, 13 of the women and 10 of the men demonstrating latent anemia. Oral iron therapy normalized the hemoglobin concentrations and led to the establishment of personal records for the competitive runners.

In reviews, Haymes,[18] Pate,[73] and Williams[64] reported the incidence of iron deficiency among athletes from various populations. Studies generally suggest that 22 to 25% of female athletes and 10% of male athletes are iron deficient. Risser et al.[74] reported that 31% of a group of varsity women athletes at two major United States universities were iron-deficient. When iron supplements are given to those who are iron-deficient, performance measures are typically improved, particularly aerobic capacity.[18,64,73,74] Supplementation of iron in those who are not deficient appears to have no benefit.[18,64] McDonald and Keen[75] reached similar conclusions in their review of iron, zinc, and magnesium.

As illustrated in Table 5–3, sodium and chloride are the dominant ions of the blood and sweat. The ionic concentration of sweat varies markedly between individuals and is strongly influenced by the rate of sweating and the athlete's state of heat acclimatization.

TABLE 5–3. ELECTROLYTE CONCENTRATIONS AND OSMOLALITY IN SWEAT, PLASMA, AND MUSCLE OF MEN FOLLOWING 2 HOURS OF EXERCISE IN THE HEAT

	ELECTROLYTES (mEq/L)				OSMOLALITY (mOsm/L)
	Na^+	Cl^-	K^+	Mg^{++}	
Sweat	40–60	30–50	4–6	1.5–5	80–185
Plasma	140	101	4	1.5	302
Muscle	9	6	162	31	302

At the high rates of sweating reported during exercise in the heat, sweat contains relatively high levels of sodium and chloride but little potassium, calcium, or magnesium. A sweat loss of nearly 4 liters, representing a 5.8% reduction in body weight, will result in sodium, potassium, chloride, and magnesium losses of 155, 16, 137, and 13 mEq, respectively.[76] On the basis of estimates of the athlete's body mineral content, these losses will lower the body's sodium and chloride content by roughly 5 to 7%. At the same time, total body levels of potassium and magnesium, two ions principally confined to the inside of the cells, will decrease by less than 1.2%.

Because the body loses more water than electrolytes during heavy sweating, the concentration of these minerals rises in the body fluids. Thus, even though there is a net loss of electrolytes from the body, plasma electrolyte concentrations actually increase. Although this might seem confusing, it simply illustrates that during periods of heavy sweating, the need to replace body water is greater than the need to replace electrolytes.

There are obvious benefits to drinking fluids during prolonged exercise, especially during hot weather. Drinking will minimize dehydration, lessen the rise in internal body temperature, and reduce the stress placed on the circulatory system.[77] It appears that the composition of fluids ingested during exercise has an effect on the rate that the fluid empties from the stomach.[78] Because little absorption of water occurs directly from the stomach, the fluids must pass into the intestine before entering the blood. In the intestine, absorption is rapid and unaffected by exercise, provided that the activity does not exceed 75% of the runner's $V_{O_{2max}}$.[78,79] Many factors affect the rate at which the stomach empties, including its volume, temperature, acidity, and the concentration of solutes (osmolality).[78]

Although large volumes of up to 600 mL empty faster from the stomach than do small portions, athletes generally find it uncomfortable to compete with a nearly full stomach, because this interferes with breathing. Taking 100 to 200 mL at 10- to 15-min intervals tends to minimize this effect.

Cold drinks have been found to empty more rapidly from the stomach than warm fluids. Although fluids at refrigerator temperatures of from 3 to 4°C reduce the temperature of the stomach from 37 to 10°C, they do not appear to cause stomach cramps. Such stomach distress occurs more often when the volume of the drink is unusually large. It has been suggested that intake of very cold fluids might affect the normal electrical activity of the heart. Although some electrocardiographic changes have been reported in a few individuals following the ingestion of very cold drinks (4°C), the medical significance of these changes has not been established. It seems that drinking cold fluids during prolonged exercise in the heat seems to pose no threat to a normal heart.

Another factor known to regulate the rate at which the stomach empties is the osmolality of the fluid. Drink osmolalities above 200 mOsm/ L tend to move out of the stomach more slowly than those below that level.[78] Thus the addition of electrolytes and/or other ingredients that raise the osmolality can actually slow the rate of fluid replacement. Solutions having high osmolalities might not have so marked a retarding effect on gastric emptying during competition, however, because more recent studies have revealed that carbohydrate-rich solutions can be emptied rather quickly from the stomach.[80] Because dehydration is the primary concern during hot-weather exercise, water seems to be the preferred fluid. Under less stressful conditions, in which overheating and large sweat losses are not as threatening, runners might use liquid feedings to supplement their carbohydrate supplies.

A number of commercially available water-electrolyte solutions are available for use during exercise and work in the heat. Unfortunately, many of the claims used to sell these drinks are based on misinterpreted and often inaccurate information. Electrolytes, for example, have long been listed as important ingredients in sports drinks. But research shows that such claims are unfounded. A single meal adequately replaces the electrolytes lost during exercise. The body needs water to bring its concentration of the electrolytes back into balance. Although the importance of minerals such as sodium, potassium, and magnesium should not be underestimated, blood and muscle biopsy studies have shown that heavy sweating has little or no sustained effect on water and electrolyte concentrations in body fluids.[76,81]

The control processes that regulate fluid volumes and electrolyte concentrations are quite effective. For example, it is normally difficult to consume too much water and dilute plasma electrolytes. Even marathoners who lose 3 to 5 L of sweat and drink 2 to 3 L of water retain normal plasma sodium, chloride, and potassium concentrations. Distance runners who run 25 to 40 km/day in warm weather and do not season their food do not develop electrolyte deficiencies. Even subjects fed only 30% as much potassium as they normally consume and made to dehydrate by losing 3 to 4 L of sweat every day for 8 days retain normal electrolyte levels.[82]

It has been suggested, however, that during ultramarathon (80 km or more) running, some individuals might become hyponatremic. A case study of two runners who collapsed after an ultramarathon race in 1983 revealed that they had blood sodium values of 123 and 118 mEq/L.[83] One of the runners experienced a grand mal seizure; the other man became disoriented and confused. An examination of the runners' fluid intake and estimates of their sodium intake (224 to 145 mEq) during the run suggested that they diluted their body sodium levels by consuming fluids that contained little sodium. Thus, in ultra-long-duration exercise with large sweat losses, the fluid replacement should include not only carbohydrate but also ample amounts of electrolytes.

☐ SUMMARY

This review has been attempted to collate the available research on the role of nutrition in optimizing athletic performance. Athletes are complex models to study. By their very nature they are unique, not representing the "normal" population, and they are greatly influenced by psychological as well as physiological factors. Often denying the athlete a certain food that he or she associates with success will result in the total failure of that athlete, irrespective of the scientific merits of the food in question. These factors must be considered as the next generation of experiments reach the planning stages. Proper questions must be asked, and the evaluative criteria must be appropriate for the questions that are being asked. Experimental designs must be improved, assuring adequate controls. Finally, statistical procedures must be carefully selected, because a 1 to 2% improvement might not reach statistical significance, but it might mean the difference between winning the gold as opposed to the silver medal.

This review has demonstrated that nutrition plays an important part in optimizing athletic performance. In most cases, however, adequate dietary intake of the essential foods, vitamins, and minerals is all that is necessary, without the need for supplementation. Although this statement would seem to stand on its own merit, most athletes have little or no idea what it means to eat a good, nutritionally sound diet. Thus education and example must be the cornerstone of any effort to improve the athlete's performance potential through sound nutritional practices.

□ REFERENCES

1. Butterfield, G.E.: Fats, carbohydrates, and protein: Why we need them, and how they are obtained. *In* Nutrition and Athletic Performance. Edited by W. Haskell, J. Scala, and J. Whittam. Palo Alto, Bull, 1982, pp. 2–15.
2. Katch, F.I., and McArdle, W.D.: Nutrition, Weight Control, and Exercise. 3rd ed. Philadelphia, Lea & Febiger, 1988.
3. Smith, N.J.: Food for Sport. Palo Alto, Bull, 1976, pp. 1–169.
4. Williams, M.H.: Nutrition for Fitness and Sport. Dubuque, IA, Wm. C. Brown, 1983, pp. 1–296.
5. Wilmore, J.H., and Costill, D.L.: Training for Sport and Activity: The Physiological Basis of the Conditioning Process. 3rd ed. Dubuque, IA, Wm. C. Brown, 1988.
6. Costill, D.L.: Carbohydrates for exercise: Dietery demands for optimal performance. Int. J. Sports Med., 9:1, 1988.
7. Costill, D.L., and Miller, J.M.: Nutrition for endurance sport: Carbohydrate and fluid balance. Int. J. Sports Med., 1:2, 1980.
8. Sherman, W.M.: Carbohydrates, muscle glycogen, and muscle glycogen supercompensation. *In* Ergogenic Aids in Sport. Edited by M.H. Williams. Champaign, IL, Human Kinetics Publishers, 1983, pp. 3–26.
9. Åstrand, P.-O.: Nutrition and physical performance. *In* Nutrition and the World Food Problem. Edited by M. Rechcigl. Basel, S. Karger, 1979, pp. 63–84.
10. Tipton, C.M.: Consequences of rapid weight loss. *In* Nutrition and Athletic Performance. Edited by W. Haskell, J. Scala, and J. Whittam. Palo Alto, Bull, 1982, pp. 176–197.
11. Black, D.R., and Burckes-Miller, M.E.: Male and female college athletes: Use of anorexia nervosa and bulimia nervosa weight loss methods. Res. Q. Exerc. Sport, *59*:252, 1988.

12. Borgen, J.S., and Corbin, C.B.: Eating disorders among female athletes. Physician Sportsmed. 15:89, 1987.
13. Dummer, G.M., Rosen, L.W., Heusner, W.W., et al.: Pathogenic weight-control behaviors of young competitive swimmers. Physician Sportsmed., 15:75, 1987.
14. Rosen, L.W., and Hough, D.O.: Pathogenic weight-control behaviors of female college gymnasts. Physician Sportsmed., 16:141, 1988.
15. Lentner, C. (Ed.): Geigy Scientific Tables, Volume 1. Units of Measurement, Body Fluids, Composition of the Body, Nutrition. Switzerland, CIBA-Geigy, 1981, pp. 232–234.
16. von Liebig, J.: Animal Chemistry and Its Application to Physiology and Pathology. London, Taylor and Walton, 1842.
17. Booth, F.W., Nicholson, W.F., and Watson, P.A.: Influence of muscle use on protein synthesis and degradation. Exerc. Sports Sci. Rev., 10:27, 1982.
18. Haymes, E.M.: Proteins, vitamins, and iron. In Ergogenic Aids in Sport. Edited by M.H. Williams. Champaign, IL, Human Kinetics Publishers, 1983, pp. 27–55.
19. Goodman, M.N., and Ruderman, N.B.: Influence of muscle use on amino acid metabolism. Exerc. Sports Sci. Rev. 10:1, 1982.
20. Dohm, G.L., Tapscott, E.B., and Kasperek, G.J.: Protein degradation during endurance exercise and recovery. Med. Sci. Sports Exerc., 19:S166, 1987.
21. Viru, A.: Mobilisation of structural proteins during exercise. Sports Med., 4:95, 1987.
22. Brooks, G.A.: Amino acid and protein metabolism during exercise and recovery. Med. Sci. Sports Exerc., 19:S150, 1987.
23. Lemon, P.W.R.: Protein and exercise: Update 1987. Med. Sci. Sports Exerc., 19:S179, 1987.
24. Lemon, P.W.R., and Nagle, F.J.: Effects of exercise on protein and amino acid metabolism. Med. Sci. Sports Exerc., 13:141, 1981.
25. Holloszy, J.O., and Booth, F.W.: Biochemical adaptations to endurance exercise in muscle. Ann. Rev. Physiol., 38:223, 1976.
26. Goldberg, A.L., Etlinger, J.D., Goldspink, D.F., and Jablecki, C.: Mechanisms of work-induced hypertrophy of skeletal muscle. Med. Sci. Sports Exerc., 7:185, 1975.
27. Horstman, D.H.: Nutrition. In Ergogenic Aids and Muscular Performance. Edited by W.P. Morgan. New York, Academic Press, 1972, pp. 343–365.
28. Yoshimura, H., Inoue, T., Yamada, T., and Shiraki, K.: Anemia during hard physical training (sports anemia) and its causal mechanism with special reference to protein nutrition. World Rev. Nutr. Dietetics, 35:1, 1980.
29. Miller, B.J., Pate, R.R., and Burgess, W.: Foot impact force and intravascular hemolysis during distance running. Int. J. Sports Med., 9:56, 1988.
30. Tarnopolsky, M.A., MacDougall, J.D., and Atkinson, S.A.: Influence of protein intake and training status on nitrogen balance and lean body mass. J. Appl. Physiol., 64:187, 1988.
31. Butterfield, G.E.: Whole-body protein utilization in humans. Med. Sci. Sports Exerc., 19:S157, 1987.
32. Carlson, L.A., Eklund, L.-G., and Oro, L.: Studies on blood lipids during exercise. IV. Arterial concentration of plasma free fatty acids and glycerol during and after prolonged exercise in normal men. J. Lab. Clin. Med., 61:724, 1963.
33. Gollnick, P.D.: Free fatty acid turnover and the availability of substrates as a limiting factor in prolonged exercise. Ann. N.Y. Acad. Sci., 301:64, 1977.
34. Havel, R.J., Naimark, A., and Borchgrevin, C.R.: Turnover rate and oxidation of free fatty acids of blood plasma in man during exercise: Studies during continuous infusion of palmitate-1-C[14]. J. Clin. Invest. 42:1054, 1963.
35. Essen, B.: Intramuscular substrate utilization during prolonged exercise. Ann. New York Acad. Sci., 301:30, 1977.

36. Saltin, B.: Metabolic fundamentals in exercise. Med. Sci. Sports Exerc., 5:137, 1973.
37. Saltin, B., and Karlsson, J.: Muscle glycogen utilization during work of different intensities. Adv. Exp. Med. Biol., 11:289, 1971.
38. Holloszy, J.O., Rennie, M.J., Hickson, R.C., et al.: Physiological consequences of the biochemical adaptations to endurance exercise. Ann. N.Y. Acad. Sci., 301:440, 1977.
39. Holloszy, J.O., Oscai, L.B., Don, I.J., and Mole, P.A.: Mitochondrial citric acid cycle and related enzymes: Adaptive response to exercise. Biochem. Biophys. Res. Com., 40:1368, 1970.
40. Mole, P.A., and Holloszy, J.O.: Exercise-induced increase in the capacity of skeletal muscle to oxidize palmitate. Proc. Soc. Exp. Biol. Med., 134:789, 1970.
41. Havel, R.J., Pernow, B., and Jones, N.L.: Uptake and release of free fatty acids and other metabolites in the legs of exercising men. J. Appl. Physiol., 23:90, 1967.
42. Rennie, M.J., and Holloszy, J.O.: Inhibition of glucose uptake and glycogenolysis by availability of oleate in well-oxygenated perfused skeletal muscle. Biochem. J., 168:161, 1977.
43. Van Handel, P.: Caffeine. In Ergogenic Aids in Sport. Edited by M.H. Williams. Champaign, IL, Human Kinetics Publishers, 1983, pp. 128–163.
44. Bergstrom, J., and Hultman, E.: Nutrition for maximal sport performance. 221:999, 1972.
45. Christensen, E.H., and Hansen, O. III.: Arbeitsfähigkeit und Ernahrung. Scand. Arch. Physiol., 81:160, 1939.
46. Bergstrom, J.: Muscle electrolytes in man: Determined by neutron activation analysis in needle biopsy specimens. A study on normal subjects, kidney patients, and patients with chronic diarrhoea. Scand. J. Clin. Lab. Invest., 14:Suppl. 68, 1962.
47. Bergstrom, J., Hermansen, L., Hultman, E., and Saltin, B.: Diet, muscle glycogen and physical performance. Acta Physiol. Scand., 71:140, 1967.
48. Bergstrom, J., and Hultman, E.: A study of the glycogen metabolism during exercise in man. Scand. J. Clin. Lab. Invest., 19:218, 1967.
49. Hermansen, L., Hultman, E., and Saltin, B.: Muscle glycogen during prolonged severe exercise. Acta Physiol. Scand., 71:129, 1967.
50. Hultman, E.: Studies on muscle metabolism of glycogen and active phosphate in man with special reference to exercise and diet. Scand. J. Clin. Lab. Invest., 19:Suppl. 94, 1967.
51. Karlsson, J., and Saltin, B.: Diet, muscle glycogen, and endurance performance. J. Appl. Physiol., 31:203, 1971.
52. Martin, B., Robinson, S., and Robershaw, D.: Influence of diet on leg uptake of glucose during heavy exercise. Am. J. Clin. Nutr., 31:62, 1978.
53. Saltin, B., and Hermansen, L.: Glycogen stores and prolonged severe exercise. In Nutrition and Physical Activity. Edited by G. Blix. Uppsala, Sweden, Almqvist & Wiksells, 1967, pp. 32-46.
54. Maughan, R.J., and Poole, D.C.: The effects of a glycogen-loading regimen on the capacity to perform anaerobic exercise. Eur. J. Appl. Physiol. Occupat. Physiol., 46:211, 1981.
55. Coggan, A.R., and Coyle, E.F.: Reversal of fatigue during prolonged exercise by carbohydrate infusion or ingestion. J. Appl. Physiol., 63:2388, 1987.
56. Coyle, E.F., Coggan, A.R., Hemmert, M.K., and Ivy, J.L.: Muscle glycogen utilization during prolonged strenuous exercise when fed carbohydrates. J. Appl. Physiol., 61:165, 1986.
57. Brouns, F.: Food and fluid related aspects in highly trained athletes. Ph.D. dissertation, State University of Limburg, Maastricht, The Netherlands, 1988.
58. Lamb, D.R., and Brodowicz, G.R.: Optimal use of fluids of varying formulations minimise exercise-induced disturbances in homeostasis. Sports Med., 3:247, 1986.

59. Murray, R.: The effects of consuming carbohydrate-electrolyte beverages on gastric emptying and fluid absorption during and following exercise. Sports Med., 4:322, 1987.
60. Piehl, K.: Time course for refilling of glycogen stores in human muscle fibres following exercise-induced glycogen depletion. Acta Physiol. Scand., 90:297, 1974.
61. Costill, D.L., Sherman, W.M., Fink, W.J., et al.: The role of dietary carbohydrates in muscle glycogen resynthesis after strenuous running. Am. J. Clin. Nutr., 34:1831, 1981.
62. Ivy, J.L., Katy, A.L., Cutler, C.L., et al.: Muscle glycogen synthesis after exercise: Effect of time of carbohydrate ingestion. J. Appl. Physiol., 64:1480, 1988.
63. Åstrand, P.-O.: Diet and athletic performance. Fed. Proc. 26:1772, 1967.
64. Williams. M.H.: Vitamin, iron and calcium supplementation: Effects on human physical performance. *In* Nutrition and Athletic Performance. Edited by W. Haskell, J. Scala, and J. Whittam. Palo Alto, CA, Bull, 1982, pp. 106–153.
65. Belko, A.Z.: Vitamins and exercise—an update. Med. Sci. Sports Exerc., 19:S191, 1987.
66. Bruce, Å., Ekblom, B., and Nilsson, I.: The effect of vitamin and mineral supplements and health foods on physical endurance and performance. Proc. Nutr. Soc., 44:283, 1985.
67. Weight, L.M., Noakes, T.D., Labadarios, D., et al.: Vitamin and mineral status of trained athletes including the effects of supplementation. Am. J. Clin. Nutr. 47:186, 1988.
68. Farrell, P.M., and Bieri, J.G.: Megavitamin E supplementation in man. Am. J. Clin. Nutr., 28:1381, 1975.
69. Ten States Nutrition Survey: Ten States Nutrition Survey 1968–1970: IV Biochemical. Washington, DC, Department of Health, Education and Welfare Pubs. No. (HMS) 72-8132, 1972.
70. Clement, D.B., and Asmundson, R.C.: Nutritional intake and hematological parameters in endurance runners. Physician Sportsmed., 10:37, 1982.
71. Ehn, L., Carlmark, B., and Hoglund, S.: Iron status in athletes involved in intense physical activity. Med. Sci. Sports Exerc., 12:61, 1980.
72. Hunding, A., Jordal, R., and Paulev, P.-E.: Runner's anemia and iron deficiency. Acta Med. Scand., 209:315, 1981.
73. Pate, R.R.: Sports anemia: A review of the current research literature. Physician Sportsmed., 11:115, 1983.
74. Risser, W.L., Lee, E.J., Poindexter, H.B.W., et al.: Iron deficiency in female athletes: Its prevalence and impact on performance. Med. Sci. Sports Exerc., 20:116, 1988.
75. McDonald, R., and Keen, C.L.: Iron, zinc and magnesium nutrition and athletic performance. Sports Med., 5:171, 1988.
76. Costill, D.L., Cote, R., and Fink, W.: Muscle water and electrolytes following varied levels of dehydration in man. J. Appl. Physiol. 40:6, 1976.
77. Pitts, R.F.: Physiology of the Kidney and Body Fluids. New York, Year Book, 1965.
78. Costill, D.L., and Saltin, B.: Factors limiting gastric emptying during rest and exercise. J. Appl. Physiol., 37:679, 1974.
79. Fordtran, J.S., and Saltin, B.: Gastric emptying and intestinal absorption during prolonged severe exercise. J. Appl. Physiol., 23:331, 1967.
80. Owen, M.D., Kregel, K.C., Wall, P.T., and Gisolfi, C.V.: Effects of carbohydrate ingestion on thermoregulation, gastric emptying and plasma volume during exercise in the heat (abstract). Med. Sci. Sports Exerc., 17:185, 1985.
81. Nielsen, B., Sjogaard, G., Ugelvig, J., et al.: Fluid balance in exercise dehydration and rehydration with different glucose-electrolyte drinks. Eur. J. Appl. Physiol., 55:318, 1986.
82. Costill, D.L., Cote, R., and Fink, W.: Dietary potassium and heavy exercise: Effects on muscle water and electrolytes. Am. J. Clin. Nutr., 36:266, 1982.
83. Frizzell, R.T., Lang, G.H., Lowance, D.C., and Lathan, S.R.: Hyponatremia and ultramarathon running. JAMA, 255:772, 1986.

BODY WEIGHT AND BODY COMPOSITION

Jack H. Wilmore

Increasing pressure is being placed on many athletes to reduce their body weight to lower and lower levels.[1,2] Suzie, a 5-ft-2-in. gymnast, is finally successful in achieving her goal weight of 115 lb after months of dieting and additional exercise, only to have her coach and her parents suggest that she might want to lose even more to improve her performance. Mary, a 50-m freestyle swimmer, has had to endure the taunts of her teammates and coach after each daily weigh-in. She has lost 20 lb in an effort to get to her competitive goal weight of 125 lb, and has only 3 more pounds to go. She is tired of wearing the "Ms. Piggy" T-shirt that is provided each swimmer who fails to meet her goal weight.

A substantial body of knowledge indicates that extra weight can be detrimental to the performance of the athlete, particularly when the body mass must be moved through space, either horizontally or vertically, as in running and jumping.[3,4] Consequently it is important for the athlete to know at what weight, or range of weights, he or she will attain optimal performance. Although weight loss generally results in an improvement in athletic performance, there is a point beyond which further weight loss leads to a deterioration in performance. At this point the health of the athlete can also be jeopardized.

It is now widely recognized that the existing weight of the athlete is not an appropriate marker or index by which goal weights for competition should be established. An important difference exists between body weight and body composition; the latter term refers to the chemical composition of the body in which the actual fat content of the body is identified. It is important for the athlete to know his or her body composition, so that fat stores can be reduced to appropriate levels. Both Suzie and Mary might have already achieved their optimal fat stores, but because of an excessive amount of fat-free mass, e.g., bone and muscle, their body weights remain above average values.

☐ OVERWEIGHT VS. OBESITY

Each of us has an optimal weight or weight range, whether it be for health promotion and disease prevention or for achieving peak performance as an athlete. How, then, do we determine our optimal weight or weight range? Before this question can be answered, it is first necessary to distinguish between the terms *overweight* and *obesity*, to highlight the difference between body weight and body composition.

These terms are often used interchangably, but this is incorrect. Overweight describes the condition that exists when body weight exceeds the standard value established for gender, height, and frame size. Table 6–1 illustrates standard weights by gender for different heights and frame sizes. For example, a 25-year-old woman shot-putter who was large-framed, 68 in. tall, and weighed 175 lb, would be 21 lb *overweight*, whereas an 18-year-old woman gymnast who was small-framed, 62 in. tall, and weighed 90 lb would be 12 lb *underweight*. In contrast to overweight, obesity refers to an abnormally high proportion of body fat. It is possible to be overweight but not overfat and to be overfat and yet fall within the normal weight range.

What determines whether you are overweight or obese? To determine whether you are overweight, simply refer to Table 6–1, knowing your correct frame size, height, and weight. Note that the tables were developed for people whose heights and weights were obtained while wearing shoes and indoor clothing. For practical purposes, the allowances for heel height and indoor clothing weight can be ignored because your height taken without shoes and weight taken without clothes will place you into approximately the same category.

Frame size is an interesting and probably accurate concept, but there is no universal agreement as to how frame size should be determined. The data included in Table 6–1 were derived primarily from the Build and Blood Pressure Study, Society of Actuaries, 1959, published by the Metropolitan Life Insurance Company in 1960. No guidance for determining frame size was provided with the initial publication of these data. In fact, frame size was not determined in the population from which the tables were derived. Rather, the data were divided into quartiles, with the lowest quartile considered small frame, the highest quartile considered large frame, and the two middle quartiles considered me-

TABLE 6–1. DESIRABLE WEIGHTS FOR MEN AND WOMEN, IN INDOOR CLOTHING,* BY HEIGHT AND FRAME SIZE

HEIGHT WITH SHOES†		SMALL FRAME	MEDIUM FRAME	LARGE FRAME
FEET	INCHES			
		WOMEN		
4	10	92–98	96–107	104–119
4	11	94–101	98–110	106–122
5	0	96–104	101–113	109–125
5	1	99–107	104–116	112–128
5	2	102–110	107–119	115–131
5	3	105–113	110–122	118–134
5	4	108–116	113–126	121–138
5	5	111–119	116–130	125–142
5	6	114–123	120–135	129–146
5	7	118–127	124–139	133–150
5	8	122–131	128–143	137–154
5	9	126–135	132–147	141–158
5	10	130–140	136–151	145–163
5	11	134–144	140–155	149–168
6	0	138–148	144–159	153–173
		MEN		
5	2	112–120	118–129	126–141
5	3	115–123	121–133	129–144
5	4	118–126	124–136	132–148
5	5	121–129	127–139	135–152
5	6	124–133	130–143	138–156
5	7	128–137	134–147	142–161
5	8	132–141	138–152	147–166
5	9	136–145	142–156	151–170
5	10	140–150	146–160	155–174
5	11	144–154	150–165	159–179
6	0	148–158	154–170	164–184
6	1	152–162	158–175	168–189
6	2	156–167	162–180	173–194
6	3	160–171	167–185	178–199
6	4	164–175	172–190	182–204

* For nude weight, deduct 5 to 7 lb.
† Height based on 2-inch heels for women and 1-inch heels for men.
Prepared by Metropolitan Life Insurance Company. Derived primarily from data of the Build and Blood Pressure Study, Society of Actuaries, 1959. New York, Metropolitan Life Insurance Company, 1960.

TABLE 6–2. FRAME SIZE BY ELBOW BREADTH IN CENTIMETERS

	FRAME SIZE		
AGE IN YEARS	SMALL	MEDIUM	LARGE
Males			
18–24	<6.7	6.7–7.6	>7.6
25–34	<6.8	6.8–7.8	>7.8
35–44	<6.8	6.8–7.9	>7.9
45–54	<6.8	6.8–8.0	>8.0
55–64	<6.8	6.8–8.0	>8.0
65–74	<6.8	6.8–8.0	>8.0
Females			
18–24	<5.7	5.7–6.4	>6.4
25–34	<5.8	5.8–6.7	>6.7
35–44	<5.8	5.8–7.0	>7.0
45–54	<5.8	5.8–7.1	>7.1
55–64	<5.9	5.9–7.1	>7.1
65–74	<5.9	5.9–7.1	>7.1

Adapted from Frisancho, A.R.: New standards of weight and body composition by frame size and height for assessment of nutritional status of adults and the elderly. Am. J. Clin. Nutr., 40:808, 1984.

dium frame. With the completion of the Build and Blood Pressure Study, Society of Actuaries, 1979, the Metropolitan Life Insurance Company published its revised standard weight tables in 1983. In this most recent publication, elbow breadth or width is suggested as the index of frame size. Table 6–2 provides an estimate of frame size from elbow breadth derived from the NHANES I and II data sets. Elbow breadth can be estimated using a ruler, but it is more accurately measured by an anthropometric caliper.

What does it mean to be overweight? It simply means that weight exceeds the range of standard weights for gender, height, and frame size. The data used to establish these standard tables were obtained from over 4 million life insurance policyholders who were predominantly white, upper middle class males. Further, heights and weights were self-reported in approximately 10% of the sample, and in the remaining 90% the policyholders were measured wearing shoes and clothing. Many health professionals considered the tables released in 1983 to be too liberal, i.e., they allowed too much weight for a given height and frame size. Therefore, many have continued using the tables published in 1960.

Most important, height/weight tables do not differentiate between the fat and fat-free components of the body's total weight. It is important to know whether the excess pounds above the standard weight represent fat stores or the lean tissue. The woman shot-putter in the previous example was 21 pounds overweight. An analysis of her body's composition, however, shows that she had only 16% body fat: 28 lb of her total weight were fat and 147 lb were fat-free or lean weight. Further analysis indicates that her large bone structure and muscle mass accounted for her 21 lb of "overweight." This illustrates the importance of knowing body composition. In fact, when determining optimal weight or optimal weight ranges, knowing body composition is far more important than knowing the degree of over- or underweight.

☐ ASSESSMENT OF BODY COMPOSITION

The body is composed of different elements that can be described either chemically or anatomically. The chemical classification includes fat, protein, carbohydrate, mineral, and water. The anatomical classification includes adipose tissue, muscle, bone, organs, and the residual. Adipose tissue is the repository for triglycerides, the storage form of fat. In addition to the stored fat, adipose tissue is comprised of a connective tissue matrix, in which the fat cells are embedded, and water.

DIRECT ASSESSMENT: CADAVER DISSECTION

Cadaver dissection, and analysis of the resulting tissue, which is the only direct method for assessing body composition, provides an extremely accurate determination of the body's composition. Although cadaver analysis is tedious, labor-intensive, and requires working under the most difficult of conditions, it still is possible to perform and the results are precise. Accurate determination of the body's composition in healthy, living humans provides a different type of challenge but one that is just as difficult.

INDIRECT ASSESSMENT: LABORATORY TECHNIQUES

Albert R. Behnke, Jr., considered by many to be the father of indirect body composition assessment, began research into indirect techniques for assessing human body composition in the 1930s. Behnke proposed a simple two-component model of body composition: fat mass and lean body mass. In Behnke's model, the lean body mass included protein, carbohydrate, mineral, water, and a small amount of fat that Behnke termed "essential fat." The essential fat was defined as fat necessary for survival.

Fat serves many useful purposes in the body in addition to being a depot for storing energy. For example, fat is used in the myelination of nerve fibers and the production of hormones, and it serves a number of important roles in general metabolism. Although the concept of essential fat is sound and important, the measurement of essential fat is problematic. How can one differentiate essential from nonessential fat? This question led scientists to abandon the concept of the lean body

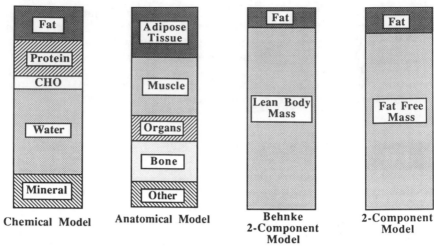

FIG. 6–1. Illustration of the chemical, anatomical, and 2-component models of body composition.

mass in favor of the fat-free body mass, the fat-free body mass including only protein, carbohydrate, mineral, and water. These different models of body composition are illustrated in Figure 6–1.

Several laboratory techniques are now available to assess body composition. These have been reviewed by Brodie, Lukaski, and Wilmore.[5–7] The present review borrows heavily from each of these reviews.

Densitometry, first developed by Behnke in the late 1930s, has been the most widely used and is generally considered the criterion technique against which all other techniques are validated. The density of the human body is determined by the ratio of its total mass to its volume (D = M/V). Mass is obtained by scale weight and volume by any one of several techniques. Volume can be obtained by measuring the volume of water displaced when a body is totally immersed, or more commonly, by the body's loss of weight when weighed under water. The difference between scale weight and underwater weight, when corrected for the density of the water, is equal to the body's volume. This volume must be corrected for any trapped air within the body, because these pockets of trapped air cause the body to be more buoyant and to weigh less when weighed under water. Gas trapped in the gastrointestinal tract is generally ignored because it is estimated to be relatively small, ~ 100 mL. The gas trapped in the lungs, however, must be measured because its contribution is major, between 0.8 and 2.0 L on average.

If the body weight, underwater weight, and lung volume at the time of the underwater weighing are each obtained correctly, the resulting body density value will be accurate. The major weakness of the densitometric technique is in the translation of body density to an estimate of relative body fat. With the two-component model, it is necessary to have an accurate estimate of the densities of the two compartments, i.e., fat-free and fat. Little disagreement exists as to the density of the fat tissue, because the density of fat among different sites appears to be consistent in the same individual as well as between individuals. The value generally used is 0.9007 g/cm^3. Unfortunately, considerable variation exists in the density of the fat-free body mass among individuals. To obtain the density of the fat-free mass, it must be assumed that the densities of the tissues, that comprise the fat-free mass are known and remain constant. Further, it is necessary to assume that they represent a constant proportion of the fat-free mass (e.g., bone represents 17% of the fat-free mass). Violations of either of these assumptions will lead to error when translating body density into relative body fat, and the size of the error can be considerable. Using data from three women athletes, this can be illustrated as follows:

	EDNA			VICKI			SUSAN		
	D_t	%	D_p	D_t	%	D_p	D_t	%	D_p
Muscle	1.065	46	0.490	1.065	41	0.437	1.065	46	0.490
Bone	1.350	17	0.229	1.350	22	0.297	1.260	17	0.214
Residual	1.030	37	0.381	1.030	37	0.381	1.030	37	0.381
D_{FFM}			1.100			1.115			1.085

D_t = density of the tissue, % = percent contribution of this tissue to the total fat-free mass, D_p = proportional density of the tissue (D_t × %/100), and D_{FFM} = density of the fat-free mass, which is the sum of the proportional densities. If Edna, Vicki, and Susan each had the same total body density of 1.060, using the standard equation of Siri, which assumes the D_{FFM} = 1.100, the relative body fat for each woman would be 17.0% body fat. This equation would be appropriate only for Edna, however, because she was the only one whose D_{FFM} = 1.100. If new equations were developed for Vicki and Susan, using the correct density of the fat-free mass specific to each of them, their relative body fat values would be 21.8% (using D_{FFM} = 1.115) and 11.5% (using D_{FFM} = 1.085) respectively. Thus, for the same body density, which is all that can be measured, the true relative body fat varied from 11.5 to 21.8%. This example might seem to exaggerate the point, but it is, in fact, very real.

The density of the fat-free mass is generally assumed to be 1.100 g/cm^3 for a chemically mature individual. Evidence now supports the use of lower values in children, females, and the aged[8] and higher values in blacks.[9] In the preceding example, Vicki is a mature black athlete and Susan is an 11-year-old white athlete. The D_{FFM} values that were obtained from the sum of the proportional densities for Vicki (1.115) and

Susan (1.085) are almost identical to the values that have been established for the black and adolescent populations. Research is progressing in this area, and population-specific equations are now available for select populations for more accurate translation of body density into relative body-fat values. The reader is referred to the excellent review by Lohman for a discussion of this issue relative to children and youth.[8]

A number of other laboratory techniques are available for the assessment of body composition. Several of these are primarily experimental, so their potential for screening of athletes or mass testing of the general population is either limited or unknown. In neutron activation analysis, one of the more experimental techniques, a beam of fast neutrons is delivered to the subject. The fast neutrons are captured by elements in the body, and unstable isotopes are produced that revert to a stable condition after emitting one or more gamma rays. The body becomes temporarily radioactive, and the gamma emissions are recorded in a whole body counter. Standard gamma spectrographic analysis is then used to measure the resulting energy. Total body nitrogen and total body potassium are examples of two elements that can be estimated.

Magnetic resonance imaging (MRI) is also primarily experimental with respect to body composition analysis, although it is widely used in clinical medicine. An external magnetic field applied across a part of the body affects the rotation of the nuclei of atoms with odd numbers of protons or neutrons. The body is then exposed to an alternating magnetic field of the same frequency. Measurement of one or more parameters of these nuclei, after removing the attenuating magnetic field, enables the formation of body images. These images are amazingly clear, giving one the impression that one is inside the body looking directly at the tissue under observation. This method, though expensive, has considerable promise for detailed body composition analyses.

Other laboratory-based techniques that have been used to measure body composition of athletes include hydrometry, spectrometry, radiography, photon absorptiometry, and total body electrical conductivity.

Hydrometry involves assessment of the body's total water content. Isotopic tracers, such as deuterium oxide and tritium oxide, are either ingested or injected and allowed a period of time for equilibration throughout the total body water (TBW). The absolute volume of the tracer is known, and the concentration of the tracer in urine, blood, or saliva is determined after the period of equilibration. All of the body's water is in the fat-free mass and generally constitutes from 72 to 74% of the fat-free mass. The constant 0.732 represents the assumed fraction of the FFM represented by the total body water. Thus FFM = TBW/0.732.

Spectrometry can be used to determine the body's total potassium content. It is well established that there are 2.66 and 2.50 grams of potassium for every kilogram of FFM in males and females respectively. The individual is placed in a whole body counter which is surrounded by liquid scintillation filled cylinders. The body's total potassium appears in three different forms: ^{39}K, ^{40}K, and ^{41}K. ^{39}K accounts for 93.2% and ^{41}K for 6.7% of the total body potassium. Although ^{40}K accounts for only 0.012% of the body's total potassium, it is a natural radioisotope that emits gamma radiation. The whole body counter is able to detect this gamma radiation as ultraviolet light pulses through the action of the scintillation fluid. Total body potassium is estimated from the ^{40}K content, because its proportion of the total remains constant. FFM is estimated by dividing the total grams of potassium by the factor 2.66 for males, and by the factor 2.50 for females.

Radiography has been used since the early 1930s to determine regional body composition. Detailed measurements on standard radiographs were used to provide estimates of thickness of bone, muscle, and fat in the extremities. In most instances, these measurements were obtained to provide a better understanding of the anatomical changes associated with growth and development in longitudinal growth studies. In 1974, Behnke[10] proposed using these measurements in the estimate of total body fatness. In 1984, Katch and Behnke[11] provided convincing evidence from a sample of 100 subjects indicating that the width of fat on a radiograph of the right upper arm at three cross-sectional sites correlated ($r = 0.89$) with relative body fat from hydrostatic weighing (densitometry), with a standard error of measurement of only 2.5%.

More recently, computer tomography (CT) has been used to determine regional body composition. A CT scanner produces a cross-sectional image of the distribution of x-ray attenuation, or transmission. Small differences in x-ray attenuation are related to differences in the physical density of tissues, allowing the construction of a two-dimensional image of the underlying tissue in the scan area.[5,6] Use of the CT procedure has become popular in differentiating visceral tissue from subcutaneous trunk adipose tissue. This has important health-related screening implications because abdominal, or upper body, obesity is highly correlated with increased risk for coronary artery disease, hypertension, lipid disorders, and diabetes. These relationships were initially established from simple waist-to-hip ratio measurements. Using CT scans, it was later possible to demonstrate that the waist-to-hip was related to relative visceral fat, thus providing some insight into possible mechanisms explaining the relationships between regional fat distribution and risk of various diseases.[12] To date, CT technology has not been used to provide estimates of total body fat.

Photon absorptiometry was used initially in the study of bone. Single-photon absorptiometry, with either an ^{125}I or a ^{241}Am source, was used to scan the radius and ulna or the femur, providing estimates of bone mineralization. With this technique, a beam of photons from the selected source is directed at the extremity; the amount that passes through the limb is inversely proportional to the mineral content of the underlying bone. Dual-photon absorptiometry, with ^{153}Gd as the source, is a more recent development. ^{153}Gd emits energy at two discrete peaks, allowing differentiation between soft tissue and bone mineral. Further, the fat content of soft tissue can be differentiated by attenuation of the ratio of

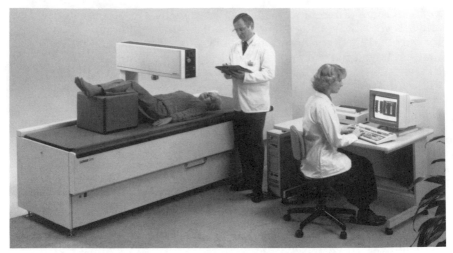

FIG. 6–2. Illustration of the dual-photon absorptiometric technique.

the response at these two energy levels. The dual-photon absorptiometric technique has recently been shown to have considerable promise for evaluation of total body fat, possibly providing the best estimate of total body fat of any indirect technique presently available.[13] The dual-photon absorptiometric device is illustrated in Figure 6–2. Typical results are shown in Figure 6–3.

Total body electrical conductivity (TOBEC) is an emerging technique based on the principle that differences in electrical conductivity and dielectric properties of fat-free and fat tissues can be used to estimate body composition. The subject is placed inside a large polaroidal coil, and a small radio-frequency current is passed through the subject's body. When a body is placed in an electromagnetic field, it perturbs the field in proportion to the quantity of conducting material present. The electrolytes in the fat-free body mass account for most of the electrical conductivity; thus total body electrical conductivity is highly correlated to the fat-free body mass. This technique has been shown, through a number of well-controlled studies, to have considerable promise for estimating total body composition.[5,6]

The densitometric techniques have major deficiencies, almost exclusively with respect to the conversion of total body density into an estimate of relative body fat, but it is my recommendation that these techniques continue to be used as the criterion against which all other techniques are evaluated. Several of the other techniques discussed in this section have considerable promise. Until they have been adequately evaluated against direct cadaver dissection methods, however, it would be premature at this time to recommend them as criterion techniques.

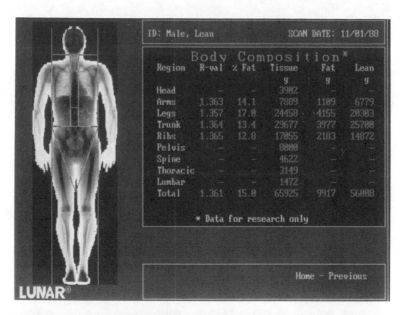

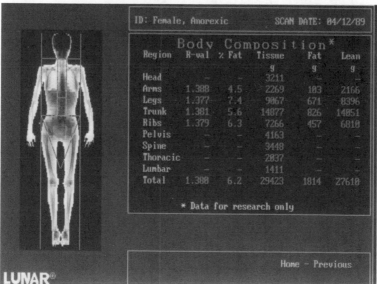

FIG. 6–3. Results obtained with the dual-photon absorptiometric technique. Courtesy of Dr. Richard B. Mazess, Lunar Radiation Corp., Madison, WI.

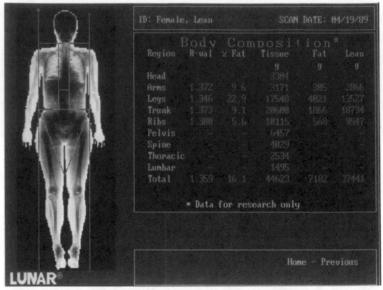

FIG. 6–3. (Continued)

INDIRECT ASSESSMENT: FIELD TECHNIQUES

There is no question that the laboratory techniques discussed in the previous section, for the most part, provide accurate estimates of body composition. Several of these techniques are still in the development stages, however, and most are impractical and prohibitively expensive for use in assessment of large numbers of individuals. This has created the need to establish a valid and reliable technique that will allow for the estimate of body composition from simple, easily obtained, and inexpensive measures.

Initially, this led to the use of skinfold, girth, and bony diameter measures in estimation of body density, fat-free mass, and fat mass. Body composition was first estimated from skinfolds in 1951. In the 1960s and 1970s, a number of investigations were conducted that resulted in the generation of numerous linear multiple regression equations for estimating body composition from anthropometric variables. In these studies, the investigators typically took anthropometric measurements at a number of sites, often including skinfolds, girths, and diameters. The resulting data were entered into a computer, and linear multiple regression techniques were then used to develop regression equations to estimate body composition. It soon became apparent that these equations were population-specific: they yielded accurate predictions only when used on populations similar in characteristics to the population from which the equation has been derived. This then led to a proliferation of equations for specific populations, including a number of equations developed for athletes in specific sports.

It is now recognized that the relationship between individual skin-folds, or the sum of skinfolds, and the total body density is curvilinear, not linear as assumed in the original studies, in which linear multiple regression techniques were used. This has led to the generation of a series of new equations based on this curvilinear relationship that are generalizable, not specific to a given population. The coefficients of correlation between hydrostatically determined body density and body density determined from skinfold estimates are nearly identical for linear and for generalized quadratic equations. Most important, however, the standard errors of estimate for the quadratic equations are usually much lower.[14] In particular, the quadratic equations minimize large prediction errors that occur at the extremes of the body-density distribution with linear regression equations. Athletes, in particular, generally have high body-densities. Linear models tend to underestimate the body density of lean athletes, resulting in overestimates of their relative body fat.

This last point is critical when working with athletes who might be at high risk for eating or weight disorders. Here is a hypothetical example. Tina is a long-distance runner who has a true relative body fat value of 11.5%, although she has never had her body composition assessed. This is an extremely low relative body fat for an average young woman, but it is approximately the mean value for elite women distance runners. She works hard to keep her weight at its present level, often denying herself when she feels hungry. Tina's coach decides to conduct body composition analyses on all her track athletes. Using skinfold calipers and a linear regression equation, she estimates Tina's body fat to be 21.4%. In this illustration, the coach now becomes the key to how this situation will develop. A knowledgeable coach will understand the limitations of body composition estimates in elite athletes and will not use this value to prescribe significant weight loss. Most coaches, however, do not understand these limitations and would likely place even an athlete such as Tina on a diet to further reduce body fat. Even providing such an athlete with a written copy of the results of a test that contains an erroneous value of this sort could set off a chain of events leading to a serious eating or weight disorder. Athletes today are well aware of the relative body fat values of the top athletes in their sport or event. The low values characteristic of the elite athlete become goals for the aspiring athlete.

Pollock and Jackson recommend that the sum of three or more skinfold sites be used in a quadratic equation to estimate body density.[14] The sum of three or more skinfolds provides an estimate of body density that is more highly correlated with the true value than estimates from individual sites. Because people have different fat patterns, selecting only one or two sites might not provide a good representation of the total body fat stores. This can be even more of an issue with athletes.

During the 1980s, two additional techniques were introduced that can be used for field testing, although initial cost of equipment is generally high. The first method, bioelectric impedance, is similar in principle to TOBEC. Electrical conduction through tissue is related to the water and

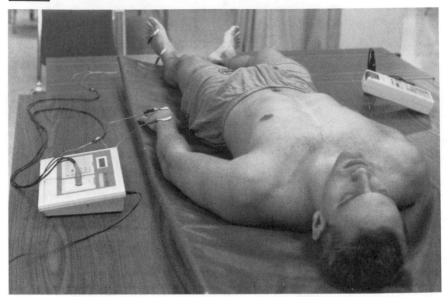

FIG. 6–4. Illustration of the bioelectric impedance technique.

electrolyte distribution of that tissue. Because the fat-free mass contains almost all of the total body water and conducting electrolytes, conductivity is much greater in the fat-free mass than in the fat mass of the body.[6] Likewise, impedance to current flow is much greater in the fat mass. Four electrodes are attached to the skin, two on the hand and two on the foot (Fig. 6–4). An excitation current of 800 μA at 50 KHz is introduced through the distal electrodes at the hand and foot, and the voltage drop is detected by the proximal electrodes. Assessments take approximately 5 minutes, and subjects can be measured while fully clothed. Correlations between bioelectric impedance and hydrostatically determined density in various populations have been relatively high (r = ~0.90 to 0.94), and the standard errors of estimate are relatively low (2.5 to 3.5%). Unfortunately, the bioelectric impedance procedure tends to overestimate relative body fat in lean athletic populations.

The second method, infrared interactance, is based on the principles of light absorption and reflection using near-infrared spectroscopy. When electromagnetic radiation strikes a material, the energy is reflected, absorbed, or transmitted depending on the scattering and absorption properties of the sample.[6] A probe is placed on the skin above the site to be measured (Fig. 6–5). The probe emits electromagnetic radiation through a central bundle of optic fibers, and optic fibers on the periphery of the same probe pick up the reflected energy and pass it on to a spectrophotometer for measurement. The depth of penetration of the electromagnetic radiation is 1 cm. The assessment requires only 2 or 3 minutes to complete, and the subject can be fully clothed during

FIG. 6–5. Illustration of the Futrex infrared interactance technique.

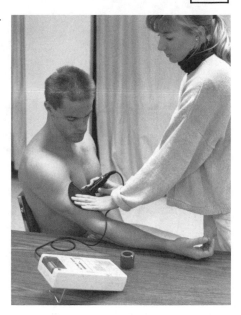

the procedure. Only limited data are available on the validity and reliability of this technique, particularly in athletic populations. A commercial model infrared interactance unit is available. According to the instructions of the manufacturer, however, only a single site (biceps) is scanned. As with skinfolds or other techniques that use regional measurements, the use of a single site to represent the total body must be questioned.

I suggest that practitioners and clinicians use skinfold calipers in the estimation of body composition in athletic populations when laboratory techniques are not available or are not practical. Further, I recommend that the Jackson and Pollock[15] equations be used for males and that the Jackson, Pollock, and Ward[16] equations be used for females, because these equations appear to be the best-generalized equations available for athletic populations.[17,18] Coefficients normally range from r = 0.85 to 0.95 (SEE ~3%) when these equations are correlated with body density determined hydrostatically in various populations. Refer to Pollock and Wilmore[19] for more specific details on how to use these equations, descriptions of the specific skinfold sites used, and equipment selection.

☐ DETERMINATION OF OPTIMAL BODY WEIGHT FOR ATHLETES

An athlete's body weight can have a negative influence on performance if it is above or below the optimal level. For athletes in contact sports, a high body weight provides a distinct advantage, but only when the excess weight is fat-free. For endurance athletes, a lower body weight appears to offer a distinct advantage, providing that the fat-free mass is not compromised. In Chapter 20, Body Weight Standards and Athletic Performance, I discuss in considerable detail the scientific basis for body weight and body composition standards for athletes in various sports. In this chapter I focus on how optimal body weight is determined.

To determine an athlete's optimal body weight, it is necessary to have an estimate of body composition. As discussed earlier in this chapter, the use of standard weight tables is not appropriate, particularly for the athletic population. This was well illustrated by Behnke in the early 1940s, shortly after he developed the underwater weighing technique for assessing body composition. He had the opportunity to assess the body composition of the members of a professional football team.[20] The average weight of these 25 men was 90.9 kg (200 lb), and the average relative body fat was 10.9%. According to the standard height-weight tables at that time, 17 of these 25 athletes would have been classified as physically unqualified for military duty and would not have qualified as first-class insurance risks. Of the 17 "overweight" athletes 11 had relative body fats less than 15.0%, a value that would be considered well within the normal range for this type of athlete. For these individuals, their "overweight" status was the result of an excess of fat-free mass. Excessive fat-free mass is typically the goal of these athletes as they prepare themselves in the weight room for competition.

Once the athlete's body composition has been assessed, optimal body weight, or a body weight range, can be determined on the basis of desired body composition. As an example, Ken is an offensive lineman on the University of Texas football team. He weighs 278 lb. and through hydrostatic weighing he has been determined to have 22.5% of his weight as fat. Data on elite offensive linemen indicate relative body fats between 14.0 and 17.0%. For Ken to reach a relative body fat of between 14% and 17%, his optimal weight range would be determined as follows:

$$
\begin{aligned}
\text{Weight} &= 278 \text{ lb} \\
\text{Fat Weight} &= 278 \text{ lb} \times 0.225 = 62.6 \text{ lb} \\
\text{Fat-Free Weight} &= 278 \text{ lb} - 62.6 \text{ lb} = 215.4 \text{ lb} \\
\text{Weight}_{17.0\%} &= 215.4 \text{ lb}/0.83 = 259.5 \text{ lb} \\
\text{Weight}_{14.0\%} &= 215.4 \text{ lb}/0.86 = 250.5 \text{ lb}
\end{aligned}
$$

where the constant 0.83 represents 17.0% fat weight and 83.0% fat-free weight, and the constant 0.86 represents 14.0% fat weight and 86.0% fat-free weight. Ken's optimal weight range would be 250.5 to 259.5 pounds, representing 14.0 to 17.0% body fat. This same procedure would be used for an athlete in any sport, event, or position within a sport. Chapter 20, Body Weight Standards and Athletic Performance, provides information on the optimal range of relative fats appropriate for the given sport, event, or position.

This chapter must be read in concert with Chapter 20 to understand fully the implications of body composition assessment in assignment of goal weights for the athletic population. Many abuses have occurred in this area, largely because of misunderstanding and lack of knowledge.

☐ REFERENCES

1. Thornton, J.S.: Feast or famine: Eating disorders in athletes. Physician Sportsmed., 18:116, 1990.
2. Brownell, K.D., Steen, S.N., and Wilmore, J.H.: Weight regulation practices in athletes: Analysis of metabolic and health effects. Med. Sci. Sports Exerc., 19:546, 1987.
3. Wilmore, J.H., and Costill, D.L.: Training for Sport and Activity: The Physiological Basis of the Conditioning Process. 3rd Ed. Dubuque, IA, Wm. C. Brown, 1988.
4. Wilmore, J.H.: Body composition in sport and exercise: Directions for future research. Med. Sci. Sports Exerc., 15:21, 1983.
5. Brodie, D.A.: Techniques for measurement of body composition, Parts I and II. Sports Med., 5:11,74, 1988.
6. Lukaski, H.C.: Methods for the assessment of human body composition: Traditional and new. Am. J. Clin. Nutr., 46:537, 1987.
7. Wilmore, J.H.: Design issues and alternatives in assessing physical fitness among apparently healthy adults in a health examination survey of the general population. In Assessing Physical Fitness and Physical Activity in Population-Based Surveys. Edited by T.F. Drury. Washington, DC, National Center for Health Statistics, Department of Health and Human Services (DHHS Publication #PHS 89-1253), 1989.
8. Lohman, T.G.: Applicability of body composition techniques and constants for children and youths. Exerc. Sport Sci. Rev., 14:325, 1986.
9. Schutte, J.E., et al.: Density of lean body mass is greater in Blacks than Whites. J. Appl. Physiol. 56:1647, 1984.
10. Behnke, A.R., and Wilmore, J.H.: Evaluation and Regulation of Body Build and Composition. Englewood Cliffs, NJ, Prentice-Hall, 1974.
11. Katch, F.I. and Behnke, A.R.: Arm x-ray assessment of percent body fat in men and women. Med. Sci. Sports Exerc., 16:316, 1984.
12. Björntorp, P., Smith, U., and Lönnroth, P. (eds.): Health Implications of Regional Obesity. Acta Med. Scand. Symposium Series No. 4, Stockholm, Almqvist & Wiksell International, 1988.
13. Wang, J., et al.: Body fat from body density: Underwater weighing vs. dual-photon absorptiometry. Am. J. Physiol. 256:E829, 1989.
14. Pollock, M.L., and Jackson, A.S.: Research progress in validation of clinical methods of assessing body composition. Med. Sci. Sports Exerc., 16:606, 1984.
15. Jackson, A.S., and Pollock, M.L.: Generalized equations for predicting body density of men. Br. J. Nutr., 40:497, 1978.
16. Jackson, A.S., Pollock, M.L., and Ward, A.: Generalized equations for predicting body density of women. Med. Sci. Sports Exerc., 12:175, 1980.
17. Sinning, W.E., et al.: Validity of "generalized" equations for body composition analysis in male athletes. Med. Sci. Sports Exerc., 17:124, 1985.
18. Sinning, W.E., and Wilson, J.R.: Validity of "generalized" equations for body composition analysis in women athletes. Res. Q. Exerc. Sport, 55:153-160, 1984.
19. Pollock, M.L., and Wilmore, J.H.: Exercise in Health and Disease: Evaluation and Prescription for Prevention and Rehabilitation. 2nd Ed. Philadelphia, W.B. Saunders, 1990.
20. Welham, W.C., and Behnke, A.R., Jr.: The specific gravity of healthy men. Body weight/volume and other physical characteristics of exceptional athletes and of naval personnel. JAMA, 118:498, 1942,

C H A P T E R

7

PHYSIQUE AND BODY COMPOSITION: EFFECTS ON PERFORMANCE AND EFFECTS OF TRAINING, SEMISTARVATION, AND OVERTRAINING

Robert M. Malina

Physique and body composition are related yet distinctly different concepts. Physique refers to the individual's body form, the configuration of the entire body as opposed to emphasis on specific features. The study of physique deals with external dimensions and characteristics of the body. Size and physique, however, do not adequately indicate tissue distribution or quantity of different tissues within the body. Quantification of tissues comprising body mass, primarily bone, muscle, fat, and viscera, is the domain of body composition assessment.

This chapter considers physique and body composition in three contexts: (1) relationships to performance, (2) the influence of training in children and adults, and (3) changes associated with semistarvation, anorexia, and overtraining.

The methods have been developed on adults, largely males, and their applicability to the growing and maturing individual, to females, or to the clinically ill, may require adjustment. Principles and methods for the assessment of physique and body composition are presented elsewhere[1,2] (see also Chapter 6).

☐ PHYSIQUE, BODY COMPOSITION, AND PERFORMANCE

Relationships between physique and body composition and physical performance can be demonstrated at two levels: (1) in empirical relationships between measures of physique and body composition and actual performances in a variety of tasks, and (2) in the physique and body composition characteristics of athletes in a variety of sports.

CORRELATION STUDIES

The following are offered as a guide in interpreting correlational studies. Correlations between zero and 0.30 are low, those between 0.30 and 0.60 are moderate, those between 0.60 and 0.85 are moderately high, and those above 0.85 are high.

PHYSIQUE. Relationships between somatotype components and body composition and performance have been considered in children, adolescents, and adults.[3-6] Correlations between endomorphy and performances requiring projection or movement of the body through space are consistently negative in all age groups and in both sexes, and range from low to moderate. These include tasks such as the standing long jump, vertical jump, dashes, pull-ups, and so on. The excess fatness associated with endomorphy represents dead weight that must be projected or moved and thus presents a mechanical disadvantage. In contrast, endomorphy is positively related to measures of static strength in males, which emphasizes the significant contribution of muscularity to endomorphy ratings and the importance of overall body size in static strength tests. The correlations tend to be low to moderate prior to adolescence (about 9 to 12 years), but consistently low during adolescence in males. Extreme endomorphs tend towards obesity, and some forms of obesity are characterized by an overgrowth of fat-free mass (FFM).[7-8]

Correlations between mesomorphy and motor performance vary among tasks but are positive and low in both sexes from childhood into young adulthood. Correlations for static strength, in contrast, are moderate in adolescent and adult males. Data for adolescent females are lacking, but in college women, correlations between mesomorphy and strength are low.

Correlations between ectomorphy and performance vary. Ectomorphy is not consistently related to motor performance during childhood, and it tends to be negatively related to strength and power tasks in adolescent and adult males. The low negative correlations for strength tasks emphasize the strength deficiency associated with extreme ectomorphy.

TABLE 7–1. MEAN SOMATOTYPES OF ADOLESCENT BOYS AND GIRLS AT THE EXTREMES OF STRENGTH AND MOTOR PERFORMANCE

PERFORMANCE MEASURE	N	MEAN SOMATOTYPE		
		ENDOMORPHY	MESOMORPHY	ECTOMORPHY
Strength—boys				
Strongest				
Weakest	10	2.5	5.0	3.5
Motor Performance—boys	10	2.5	3.5	4.5
High				
Low	10	3.0	5.2	3.1
Motor Performance—girls	9	4.6	4.5	2.9
High				
Low	8	4.9	3.7	2.7
	8	5.6	3.0	2.8

Adapted from Jones, University of California Press, 1949, pp. 145 and 147; Espenschade, A.: Motor Performance in Adolescence. Monographs of the Society for Research in Child Development, Vol. 5, No. 1. University of Chicago Press, 1940, pp. 79–88; and Espenschade, A., and Eckert, H.M.: Motor Development. Columbus, OH, Merrill, 1967, p. 147.

Among college women, ectomorphy is apparently not a significant factor in performance.

Overall, correlations between somatotype components and performance tend to be low to moderate in magnitude. They rarely exceed 0.5; hence, explained variances are low and have limited predictive utility. It can thus be inferred that physique does not markedly influence performance. The situation might be somewhat different, however, at the extremes of physique. Extreme ectomorphs tend to be deficient in muscle mass and strength, whereas extreme endomorphs have excess fat, which has negative consequences for performance both mechanically and metabolically (see below). On the other hand, certain physiques can occur at the extremes of performance. Mean somatotypes of the strongest and weakest boys and the highest and lowest performers in a series of motor tests among adolescents in the Oakland Growth Study[9–11] are shown in Table 7–1. The strongest boys at 17 years of age were dominant mesomorphs, and the weakest were dominant ectomorphs. Boys who excelled in motor performance were also dominant mesomorphs, whereas low-performing boys were equally high in both endomorphy and mesomorphy. Strength data for girls were not reported, but the high-performing girls were slightly more mesomorphic and less endomorphic than the poor performers.

BODY COMPOSITION. A major component of FFM is skeletal muscle, the major work-performing tissue of the body. Hence one would expect positive associations between FFM and performance. Absolute FFM is particularly related to static strength, as might be expected from the association between strength and the cross-sectional area of a muscle. Absolute FFM is also important in performances that require that force be exerted against an object, such as throwing a ball, putting a shot, or weight lifting. In both strength and object-projection tasks, a large FFM is important. On the other hand, a large FFM can be a limiting factor in tasks in which the body must be projected as in a vertical jump or moved across space as in a run.

Relationships between FFM and performance, however, vary with age. Among 7- to 12-year-old boys, for example, both absolute FFM and relative FFM are moderately related to about the same extent to performances in the 50-yard dash, the standing long jump, and the vertical jump.[12,13] Correlations approach 0.5 (the sign of correlations for the dash are inverted because a lower time is a better score). At these preadolescent ages, absolute FFM is more closely related to distance throwing performance than relative FFM, indicating the role of absolute body size.[12] Among adult males, on the other hand, absolute FFM is not related to the standing long jump and pull-ups ($r = 0$ and -0.1), and relative FFM is moderately related at the same magnitude ($r = 0.5$) as in preadolescent boys.[14]

As might be anticipated, strength is significantly related to FFM during male adolescence. Correlations between FFM and grip strength, for example, reach 0.9 in samples of boys from 9 to 14 years[15] and from 12 to 18 years.[16] When age, stature, and weight are statistically controlled, the correlation between FFM and grip strength approaches 0.6 in the 9- to 14-year-old boys. Several studies of adult males[4] indicate slightly lower correlations between FFM and strength (about 0.5), but statistically controlling stature and weight does not alter the relationship as in boys.

Data for 7- to 12-year-old girls are generally consistent with those for boys, though the data are limited to a single study. Absolute FFM has a moderately high relationship to performance in the 50-yard dash, the standing long jump, and the vertical jump (0.6 to 0.7), and the relationships for relative fatness are low but negative (-0.2 to -0.3).[17] Data relating FFM to strength and motor performance of adolescent and young adult females are lacking.

In contrast to FFM, fat mass (FM) generally has a negative influence on performance. From a mechanical perspective, excess fat represents an inert load (dead weight) that must be moved. Hence relative fatness and skinfold thicknesses are inversely related to performance tasks that require the projection or movement of the body through space. The negative correlations range from low to moderate for the standing long and vertical jumps, dashes, distance runs, shuttle runs, pull-ups, and so on. In the runs, correlations are reversed because a greater relative fatness is associated with slower times, i.e., poorer performance. The correlations are reasonably consistent from childhood through adolescence into young adulthood in both sexes.[4,5,13,17] It is also likely that when FM is low, as it is in many athletes, FFM is of more functional significance in performance than FM.

As in physique, the influence of fatness on performance is more apparent at the extremes of fatness. This is shown for 12 and 18 year old Belgian males in Figure 7–1. The performances of the fattest 5% and leanest 5% (based on the sum of four skinfolds) are compared to age-specific reference data for Belgian males. With the exception of static strength (arm pull), the performances of the fattest boys were significantly poorer than those of the leanest boys. The advantage of a large body size associated with fatness is apparent in arm-pull strength. All of the other performance tasks require that the body be supported off the ground (bent arm hang), moved rapidly (shuttle run), or projected (vertical jump) and that parts of the body be lifted (leg lifts). In addition, pulse recovery after a 1-min step test was poorer in the fattest relative to the leanest boys. This probably reflects a metabolic consequence of the additional work performed during the test. In contrast, the fattest and leanest boys did not differ in speed of upper limb movement (plate tapping), flexibility of the lower back (sit and reach), or eye-hand coordination (stick balance).[18]

From a metabolic perspective, excess fatness is associated with reduced capacity for physical work, both directly and indirectly. Excess fat represents an inert load that does not contribute to work. It can also interfere with cardiovascular and respiratory function and perhaps increases the metabolic cost of performing work that requires the body to be moved.[19–22] The negative influence of excess fatness on performance is especially apparent in obesity. Although maximal oxygen uptakes reached by obese children, adolescents, and adults might be similar to maximal oxygen uptakes reached by the nonobese, maximal levels are reached at lower speeds and after a shorter period of exercise in the obese.

PHYSIQUE AND BODY COMPOSITION OF ATHLETES

PHYSIQUE. Athletes in a given sport tend to have, on average, reasonably similar somatotypes and also show a more limited range of variability in somatotype compared to the general population. This would seem to suggest that success in some sports is related in part to physique. With the exception of throwing events in track and field and the higher weight categories in weight lifting and related activities, endomorphy is rather low in most athletes and mesomorphy is well developed, whereas ectomorphy is more variable.[23] Moreover, data for early adolescent and adolescent athletes (about 12 to 18 years of age) suggest that those who are successful tend to have, on average, somatotypes that are similar to those of adult athletes in the respective sports.[24] As in adult athletes, somatotypic variation is less among younger athletes compared to the general population of youth. Younger athletes, however, tend to be less endomorphic (particularly females), less meso-

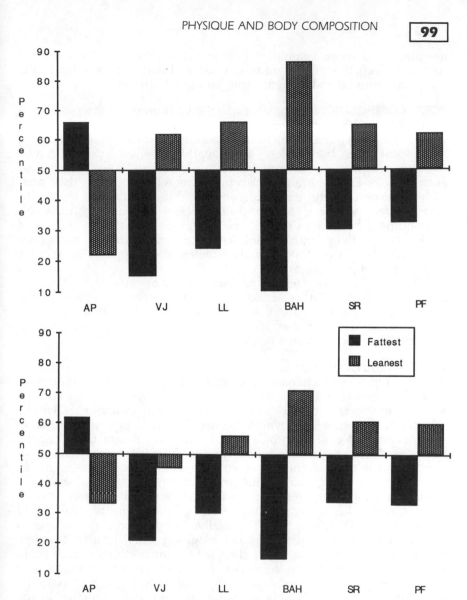

FIG. 7–1. Performance of the fattest 5% and leanest 5% of 12-year-old boys (A) and 18-year-old boys (B) relative to age-specific percentiles for Belgian boys: AP = arm pull strength, VJ = vertical jump, LL = leg lifts, BAH = bent arm hang, SR = shuttle run, PF = pulse frequency. Redrawn after Beunen, G., Malina, R.M., Ostyn, M., et al.: Fatness, growth and motor fitness of Belgian boys 12 through 20 years of age. Hum. Biol., 55:599, 1983.

morphic, and more ectomorphic than adult athletes. The latter, of course, reflects the role of growth in size and body composition in the transition from late adolescence into young adulthood.

BODY COMPOSITION. Estimates of relative fatness in adolescent and young adult athletes in several sports indicate that athletes as a group have less relative fatness than non-athletes of the same age and sex.[2,25–28] Adolescent males, both athletes and nonathletes, show a decline in relative fatness during adolescence, but the athletes have less relative fatness at most ages. Female athletes also have less relative fatness than nonathletes, especially during adolescence, and it appears that the difference between female athletes and nonathletes is greater than the corresponding difference in males. Relative fatness, on the average, does not increase with age during adolescence in female athletes, but it does in nonathletes. In contrast to male athletes, there appears to be more variation among female athletes.

Within a given sport, female athletes tend to be fatter than male athletes, and the magnitudes of the differences are similar to those in the nonathletic population. There are thus important biological influences that either override or that are as important as training for sport in determining an individual's level of fatness.

FAT DISTRIBUTION. Different sports or events within a sport require different types of mechanical efficiency. Thus a question of interest is possible variation in the distribution of subcutaneous fat among athletes in different sports. This question was addressed in a sample of Olympic athletes at the Montreal Olympic Games.[29] Results of a principal components analysis of six skinfolds indicate that fatness, the first principal component, is more influenced by sport, and by inference, training for sport, than is the distribution of subcutaneous fat on the extremities relative to the trunk, the second principal component. Sex, age, and ethnicity are more important than sport in determining the second component, and sex is more important than age and ethnicity. This would suggest that the major factor in the relative distribution of subcutaneous fat on the trunk and extremities is biological (genetic) rather than environmental. Two trends in the data for Olympic athletes merit replication and further study, however. Runners of short distances and jumpers of both sexes, and male weight lifters had the most centrally distributed fat, i.e., relatively more fat on the trunk compared to the extremities, whereas swimmers and rowers had the most extremity-oriented fat distribution. Variation in subcutaneous fat distribution by sport and by event within a sport clearly merits further study.[30]

☐ EFFECTS OF TRAINING ON PHYSIQUE AND BODY COMPOSITION

Because growing and maturing individuals are not miniature adults, the influence of training on physique and body composition is considered separately for children and adults.

TRAINING DURING CHILDHOOD AND ADOLESCENCE

Many athletes begin formal training during childhood and adolescence; hence it is important to consider the effects of training on physique and body composition relative to those associated with normal growth and maturation. Changes that accompany normal growth and maturation are described elsewhere.[2]

PHYSIQUE. In a small sample of boys from 11 to 18 years of age (n = 39) participating in three different activity programs (6 h/wk, 4 h/wk, and 2.5 h/wk), distributions of somatotypes did not differ among the 3 activity groups.[31] Somatotypes changed over adolescence, but the changes occurred in a random manner and were not associated with training. Thus regular training during growth does not appear to have a significant effect on somatotype. Mesomorphy increased between 18 and 24 years of age even though the young men had ceased regular training.[32]

In the preceding longitudinal study, specific intensities of the training programs were not indicated. Some types of training, however, result in muscular hypertrophy of the body parts specifically exercised, e.g., thoracic and arm musculature in male gymnasts, shoulder musculature in young swimmers, and arm musculature in weight training programs. Such changes are sometimes extreme, giving the impression of altered physique. The changes are rather localized, however, and do not markedly alter an individual's somatotype.[33,34]

BODY COMPOSITION. Most studies that consider the effects of regular training on body composition are short term, and only a few span the years during childhood and adolescence. Youngsters who are regularly engaged in physical activity programs, be they formal training for sport or recreational activities, generally have more FFM and less FM than those who are not regularly active.[2] Changes in FFM and relative fatness of small samples of boys who were engaged in different levels of sports training over 7 years from age 10 to age 17 are shown in Figure 7–2. The groups differed somewhat in body composition at the start of training, but during the study and at its end, the most active boys had significantly more FFM and less FM than the moderately and least active boys.[35] The latter two groups differed only slightly in FFM, but the least active boys had greater relative fatness. The negligible differences in FFM between the moderately active and least active boys would seem to suggest a need for a more intense training stimulus to produce changes in FFM during growth. These trends, however, need to be viewed with some caution. The 3 groups varied in maturity status. The most active boys reached peak height velocity (maximum growth during the adolescent spurt) earliest, followed by the moderately active and then the least active.[36] This trend is consistent with differences in skeletal maturity among the 3 activity groups at 14 and 15 years of age.[35] In addition to training, the differences in FFM could reflect maturity-as-

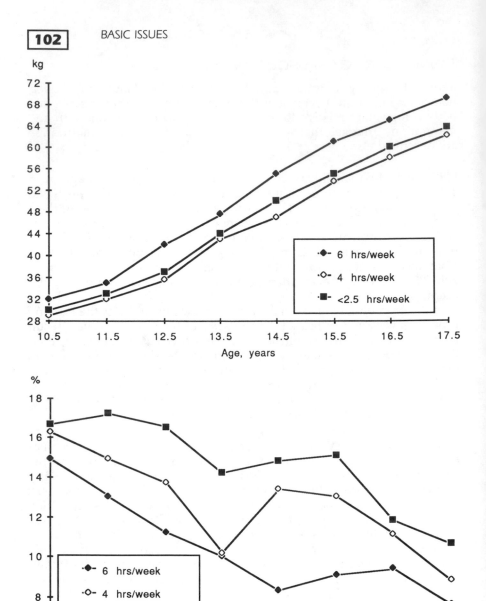

FIG. 7–2. Changes in fat-free mass (A) and relative fatness (B) of Czechoslovak boys followed longitudinally from age 10 to age 17 and exposed to different levels of training. Redrawn after Parizkova, J.: Particularities of lean body mass and fat development in growing boys as related to their motor activity. Acta Paediatr. Belg. (Suppl.), *28*:233, 1974.

sociated variation and selection for sport. Longitudinal observations on female gymnasts between 12 and 17 years of age and female swimmers between 12 and 15 years of age indicate similar trends, particularly for fatness.[21]

The increase in FFM observed in youth who regularly trained over several years would seem to suggest an increase greater than that expected with normal growth and maturation, although other factors might be involved. The persistence of training-associated changes in body composition after the cessation of training, however, is not ordinarily considered.

Much of the variation in body composition associated with regular activity or inactivity is associated with fatness, which fluctuates inversely with training. Changes in response to short-term training programs most likely reflect fluctuating levels of fatness with minimal or no changes in FFM.[28]

TRAINING DURING ADULTHOOD

PHYSIQUE. Mean somatotypes of young adult males (18 to 25 years) before and after 4 months of weight training and of university female swimmers (18 to 23 years) during a competitive season are summarized in Table 7–2. Training during the swim season also included high-repetition, low-resistance weight training. Changes in somatotype with training were minor. Among males, on average, mesomorphy increased

TABLE 7–2. SOMATOTYPES OF YOUNG ADULT MALES BEFORE AND AFTER 4 MONTHS OF WEIGHT TRAINING AND OF UNIVERSITY FEMALE SWIMMERS DURING A SEASON. SOMATOTYPES OF THE MALES ARE BASED ON SHELDON'S METHODS, AND THOSE OF FEMALES ARE BASED ON THE HEATH-CARTER ANTHROPOMETRIC METHOD

TEST SUBJECT	ENDOMORPHY MEAN	ENDOMORPHY SD	MESOMORPHY MEAN	MESOMORPHY SD	ECTOMORPHY MEAN	ECTOMORPHY SD
Males						
Before	2.7	0.9	4.9	0.6	3.1	1.0
After	2.7	0.8	5.1	0.6	3.1	1.1
Female swimmers						
October	3.6	0.8	3.5	0.7	3.3	0.8
December	3.3	0.6	3.6	0.7	3.6	0.8
March	3.1	0.8	3.5	0.7	3.5	0.8

Adapted from Tanner, J.M.: The effect of weight-training on physique. Am. J. Phys. Anthropol., *10*:427, 1952, and Meleski, B.W., and Malina, R.M.: Changes in body composition and physique of elite university-level swimmers during a competitive season. J. Sports Sci., *3*:33, 1985.

slightly in response to weight training, and endomorphy and ectomorphy were unchanged. Changes with weight training occurred primarily in the upper arm and shoulder girdle but were not sufficient to alter estimates of somatotype.[37] All changes in somatotype components varied within +0.5 and −0.5 units, and the majority were unchanged with training. Among female swimmers small changes occurred, on average, in endomorphy (decrease) and ectomorphy (increase), while mesomorphy was virtually unchanged. Changes in somatotype components ranged between +1.5 and −1.0 units, but most of the changes occurred in endomorphy and ectomorphy. Mesomorphy was unchanged in the majority of swimmers. All skinfold thicknesses decreased with training in the swimmers and thus influenced endomorphy in the Heath-Carter method. Limb circumferences behaved differently during the swim season. On average, arm girth increased and calf girth decreased, resulting in negligible changes in the anthropometric estimate of mesomorphy.[38] The preceding results thus suggest limited changes in somatotype, if any, with training. Athletes are a select group, however, sometimes on the basis of physique, and are ordinarily better trained than the general population at the start of training. Hence one might expect minimal changes.

BODY COMPOSITION. Changes in FFM with regular training in adults are variable. Studies that incorporate intense training programs generally show significant increases in FFM.[39] The literature on changes in FFM with training is confounded in part by the fact that athletes are a select sample, are leaner than the general population, and in some sports have a larger FFM than the nonathletic population. Further, many training studies are of relatively short duration and do not quantify the intensity of the program. In contrast to FFM, absolute and relative fatness ordinarily decline in association with regular training in both athletes and nonathletes.

Changes in body composition of female swimmers during a swim season are summarized in Table 7–3. Weight training, with emphasis on high repetition and low resistance, typically preceded swim training early in the season. Changes in body composition during the season occurred primarily in the first part, when training was more intense, and were maintained during the second part. Correlations between body composition at the beginning of intensive training (October) and after about 10 weeks (December) and after 24 weeks (March) were moderate and negative. Thus swimmers with higher absolute and relative fatness at the start of training experienced greater absolute and relative fat losses with training, whereas those with a smaller FFM experienced greater gains in FFM with training.[38]

The changes in body composition of female swimmers during a swim season are generally consistent with those observed in college-age female and male athletes and nonathletes, and they indicate similar responses in males and females. Much of the comparative literature on changes in body composition with training, however, reports only dif-

TABLE 7–3. CHANGES IN BODY WEIGHT AND COMPOSITION OF FEMALE SWIMMERS DURING A SEASON

MEASURE	OCTOBER–DECEMBER		DECEMBER–MARCH	
	MEAN	SD	MEAN	SD
Body weight, kg	− 1.3	1.8	0.8	1.2
Fat-free mass, kg	1.1	1.8	0.0	1.1
Fat mass, kg	− 2.4	1.2	0.8	1.5
Fat, %	− 3.8	1.9	1.2	2.0

Adapted from Meleski, B.W., and Malina, R.M.: Changes in body composition and physique of elite university-level swimmers during a competitive season. J. Sports Sci., 3:33, 1985.

ferences between means, so that it is difficult to evaluate individual variation in changes. In an analysis of reported data,[40] differences between pre- and post-training means in 9 studies of males 18 to 23 years of age ranged from − 0.2 kg to + 1.4 kg for FFM (overall mean + 0.8 kg) and − 0.4% to − 3.0% for relative fatness (overall mean − 1.7%). Differences in 10 studies of females 18 to 22 years of age ranged from − 1.7 kg to + 1.5 kg for FFM (overall mean + 0.3 kg) and − 2.1% to + 3.1% for relative fatness (overall mean − 0.4%). Training protocols varied among studies, however, as did the quality and level of training among athletes used as subjects.

FAT DISTRIBUTION. Evidence for young adult males suggests greater reductions in trunk than in extremity skinfolds after 20 weeks of aerobic training[41] and after 15 weeks of high-intensity training.[42] In contrast, reduction in subcutaneous fat with training in females is evenly distributed between extremity and trunk skinfolds.[42] Further study is needed to clarify these observations.

☐ **PHYSIQUE, BODY COMPOSITION, AND PERFORMANCE IN SEMISTARVATION, ANOREXIA, AND OVERTRAINING**

Emphasis on low body weight and leanness in several sports leads to the development of eating disorders, especially anorexia, in some athletes. On the other hand, given the premium on excellence in sport, the drive for high levels of performance leads some athletes to overtrain. The prevalence of eating disorders and overtraining among athletes, however, is not known with certainty.

SEMISTARVATION AND ANOREXIA

The morbid fear of becoming fat and the obsessive pursuit of thinness that characterizes anorexia nervosa often result in severe undernutrition similar to that observed under conditions of partial or total starvation.

TABLE 7–4. MEAN SOMATOTYPES BEFORE AND AFTER 6 MONTHS OF SEMISTARVATION IN ADULT MALES IN THE MINNESOTA EXPERIMENT

TIME OF MEASUREMENT	ENDOMORPHY	MESOMORPHY	ECTOMORPHY
Before	3.47	3.94	3.42
After	1.82	2.81	5.71

Adapted from Keys, A., Brozek, J., Henschel, A., et al.: The Biology of Human Starvation. Minneapolis, University of Minnesota Press, 1950.

Hence the parallels between anorexia and starvation merit consideration, recognizing of course that the two conditions are not identical. The Minnesota Experiment[43] provides data on the effects of 6 months of semistarvation on adult males (25.5 ± 3.5 years of age), which to some extent parallel observations on anorectic patients. Average daily intake during the experiment was 1530 kcal, including about 50 g of protein and 30 g of fat.

PHYSIQUE. Individuals in the Minnesota Experiment lost, on average, about 25% of their original body weight after 6 months of semistarvation. Given such weight loss, one might expect changes in somatotype. Endomorphy and mesomorphy declined by about 48% and 29% respectively, and ectomorphy increased by about 67% (Table 7–4). These changes suggest that endomorphy and ectomorphy are strongly influenced by the amount of subcutaneous tissue.

Similar loss of body weight characterizes anorexia—for example, losses of about 25% relative to premorbid weights[44] and about 68% of ideal weight,[45,46] in adolescent and adult patients. Somatotype data for anorectics are not available, but one can assume changes in the same direction as those reported in the Minnesota Experiment.

BODY COMPOSITION. In the Minnesota Experiment, relative fatness decreased from 13.5% to 5.2%, and FM and FFM decreased by about 7 kg and 9 kg, respectively. The data also indicate a decrease in muscle mass, though not to the same extent as FM. During 3 months of rehabilitation, relative fatness increased from 5.2% to 10.5%, and both FM and FFM increased by about 3 to 4 kg. The gain in FM during rehabilitation was about 49% of the loss, and the gain in FFM was about 31% of the initial loss.

Changes in body composition in anorectic patients are similar to those observed in the Minnesota Experiment. Both FFM and FM decrease in anorexia nervosa, although the decrease in FM is greater. Estimates of fatness in anorexia are largely based on skinfold thicknesses, which are well below reference data for adolescent and adult control subjects.[44-46] The evidence thus indicates severe fat store depletion. Estimates of FFM are also reduced in anorectic adolescents and young adults, but changes in hydration and chemical composition of FFM in anorexia possibly confound the estimates. Among 10 female anorectics 13 to 22 years of age, FFM (^{40}K) was about 82% of that expected for age and stature,[46] whereas among male (n = 5) and female (n = 10) anorectics 12 to 17 years of age, the absolute amount of potassium was reduced but potassium per unit body weight was within normal limits.[44] Ten young adult female anorectic patients had total body water and ^{40}K contents that approximated only about 74% and 88%, respectively, of mean values for control women.[45] The reduction in FFM in anorexia included moderately severe muscle wasting as indicated by estimated midarm muscle circumference.

PERFORMANCE. Functional consequences of alterations in body composition with semistarvation include physical performance. Oxygen consumption during a standard task of moderate intensity was reduced by 28% after 6 months of semistarvation, and energy expenditure per minute during work (corrected for basal metabolic rate) decreased by 23%. The decreases in these two indicators of performance are similar to the decrease in body weight (24%) during semistarvation. After 12 weeks of rehabilitation, oxygen consumption and energy expenditure per minute during work were still reduced relative to control values by 19% and 17%, respectively. In contrast to moderate work, the capacity to perform maximally deteriorated markedly during semistarvation. Performance on a treadmill run (7 mph, 8.6% grade) to exhaustion or on a maximum run of 5 min decreased by 72% after 6 mo and was still decreased by 45% after 12 wk of rehabilitation. In contrast to prolonged semistarvation, acute caloric restriction (420 and 500 kcal per day) for 10 days in young adult males had a negligible effect on oxygen uptake during submaximal and maximal work.[47]

Muscular strength, speed, and coordination also decreased during semistarvation. Grip and back dynamometric strength declined by 28% and 30%, respectively, manual speed (repeated passing of a ball bearing through a vertically held pipe) and tapping speed (wrist movements) by about 5%, and coordination (pattern tracing) by about 17%. Relative changes in static strength with semistarvation are thus more marked than those for fine motor skills. During 12 weeks of rehabilitation, grip and back strength recovered about 33% and 25%, respectively, of initial strength, manual speed and two measures of coordination recovered 87%, 53%, and 63%, respectively, and tapping speed recovered completely. Strength apparently shows minimal recovery after semistarvation, whereas fine motor performances show greater recovery. In contrast to the prolonged semistarvation of the Minnesota Experiment, 2 weeks of limited activity (seclusion in a narrow room) and restricted energy intake (1388 kcal/day in males, 1055 kcal/day in females) resulted in reductions of arm and leg strength of 27% in males and 28% in females relative to control values.[48]

Generally similar changes in performance occur in anorexia. Maximal aerobic power is reduced by about 40 to 45% in adolescent anorectic patients,[49] and the reduction is greater than that associated with changes in body size and composition. Electrical stimulation of the adductor pollicis in young adult anorectic patients indicates altered muscle function, including reduced power, increased fatigability, and slower relaxation rates.[50] With the exception of power, the indicators of muscle function were restored to normal after 8 weeks refeeding.

Results of the Minnesota Experiment and observations on anorectic patients are generally parallel. More important, perhaps, recovery of functional capacity during rehabilitation is a slow process and might not be complete. More specific effects of anorexia on athletic performance need further study.

☐ OVERTRAINING

Overtraining refers to excessive training without adequate time for recovery. It can be short-term or chronic, and when it is chronic it results in an array of behavioral, emotional, and physiological symptoms.[51] Information on changes in physique, body composition, and performance with overtraining is limited. Data are lacking for physique, but the evidence indicates weight loss, decreased performance, and slow recovery after training.[51] Reduction of FFM and FM probably accompany weight loss, and a reduction in efficiency and maximal working capacity accompany the decrease in performance.

☐ REFERENCES

1. Carter, J.E.L., and Heath, B.H.: Somatotyping—Development and Applications. Cambridge, Cambridge University Press, 1990.
2. Malina, R.M., and Bouchard, C.: Growth, Maturation, and Physical Activity. Champaign, IL, Human Kinetics, 1991.
3. Malina, R.M., and Rarick, G.L.: Growth, physique, and motor performance. In Physical Activity: Human Growth and Development. Edited by G.L. Rarick. New York, Academic Press, 1973, pp. 124–153.
4. Malina, R.M.: Anthropometric correlates of strength and motor performance. Exerc. Sport Sci. Rev., 3:249, 1975.
5. Boileau, R.A., and Lohman, T.G.: The measurement of human physique and its effect on physical performance. Orthop. Clin. North Am., 8:563, 1977.
6. Beunen, G., Claessens, A., Ostyn, M., et al.: Motor performance as related to somatotype in adolescent boys. In Children and Exercise XI. Edited by R.A. Binkhorst, H.C.G. Kemper, and W.H.M. Saris. Champaign, IL, Human Kinetics, 1985, pp. 279–284.
7. Forbes, G.B.: Lean body mass and fat in obese children. Pediatrics, 34:308, 1964.

8. Seltzer, C.C., and Mayer, J.: Body build and obesity—who are the obese? JAMA, *189*:677, 1964.
9. Jones, H.E.: Motor Performance and Growth: A Developmental Study of Static Dynamometric Strength. Berkeley, University of California Press, 1949.
10. Epenschade, A.: Motor Performance in Adolescence. Monographs of the Society for Research in Child Development, Vol. 5, No. 1. University of Chicago Press, 1940, pp. 1–126.
11. Epenschade, A.S., and Eckert, H.M.: Motor Development. Columbus, OH, C.E. Merrill, 1967.
12. Ismail, A.H., Christian, J.E., and Kessler, W.V.: Body composition relative to motor aptitude for preadolescent boys. Res. Q., *34*:463, 1963.
13. Slaughter, M.H., Lohman, T.G., and Misner, J.E.: Relationship of somatotype and body composition to physical performance in 7- to 12-year old boys. Res. Q., *48*:159, 1977.
14. Leedy, H.E., Ismail, A.H., Kessler, W.V., and Christian, J.E.: Relationships between physical performance items and body composition. Res. Q., *36*:158, 1965.
15. Malina, R.M., Little, B.B., and Buschang, P.H.: Estimated body composition and strength of chronically mild-to-moderately undernourished rural boys in southern Mexico. In Human Growth, Physical Fitness and Nutrition. Edited by R.J. Shephard and J. Parizkova. Basel, S. Karger, 1991, pp. 119–132.
16. Forbes, G.B.: Toward a new dimension in human growth. Pediatrics, *36*:825, 1965.
17. Slaughter, M.H., Lohman, T.G., and Misner, J.E.: Association of somatotype and body composition to physical performance in 7–12 year-old girls. J. Sports Med. Phys. Fit., *20*:189, 1980.
18. Beunen, G., Malina, R.M., Ostyn, M., et al.: Fatness, growth and motor fitness of Belgian boys 12 through 20 years of age. Human Biol., *55*:599, 1983.
19. Buskirk, E.R., and Taylor, H.L.: Maximal oxygen intake and its relation to body composition with special reference to chronic physical activity and obesity. J. Appl. Physiol. *11*:72, 1957.
20. Dempsey, J.A., Reddan, W., Balke, B., and Rankin, J.: Work capacity determinants and physiologic cost of weight-supported work in obesity. J. Appl. Physiol., *21*:1815, 1966.
21. Parizkova, J.: Body Fat and Physical Fitness. The Hague, Martinus Nijhoff, 1977.
22. Cooper, D.M., Poage, J., Barstow, T.J., and Springer, C.: Are obese children truly unfit? Minimizing the confounding effect of body size on the exercise response. J. Pediatr. *116*:223, 1990.
23. Carter, J.E.L.: Somatotypes of Olympic athletes from 1948 to 1976. In Physical Structure of Olympic Athletes. Part II. Kinanthropometry of Olympic Athletes. Edited by J.E.L. Carter. Basel, S. Karger, 1984, pp. 80–109.
24. Carter, J.E.L.: Somatotypes of children in sports. In Young Athletes: Biological, Psychological, and Educational Perspectives. Edited by R.M. Malina. Champaign, IL, Human Kinetics, 1988, pp. 153–165.
25. Malina, R.M., Meleski, B.W., and Shoup, R.F.: Anthropometric, body composition, and maturity characteristics of selected school-age athletes. Pediatr. Clin. North Am., *29*:1305, 1982.
26. Wilmore, J.H.: Body composition in sport and exercise: Directions for future research. Med. Sci. Sports Exerc., *15*:21, 1983.
27. Wilmore, J.H.: Advances in body composition applied to children and adolescents in sport. In Young Athletes: Biological, Psychological, and Educational Perspectives. Edited by R.M. Malina. Champaign, IL, Human Kinetics, 1988, pp. 141–151.
28. Boileau, R.A., Lohman, T.G., and Slaughter, M.H.: Exercise and body composition of children and youth. Scand. J. Sports Sci., *7*:17, 1985.

29. Malina, R.M., Mueller, W.H., Bouchard, C., et al.: Fatness and fat patterning among athletes at the Montreal Olympic Games, 1976. Med. Sci. Sports Exerc. *14:*445, 1982.
30. Carter, J.E.L., and Yuhash, M.S.: Skinfolds and body composition of Olympic athletes. *In* Physical Structure of Olympic Athletes. Part II. Kinanthropometry of Olympic Athletes. Edited by J.E.L. Carter. Basel, S. Karger, 1984, pp. 144–182.
31. Parizkova, J., and Carter, J.E.L.: Influence of physical activity on stability of somatotypes in boys. Am. J. Phys. Anthropol., *44:*327, 1976.
32. Carter, J.E.L., and Parizkova, J.: Changes in somatotypes of European males between 17 and 24 years. Am. J. Phys. Anthropol., *48:*251, 1978.
33. Malina, R.M.: The effects of exercise on specific tissues, dimensions, and functions during growth. Stud. Phys. Anthropol. *5:*21, 1979.
34. Malina, R.M.: Human growth, maturation, and regular physical activity. Acta Med. Auxol., *15:*5, 1983.
35. Parizkova, J.: Particularities of lean body mass and fat development in growing boys as related to their motor activity. Acta Paediatr. Belg. (Suppl.), *28:*233, 1974.
36. Sprynarova, S.: The influence of training on physical and functional growth before, during and after puberty. Europ. J. Appl. Physiol., *56:*719, 1987.
37. Tanner, J.M.: The effect of weight-training on physique. Am. J. Phys. Anthropol., *10:*427, 1952.
38. Meleski, B.W., and Malina, R.M.: Changes in body composition and physique of elite university-level swimmers during a competitive season. J. Sports Sci., *3:*33, 1985.
39. Forbes, G.B.: Body composition in adolescence. *In* Human Growth. Volume 2. Postnatal Growth. Edited by F. Falkner and J.M. Tanner. New York, Plenum, 1978, pp. 239–272.
40. Wilmore, J.H.: Appetite and body composition consequent to physical activity. Res. Q., *54:*415, 1983.
41. Despres, J.P., Bouchard, C., Tremblay, A., et al.: Effects of aerobic training on fat distribution in male subjects. Med. Sci. Sports Exerc., *17:*113, 1985.
42. Tremblay, A., Despres, J.P., and Bouchard, C.: Alteration in body fat and fat distribution with exercise. *In* Fat Distribution During Growth and Later Health Outcomes. Edited by C. Bouchard and F.E. Johnston. New York, Alan R. Liss, 1988, pp. 297–312.
43. Keys, A., Brozek, J., Henschel, A., et al.: The Biology of Human Starvation. Minneapolis, University of Minnesota Press, 1950.
44. Fohlin, L.: Body composition, cardiovascular and renal function in adolescent patients with anorexia nervosa. Acta Paediatr. Scand., Suppl. 268, 1977, pp. 1–17.
45. Dempsey, D.T., Crosby, L.O., Lusk, E., et al.: Total body water and total body potassium in anorexia nervosa. Am. J. Clin. Nutr., *40:*260, 1984.
46. Forbes, G.B., Kreipe, R.E., Lipinski, B.A., and Hodgman, C.H.: Body composition changes during recovery from anorexia nervosa: Comparison of two dietary regimes. Am. J. Clin. Nutr. *40:*1137, 1984.
47. Daws, T.A., Consolazio, F., Hilty, S.L., et al.: Evaluation of cardiopulmonary function and work performance in man during caloric restriction. J. Appl. Physiol., *33:*211, 1972.
48. Wirths, W.: Muskelfunktionsprufungen mit Hilfe von Dynamometermessungen unter Einfluss mangelnder Aktivitat und restriktiver Calorien- und Eiweissaufnahme. Int. Z. Angew. Physiol., *27:*116, 1969
49. Davies, C.T.M., Von Dobeln, W., Fohlin, L., et al.: Total body potassium, fat free

weight and maximal aerobic power in children with anorexia nervosa. Acta Paediatr. Scand., *67*:229, 1978.

50. Russell, D.McR., Prendergast, P.J., Darby, P.L., et al.: Comparison between muscle function and body composition in anorexia nervosa: The effect of refeeding. Am. J. Clin. Nutr., *38*:229, 1983.

51. Kuipers, H., and Keizer, H.A.: Overtraining in elite athletes: Review and directions for the future. Sports Med., *6*:79, 1988.

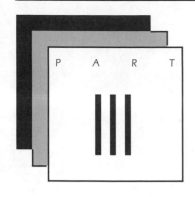

CAUSES, PATHOLOGY, AND PREVALENCE OF EATING AND WEIGHT PROBLEMS IN ATHLETES

C H A P T E R

8

PATHOLOGY AND DEVELOPMENT OF EATING DISORDERS: IMPLICATIONS FOR ATHLETES

G. Terence Wilson and Kathleen L. Eldredge

Strictly speaking, the term *eating disorders* refers to the clinically diagnosable syndromes of anorexia nervosa and bulimia nervosa. Tables 8–1 and 8–2 detail the diagnostic criteria for these disorders.[1] The prevalence of these disorders in the general population is estimated to be approximately 1% for anorexia nervosa and 1 to 3% for bulimia nervosa, although definitive epidemiological evidence is still unavailable.[2] It would be shortsighted, however, to focus solely on these diagnostic entities. More common partial or subclinical forms of these disorders that meet some but not all of the formal diagnostic criteria have been identified.[3,4] Even more broadly, we believe that it is important to address what could be called disordered eating, which, even if not as severe as the full or partial syndromes, is both a problem in its own right and a risk factor for developing a full-fledged disorder. We share the widely held view that eating disturbances lie on a continuum ranging from normative concerns about body weight and shape, to rigid dieting, to subclinical, and to diagnosable eating disorders.[5,6]

The specific causes of the eating disorders remain to be established. Nonetheless, there is increasing consensus on some of the critical ele-

TABLE 8–1. DSM-III-R DIAGNOSTIC CRITERIA FOR ANOREXIA NERVOSA

A. Refusal to maintain body weight over a minimal normal weight for age and height, e.g., weight loss leading to maintenance of body weight 15% below that expected; or failure to make expected weight gain during period of growth, leading to body weight 15% below that expected.
B. Intense fear of gaining weight or becoming fat, even though under-weight.
C. Disturbance in the way in which one's body weight, size, or shape is experienced, e.g., the person claims to "feel fat" even when emaciated, believes that one area of the body is "too fat" even when obviously under-weight.
D. In females, absence of at least three consecutive menstrual cycles when otherwise expected to occur (primary or secondary amenorrhea).

From American Psychiatric Association: Diagnostic and Statistical Manual of Mental Disorders. 3rd ed., revised. Washington, DC, American Psychiatric Association, 1987, pp. 67–68.

TABLE 8–2. DSM-III-R DIAGNOSTIC CRITERIA FOR BULIMIA NERVOSA

A. Recurrent episodes of binge eating (rapid consumption of a large amount of food in a discrete period of time).
B. A feeling of lack of control over eating behavior during the eating binges.
C. The person regularly engages in either self-induced vomiting, use of laxatives or diuretics, strict dieting or fasting, or vigorous exercise in order to prevent weight gain.
D. A minimum average of two binge eating episodes a week for at least three months.
E. Persistent overconcern with body shape and weight.

From American Psychiatric Association: Diagnostic and Statistical Manual of Mental Disorders. 3rd ed., revised. Washington, DC, American Psychiatric Association, 1987, pp. 68–69.

ments that are responsible for the development and maintenance of these disorders.

☐ AN INTEGRATIVE MODEL OF EATING DISORDERS

THE PSYCHOSOCIAL CONTEXT

A striking feature of eating disorders is that they are largely confined to women. Fundamental to explaining this dramatic gender difference and to understanding the nature of eating disorders is the current cultural context. That the present cultural milieu defines the ideal female body shape as slim and lithe has been repeatedly documented, and is reviewed in Chapter 10. Conforming to the slim ideal is particularly important among white middle and upper class women. Obesity is strongly and inversely correlated with socioeconomic status,[7] and the desire to be thin is positively correlated with socioeconomic status for women, but not men.[8] White adolescent girls from higher-income families become leaner during adolescence than black females and their peers from lower-income families, presumably because they deliberately restrict food intake.[9] Significantly, eating disorders are most common among the very population—white, upper socioeconomic females—that is most invested in dieting to achieve slimness. There is an overall correlation between cultural pressure to be thin and prevalence of eating disorders, both across and within different ethnic groups.[5] It is also well documented that eating disorders occur more frequently in occupations (e.g., modeling) and other life activities (e.g., ballet dancing) that place pressure on females to be thin.[10] We discuss the role of athletics in this regard later in this chapter.

DIETING

Psychosocial pressure to be thin often conflicts with biological reality. Body weight and shape are heavily influenced by biological variables that predestine women to be fatter than men and certainly fatter than the current psychosocial thin ideal. Confronted with this dilemma, women resort to often unrealistic and unhealthful diets. The result is a pattern of repeated "on a diet/off a diet" cycles that have a variety of negative biological and psychological effects.

Available evidence strongly suggests that dieting is closely linked to development of disordered eating or an eating disorder.[5,11,12] First, patients with bulimia nervosa almost invariably report the onset of binge-eating following a severe diet.[13] Second, laboratory research has shown that dieters, or what Herman and Polivy[11] have termed restrained eaters, differ from nondieters or unrestrained eaters in the amount of food they eat after having consumed an actual or perceived high-calorie preload.[14] In these studies unrestrained eaters typically regulate their eating so that following a preload they eat less in a subsequent taste test then those who do not receive a preload. Restrained eaters typically regulate their intake in the absence of a preload, but they eat significantly more in a taste test following consumption of a preload versus no preload, or they simply fail to regulate (decrease) their consumption. This pattern of disinhibited eating has been termed counterregulation. Restrained eaters show the same dietary disinhibition under the influence of negative emotional scales.[11,14] And third, a prospective study of 1010 high-school girls in London showed that dieters were significantly more likely than nondieters to develop an eating disorder 1 year later.[15] Only a minority of the girls who were dieting at the beginning of the study subsequently were diagnosed as having an eating disorder, but they were a significant minority.

NOT ALL DIETERS ARE ALIKE. In linking dieting to the development of disordered eating and eating disorders it is important to note that there are different types of dieting and dieters.[16] Dieters vary both in the pattern and content of daily eating behavior.[17] A subgroup of restrained eaters who appear to have achieved stable, long-term weights that are lower than their previous weights have been called "successful dieters" or "weight suppressors" by Lowe and Kleifield.[18] They differ functionally from other restrained eaters in not showing counterregulation in the laboratory. As Tuschl[16] concludes, "some forms of dietary restraint are more apt to disarrange intake regulation than others. It can be hypothesized that the more chaotic the everyday eating behavior, the higher the risk of developing bulimia" (p. 108).

HOW IS DIETING LINKED TO THE DEVELOPMENT OF EATING DISORDERS? Although we know that dieting is closely linked to the onset of eating disorders, the precise nature of this relationship remains to be established. Some investigators consider dieting to be a necessary but not sufficient cause of eating disorders.[5,11,19] Blundell,[20] however, questions whether "dieting is a genuine precursor (i.e., a necessary precondition) or is it simply an inevitable antecedant (with no causal significance)?" (p. 114). Although available data do not provide a definitive answer to this question, there is no doubt that dieting can have several negative biobehavioral effects.

Dieting has a variety of biological, cognitive, and affective consequences that predispose to binge-eating. At the biological level, normal-weight dieters, compared with nondieters, show a significantly increased rate of eating, greater overall consumption, and elevated insulin levels (the latter being associated with increased hunger) following a small caloric preload. Compared with unrestrained eaters, restrained eaters have a higher body mass index (BMI) even though they consume fewer calories on a daily basis. The reason is that they are more metabolically efficient.[16] Patients with bulimia nervosa similarly show a lower resting metabolic rate than age-matched controls.[21] Whether this metabolic efficiency is a biological predisposition to a higher BMI or the consequence of repeated cycles of weight gain and loss,[22] it makes it more difficult for the dieter to conform to the body shape and weight in vogue. The behavioral consequence is even more restrained caloric consumption with enhanced vulnerability to binge-eating.

Psychologically, the unrealistically rigid standards of dietary restraint, coupled with the sense of deprivation, leaves one vulnerable to loss of control of eating following any perceived transgression of the diet.[11] The mere perception that they have eaten a high calorie, forbidden food (regardless of actual caloric content) suffices to trigger counterregulation in restrained eaters in laboratory studies.

The extent of the binge-eating, once initiated, can be influenced by physiological factors, such as impaired satiety signals that result from the skipping of meals and the artificially limited energy content of restrained eaters' diets. For example, terminating a meal because a cognitively imposed limit has been reached as opposed to physiologically-based satiety might weaken or extinguish the conditioned satiety signals that are the longer-term learned consequences of food intake.[16,23] Binge-eating that is followed by self-induced vomiting is a still more extreme means of dysregulating conditioned satiety.[12]

Dieting can cause stress or make the dieter more vulnerable to its effects.[24] To the extent that stress is a precipitant of binge-eating, as bulimic patients report[25] and experimental studies have suggested,[26,27] then this is another indirect means by which dieting contributes to disordered eating.

BINGE-EATING AND PURGING. Binge-eating leads to attempts to counteract the perceived effect of the food on weight, as shown in Figure 8–1. These weight control behaviors include self-induced vomiting, laxative or diuretic use, excessive exercise, and strict dieting. The immediate effect of these behaviors is to reduce anxiety about weight gain, but this is quickly followed by guilt and self-deprecation. The individual vows to redouble efforts at dietary control to avoid future binge/purge episodes, and thereby unwittingly sets the occasion for subsequent loss of control.

PSYCHOPATHOLOGY

Dieting is an important, perhaps even a necessary condition for development of an eating disorder, but it is not sufficient. Estimates of dieting to influence body weight and shape among adolescent and young adult females in the United States range anywhere from 30 to 60%.[28] Yet as we note above, it is only a small minority of women who develop an eating disorder. Some other factor or set of factors must interact with dieting-induced mechanisms to cause eating disorders.

Risk factors for eating disorders range from genetic predisposition, through personality and individual psychopathology, to familial influences.

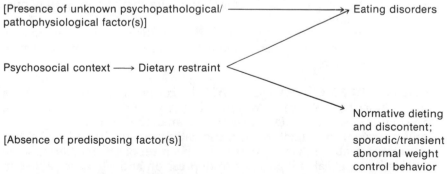

FIG. 8–1. Hypothesized interaction of dieting with undetermined psychopathological factors in causing eating disorders.

GENETIC INFLUENCES. There is good evidence of genetic determination in anorexia nervosa. For example, identical twins are far more likely to be concordant for anorexia nervosa than fraternal twins.[29] The data are not definitive, but they similarly suggest a genetic influence in bulimia nervosa.[30,31] Strober et al.[32] have shown that patients with anorexia nervosa are significantly more likely to have relatives with this disorder than patients with major depression. The relative roles of genetic and environmental factors in this familial transmission of anorexia nervosa are unclear. The nature of any genetic vulnerability and how it interacts with environmental influences is unknown. Hypotheses include a deficiency in particular neurotransmitters involved in the regulation of eating and a tendency to emotional instability and loss of behavioral control.[5]

BIOLOGICAL MECHANISMS. A popular biological hypothesis is that the binge-eating and frequent depressive mood in bulimia nervosa is a product of a serotonin deficiency in the brain. Dieting does produce a greater decrease in the brain serotonin of women than men,[33] and the drugs that are most frequently used to treat patients with bulimia nervosa—imipramine, desipramine, and fluoxetine—have serotonergic properties. Nonetheless, the serotonin hypothesis cannot be supported.

The serotonin hypothesis predicts that bulimic patients are hyposerotonergic. Yet Kay et al.[34] have shown that 5-HIAA levels in the cerebrospinal fluid of patients with bulimia nervosa do not differ from those of normal controls. The hypothesis predicts that bulimics preferentially consume carbohydrates during their binges to enhance brain serotonin as a form of self-medication. But Walsh et al.,[35] among others, have shown that this does not occur. Their experimental analyses of eating behavior of women with and without bulimia nervosa in the laboratory showed that the main difference between bulimics and controls was not in the macronutrient composition of what was eaten but in the total amount consumed. Similarly, Jansen et al.[36] in a study of outpatients' food diaries, showed that contrary to the hypothesis, (a) bulimics' carbohydrate intake during binges did not differ from that during nonbinge eating, and (b) carbohydrate intake during nonbinge eating in bulimics is low.

There is similarly little empirical support for the view that endogenous opioid system influences can explain the development or maintenance of eating disorders.[37]

ASSOCIATED PSYCHOPATHOLOGY. Clinical cases of anorexia nervosa and bulimia nervosa are characterized by a wide range of co-occurring psychiatric disorders.[38] Depression and anxiety disorders are particularly prevalent in patients with these eating disorders, and high rates of substance abuse disorder have also been reported. Similarly, some studies have revealed high rates of depression and substance abuse in the first-degree family members of patients with anorexia and bulimia nervosa.[39]

These findings have led some investigators to suggest that underlying both eating disorders and depression is a common biological cause. Despite the co-occurrence of depression and eating disorders, however, the consensus is that neither anorexia nor bulimia nervosa is a form of an underlying depressive disorder.[40] For example, therapy outcome studies with bulimic patients consistently show that co-occurring psychiatric disorders typically disappear following successful treatment of the eating disorder, suggesting that they are secondary consequences of the eating disorder.[41] Another popular view is that eating disorders are expressions of an underlying addictive disorder. Although high rates of substance abuse have been reported in patients with eating disorders, and in their family members, there is as yet no convincing evidence of any significant co-occurrence between these problems in unselected community samples. It could be that patients with eating disorders who seek treatment are those with more than one type of disorder.[37]

To summarize, the evidence indicates that eating disorders are primary disorders in their own right, and not simply different forms or expressions of some other psychiatric disorder such as depression or substance-abuse disorder. Nevertheless, dieters who go on to develop an eating disorder must have some psychological or biological vulnerability that combines with the negative effects of dieting to precipitate the clinical eating disorder.

Patients with eating disorders share with "normal nonbulimic dieters a concern with body weight and shape but differ on a number of measures of maladaptive functioning, including personal ineffectiveness and interpersonal distrust,[42] coping skills,[43] and vulnerability to negative emotional states.[26,44]

☐ IMPLICATIONS FOR ATHLETES

WHY ATHLETES ARE AT RISK FOR EATING DISORDERS

It follows from the model described here that one would predict, on the one hand, higher rates of abnormal weight control behavior (e.g., binge-eating, vomiting, and laxative and diuretic misuse) and, on the other hand, more diagnosable eating disorders among athletes—or perhaps more accurately, certain types of athletes. In general, athletes with higher socioeconomic backgrounds, who are white, and who come from a specific subculture that emphasizes the importance of physical appearance will be more at risk for developing disordered eating and eating disorders. More specifically, because particular occupations and significant life activities appear linked to prevalence of eating disorders, one would expect to see higher rates of eating problems in athletes who participate in sports that demand thinness or weight loss (e.g., gymnastics). There are data to support this speculation. For example, Borgen and Corbin[45] found evidence for higher levels of symptoms associated with eating disorders among female athletes in sports that emphasized thinness as compared to sports with no or minimal emphasis on thinness. Similarly, Davis and Cowles[46] found female athletes in thin-build sports to have greater diet and weight concerns, dissatisfaction, and more emotional lability than athletes in normal-build sports, even though they were actually thinner. Pressure to be slim in such sports would be heightened by the philosophy and training practices of coaches and athletes who believe that thinner athletes often attain greater success.

The same pressure on women to appear slim can be seen in sports in which thinness is demanded for esthetics rather than performance, such as cheerleading. It is not uncommon that cheerleaders and majorettes must attain arbitrarily derived and often unrealistically low weight goals in order to participate at sporting events. Humphries and Gruber[47] studied a group of university majorettes to view the relationship between eating behaviors and weight goals set for them by faculty advisors and coaches. All of the women studied were found to have nutritionally and calorically deficient diets, and they all believed themselves to be overweight. In order to attain their target weights at weigh-ins, many women reported fasting, engaging in heavy exercising, taking saunas, and occasionally using diet pills and diuretics. After meeting their weight goals, athletes then reported engaging in episodic binge-eating, only to begin the cycle of fasting and other weight-control methods prior to the following week's weigh-in.

Several specific features of athletic competition are relevant to the development of disordered eating. Body weight and shape are strongly genetically determined.[48] Attaining a thin body is particularly difficult for individuals with a personal or family history of overweight, and there is evidence that a personal history of higher weight is associated with the development of eating disorders.[15] The greater the extent to which an athlete's body deviates from the "ideal" for a particular sport, then, the greater the risk that the athlete will develop an eating disorder.

Support for personal or familial history of overweight as a risk factor for disordered eating because it poses an obstacle to achieving the thinness demanded by an activity such as ballet comes from a study by Hamilton et al.[49] They studied the weight-control behavior of 49 female ballet dancers from national ballet companies classified as either "selected" (i.e., whose members were drawn from company schools, indicating that they had survived years of competitive cuts) or "less selected" (i.e., whose members were drawn from general auditions). Not only did the dancers from less-selected companies have a higher prevalence of anorexia, bulimia, and purging than members of selected companies (46% vs. 11%), but they also reported a higher frequency of having a close family member who is obese (42% vs. 5%). The authors of this study suggested on this basis that dancers who survive stringent early selection processes might be less susceptible to the development of eating problems because they are more naturally suited to ballet's thin body ideal. Consistent with this suggestion is another study by these authors showing that dancers 20% below ideal weight who had no eating problems consumed significantly more calories than dancers closer to their ideal weight.[50]

The competitive nature of sports is probably also associated with development of abnormal weight control behavior and eating disorders. In serious athletic competition, winning, as Vince Lombardi said, is not everything—it is the only thing. Many athletes develop an all-or-nothing view of their efforts. This dichotomous thinking style is consistent with the thinking style evidenced by individuals with eating disorders. For example, a bulimic might believe that even a minor dietary transgression represents loss of control and personal failure and consequently go on a binge. Furthermore, in serious competition, winning requires not only natural ability, but also determined efforts to achieve ever higher standards of performance. Perfectionism is another attitudinal style shared by athletes and individuals with eating disorders. It is possible that the perfectionist standards guiding athletes in competitive sports increases those athletes' vulnerability to the development of eating disorders.

Animal research has shown that dietary restriction induces an increase in physical activity, which in turn produces a reduction in food intake. Epling and Pierce[51] have interpreted these data to suggest that some athletes, by combining high levels of physical activity with dietary restriction to reduce weight, might be at greater risk for developing an eating disorder than individuals who are subject to either factor alone.

Finally, the onset of eating disorders is typically in adolescence and young adulthood. This, of course, is the age range during which serious athletic participation and competition are most likely. Understanding why eating disorders occur during adolescence and young adulthood should explain why athletes at this stage of their biopsychosocial development might be at particular risk. This is a period during which females have lower self-esteem and are more vulnerable to affective disturbance than males. Postpubertal changes in body weight and shape are more stressful for females than males. In contrast to males, the self-images of female adolescents are more interpersonally oriented.[6] Because interpersonal success is closely linked to physical attractiveness, body weight and shape become critical determinants of self-acceptance and self-esteem. Consequently, for females far more than males, any emotional problem is likely to embroil their body image and attempts to influence it.

DISTINGUISHING BETWEEN EATING DISORDERS AND TRANSIENT ABNORMAL EATING BEHAVIORS

It is most important, as King[4] points out, "to distinguish between behaviours (no matter how extreme) aimed principally at maintaining a low weight for reasons such as a vocation and the central psychopathology of an eating disorder" (p.25). Thus it is vital to assess the functional significance of abnormal weight control behavior for a given athlete. Recall that a defining feature of eating disorders is the set of core attitudes about the importance of body weight and shape to personal identity and self-evaluation. Many athletes, particularly men but also women, diet to achieve a leaner body and show intense preoccupation with their weight. This concern is secondary to their goal of enhancing athletic performance. Abnormal weight control behavior and its sequelae might well constitute a problem in their own right, and even a risk factor for eating disorders, but they are not the same as the diagnosable clinical phenomena.

Pressure to be slim encourages dieting, which in turn increases the likelihood of abnormal weight control behavior, but only a minority of athletes who engage in such behavior develop eating disorders. One factor that might tip this balance is general psychopathology, perhaps because it is associated with heightened importance of weight and shape to self-evaluation. Davis and Cowles,[46] in their study of female athletes in thin-build and normal-build sports, used regression analysis to show that 38% and 46%, respectively, of the variance in measures of drive for thinness and body dissatisfaction were accounted for by age, body mass index, participation in thin-build sports, and neuroticism. Although less than conclusive, these results fit with studies of nonathletes that found levels of general psychopathology to be associated with the development of eating disorders.[15]

In evaluating research on the association between psychopathology and eating disorder symptoms, it is important not to infer causation from correlation. Just as it is possible that high levels of psychopathology predispose athletes to develop eating disorders, it is also quite possible that efforts to achieve unrealistically low body weights facilitates the development of specific and general psychopathology. Only long-term prospective studies can clarify the direction of this relationship.

Specific implications follow from this distinction between eating disorders and isolated abnormal eating and weight-related behavior. If an athlete engages in abnormal weight control behavior strictly for instrumental reasons, one would not expect such behavior to persist during the off-season when the immediate press of athletic performance is removed or diluted. Consistent with this view, King and Mezey[52] found that male jockeys showed a variety of abnormal weight control behaviors during the racing season that they did not show in the off-season. The authors interpreted this reversal to the absence of a pathological preoccupation with body weight.

Another implication is that to the extent that men are more likely than women to engage in weight control behavior for purely instrumental purposes, female athletes are more likely than their male peers to develop an eating disorder. A related implication concerns race. White female athletes, we hypothesize, are more likely to couple concerns about body image and self-concept than their black counterparts. Accordingly, white athletes are at greater risk. Although there are few data to test this prediction, Rosen et al.[53] reported an analysis of abnormal weight control behavior by race showing a higher frequency among whites than blacks in the college athletes they studied.

☐ SUMMARY

Eating disorders occur within a context of psychosocial pressures to conform to an ideal body weight and shape. These pressures affect women in particular and perhaps explain why eating disorders occur primarily in women. This psychosocial pressure drives women to dieting that is often unhealthful. Dieting is closely linked to the onset of eating disorders and might even be a necessary but not sufficient condition for their development. In the service of improving either their performance or appearance, both male and female athletes are likely to engage in abnormal eating and weight control behavior. Athletic activities that are most likely to be associated with abnormal eating and weight control behavior include those that place a demand on thinness and those in which individual athletes have to fight their biologically natural body weight in the service of meeting a culturally determined, often arbitrarily determined ideal weight.

To a large extent, these abnormal behaviors are confined to the season of athletic participation and performance and seem readily reversible on termination of the athletic activity. A minority of these athletes get caught up in their abnormal weight control behavior and develop a subclinical or clinical eating disorder. Women, far more than men, are at risk for becoming ensnared in serious eating disturbances. The reason is that they are more likely than men to have overconcern about body weight and shape as it affects their self-evaluation. Future research needs to more carefully address the assessment of these cognitive and additudinal concerns in arriving at estimates of the prevalence of disordered eating and eating disorders among athletes. More thorough and detailed assessment might then usefully inform preventive and treatment strategies for this population.

☐ REFERENCES

1. American Psychiatric Association: Diagnostic and Statistical Manual of Mental Disorders. 3rd ed., revised. Washington, DC, American Psychiatric Association, 1987.
2. Fairburn, C.G., Phil, M., and Beglin, S.J.: Studies of the epidemiology of bulimia nervosa. Am. J. Psychiatry, 147:401, 1990.
3. Bunnell, D.W., Shenker, I.R., Nussbaum, M.P., et al.: Subclinical versus formal eating disorders: Differentiating psychological features. Int. J. Eat. Dis., 9:357, 1990.
4. King, M.B.: Eating disorders in a general practice population: Prevalence, characteristics and follow-up at 12 to 18 months. Psychol. Med., Supp. 14., 1989.
5. Hsu, L.K.G.: Eating disorders. New York, Guilford Press, 1990.
6. Striegel-Moore, R.H., Silberstein, L.R. and Rodin, J.: Toward an understanding of risk factors for bulimia. Am. Psychol., 41:246, 1986.
7. Rand, C.S.W., and Kuldau, J.M.: The epidemiology of obesity and self-defined weight problem in the general population. Int. J. Eat. Dis., 9:329, 1990.
8. Dornbusch, S.M., Carlsmith, J.M., Duncan, P.D., et al.: Sexual maturation, social class, and the desire to be thin among adolescent females. Dev. Behav. Pediatrics, 5:308, 1984.

9. Garn, S.M., and Clark, D.C.: Trends in fatness and the origins of obesity. Pediatrics 57:443, 1976.

10. Garner, D.M., Garfinkel, P.E., Rockert, W., and Olmsted, M.P.: A prospective study of eating disturbances in the ballet. Psychother. Psychosom., 48:170, 1987.

11. Herman, C.P., and Polivy, J.: Restraint and excess in dieters and bulimics. In The psychobiology of bulimia nervosa. Edited by K.M. Pirke, W. Vandereycken, and D. Ploog. Berlin, Springer-Verlag, 1988.

12. Wardle, J.: Compulsive eating and dietary restraint. Br. J. Clin. Psychol., 26:47, 1987.

13. Pyle, R.L., Mitchell, J.E., Eckert, E.D., et al: Maintenance treatment and 6-month outcome for bulimic patients who respond to initial treatment. Am. J. Psychiatry, 147:871, 1990.

14. Ruderman, A.J.: Dietary restraint: A theoretical and empirical review. Psychol. Bull., 99:247, 1986.

15. Patton, G.C.: The spectrum of eating disorder in adolescence. J. Psychosom. Res., 32:579, 1988.

16. Tuschl, R.J.: From dietary restraint to binge eating: Some theoretical considerations. Appetite, 14:105, 1990.

17. Tuschl, R.J., Laessle, R.G., Platte, P., and Pirke, K.M.: Differences in food-choice frequencies between restrained and unrestrained eaters. Appetite, 14:9, 1990.

18. Lowe, M.R., and Kleifield, E.: Cognitive restraint, weight suppression, and the regulation of eating. Appetite, 10:159, 1988.

19. Wilson, G.T.: Bulimia nervosa: A cognitive-social learning analysis. In Perspectives in Behavioral Medicine. Edited by A.J. Stunkard and A. Baum. New York, Erlbaum, 1989, pp. 137–145.

20. Blundell, J.E.: How culture undermines the biopsychological system of appetite control. Appetite, 14:113, 1990.

21. Devlin, M.J., Walsh, B.T., Kral, J.G., et al: Metabolic abnormalities in bulimia nervosa. Arch. Gen. Psychiatr., 1990, 47:144–148, 1990.

22. Blackburn, G.L., Wilson, G.T., Kanders, B.S., et al: Weight cycling: The experience of human dieters. Am. J. Clin. Nutr., 49:1105, 1989.

23. Booth, D.A.: Culturally coralled into food abuse: The eating disorders as physiologically reinforced excessive appetites. In Psychology of Bulimia Nervosa. Edited by K.M. Pirke, W. Vandereycken, and D. Ploog. Berlin, Springer-Verlag, 1988.

24. Rosen, J.C., Tacy, B., and Howell, D.: Life stress, psychological symptoms and weight reducing behavior in adolescent girls: A prospective analysis. Int. J. Eat. Disorders, 9:17, 1990.

25. Johnson, C., and Larson, R.: Bulimia: An analysis of moods and behavior. Psychosom. Med., 44:341, 1982.

26. Cattanach, L., Malley, R., and Rodin, J.: Psychologic and physiologic reactivity to stressors in eating disordered individuals. Psychosom. Med., 50:591, 1988.

27. Lingswiler, V.M., Crowther, J.H., and Stephens, M.A.P.: Affective and cognitive antecedents to eating episodes in bulimia and binge eating. Int. J. Eat. Disorders, 8:533, 1989.

28. Drewnowski, A., and Yee, D.K.: Men and body image: Are males satisfied with their body? Psychom. Med., 49:626, 1988.

29. Holland, A.J., Sicotte, N., and Treasure, J.: Anorexia nervosa: Evidence for a genetic basis. J. Psychosom. Res., 32:561, 1988.

30. Fichter, M.M., and Noegel, R.: Concordance for bulimia nervosa in twins. Int. J. Eat. Disorders, 9:255, 1990.

31. Hsu, L.K.G., Chesler, B.E., and Santhouse, R.: Bulimia nervosa in eleven sets of twins: A clinical report. Int. J. Eat. Disorders, 9:275, 1990.

32. Strober, M., Lampert, C., Morrell, W., et al: A controlled family study of anorexia

nervosa: Evidence of familial aggregation and lack of shared transmission with affective disorders. Int. J. Eat. Disorders, 9:239, 1990.

33. Goodwin, G.M., Fairburn, C.G., and Cowen, P.J.: Dieting changes serotonergic function in women, not men: Implications for the aetiology of anorexia nervosa? Psychol. Med., 17:839, 1987.

34. Kay, W.H., Balenger, J.C., Lydiard, R.B., et al: CSF monoamine levels in normal-weight bulimia: Evidence for abnormal noradrenergic activity. Am. J. Psychiatry, 147:225, 1990.

35. Walsh, B.T., Kissileff, H.R., Cassidy, S.M., and Dantzic S.: Eating behavior of women with bulimia. Arch. Gen. Psychiatry, 45:471, 1988.

36. Jansen, A., Van Den Hout, M.A., and Griez, E.: Does bingeing restore bulimics' alleged 5-HT-deficiency? Behav. Res. Ther., 27:555, 1989.

37. Wilson, G.T.: Bulimia nervosa as an addiction: Theoretical and therapeutic considerations. Adv. Behav. Res. Ther., in press.

38. Laessle, R., Wittchen, H., Fichter, M., and Pirke, K.: The significance of subgroups of bulimia and anorexia nervosa: Lifetime frequency of psychiatric disorders. Int. J. Eat. Disorders. 8:569, 1989.

39. Kassett, J.A., et al.: Psychiatric disorders in the first-degree relatives of probands with bulimia nervosa. Am. J. Psychiatry, 146:1468, 1989.

40. Levy, A.B., Dixon, K.N., and Stern, S.I.: How are depression and bulimia related? Am. J. Psychiatry, 146:162, 1989.

41. Garner, D.M., Olmsted, M.P., Davis, R., et al: The association between bulimic symptoms and reported psychopathology. Int. J. Eating Disorders, 9:1, 1990.

42. Garner, D.M., Olmsted, M.P., Polivy, J., and Garfinkel, P.E.: Comparison between weight-preoccupied women and anorexia nervosa. Psychom. Med., 46:255, 1984.

43. Lehman, A.K., and Rodin, J.: Styles of self-nurturance and disordered eating. J. Consult. Clin. Psychol., 57:117, 1989.

44. Laberg, J.C., Wilson, G.T., Eldredge, K., and Nordby, H.: Effects of mood on heart rate reactivity in bulimia nervosa. Int. J. Eat. Disorders, 10:169, 1991.

45. Borgen, J.S., and Corbin, C.B.: Eating disorders among female athletes. Physician Sportsmed. 15:89-95, 1987.

46. Davis, C., and Cowles, M.: A comparison of weight and diet concerns and personality factors among female athletes and nonathletes. J. Psychosom. Res. 33:527-536, 1989.

47. Humphries, L.L., and Gruber, J.J.: Nutrition behaviors of university majorettes. Physician Sportsmed., 14:91, 1986.

48. Stunkard, A.J.: Perspectives on human obesity. In Perspectives in Behavioral Medicine. Edited by A.J. Stunkard and A. Baum. Hillsdale, NJ, Erlbaum, 1989.

49. Hamilton, L.H., Brooks-Gunn, J., Warren, M.P., and Hamilton, W.G.: The role of selectivity in the pathogenesis of eating problems in ballet dancers. Med. Sci. Sports Exerc., 20:560, 1988.

50. Hamilton, L.H., Brooks-Gunn, J., and Warren, M.P.: Nutritional intake of female dancers: A reflection of eating problems. Int. J. Eat. Disorders, 5:109, 1986.

51. Epling, F.W., and Pierce, D.W.: Activity-based anorexia: A biobehavioral perspective. Int. J. Eat. Disorders, 475, 1988.

52. King, M.B., and Mezey, G.: Eating behaviour of male racing jockeys. Psychol. Med., 17:249, 1987.

53. Rosen, L.W., and Hough, D.O.: Pathogenic weight-control behaviors of female college gymnasts. Physician Sportsmed. 16:141, 1988.

PREVALENCE OF EATING DISORDERS IN ATHLETES

Kelly D. Brownell and Judith Rodin

The late 1980s and early 1990s have seen an impressive increase in the attention given to eating disorders in athletes. Numerous case studies and anecdotal reports show athletes who struggle with inner turmoil, intense external pressures to succeed, and a fanatic concern with body weight and shape. Press reports have painted a picture of an epidemic that is being denied by coaches, athletic officials, and parents.

At the center of this maelstrom are the athletes themselves. They exist in a world where they are expected to perform and where victory is determined by hundredths of a second. Having a low body weight and the ideal body shape is thought to confer a competitive advantage. Many athletes have psychological qualities similar to those found in nonathletes with eating disorders. For these reasons, it is natural to assume that eating disorders occur with increased frequency in athletic populations and that the prevalence would be greatest in sports in which low body weight is related to performance or appearance. Can this assumption be justified?

The purpose of this chapter is to review existing evidence on the prevalence of eating disorders in athletes and discuss the implications of these findings for both research and day-to-day work with athletes. It is only with studies with proper controls and adequate methods that we can define the true nature and severity of the problem.

◻ DEFINING THE EATING DISORDERS

As described in Chapter 8, there are two eating disorders: anorexia nervosa and bulimia nervosa, each with a specific diagnosis. To deal only with these "clinical" entities, however, would miss a great many "subclinical" problems such as preoccupation with food, obsessive thinking about weight, and disturbed body image. As Wilson and Eldredge point out in Chapter 8, the prevalence of anorexia nervosa in the general population is thought to be approximately 1%; the prevalence of bulimia nervosa is between 1 and 3%. The number of people who suffer with eating and weight problems but who do not meet strict diagnostic criteria is much, much greater.

This issue of definition is important in interpreting studies on the prevalence of eating disorders in athletes. Some studies use measures derived from strict diagnostic definitions established by the American Psychiatric Association, whereas others rely on questions developed by investigators who might be interested in only one aspect of the problem (e.g., body image disturbance). These differences, which might be described as a methodologic morass, lead to widely differing estimates of the problem.

In dealing with anorexia nervosa and bulimia nervosa, it is helpful to distinguish warning signs from the diagnostic criteria used to establish that an individual has the disorder. The diagnostic criteria from the Diagnostic and Statistical Manual (DSM III-R) of the American Psychiatric Association[1] are the most widely accepted standards for establishing diagnoses of anorexia and bulimia. These are detailed in Chapter 8.

There has been increasing concern that great numbers of athletes might have eating disturbances, whether or not they actually meet the DSM III-R criteria. In 1990, the National Collegiate Athletic Association (NCAA) publicized a list of warning signs designed specifically for athletes (Table 9-1). These differ to a small extent from what might be recommended for the population in general.

It is evident from the diagnostic criteria and the warning signs that prevalence figures must be considered in the context of how eating disorders are defined. In addition, some of the criteria and signs are difficult to evaluate in light of demands of the sport. For example, "relentless, excessive exercise" can be difficult to define when top athletes are training so vigorously for a sport. With these issues in mind, we can now examine what is known about the prevalence of eating problems in athletes.

◻ PREVALENCE FIGURES

To date, there has been no large-scale prevalence study on eating disorders in athletes. For the most part, small-scale studies have been done using participants in a single sport, in many cases without proper age-matched, nonathlete controls. Therefore it is simply not possible to make

TABLE 9–1. WARNING SIGNS FOR ANOREXIA NERVOSA AND BULIMIA DISTRIBUTED TO COACHES, ATHLETES, AND ATHLETIC OFFICIALS BY THE NATIONAL COLLEGIATE ATHLETIC ASSOCIATION

WARNING SIGNS FOR ANOREXIA NERVOSA
Dramatic loss in weight
A preoccupation with food, calories and weight
Wearing baggy or layered clothing
Relentless, excessive exercise
Mood swings
Avoiding food-related social activities
WARNING SIGNS FOR BULIMIA NERVOSA
A noticeable weight loss or gain
Excessive concern about weight
Bathroom visits after meals
Depressive moods
Strict dieting followed by eating binges
Increasing criticism of one's body

definitive estimates of the prevalence of eating disorders in any sport, much less across the range of sports that might be considered "high risk."

In the absence of the proper studies with the proper controls, we must rely on the research currently available in the field. Keeping the methodological weaknesses in mind, these studies are informative and begin to form a picture of which sports might be most affected, which measures might be useful in establishing prevalence, and how associated body image and psychological variables might be related.

Table 9–2 presents a summary of studies available in the area.[2–24] These studies are first reviewed without regard to sample size, validity of measures, or use of appropriate controls. Because relatively little work has been done, it is useful to examine all the available research to help identify where possible eating problems exist and to highlight research needs for the future. Then we will describe the methods and types of studies that are necessary to establish the true prevalence of eating disorders in athletes.

DATA ON ANOREXIA NERVOSA AND BULIMIA NERVOSA

MEASURES. The measure used most frequently in the studies listed in Table 9–2 was the Eating Attitudes Test (EAT).[25] The original version of the EAT contained 40 questions (EAT-40), but a more recent and widely used version contains 26 items (EAT-26). A score of 20 or higher on the EAT-26 and 30 or higher on the EAT-40 are typical of scores obtained on patients with anorexia nervosa. The EAT has people rate how well a statement applies to them on a 6-point scale ranging from "rarely" to "always." Examples of statements are "I am terrified about being overweight," "I feel that food controls my life," and "I vomit after I have eaten." This instrument is used frequently for nonclinical samples and identifies eating and weight concerns, preoccupation with food, and some behaviors associated with eating disorders. High reliability and validity have been reported for this measure.[25]

The Eating Disorder Inventory (EDI)[26] was also used in a number of studies. It is a 64-item questionnaire with 8 subscales. The first 3 subscales (Drive For Thinness, Bulimia, and Body Dissatisfaction) assess behaviors and attitudes regarding body image, eating, and dieting. The remaining 5 subscales, Interpersonal Distrust, Perfectionism, Interoceptive Awareness, Maturity Fears, and Ineffectiveness, assess psychopathology related to anorexia nervosa. The EDI is used with both clinical and nonclinical samples and can be useful for diagnostic screening. This instrument has also been shown to be valid and reliable.[26]

In addition to these measures, many studies used questionnaires developed by the authors. In most cases, these contained questions on dieting, preoccupation with weight, and attitudes about eating. Several studies provided descriptions of anorexia and bulimia and then asked the subjects to report whether they had ever had these problems. These questionnaires are difficult to evaluate because the questions were not provided in most cases, and information on reliability and validity was not presented.

RESULTS. In studies in which eating disorders were described and subjects were asked whether they had the problems, there was a higher than expected prevalence of anorexia given rates in the general population.[4,11,12] All three of these studies were with ballet dancers.

In studies in which athletes and controls were compared using more standard measures (EAT and EDI), the results were inconsistent, some studies showing no differences, at least one showing lower rates in athletes, and others showing greater prevalence. Of those studies in which athletes and controls did not differ on overall scores,[3,8,9,23,24] it is sometimes difficult to determine whether the lack of differences is due to weaknesses in the studies. For instance, Frusztajer et al.[9] studied 10 ballet dancers with stress fractures, 10 dancers without fractures, and 10 nondancer controls. With so few subjects, it is difficult to address the issue of prevalence. These authors found that the dancers with stress fractures had a nonsignificant increase in EAT scores compared to the other two groups. Evers,[8] studying university dancers, did not find significant differences in EAT scores when comparing the dancers to nonathletic controls. However, 33% of the dancers and 14% of the controls scored in the range symptomatic of anorexia, which is surprisingly high given overall prevalence rates typically reported in the general population.

At least one study reported that athletes had fewer eating problems than did controls. Kurtzman et al.[16] studied various student populations at UCLA. The athletes generally had lower scores on eating disorder variables than subjects in 5 comparison groups. No statistical compar-

TABLE 9–2. SUMMARY OF STUDIES ON EATING DISORDERS IN ATHLETES

STUDY	SPORT	SUBJECTS	MEASURES	OUTCOME
Black and Burckes-Miller[2]	Female and male athletes from 8 sports	695 athletes (55% female) from 8 sports. Mean age = 19 (range = 16–25)	41-item questionnaire mailed to coaches in 21 colleges in midwest. Coaches administered it to athletes	59% lost weight by "excessive" exercise, 24% by consuming less than 600 cal/d, 12% by fasting, 11% by using fad diets, 6% by vomiting, 4% by using laxatives, and 1% by using enemas. Relatively few gender differences, but trend for males to use exercise and females to use dieting to lose weight
Borgen and Corbin[3]	Female athletes from 7 sports	79 females athletes in sports emphasizing leanness (ballet, body building, cheerleading, gymnastics) or sports with no emphasis (swimming, track and field, volleyball). 101 nonathlete controls	EDI	No overall differences between athletes and controls. Athletes in sports emphasizing leanness had a higher percentage of elevated scores than athletes in other sports
Brooks-Gunn et al.[4]	Ballet dancers	55 female dancers in national and regional companies	EAT-26	33% had anorexia or bulimia in the past. 50% of amenorrheic subjects reported anorexia, compared to 13% of normal cycling women
Davis and Cowles[5]	Various sports	64 female athletes in 'thin-build" sports (e.g., gymnastics); 62 females in "normal-build" sports (e.g., volleyball); 64 female univ. student controls	EDI	Overall EDI scores not different among groups. Athletes in thin-build sports had greater weight concerns, more body dissatisfaction, and more dieting than normal build athletes and controls, even though body weights were lower
Dummer et al.[6]	Swimmers	487 girls and 468 boys, ages 9–18, at a competitive swimming camp	Questionnaire on dieting and weight control practices	15.4% of the girls (24.8% of the postmenarcheal girls) and 3.6% of boys used pathogenic weight loss techniques. Girls were more likely than boys to perceive themselves heavier than they were

Study	Group	Sample	Measures	Results
Enns et al.[7]	Wrestlers, swimmers, Nordic skiers	26 male wrestlers, 21 male swimmers, and cross-country skiers	EAT-40, restraint questionnaire, body image assessment	Higher EAT scores in wrestlers, due to higher scores on weight fluctuation and dieting. No overall differences in estimates of body size; a small subsample of wrestlers who scored high on restraint and EAT scores had distortions of body size
Evers[8]	Dancers	21 female university dancers and 29 female university controls	EAT-40	33% of dancers and 14% of controls scored in the range symptomatic of anorexia on the EAT. Difference in overall EAT scores not significant
Frusztajer et al.[9]	Ballet dancers	10 female ballet dancers with stress fractures, 10 dancers without fractures, and 10 nondancer controls	EAT-26, structured interview on DSM-III criteria for eating disorders	Nonsignificant trend for stress-fracture dancers to have higher EAT scores than other 2 groups. Greater incidence of eating disorders in stress-fracture group
Garner et al.[10]	Ballet dancers	35 female ballet students, ages 11–14, followed 2–4 years	EDI	At follow-up, 26% of subjects had anorexia nervosa and 14% had bulimia nervosa or a "partial syndrome." The "drive for thinness" and "body dissatisfaction" scales of the EDI predicted eating disorders at follow-up
Hamilton et al.[11]	Ballet dancers	55 white and 11 black female dancers in national and regional companies (mean age = 24.9)	EAT-26	15% of white dancers reported anorexia and 19% reported bulimia; none of the black dancers reported anorexia or bulimia
Hamilton et al.[12]	Ballet dancers	32 female ballet dancers from 4 national U.S. companies, 17 dancers from national company in China (mean age = 24.6)	Variation in EAT-26, subjects given description of eating disorders and asked if they had the problem	American dancers from less-selected companies had more eating problems, more anorexic behaviors, and more familial obesity than the highly-selected American or Chinese dancers
Humphries and Gruber[13]	Majorettes	11 varsity majorettes	24-hour dietary recall, interviews on eating and weight practices. No standardized measures	Based on clinical observations, all subjects had distorted body image due to low weight standards. Subjects reported eating and drinking little for several days prior to weigh-ins, high levels of exercise, and using sauna, diet pills, and diuretics

TABLE 9-2. SUMMARY OF STUDIES ON EATING DISORDERS IN ATHLETES (*continued*)

STUDY	SPORT	SUBJECTS	MEASURES	OUTCOME
Kiernan et al.[14]	Runners	4551 (1911 females, 2640 males) respondents to survey in *Runners World* magazine	EAT-26 questions on eating and diet concerns	Mean EAT score = 9.0 for males, 14.1 for females. 8% of males and 24% of females scored ≥20 on EAT. 15% of males who ran ≥45 mi/wk scored ≥20, compared to 7% of males who ran less. 24% of females who ran ≥40 mi/wk scored ≥20, compared to 23% of those who ran less
King and Mezey[15]	Jockeys	10 male jockeys from England (mean age = 22.9) (mean weight = 108.5 lb)	EDI, EAT-26	Poor response rate to full battery of tests (from 58 stables, only 10 subjects responded). Mean EAT score was 14.9, higher than expected in young males. The majority reported food avoidance, saunas, and laxative abuse. Diuretics and appetite suppressants were used. Binges were common, but vomiting was unusual
Kurtzman et al.[16]	Athletes from unspecified sports	126 female athletes from unspecified sports, 590 students from other groups (e.g. sororities, classes)	EDI, questionnaire with eating disorder diagnosis questions	Athletes had generally lower scores on all eating disorders measures than other groups, but statistical tests not performed
Mallick et al.[17]	Female athletes from different sports	87 female athletes from track, swimming, gymnastics, and ballet; 41 females with eating disorders; 120 female high school and jr. high controls	Self-reports of dieting, vomiting, and eating disorders	Frequent dieting, vomiting, and self-reported anorexia more common in athletes than normal controls but less common than eating disorders subjects; but no statistical comparisons performed
Pasman and Thompson[18]	Obligatory runners and weightlifters	15 males and 15 females in each of 3 groups; obligatory runners, obligatory weightlifters, and sedentary controls	Body size estimation, 3 subscales on EDI	Runners and weightlifters had greater eating disturbances than controls; females had greater eating pathologies than males

Study	Sport	Sample	Measure	Findings
Rosen and Hough[19]	Gymnastics	42 female college gymnasts	Questionnaire on dieting and weight-control practices	All subjects were dieting (50% for appearance, 50% for performance). 62% used at least 1 pathogenic weight method (e.g., vomiting, diet pills, fasting). 66% were told they were too heavy by coaches
Rosen et al.[20]	Varsity level female athletes from 10 sports	182 female varsity athletes	Questionnaire on dieting and weight-control practices	32% engaged in at least 1 pathogenic weight-control practice. The percentages were 14% for vomiting, 16% for laxatives, 25% for diet pills, 5% for diuretics, 20% for regular binges, and 8% for excessive weight loss
Rucinski[21]	Ice-skaters	17 male (mean age = 21.1) and 23 female (mean age = 17.6) figure skaters from mid-Atlantic training facility	EAT-40	Mean EAT scores were 29.3 for women and 10 for men. 48% of women and none of the men had EAT scores in anorexia range (>30)
Steen and Brownell[22]	Wrestlers	63 male college wrestlers and 378 high school wrestlers	Questionnaire on dieting and weight-control practices	63% of college and 43% of high school wrestlers were preoccupied with food during the season (19% and 14% in the off season). 41% of college and 29% of high school wrestlers reported eating out of control between matches. 52% of college and 26% of high school wrestlers reported fasting at least once a week
Warren et al.[23]	Female athletes from 7 sports	82 female athletes from gymnastics, cross-country, basketball, golf, volleyball, swimming, and tennis; 52 nonathlete controls	EAT-40, EDI	None of athletes scored in disturbed range. No overall differences between athletes and controls. Cross-country runners showed less and gymnasts showed more eating disturbance than controls, but only on selected scales
Weight and Noakes[24]	Runners	125 female distance runners, 25 nonrunning controls	EAT-26, EDI	No greater incidence of eating problems in runners than controls. Elite runners were more likely than other runners to have problems

isons were provided, however. Mallick et al.[17] compared female athletes to females with eating disorders and to controls. The athletes scored best on psychological tests. Pathological eating patterns were more common among athletes than controls and less common among athletes than among eating-disordered patients, but no statistical comparisons were made.

The most frequently reported finding is of a greater array of eating-related problems among athletes. Studies examining pathological *behaviors* and *attitudes*[2,3,5,6,12–15,17–20,22] are fairly consistent in showing one of the following: (1) higher than expected occurrence of problems in athletes, given rates in the general population; (2) more frequent problems in athletes than controls; or (3) more problems in sports in which weight is an issue (e.g., gymnastics) than in sports in which weight is not as important (e.g., basketball).

An example of descriptive studies on behaviors and attitudes is a survey we conducted in *Runner's World* magazine (Table 9–3).[27] A total

TABLE 9–3. BODY WEIGHT AND DIETING CONCERNS IN 4551 RESPONDENTS TO SURVEY IN *RUNNER'S WORLD* MAGAZINE[14,27]

QUESTION	PERCENT GIVING THIS RESPONSE	
	FEMALES (N = 1911)	MALES (N = 2640)
Do you consciously watch your weight? ("often" or "always")	73	64
How satisfied are you with your current body size and shape? ("moderately satisfied" or worse)	57	37
How easy or difficult is it for you to maintain optimal weight? ("somewhat" or "very" difficult)	52	39
Do you ever feel out of control while you are eating or have the feeling that you won't be able to stop eating? ("sometimes," "often," or "always")		
While in training	43	33
While not training	59	46
In the days before a race	30	20
After a race	38	44
Have you ever eaten a large amount of food rapidly and felt that this incident was excessive and out of control (aside from holiday feasts)	64	45
Questions From Eating Attitudes Test ("often," "usually," or "always")		
I am terrified about being overweight	48	22
I find myself preoccupied with food	36	16
I feel extremely guilty after eating	20	7
I am preoccupied with a desire to be thinner	48	24
I give too much time and thought to food	35	13

of 4551 surveys were returned and analyzed from 2640 males and 1911 females. The responses showed high levels of weight and eating concerns. For instance, 48% of women and 22% of men reported they were often, usually, or always terrified about being overweight. These results must, of course, be viewed with caution because of the way the data were obtained. Only readers who chose to complete the survey were included. Even though the large number of responses would indicate concern about weight among many runners, the extent to which this is true of runners in general is not known.

A subsequent analysis using these same *Runner's World* data revealed intriguing differences between runners with higher or lower intensity training regimens.[14] Using scores above 20 on the EAT (scores above 20 indicate disturbed eating patterns), we examined both male and female runners. Of the males who ran 45 miles a week or more, 15% scored above this level, compared to 7% of those who ran less. The same difference was not true of the females: 24% of those who ran 40 or more miles a week scored above this level, compared to 23% of those who ran less. These data show that training intensity might be a relevant variable in defining risk and that there might be important differences in this regard between males and females.

Two studies by Rosen and colleagues[19,20] exemplify the approach of collecting data on athletes only, and show that eating problems are important, irrespective of what would occur in a comparison group. In a study with 42 collegiate gymnasts,[19] these authors found that all were dieting and that 62% used at least one pathogenic weight control method. These figures indicate serious problems, and comparisons with nonathletic controls are not necessary to make this point. A study of 10 male jockeys in England[15] is an example of reporting rates of eating problems and comparing them with what might be expected in the general population. This study found a mean score on the EAT of 14.6 for the jockeys, higher than the authors proposed would occur for young males in general. Again, the issue of small sample size compromises interpretation of the results.

The claim that eating disorders are a problem among athletes is supported by studies in which different groups of athletes are compared.[3,5,7,12] Davis and Cowles,[5] for example, compared athletes in "thin-build" sports to athletes in "normal-build" sports. There were no overall differences in EAT scores, but the thin-build athletes had greater weight concerns, more body dissatisfaction, and dieted more than the comparison athletes, even though their weights were lower.

GENDER DIFFERENCES. It appears there are clear gender differences in the prevalence of eating disorders in the general population (see Chapter 8). Most studies have been done with females, so it is difficult to establish precise prevalence figures for males. Andersen, in his chapter on eating disorders in males (Chapter 12), presents a compelling argument that more males are afflicted than previously believed. Given available studies, however, it would appear that females are more susceptible than males.

The vulnerability of females to eating disorders has several likely explanations (Chapter 10). Social factors focus more pressure on females than males to be lean. The pressure is extreme (during adolescence) at the very time females naturally increase their body fat. These reasons argue for gender as an important issue to study with regard to causes, prevalence, and treatment of eating disorders.

It is not clear whether the gender differences in the general population also exist in athletes. There are more studies with female than male athletes (Table 9–2). This could reflect greater problems in females or the bias of researchers who expect to find more problems in females. Studies are needed in which prevalence is defined in males and females in the same sports, at equivalent levels of training and competition.

A NOTE ON TRUTHFUL RESPONDING. Each of the studies discussed above used questionnaires to assess eating problems. Several of the measures, such as the EDI and the EAT, have been validated,[25,26] but not with athletes. In a number of cases, authors have developed their own questionnaires but have not presented validity information.

We, along with our co-editor on this book (J.H.W.), have had several experiences that underscore possible problems with validity:

Example 1. Questionnaires were given to a group of 110 elite female athletes representing 7 different sports. Anonymity was guaranteed, and coaches and athletic officials were not to see the questionnaires. Of the 87 respondents, not one scored in the disordered eating range of the EAT, and there were few indications of serious disorders in other parts of the questionnaire. In the 2 years following this study, we learned that 18 of these athletes had received either inpatient or outpatient treatment for eating disorders.

Example 2. In a study of nationally ranked distance runners, the EDI was administered to 9 amenorrheic and 5 eumenorrheic runners. Three subjects were identified as having "possible" problems, but not clear eating disorders. Of the 9 amenorrheic runners, 4 were subsequently diagnosed as having anorexia nervosa, 2 as having bulimia nervosa, and 1 as having both. None of the 5 eumenorrheic runners was later diagnosed as having an eating disorder.

These examples show that self-reports have questionable validity, at least with certain athletes under some circumstances. There are two implications. First, prevalence figures from existing studies might underestimate the extent of the problem. Methodological differences, perhaps in whether athletes believe they can be identified from questionnaire responses, might explain in part why some studies show increased levels of eating problems and others do not. Second, research is clearly needed to validate instruments used with athletes and to identify the conditions under which truthful responses are likely to be given.

CONCLUSIONS. The groups of athletes that have been studied show more problems with eating, dieting, and body image than one would expect in nonathletic individuals of the same age. It appears that the problems are greatest in sports in which there is a need to be thin for reasons of either performance or appearance. This is the case when specific behaviors such as binge eating or attitudes such as weight preoccupation are studied. Studies comparing athletes to controls using more standardized measures such as the EAT and EDI are more inconclusive.

There appear to be particular problems in certain sports. Dancers have been the most frequently studied group, followed by gymnasts and runners. These studies suggest pathogenic behaviors and attitudes, and in some cases, elevated survey scores indicative of eating disorders. Even using this method of comparing sports, studies are not entirely consistent, perhaps because of divergent methods. One study, for example, specifically targeted swimmers because of their strong concerns with weight and shape,[6] whereas another used swimmers as controls because they are in a sport that does "not emphasize leanness."[3] Studies on some groups that might be at high risk, such as figure skaters and jockeys, are sketchy and provide only suggestive information.

One question that is difficult to answer from existing studies is whether elite athletes are at greater risk for eating disturbances than are nonelite athletes. We assume that the factors that create risk (e.g., intense pressure to be lean, perfectionism) are most pronounced in elite athletes. Few studies specify the level of proficiency of the subjects, so we can only speculate about whether eating problems are more common in the most highly trained athletes. Future studies should more carefully specify the competitive and training levels of the subjects.

A number of methodological issues call into question the extent to which the results from existing studies can be used to evaluate eating problems in athletes. These are discussed in more detail in the Research Needs section. The large-scale prevalence studies needed to estimate the prevalence of eating disorders in athletes have not been done. Studies have used different measures, different groups of athletes, and various control groups, so the data can be considered only suggestive. There is sufficient indication of serious methodological problems to warrant extreme caution in interpreting the present data until studies are done in which appropriate sample sizes and controls are used.

☐ OBLIGATORY EXERCISE AND EATING DISORDERS

In 1983, Yates et al.[28] published a paper in the *New England Journal of Medicine* that generated great publicity. These authors compared the behavior and psychological characteristics of obligatory male runners with those of patients with anorexia nervosa. An obligatory runner, as defined subsequently by Blumenthal et al.,[29] is someone who exercises compulsively, maintains a rigid schedule of intense exercise, resists temptations to lapse into nonexercising, feels guilty when the schedule is violated, increases exercise further to compensate for lapses, exercises even when ill or tired, is preoccupied with exercise, and keeps detailed records of exercise.

In the study by Yates et al.[28], runners were interviewed during workouts, at races, at a sports medicine clinic, and by telephone. These authors noted that individuals with anorexia nervosa share a compulsive, driven search with the runners but pursue a specific body shape and weight, not a level of conditioning. Both the runners and anorectics were said to share personality traits and behavior patterns. Both reportedly had problems with self-identity, became depressed when their diet and exercise regimens were interrupted, and tended to be introverted, hardworking high achievers. Yates et al. claimed that "athletes with a penchant for profound exertion are at high risk for depression, anorexia, and other disorders."

Given the strident conclusions of the authors and the widely publicized nature of the findings, a number of authors responded by criticizing the study and by conducting studies of their own.[24,29-33] The methods of the study were roundly criticized.[29,30,34] Among the problems were that the authors collected all their information by interview and did not keep precise notes or make tape recordings. No standardized psychological instruments were used; instead the authors relied on clinical impressions from "more than 60 interviews" to generate a composite picture of the runners' behaviors and personality characteristics. "Obligatory" running was never operationally defined. There were no raters or blinding procedures, as would be expected when evaluating interview material. Yates et al. provided three case histories in their paper, but they later admitted that the histories did not represent specific individuals but were derived to represent what the authors thought were "typical" subjects.

We go into such detail on the methods of the Yates et al. study because of the serious picture it paints of the habitual runner. With such weak methods, it is surprising that the study was published, especially in such a visible outlet. Be that as it may, what are the findings of studies with better methods that have addressed this issue?

Blumenthal et al.[29] compared personality profiles of male and female obligatory runners and female anorectics, using the Minnesota Multiphasic Personality Inventory (MMPI). Obligatory running was more precisely defined than in the Yates et al. study, and the anorectics were diagnosed using DSM-III criteria. Anorectic patients scored significantly higher on 8 of 10 subscales of the MMPI, including the scale measuring depression. The anorectics also scored lower on ego strength. 79% of the anorectics scored in the clinical range on at least one subscale, compared to 37% of the runners. The scales on which the runners had elevated scores are generally not thought to reflect psychopathology. Similar findings have been reported by other authors.[24,31-33] In addition, the exercise literature is consistent in showing that mood improves following exercise, although studies using standardized psychological tests show less consistent results.[30,35]

Given the weak methods of Yates et al.[28] and the presence of conflicting findings,[24,29-33] there is little support for the notion that running is an analogue of anorexia nervosa. There are, in fact, several conceptual models by which excessive exercise could be linked to eating disorders.[34] It is possible, and even likely, that some psychological characteristics in some athletes overlap with those of persons with eating disorders. The most fruitful research would be to find *which* athletes develop eating problems and the conditions under which they do so.

☐ RESEARCH NEEDS

There are a number of pressing needs for research on eating and weight problems in athletes (Table 9–4). They involve methodological improvements in studies, examination of larger and new populations, and longitudinal studies to examine risk factors.

The greatest need in this field is for a large-scale epidemiologic study of the prevalence of eating disorders in athletes. Existing studies typically focus on one sport, so our entire body of knowledge consists of a handful of studies with dancers, a few studies with runners and gymnasts, and sporadic attempts to study other sports. Most studies have small sample sizes, so it is simply not possible to determine with any certainty which sports bring the greatest risk, whether certain individuals are at increased risk, whether there are relevant age or training factors, whether there are sex differences, and so forth. Such a large-scale study would probably involve more than one site, so coordination

---

TABLE 9–4. RESEARCH NEEDS PERTAINING TO THE PREVALENCE OF EATING DISORDERS IN ATHLETES

1. Carry out large-scale, epidemiologic studies using consistent measures to define the prevalence of eating disorders in various athletic populations
2. Studies on prevalence should have the proper control groups. This should include groups of age- and sex-matched controls not involved in sports, and in some cases, athletes from sports with equivalent training but less emphasis on weight
3. Examine both anorexia nervosa and bulimia nervosa, in addition to the range of *behaviors* and *attitudes* associated with eating disturbances
4. Identify sports that bring the greatest risk for eating and weight problems
5. Identify the psychological predisposing factors that place individual athletes at risk
6. Identify the physiological factors that place an individual athlete at risk. Examples might be genetic predisposition to be heavy, low metabolic rate, and extreme energy efficiency
7. Examine sex differences in the prevalence and development of eating disorders. This would involve studies of males and females in sports in which weight is emphasized (e.g., gymnastics, figure skating, and distance running).
8. Within sports, study athletes at varying levels of training and proficiency
9. Study young athletes early in their training to identify early risk factors
10. Validate self-report measures with athletes and identify the conditions under which self-reports of eating disturbances are most likely to be accurate

would be important to ensure consistency of measures, appropriate documentation of methods, and a common statistical approach.

Existing studies on eating disorders in athletes can be considered only suggestive because of small sample sizes, absence of control groups, use of untested measurement instruments, and lack of statistical comparisons. Therefore improved methods are one of the most important research needs in the area. The choice of control groups is one important consideration. One necessary control group is nonathletic individuals of the same age and sex. This provides a baseline for the relevant population against which to judge measures on athletes. Without this comparison, high rates of eating problems can be unjustly attributed to athletics.

In seeking out nonathletic controls, it will be helpful to match on or control for psychological factors known to be related to the eating disorders. Having controls from the general student body in a study of college athletes is less informative than seeking students with the psychological characteristics that might place a person at risk. Selecting perfectionistic, high-achiever students as controls, for instance, might help determine if the sports themselves create problems or whether the psychological predisposing factors are operating.

Controls are necessary to determine cause and effect relationships between athletics and eating disorders. This does not diminish the importance of the disorders to those afflicted, however. Let us say, for example, that the rate of eating disorders in a group of gymnasts is the same as in the general student population. This argues against gymnastics causing the eating problems but still leaves a serious disorder for the gymnast with the problem. This argues for a comprehensive program for screening, monitoring, and managing these problems with athletes who have them.

There are a number of additional research needs we can identify, shown in Table 9–4. Studies examining athletes at various levels of proficiency within sports will be important to separate training and athletic ability effects. There are some data showing this is important in the comparison of dancers from more-selective or less-selective companies by Hamilton et al.[12] Longitudinal studies with young athletes might be helpful in identifying risk factors. In addition, most work has focused on psychological and cultural risk factors. There might be physiological risk factors such as family history of obesity,[12] reduced metabolic rate, and lowered energy cost of exercise. Finally, studies validating self-report measures of eating disturbances in athletes will be important. Given the nature of the disorders (denial, shame, secrecy) and the athletes' fear that discovery will have adverse consequences (disapproval from coach, interruption of competition), athletes might not be forthcoming in all circumstances.

◻ SUMMARY

Considering the relatively small number of studies and the methodological problems inherent in some studies, it is important to be cautious in drawing conclusions about eating disorders in athletes. No studies have used the American Psychiatric Association criteria[1] applied across athletes and controls. Existing studies vary in whether they measure behavior, attitudes, body image, or factors thought to be associated with eating disorders. The literature is scattered, inconsistent, and in some cases, inconclusive, so it is only possible to suggest relationships that might exist with regard to eating problems in athletes.

These cautions notwithstanding, one cannot ignore the reports of athletes with serious eating disorders. Even though the exact prevalence is not known, the studies reviewed here show that many athletes have problems. Among the documented problems are pathogenic eating and weight control practices, psychological factors such as preoccupation with food and a drive to be thin, and scores on questionnaires that place athletes in the same range as patients with diagnosed eating disorders.

There is abundant reason to believe that some athletes are at risk for eating problems due to the nutritional or weight demands of the sport. Some types of individuals, however, by virtue of particular psychological or biological characteristics, might be at greater risk than others. In no studies, even those showing the strongest differences between athletes and controls, did all athletes show equivalent severity of eating disorders, problematic behavior, or disturbed attitudes. Thus it is crucial that studies now ask what makes risk become reality in some individuals. We believe that much more work remains to be done, but the topic is important, the stakes are high in terms of health and athletic performance, and coaches and athletic officials will be under increasing pressure to identify and manage eating and weight problems in their athletes.

☐ REFERENCES

1. American Psychiatric Association: Diagnostic and Statistical Manual of Mental Disorders (DSM-III-R). 3rd ed. Revised. Washington, DC, American Psychiatric Association, 1987.
2. Black D.R., and Burckes-Miller, M.E.: Male and female college athletes: Use of anorexia nervosa and bulimia nervosa weight loss methods. Res. Q., *59*:252, 1988.
3. Borgen J.S., and Corbin C.B.: Eating disorders among female athletes. Phys. Sportsmed., *15*:89, 1987.
4. Brooks-Gunn, J., Warren, M.P., and Hamilton, L.: The relation of eating problems and amenorrhea in ballet dancers. Med. Sci. Sports Exerc., *19*:41, 1987.
5. Davis, C., and Cowles, M.: A comparison of weight and diet concerns and personality factors among female athletes and non-athletes. J. Psychosomat. Res., *33*:527, 1989.
6. Dummer, G.D., Rosen, L.W., Heusner, W.W., et al.: Pathogenic weight control behaviors of young competitive swimmers. Phys. Sportsmed., *15*:75, 1987.
7. Enns, M.P., Drewnowski, A., and Grinker, J.A.: Body composition, body size estimation, and attitudes toward eating in male college athletes. Psychosomat. Med., *49*:56, 1987.
8. Evers, C.L.: Dietary intake and symptoms of anorexia nervosa in female university dancers. J. Am. Dietet. Assoc., *87*:66, 1987.
9. Frusztajer, N.T., et al.: Nutrition and the incidence of stress fractures in ballet dancers, Am. J. Clin. Nutr., *51*:779, 1990.

10. Garner, D.M., Garfinkel, P.E., Rockert, W., and Olmstead, M.P.: A prospective study of eating disturbances in the ballet. Psychother. Psychosom., *48:*170, 1987.
11. Hamilton, L.H., Brooks-Gunn, J., and Warren, M.P.: Sociocultural influences on eating disorders in professional female ballet dancers. Int. J. Eating Dis., *4:*465, 1985.
12. Hamilton, L.H., Brooks-Gunn, J., Warren, M.P., and Hamilton, W.G.: The role of selectivity in the pathogenesis of eating problems in ballet dancers. Med. Sci. Sports Exerc., *20:*560, 1988.
13. Humphries, L.L., and Gruber, J.L.: Nutrition behaviors of university majorettes. Phys. Sportsmed., *14:*91, 1986.
14. Kiernan, M., Crandell, C., Rodin, J., et al.: Eating and weight concerns in male and female runners at varying levels of training. Unpublished manuscript.
15. King, M.B., and Mezey, G.: Eating behaviour of male racing jockeys. Psychol. Med., *17:*249, 1987.
16. Kurtzman, F.D., et al.: Eating disorders among selected female student populations at UCLA. J. Am. Dietet. Assoc., *89:*45, 1989.
17. Mallick, M.J., Whipple, T.W., and Huerta, E.: Behavioral and psychological traits of weight-conscious teenagers: A comparison of eating-disordered patients and high- and low-risk groups. Adolescence, *22:*157, 1987.
18. Pasman, L., and Thompson, J.K.: Body image and eating disturbance in obligatory runners, obligatory weightlifters, and sedentary individuals. Int. J. Eating Dis., *7:*759, 1988.
19. Rosen, L.W., and Hough, D.O.: Pathogenic weight-control behaviors of female college gymnasts. Physician Sportsmed., *16:*141, 1988.
20. Rosen, L.W., McKeag, D.B., Hough, D.O., and Curley, V.: Pathogenic weight-control behavior in female athletes. Physician Sportsmed., *14:*79, 1986.
21. Rucinski, A.: Relationship of body image and dietary intake of competitive ice skaters. J. Am. Dietet. Assoc., *89:*98, 1989.
22. Steen, S.N., and Brownell, K.D.: Current patterns of weight loss and regain in wrestlers: Has the tradition changed? Med. Sci. Sports Exerc., *22:*762, 1990.
23. Warren, B.J., Stanton, A.L., and Blessing, D.L.: Disordered eating patterns in competitive female athletes. Int. J . Eating Dis., *9:*565, 1990.
24. Weight, L.M., and Noakes, T.D.: Is running an analog of anorexia? A survey of the incidence of eating disorders in female distance runners. Med. Sci. Sports Exerc., *19:*213, 1987.
25. Garner, D.M., and Garfinkel, P.E.: The Eating Attitudes Test: An index of the symptoms of anorexia nervosa. Psycholog. Med., *9:*273, 1979.
26. Garner, D.M.: Eating Disorder Inventory—2: Professional Manual. Odessa, FL: Psychological Assessment Resources, Inc., 1991.
27. Brownell, K.D., Rodin, J., and Wilmore, J.H.: Eat, drink, and be worried? Runner's World, *23:*28, 1988.
28. Yates, A., Leehey, K., and Shisslack, C.M.: Running—an analogue of anorexia? N. Engl. J. Med., *308:*251, 1983.
29. Blumenthal, J.A., O'Toole, L.C., and Chang, J.L.: Is running an analogue of anorexia nervosa? JAMA, *252:*520, 1984.
30. Blumenthal, J.A., Rose, S., Chang, J.L.: Anorexia nervosa and exercise: Implications from recent findings. Sports Med., *2:*237, 1985.
31. Knight, P.O., et al.: Gender comparison in anorexia nervosa and obligate running. Med. Sci. Sports Exerc., *19:*S66, 1987.
32. Wheeler, G.D., et al.: Are anorexic tendencies prevalent in the habitual runner? Br. J. Sports. Med., *20:*77, 1986.
33. Nudelman, S., Rosen, J.C., and Leitenberg, H.: Dissimilarities in eating attitudes, body

image distortion, depression, and self-esteem between high-intensity male runners and women with bulimia nervosa. Int. J. Eat. Dis., 7:625, 1988.

34. Eisler, I., and le Grange, D.: Excessive exercise and anorexia nervosa. Int. J. Eat. Dis., 9:377, 1990.

35. Rodin J., and Plante, T.: The psychological effects of exercise. In Biological Effects of Physical Activity. Edited by R.S. Williams and A.G. Wallace. Champaign, IL, Human Kinetics Press, 1987, pp. 127–137.

SOCIAL FACTORS AND THE IDEAL BODY SHAPE

Judith Rodin and Lynn Larson

People in Western society strive for physical perfection. Although physical appearance has meant status and esteem since the time of the Greeks, modern society goes to new lengths to reward those thought to embody the ideal. Physical appearance is a key factor in how people judge one another. Appearance determines much of our initial attraction to others, and though standards for physical attractiveness vary across different cultures,[1] appearance matters in almost every culture.

Research supports the hypothesis that "what is beautiful is good"—that physically attractive individuals possess many positive attributes, which include having a more desirable personality, and being more satisfied and successful socially, professionally, and maritally.[2–4] When attractiveness is defined as a desirable physique, men and women of all ages have a more favorable view of people who approximate their idea of physical perfection.[5–7] One need only look at the multibillion dollar industry to help people be more attractive—cosmetics, fashions, diets, exercise regimes and various forms of plastic surgery—to realize the extent to which there is societal pressure to look good.

Much has been written about why women are particularly vulnerable to these societal pressures.[8,9] Male and female athletes, however, have been virtually unrecognized by researchers as a group also at risk. In addition to the general demand on all individuals to achieve or to maintain an ideal body shape, pressures on athletes to improve their performance and physique often result in a heightened focus on appearance. This emphasis is especially strong in those sports in which the maintenance of a low weight, a low percentage of body fat, or a lean physique influences performance, or in those in which appearance might influence judges' decisions regarding quality of performance.[10]

This chapter examines societal pressures to achieve an ideal body shape and the ways in which developmental and psychological factors interact with these sociocultural influences. We show that these pressures are especially strong for women and, hence, women athletes. We consider how the pressure to have the ideal body shape is intense for many athletes; and finally, each section ends by considering which athletes are particularly affected by these pressures. The focus is on those athletes who compete seriously in their respective sports, because this group might differ markedly in terms of psychological and physiological characteristics from those individuals who exercise merely for weight control or health reasons. Since there is relatively little research in this area, we must speculate in some cases. We hope thereby to stimulate further studies.

□ SOCIOCULTURAL INFLUENCES

SOCIAL IMPORTANCE OF ATTRACTIVENESS

Being attractive is extremely important in our society. Because attractiveness is defined primarily by physical appearance, concern about weight and body shape runs high. This concern takes a different form as a function of gender—women generally want to lose weight, whereas men are equally likely to want to gain, lose, or simply redistribute their weight.[11-13]

In the last few decades, there has been a marked trend toward an increasingly thin ideal in women's beauty. For example, comparing measurements of contestants in the Miss America Pageant between 1959 and 1978, Garner et al.[14] documented a significant decrease in body weight and in measurements over the 20-year period. Since 1970, the winners have been significantly thinner than the other contestants. These investigators also found that the body sizes of *Playboy* Magazine centerfold models have decreased over recent years. During this same period, however, the average woman under 30 years of age has increased in body weight.[15] In other words, over the past 20 years, women have become heavier while the beauty ideal has become leaner.

Until recently it was rare for men in Western cultures to be judged by rigid criteria concerning physical appearance. But now we only have to examine magazines or the television to know that we celebrate the young, lean, and muscular male body. Men's fashions have changed to accentuate a new physique, which is thought to be more muscular and trim than it was in the past. Today, men serve as marketing targets for products such as diet soda and cosmetics which only a few years ago would have been considered feminine.[16]

A recent study of more than 1000 male business school graduates showed a strong relationship between weight, height, and income.[17] Those who were at least 20% overweight made $4000 less per year, and leaner men earned higher salaries over time. Taller male executives earned about $600 more per inch than shorter executives.

In 1986, *Psychology Today* published the results of a survey on appearance and weight.[18] Only 12% of the readers indicated that they had little concern about their appearance and didn't do much to improve it. People who return a survey on body image might be likely to care more than most about their appearance, but the results are similar to those from studies in which participants are selected at random.[19,20] People feel intense pressure to look good.

An earlier survey on body image was published in *Psychology Today* in 1973.[21] The respondents of the 1970s were more satisfied with their bodies than were those of the 1980s. Men are more concerned about how they look now than they used to be, but for both sexes, *the pressure to look good has intensified in the last 15 years.* Consider (Table 10–1), which compares the two *Psychology Today* surveys. Dissatisfaction has grown for every area of the body.

The 1986 survey also shows how important weight is to body image. Over 40% of the men and 50% of the women were unhappy with their weights. Men were most dissatisfied with their stomachs and women with their thighs, namely, those areas most often affected by weight gain for each sex.

Adolescents and children are following suit. In the early 1970s, a sur-

TABLE 10–1. UNHAPPY BODIES: PERCENTAGE OF PEOPLE DISSATISFIED WITH BODY AREAS OR DIMENSIONS

1972 SURVEY			1987 SURVEY		
FACTOR	MEN	WOMEN	FACTOR	MEN	WOMEN
Height	13	13	Height	20	17
Weight	35	48	Weight	41	55
Muscle tone	25	30	Muscle tone	32	45
Overall face	8	11	Face	20	20
Breast/chest	18	26	Upper torso	28	32
Abdomen	36	50	Mid torso	50	57
Hips and upper thighs	12	49	Lower torso	21	60
Overall appearance	15	25	"Looks as they are"	34	38

Data from Cash, T.F., Winstead, B.A., and Janda, L.M.: The great American shape-up. Psychol. Today, *20:*30, 1986, and from Berscheid, E., Walster, E., and Bornstedt, G.: The happy American body: A survey report. Psychol. Today, *7:*119, 1973.

vey of teenagers found that only 6% worried about their weight,[22] while a survey in the 1980s found that 31% of the teenagers—both boys and girls—worry that they weigh too much.[23] In another recent study of almost 500 San Francisco schoolgirls, mostly from middle income families, 81% of the 10-year-olds reported that they had already dieted at least once.[24]

ATTRACTIVENESS NOW EQUALS FITNESS

The look for the 90s woman is still lean, but now there is the added pressure to be fit. *American Health* magazine's account of a recent Gallup survey suggests that the model Elle Macpherson is our new ideal. She's fit and sinewy. The *Ameican Health* report asserts, "La cream puff is finally out; strong and sensuous is in."[25] For males today, actors, such as Mel Gibson, and male mannequins project a muscular, macho ideal. The newest window dummies are 6 feet 2 inches tall, have 42-inch chests, and need a size-42 suit, which is quite different from the old industry standard, size 38 regular.

THE FITNESS MOVEMENT

The emphasis on health and fitness is certainly another social force pushing increased body awareness. Health clubs, corporate fitness programs, video workouts, and triathalons are the hallmarks of the 1990s. Over 50,000 businesses in the United States are implementing programs to promote physical fitness among their employees.[26] Over a billion dollars was spent on exercise devices last year, most of it on equipment for the home.[26]

A recent Harris survey[27] reported that approximately 15% of U.S. adults participate regularly in high-level physical activity (energy expenditure of more that 2100 calories per week). This translates into an hour of walking at 3 miles per hour every day, a daily 20- to 30-minute run at 6 miles per hour, or 1 hour of swimming at 1 mile per hour for 5 days per week. About 20% more adults participate regularly in moderate activity.

In 1989, Clifford Adelman, a researcher in the U.S. Department of Education, studied the "thirtysomething" generation, that is, people who had been in the high school graduating class of 1972. He reported in the *New York Times*:

> Nearly 30 percent of the class took courses in aerobics, jogging, body-building, karate, yoga and the care of athletic injuries. Instead of studying subjects necessary to maintaining a technological economy in a world marketplace, the class of '72 maintained its physical well-being.[28]

Women might feel they are getting more from the fitness boom than men, perhaps because they started with so much less. Denied most athletic outlets, traditionally encouraged to be weaker and slower, women have embraced the fitness mentality. They were spending a larger percentage of the fitness dollar than men by 1984, the year the Olympic Games staged its first marathon for women.

In her review of the 80s at the turn of the decade, columnist Vida Roberts concluded:

The body was the strongest fashion statement for the 80's. It was the essential element of style, with clothes mere accessories. And it was a fashion of our own design that we could stretch, pump and diet into shape. Cher promised it was so if we would "just do it." The decade allowed no excuse for droopy thighs or flabby midriffs.

But being fit was not enough, you had to look good. As the workouts started to work, the healthy set bagged their sweat suits, and the run on sexy active wear was on.

They preened and fluttered in the spa mirrors like iridescent tropical birds in full mating plumage. The look was tight, the colors were hot and bodies gleamed with Lycra and Spandex. There were unitards and "legotards" and bike pants and running tights. Workout clothes climbed high on the thigh, disappeared at the midriff, plunged at the bosom, rode high on the fanny.

They looked so good, that the stretch look went public and into the streets.[29]

Now, in the 90s, we have entered the era of strength. More and more people are weight training. Sales of free weights and strength machines topped $300 million in the United States in 1988–89.[30] The exercise machine manufacturers have redesigned their weight equipment so that they can be used by smaller bodies—presumably women.

Managing weight and fitness are now seen as forms of health promotions; and the modern burdens of illness, such as heart disease, are viewed as preventable by appropriate changes in behavior. Looking healthy signifies being healthy. The body reflects our ability to engage in self-corrective behavior.[16] Athletes both enjoy and feel the burden of the emphasis on fitness.

Athletes probably constitute the group that most closely embodies the ideal of physical perfection, but they are likely to be under a sometimes onerous societal pressure to achieve this ideal. An array of athletic events receives extensive media coverage, and "good-looking" athletes are used to endorse a wide variety of products. This focus on the body can place additional pressure on athletes to achieve unrealistic body size and weight goals. Many athletes feel that society expects this of them.

It is reasonable to assume that the athletes most affected by this pressure compete in those sports in which esthetic appearance is important (e.g., gymnastics, diving, figure skating, and ballet). In one study,[31] female athletes participating in sports in which a thin body build was an advantage for performance (e.g., gymnastics, synchronized swimming, figure skating, long-distance running, and ballet) were compared to nonathletic college women and to athletes participating in sports permitting a more normal body build (e.g., field hockey, basketball, volleyball, sprinting, and downhill skiing). Athletes in the thin-body-build sports had greater weight and diet concerns and were less emotionally satisfied than subjects in the other two groups, despite being significantly thinner.

More comparative studies of athletes would help to shed light on the role of cultural factors in the overemphasis on body weight and shape. The ways in which a focus on physical strength and skills might affect body image and eating behaviors, as well as the ways in which weight concerns influence exercise patterns, are issues worthy of further study. Some of these issues are discussed by Brownell and Rodin in Chapter 9.

ATTRACTIVENESS, BODY IMAGE, AND SELF-WORTH

Attractiveness figures prominently in an individual's feelings of self-worth.[32] The high value society places on appearance enhances an attractive individual's self-confidence and challenges an unattractive individual's sense of self-worth. More-attractive individuals are likely to have been more popular and rewarded as children and to be more successful in school, career, and intimate relationships.[9,33] Perhaps the cultural view of attractiveness is what mediates actual attractiveness and self-worth. On the other hand, individuals who suffer from low self-esteem might perceive deficiencies in all areas relevant to self-worth, including appearance.

Attractiveness relates to self-acceptance for both sexes, but attractiveness and body attitudes are a more salient component of self-concept for females than for males.[34] This begins at least by adolescence. Simmons and Rosenberg[35] found that adolescent girls were more concerned with their looks than boys, and they also perceived themselves as less attractive. Girls who perceived themselves to be less good-looking had lower self-esteem scores than girls who were more satisfied with their appearance.

The relationship between appearance and self-worth can be particularly pertinent for athletes of both sexes. An athlete's self-worth may be contingent on his or her sense of physical self, because this is a major focal point in life. In addition, the athlete's physical shape and build may be directly related to the quality of athletic performance, which undoubtedly is important for self-worth. Again, this is likely to vary across different sports.

☐ DEVELOPMENTAL DETERMINANTS OF BODY IMAGE

Throughout the life span, socialization conspires to influence body image. As people grow and develop, the body is the centerpiece around which change and expectations revolve. These experiences differ, early on, between men and women.

Females begin life with slightly more fat than males, and this difference increases over the life cycle. Furthermore, natural development for women involves several milestones, not experienced analogously by men, which are characterized by increased fat storage: At puberty, pregnancy, and menopause, the physiological changes women undergo promote weight gain. Assuming that body size and weight are normally distributed, only a minority of women can be expected to match "naturally" the extremely thin ideal; the great majority will have varyingly heavier bodies.

ADOLESCENCE

The profound biological changes associated with puberty render the body the most salient aspect of the adolescent's sense of self. Coming to terms with the vital adolescent question "Who am I?" involves forming a new body image and integrating the new physical self into one's self concept. The adolescent is forced to form a new body image appropriate to the maturing self. This makes the adolescent particularly sensitive to sociocultural norms concerning appearance. In the context of these norms, pubertal development can create a particular problem for girls.

Before puberty girls have about 10 to 15% more fat than boys, and after puberty this difference increases to about 50% more fat.[36] Girls gain weight at puberty primarily in the form of fat tissue, while boys' growth spurt is predominantly due to an increase in lean tissue.[37,38] Many adolescent females despair the increase in body fat associated with normal sexual development.

Given the ideal of the "thin prepubertal look" for women[39] and the tall, muscular look for men, it is not surprising that adolescent girls express lower body esteem than adolescent boys[40,41] and greater dissatisfaction with their weight.[42] Physical maturation brings boys closer to the masculine ideal, but it takes girls further away. When boys do report dissatisfaction with their weight, they want to be heavier; girls want to be thinner.[41,43,44]

By adolescence substantial numbers of girls are dieting—far more girls than boys.[23,24] The higher their social class, the thinner the adolescents want to be.[42] In a study of over 500 adolescents in San Francisco,[44] boys' stage of pubertal development was related to the physique they chose as their ideal. Those who were more mature and larger in body size defined their ideal figure as larger. For the girls, however, perceived body size and preferred body size did not develop in tandem, which resulted in increased body dissatisfaction; and girls at more advanced pubertal levels showed a greater discrepancy between current and ideal figures than did less-developed girls. When they are matched for age, postmenarchal girls have higher rates of eating disorders than prepubertal girls,[45] a finding which emphasizes the problems that can develop with concerns over the pubertal increase in fat.

For the athlete, this rapid change in body build and physique can affect sports performance as well as overall body satisfaction. More specifically, the addition of muscle and bone mass in males can be advantageous for athletic performance, while the increase in adipose tissue in females can be disadvantageous, particularly in such sports as gymnastics, ballet, and figure skating, in which appearance is important to performance.

Another factor that has been found to contribute to excessive body preoccupation and disordered eating in adolescents is high achievement orientation.[45] Because many young athletes have high achievement needs, they are likely to make appearance another important domain in which to excel. A study of 487 highly competitive adolescent swimmers supports this hypothesis.[46] Even though there was minimal coaching pressure to lose weight and the demands of the sport did not require extreme thinness, 60% of the average-weight girls and 17% of the underweight girls were dieting.

Feltz and Ewing[47] describe four primary achievement goals in adolescent athletes: (1) for the ability-oriented athlete, to demonstrate his or her ability to others; (2) for the mastery-oriented athlete, to master the situation by improving or perfecting a skill; (3) for the social-approval-oriented athlete, to gain approval from others for working hard to accomplish a task; and (4) for the venture-oriented athlete, to experience the risk or adventure associated with sports. One would expect that the ability-oriented and approval-oriented athletes would be more susceptible to societal pressure regarding the ideal physique than would athletes motivated by mastery orientation or venture orientation.

ADULTHOOD

The aging process has important implications for weight regulation. Basal metabolic rate declines with age, lean body mass decreases, and body fat increases. Young and coworkers,[48,49] for example, reported that in a sample of 94 normal-weight women between 16 and 70 years of age, mean body fat increased after the 40th year, from 23.1% during the fourth decade, to 46% during the fifth decade, to 55.3% during the sixth decade. Furthermore, women experience a larger increase in fat with age than men and seem to undergo a relatively greater slowdown of their metabolism.[50-53]

Little research has been done on the effects of aging on an athlete's body image. Because a significant part of an athlete's self-image is likely to depend on body competence, aging can be especially difficult. Athletes who have participated in sports in which aging prevents active participation, such as organized team sports, are likely to experience greater difficulty than athletes who can continue in individual sports such as swimming, running, and tennis. The effects of aging on an athlete's sense of self-efficacy and body image require further research.

□ **PSYCHOLOGICAL DETERMINANTS OF BODY IMAGE**

In order to fully understand body image, it is important to portray not only the societal pressures and developmental changes, but also to consider the inner world of body preoccupation—the psychological determinants of body image.

DEFINITION OF BODY IMAGE

Body image is our subjective experience with our body and the way we organize this experience.[54] It is the picture of our body in our mind.

There are fundamental differences in the meaning of the body to men and women. Men tend to see their bodies as functional and active—as tools that need to be in shape and ready for use. Women view their bodies more along esthetic and evaluative dimensions,[55–58] Little is known about whether women's esthetic and evaluative view of their bodies becomes more instrumental through athletic participation.

BODY FOCUS

The body figures as a central element in self concept.[54,55] Heightened focus on the body further increases its influence on a person's sense of self. The clearest demonstration of this involves studies in which people are given a mirror or shown videotapes of themselves and asked to focus their attention on their bodies.[59,60] People react to their mirror image by becoming more aware of all aspects of themselves, even those that are not visible. This kind of increased body awareness lowers self esteem. The more people focus on their bodies, the more they scrutinize themselves and feel guilty. Although there are some exceptions, the experience of looking at our bodies in the mirror tends to provoke negative feelings, not only toward the body but also toward the self inside. Other studies show that intensified self awareness also leads to increased conformity,[60] that is, the more people focus on the body and its flaws, the more they try to be like everyone else.

Athletes certainly possess a high degree of body awareness. They are forced to focus on particular body parts or to view videotapes of themselves in order to improve performance. Research on body awareness indicates that this high degree of bodily focus should heighten body shape preoccupation.

With performances in many sports reaching new heights, small differences distinguish champions from other competitors. Athletes might see even a slight imperfection in body size or shape as something of monumental significance. For example, wrestlers who scored high on scales of disordered eating showed distortions in body size estimations.[61] Swimmers and Nordic skiers who participated in this study did not have comparable distortions, which suggests that it is those athletes most preoccupied with body size who have a distorted sense of their own shape and size. A study of adolescent ballet dancers found that the dancers had significantly more distorted body images than did the age-matched nonathlete control group.[62] Because athletes work to improve their bodies for their sport, they are likely to have strong beliefs that their bodies are malleable. Depending on the individual, this could either be reassuring or lead to excessive preoccupation with weight and body image.

PRIVATE AND PUBLIC ASPECTS OF THE SELF

Psychologists increasingly believe that there are at least two sides of the self.[63] The private self consists of personally-held feelings and attitudes, covert thoughts, and other aspects of the self that are not easily available to others. The public self is the socially apparent self and it consists of acts from which others form impressions—one's overt behavior, mannerisms, stylistic quirks, and expressions. Central to the public self, of course, is the body. But not everyone is alike.

Theorists working in this area believe that people differ in the degree to which they attend to one or another area of the self.[63] People high in public self-consciousness are likely to be more intensely affected by weight and body shape concerns. They attach greater importance to those aspects of the self that contribute to their outward, social persona, especially to their physical features and appearance.

Research on the effects of exercise training in women suggests that exercise leads to increased consciousness of bodily sensations and body competence, but no change in public self-consciousness.[64] This research was done, however, on sedentary individuals participating in a structured athletic regime, results might differ substantially for elite athletes.

☐ SUMMARY

The studies revealed in this chapter suggest that cultural and social factors emphasize and reward an unrealistic body shape. Currently, it appears that thinness is joined by fitness in the body shape ideal. Developmental factors appear to conspire against females in particular, so for many women physiological maturation is in conflict with the prevailing cultural imperative. Psychological factors related to self concept show how important body image can be, how it figures as a central determinant in people's overall sense of self-worth. Finally, our own review and the few studies that currently exist suggest that for a number of reasons athletes are under extraordinary pressure, both culturally and psychologically, to achieve and to maintain the ideal body. With these pressures, it is understandable that athletes have more than their share of eating and weight problems (as other chapters show).

Areas in which further research is needed include comparative studies of nonathletic individuals, recreational athletes, and elite athletes as well as studies of the effects of participation in various sports on (1) over-concern with body weight and shape, (2) the relationship between appearance and self-worth, (3) the effects of aging on an athlete's body image, and (4) the relationship between an increase in body focus and preoccupation with weight and body image. More research in these areas will aid us in better understanding when athletic participation increases the pressures and risk for heightened body preoccupation and possibly disordered eating.

◻ REFERENCES

1. Ford, C.S., and Beach, F.A.: Patterns of Sexual Behavior. New York, Harper and Row, 1951.
2. Berscheid, E., and Walster E.H.: Interpersonal Attraction. 2nd ed. Reading, MA, Addison-Wesley, 1978.
3. Dion, K., Berscheid, and E., Walster E.: What is beautiful is good. J. Pers. Soc. Psychol., 24:285, 1972.
4. Wrightman, L.S., and Deaux, R.: Social Psychology in the 80's. 3rd ed. Monterey, CA, Brooks-Cole, 1981.
5. Diabase, W.J., and Hjelle, L.A.: Body-image stereotypes and body-type preferences among male college students. Percept. Mot. Skills, 27:1143, 1968.
6. Lerner, R.M., and Korn S.L.: The development of body-build stereotypes in males. Child Dev., 43:908, 1972.
7. Lerner, R.M., Karabenick, S.A., and Meisils, M.: Effects of age and sex on the development of personal space schemata towards body build. J. Genet. Psychol., 127:91, 1975.
8. Rodin, J., Silberstein, L., and Striegel-Moore, R.: Women and weight: A normative discontent. Neb. Symp. Motiv., 32:268, 1984.
9. Garner, D.M., Rockert, W., Olmsted, M.P., et al.: Psycho-educational principles in the treatment of bulimia and anorexia nervosa. In Handbook of Psychotherapy for Anorexia Nervosa and Bulimia. Edited by D.M. Garner and P.E. Garfinkel. New York, Guilford, 1985, pp. 513–572.
10. Brownell, K.D., Steen, S.N., and Wilmore J.H.: Weight regulation practices in athletes: Analysis of metabolic and health effects. Med. Sci. Sports Exerc., 19:546, 1987.
11. Drewnowski, A., and Yee, D.K.: Men and body image: Are males satisfied with their body weight? Psychosom. Med., 49:626, 1987.
12. Fallon, A.E., and Rozin, P.: Sex differences in perceptions of body shape. J. Abnorn. Psychol., 94:102, 1985.
13. Silberstein, L.R., Striegel-Moore, R.H., Timko, C., and Rodin, J.: Behavioral and psychological implications of body dissatisfaction: Do men and women differ? Sex Roles, 19:219, 1988.
14. Garner, D.M., Garfinkel, P.E., Schwartz, D., and Thompson, M.: Cultural expectations of thinness in women. Psychol. Rep., 47:483, 1980.
15. Metropolitan Life Insurance Company: Statistical Bulletin, 64:2, 1983.
16. Rodin, J.: Body Traps. New York, William Morrow, in press.
17. Frieze, I.M., Olson, J.E., and Good, D.C.: Perceived and actual discrimination in the salaries of male and female managers. J. Appl. Soc. Psychol., 20:63, 1990.
18. Cash, T.F., Winstead, B.A., and Janda, L.M.: The great American shape-up. Psychol. Today, 20(4):30, 1986.
19. Cash, T.F., Rissi, J., and Chapman, R.: Not just another pretty face: Sex roles, locus of control, and cosmetic use. Pers. Soc. Psychol. Bull., 11:253, 1985.

20. Gillan, B.: Physical attractiveness: A determinant of two types of goodness. Pers. Soc. Psychol. Bull., 7:277, 1981.

21. Berscheid, E., Walster, E., and Bornstedt, G.: The happy american body: A survey report. Psychol. Today, 7(6):119, 1973.

22. Sternlieb, J.J., and Munson, L.: A survey of health problems, practices and needs of youth. Pediatrics, 49:177, 1972.

23. Feldman, W., Hadgson, C., Corber, S., and Quinn, A.: Health concerns and health-related behaviors of adolescents. J. Can. Med. Assoc., 134:489, 1986.

24. Mellin, L.M., Scully, S., and Irwin, C.E.: Disordered eating characteristics in preadolescent girls. Paper presented at the meeting of the American Dietetic Association, Los Angeles, CA, October 1986.

25. Britton, A.G.: Thin is out, fit is in. Am. Health, 7(6):66, 1988.

26. Rodin, J., and Plante, T.: The psychological effects of exercise. In Biological Effects of Physical Activity. Edited by R.S. Williams and A.G. Wallace. Champaign, IL, Human Kinetics Books, 1989, pp. 127–137.

27. Lipsite, R.: What price fitness? N.Y. Times Magazine, February 16, 1986, p.32.

28. Adelman, C.: On the paper trail of the class of '72. N.Y. Times, July 22, 1989, p. 25.

29. Roberts, V.: Remembering the 80s. Baltimore Evening Sun, December 26, 1989, p. D10.

30. Rippe, J.M., and Groves, D.: Cross training: More than just the sum of its parts. Am. Health, 8(7):92, 1989.

31. Davis, C., and Cowles, M.: A comparison of weight and diet concerns and personality factors among female athletes and non-athletes. J. Psychosom. Res., 33:527, 1989.

32. Adams, G.R.: Physical attractiveness research. Hum. Dev., 20:217, 1977.

33. Story, I.: Factors associated with more positive body self-concepts in preschool-children. J. Soc. Psychol., 108:49, 1979.

34. Lerner, R.M., and Karabenick, S.A.: Physical attractiveness, body attitudes, and self-concept in late adolescents. J. Youth Adolescence, 3:307, 1974.

35. Simmons, R.G., and Rosenberg, F.: Sex, sex roles, and self-image. J. Youth Adolescence, 4:229, 1975.

36. Beller, A.S.: Fat and Thin: A Natural History of Obesity. New York, Farrar, Straus and Giroux, 1977.

37. Tanner, J.M.: Sequence and tempo in the somatic changes in puberty. In Control of the Onset of Puberty. Edited by M.M. Grumbach, G.D. Grave, and F.E. Mayer. New York, Wiley, 1974, pp. 100–115.

38. Faust, M.S.: Alternative constructions of adolescent growth. In Girls at Puberty. Edited by J. Brooks-Gunn and A.C. Petersen. New York, Plenum, 1983, pp. 105–125.

39. Simmons, R.G., Blyth, D.A., and McKinney, K.L.: The social and psychological effects of puberty on white females. In Girls at Puberty, Edited by J. Brooks-Gunn and A.C. Petersen. New York, Plenum, 1983, pp. 229–278.

40. Marino, D.D., and King, J.C.: Nutritional concerns during adolescence. Pediatr. Clin. North Am., 27:125, 1980.

41. Dornbusch, S.M., Carlsmith, M.J., Duncan, P.D., et al.: Sexual motivation, social caste, and the desire to be thin among the adolescent females. Dev. Behav. Pediatr., 5:308, 1984.

42. George, R.S., and Krondl, M.: Perceptions and food use of adolescent boys and girls. Nutr. Behav., 1:115, 1983.

43. Tobin-Richards, M.H., Boxer, A.M., and Petersen, A.C.: The psychological significance of pubertal change: Sex differences in perceptions of self during early adolescence. In Girls at Puberty. Edited by J. Brooks-Gunn and A.C. Petersen. New York, Plenum, 1983, pp. 127–154.

44. Cohn, L., Adler, N., Irwin, C., et al.: Body-figure preferences in male and female adolescents. J. Abnorm. Psychol., 3:276, 1987.

45. Striegel-Moore, R.H., Silberstein, L.R., Grunberg, N.E., and Rodin, J.: Competing on all fronts: Achievement orientation and disordered eating. Sex Roles, 19:219, 1990.
46. Dummer, G.M., Rosen, L.W., Heusner, W.W., et al.: Pathogenic weight-control behaviors of young competitive swimmers. Physiol. Sportsmed., 15:75, 1987.
47. Feltz, D.L., and Ewing, M.E.: Psychological characteristics of elite young athletes. Med. Sci. Sports Exerc., 19:S98, 1987.
48. Young, C.M., Blondin, J., Tensuan, R., and Fryer, J.H.: Body composition studies of "older" women, thirty–seventy years of age. Ann. N.Y. Acad. Sci., 110:589, 1963.
49. Young, C.M., Martin, M.E.K., Chihan, M., McCarthy, M., et al.: Body composition of young women: Some preliminary findings. J. Am. Dietet. Assoc., 38:332, 1961.
50. Bray, G.A.: The Obese Patient. Philadelphia, Saunders, 1976.
51. Forbes, G., and Reina, J.C.: Adult lean body mass declines with age: Some longitudinal observations. Metabolism, 19:653, 1970.
52. Parizkowa, J.: Body composition and exercise during growth and development. In Physical Activity: Human Growth and Development. Edited by G.L. Rarick. New York, Academic Press, 1973, pp. 55–72.
53. Wessel, J.A., Ufer, A., Van Huss, W.D., and Cederquist, D.: Age trends of various components of body composition and functional characteristics of women aged 20–69 years. Ann. N.Y. Acad. Sci., 110:608, 1963.
54. Fisher, S.: Development and Structure of the Body Image Vol. 1. Hillsdale, NJ: Lawrence, 1986.
55. Franzoi, S.L., and Shield, S.A.: The body esteem scale: Multidimensional structure and sex differences in a college population. J. Pers. Assess., 48:173, 1984.
56. Kurtz, R.M.: Sex differences and variation in body attitudes. J. Consult. Clin. Psychol., 33:625, 1969.
57. Lerner, R.M., Orlos, J.B., and Knapp, J.R.: Physical attractiveness, physical effectiveness and self-concept in late adolescents. Adolescence, 11:313, 1976.
58. Bearen, S.I.: Attitudes to appearance in adolescence. J. Hum. Nutr., 35:335, 1981.
59. Scheier, M.F., and Carver, C.S.: Self-focused attention and the experience of emotion: Attraction, repulsion, elation, and depression. J. Pers. Soc. Psychol., 35:625, 1979.
60. Scheier, M.F., and Carver, C.S.: Self-directed attention, awareness of bodily states and suggestibility. J. Pers. Soc. Psychol., 37:1576, 1979.
61. Enns, M.P., Drewnowski, A., and Grinker, J.A.: Body composition, body size estimation, and attitudes towards eating in male college athletes. Psychosom. Med., 49:56, 1987.
62. Braisted, J.R., Mellin, L., Gong, E.J., and Irwin, C.E.: The adolescent ballet dancer: Nutritional practices and characteristics associated with anorexia nervosa. J. Adolesc. Health Care, 6:365, 1985.
63. Fenigstein, A., Scheier, M.F., and Buss, A.H.: Public and private self-consciousness: Assessment and theory. J. Clin. Psychol., 43:522, 1975.
64. Skrinar, G.S., Bullen, B.A., Cheek, J.M., et al.: Effects of endurance training on body-consciousness in women. Percept. Mot. Skills, 62:483, 1986.

C H A P T E R

11

WEIGHT CYCLING IN ATHLETES: EFFECTS ON BEHAVIOR, PHYSIOLOGY, AND HEALTH

Kelly D. Brownell and Suzanne Nelson Steen

Weight cycling is defined as repeated cycles of weight loss and gain. There has been growing recognition that this weight change pattern is common to many groups of athletes and that important effects are likely to occur in behavior, physiology, and health.[1] In this chapter we describe these patterns in various groups of athletes, discuss the effects of weight cycling, and then integrate this information to underscore what is and is not known in this area.

☐ IMPORTANCE OF THE ISSUE FOR ATHLETES

WEIGHT CONCERN AND WEIGHT CYCLING

Athletes in many sports are concerned about their weight. Some are concerned for reasons of appearance and others for reasons of performance. Distance runners and swimmers are examples of athletes in whom lower weight is thought to confer a competitive advantage. Gymnasts, figure skaters, and divers, on the other hand, might feel that weight is important for performance, but they must also be concerned with appearance. Performance is rated by judges, and the degree to which an athlete meets the prevailing ideal for body shape can influence ratings.

For many athletes, weight can become the focal point of their athletic existence. Some develop frank eating disorders, others have subclinical eating problems, and others devote inordinate attention and energy to how they look and what they weigh. The psychological consequences of this are discussed in detail in Chapters 8, 10, and 12.

The need to be lean, either real or perceived, leads to a diverse set of dieting practices. There has long been concern with some of these practices,[2,3] particularly the rapid weight loss typical of some sports such as wrestling. Weight cycling, in contrast, is a relatively new area of study, so the issue has only recently been discussed with reference to its effects on athletes. As we indicate below, there is need for further research because of the potential importance of the issue to the performance, psychological well-being, and health of the athlete.

PATTERNS OF WEIGHT CHANGE

The concern with weight in athletes is manifested in a number of different weight-change patterns. One notable pattern is the rapid loss and gain necessitated by competition in specific weight categories. High school and collegiate wrestlers, for example, must make a specific weight in order to compete. Failure to "make weight" results in a forfeit. Many wrestlers lose weight rapidly prior to a match, regain rapidly after competition, and then repeat the cycle for the next match.

These rapid and frequent cycles are not specific to wrestlers. Lightweight rowers, boxers, and jockeys must also meet weight standards to compete. Athletes in these sports vary considerably in the manner in which they cycle (e.g., frequency, magnitude, rapidity, and type of food and fluid restriction).

Another pattern of weight change can result from training differences between the season and the off-season. Some athletes, such as football players, can alter their training and eating habits after the season ends; they then must make equally dramatic changes to prepare for the subsequent season. Weight might be relatively constant within a season but vary between seasons.

A third pattern occurs in athletes who wish to keep weight at a certain level but have difficulty accomplishing this. An example might be a distance runner who wishes to have a low weight because of an expected improvement in performance. The runner is inclined to weigh more, perhaps because of genetics and accompanying metabolic factors. When weight increases, restricted eating or additional exercise might be necessary to restore the desired weight. Such individuals frequently engage in cycles of conflict with their own bodies, in which they keep weight low for periods but then gain weight when their restraint weakens or when physiological processes seek to restore a higher weight.

☐ CYCLING PATTERNS IN ATHLETES

Weight and body composition data are available in abundance for many groups of athletes.[4] Most studies on this issue, however, examine average weights and typical body composition figures for a specific group of athletes, usually at a point of peak training. The object of these studies has been to determine the weights and percent body fat levels characteristic of various athletes, and to help define the levels associated with top performance.

Relatively little information is available on weight *change* in athletes. The existing studies are likely to have self-reported, retrospective reports of weight over a circumscribed time, perhaps a single competitive season. The accuracy of such information is not known. The results of these studies are informative, however, and are typically consistent with what little prospective information is available. There is clearly a need for longitudinal studies in which athletes are followed over the course of several seasons.

WEIGHT-CHANGE PATTERNS IN WRESTLERS

Wrestling has been the sport most thoroughly studied with respect to weight changes. Wrestlers typically restrict food and fluid intake to qualify to wrestle in a weight classification that is below their natural weight. This occurs for several reasons. First, many coaches and wrestlers believe that losing weight is advantageous because it permits the competitor to wrestle a smaller opponent. This can provide an advantage in leverage and strength. Second, weights of high school and college students tend to cluster in the middle weight categories, in which there is greatest competition for positions on the team. Some wrestlers have to drop one or more weight categories in order to make the team. Third, an individual might be on a team that has better wrestlers in certain weight categories, so there is no choice but to drop weight. For many or even most wrestlers, cutting weight is not easy and requires constant attention and effort. Because weight gain occurs between matches, we can infer that the low weight is difficult to maintain.

Studies have shown the array of approaches wrestlers use to lose weight, including the use of a sauna, heated wrestling room, rubber sweat suit, fasting, and even vomiting, laxatives, and diuretics.[5-8] Both the American College of Sports Medicine[2] and the American Medical Association[3] have developed position statements warning of the practices leading to rapid and frequent weight loss.

HISTORY OF WEIGHT RESEARCH WITH WRESTLERS. Steen and Brownell[8] traced the history of weight change research in wrestlers. There have been published papers on the topic since the 1940s, the earliest reports focusing on both performance and health. The health effects gained increasing attention in the 1950s. Only in recent years has there been interest in the effects of repeated cycles of loss and regain on behavior and metabolism.

In 1943, Tuttle[9] studied the effects of weight loss on performance in six wrestlers at the University of Iowa, because "the practice of voluntary weight loss by dehydration and the withholding of food so as to make wrestling weights raises the question as to the effect this procedure has on performance." Doscher[10] expressed similar concerns after surveying coaches about rapid weight loss and performance.

> . . . Purposefully shedding a number of pounds of body weight and then engaging in very strenuous combat is not a normal procedure . . . done obviously to increase a competitor's chance of winning a match. However because such reduction in weight usually involves one of the following— interference with the laws of good nutrition, excessive exercise, artificial methods of dehydration—many interested persons question the effect of such rigorous procedures on the performance and health of the athlete.[10]

As concerns on health effects were raised, legislative efforts were proposed to control weight-loss practices in wrestlers. One such effort occurred in Iowa in 1967. A local medical society passed a resolution to abolish wrestling in their county, the belief being that weight-loss practices were unhealthy. Months of debate followed, ending in the recognition that few studies had been done to document the frequency and nature of these practices. What followed were a series of studies by Tipton and colleagues at the University of Iowa to evaluate the extent of the problem.[5,11,12]

In 1970, Tipton and Tcheng[5] measured body weight changes in 747 wrestlers from 30 high schools in Iowa. For the 17 days before competition, the average weight loss was 3.1 kg (4.9% of body weight), most of the weight loss occurring in the last 10 days. The percentages of wrestlers who used a particular weight loss practice "a lot" were 16% for decreased food intake, 14% for decreased fluid, 31% for increased exercise, 23% for exercise in a hot environment, and 5% for use of rubber suits.

CURRENT PRACTICES AMONG WRESTLERS. Steen and Brownell[8] studied weight-change patterns in 63 college wrestlers and 378 high school wrestlers with a questionnaire that examined the frequency and magnitude of weight loss, dieting patterns, weight-loss methods, preoccupation with food, and emotions associated with weight loss. The study revealed clear patterns of frequent, rapid, and large cycles of weight loss and gain.

The average weekly weight losses are shown Figure 11-1 for the high school wrestlers and Figure 11-2 for the college wrestlers. The numbers are striking. Of the high school wrestlers, 30% lost at least 2.7 kg in a

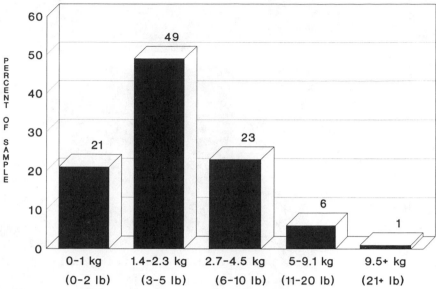

FIG. 11–1. Percent of high school wrestlers with weekly weight fluctuation (in kg) in specific weight categories. From Steen, S.N., and Brownell, K.D.: Patterns of weight loss and regain in wrestlers: Has the tradition changed? Med. Sci. Sports Exerc., 22:762, 1990

typical week of the wrestling season. The figure for college wrestlers was 87%. Fully 43% of the college wrestlers reported losing at least 5 kg in a typical week.

These typical weekly fluctuations translated into large total lifetime fluctuations (see Table 11-1). Sixty percent of the high school wrestlers had already lost 0.5 to 4.5 kg 6 or more times in their life; 90% of the college wrestlers made the same reports. Sixty-nine percent of the college wrestlers reported losing 5-9.1 kg at least 11 times; 8% reported this occurred 100 times or more.

The wrestlers in this study[8] were asked about methods they used to make weight. A variety of aggressive methods were used. These included dehydration, food restriction, fasting, and to some degree, the use of vomiting, laxatives, and diuretics. Despite warnings from national organizations,[2,3] 78% of college and 45% of the high school wrestlers used the sauna, and 90% of the college and 57% of the high school wrestlers used a rubber suit. Rates of vomiting, laxatives, and diuretics were low (0 to 6%), but given the potential complications, the numbers cannot be ignored.

From these figures it would appear that little has changed from the 1940s, when data on rapid and frequent weight losses in wrestlers were first published. This has occurred despite a growing body of literature documenting untoward health effects.[2,3,5,11–15] Aggressive practices are

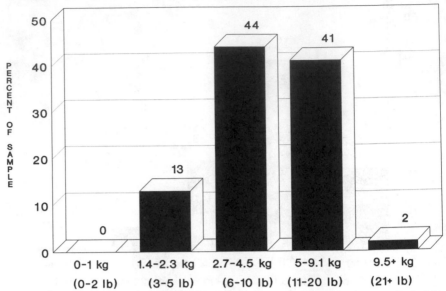

FIG. 11–2. Percent of college wrestlers with weekly weight fluctuations (in kg) in specific weight categories. From Steen, S.N., and Brownell, K.D.: Patterns of weight loss and regain in wrestlers: Has the tradition changed? Med. Sci. Sports Exerc., *22*:762, 1990.

TABLE 11–1. PERCENTAGES OF HIGH SCHOOL (HS) AND COLLEGE (COL) WRESTLERS WHO REPORTED WEIGHT CYCLING, BY NUMBER OF TIMES AND WEIGHT LOST

		NUMBER OF TIMES						
KILOGRAMS LOST		**0**	**1–5**	**6–10**	**11–20**	**21–50**	**51–100**	**100+**
0.5–4.5 kg	HS	8	32	18	15	18	5	4
(1–10 lb)	Col	3	7	3	2	25	25	35
5–9.1 kg	HS	40	42	9	8	1	0	0
(11–20 lb)	Col	8	18	5	27	22	12	8
9.5–18.2 kg	HS	84	15	1	0	0	0	0
(21–40 lb)	Col	60	27	2	7	0	5	0
18.6+ kg	HS	99	1	0	0	0	0	0
(41+ lb)	Col	98	0	0	0	2	0	0

From Steen, S.N., and Brownell, K.D.: Med. Sci. Sports Exerc., *22*:762, 1990.

used to accomplish the weight losses, in the face of warnings from professional and medical groups.[2,3] Legislation defining a minimum weight for competition, perhaps based on an individual's percent body fat, might be the only means for altering these practices.

WEIGHT-CHANGE PATTERNS IN OTHER ATHLETES

Relatively little is known about weight-fluctuation patterns in groups other than wrestlers. There is some research on dietary intake and typical weights of competitors in various sports,[4,16] but studies have not focused on weight *change*. There are also studies on dieting practices and eating disorders, particularly in some groups such as gymnasts, swimmers, and dancers (see Chapter 9), but again, these studies have not addressed the issue of weight change over time. Studies systematically documenting weight-cycling practices in athletes are urgently needed.

◻ EFFECTS OF WEIGHT CYCLING

Research on weight cycling is relatively new, so there are currently more questions than answers regarding the effects of weight cycling on the behavior, metabolism, health, and performance of the athlete. Some studies have been done, however, and pertinent information is available from research on nonathletes and even animals.

EFFECTS ON PSYCHOLOGY, BEHAVIOR, AND WEIGHT

PSYCHOLOGICAL FACTORS AND WEIGHT PREOCCUPATION. Studies on athletes in sports in which weight fluctuates have shown sufficient psychological distress to warrant further study. In one study of wrestlers,[8] the percentages reporting problems for college and high school wrestlers respectively were 66 and 45% for anger, 33 and 24% for anxiety, and 24 and 24% for depression (Fig. 11-3). These data show that psychological distress occurs in wrestlers in general, but cycling and noncycling wrestlers have not been compared. Comparisons of cycling athletes with noncycling athletes in the same sport, and with age-matched nonathletes, will be necessary to identify the important associations.

Weight cycling might also be associated with problematic thoughts and perceptions about eating. In research with wrestlers,[8,17] 63% of the college wrestlers and 43% of the high school wrestlers reported that they were often or always preoccupied with food. The percentages dropped to 19% and 14% in the off-season. After a match, 41% of the college wrestlers and 29% of the high school wrestlers felt their eating was often or always out of control. These figures dropped to 10% and 20% in the off-season. Again, however, cycling and noncycling wrestlers were not compared.

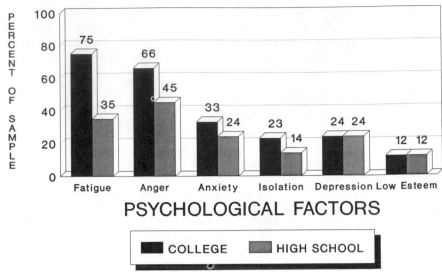

FIG. 11–3. Percent of high school and college wrestlers reporting psychological effects of weight loss. From Steen, S.N., and Brownell, K.D.: Patterns of weight loss and regain in wrestlers: Has the tradition changed? Med. Sci. Sports Exerc., *22*:762, 1990.

The differences in these studies between in-season and off-season reports of weight concerns and eating preoccupation are interesting. They suggest a carryover of problems to the off-season for only some of the athletes. Not having the right comparisons, it is difficult to know whether the off-season problems are higher than would be expected in males that age. We believe that there is some increase in eating problems in wrestlers and that repeated dieting predisposes some individuals to psychological problems related to food and weight.

PATTERNS OF WEIGHT CHANGE. Some of the early animal work on weight cycling began with the hypothesis that repeated dieting would make the body more energy-efficient, so that with successive cycles, weight loss would occur more slowly and gain would occur more rapidly.[18] The animal literature has produced inconsistent findings on this topic, and to date only one study in humans has addressed this issue in detail. Blackburn and colleagues[19] studied dieters who had been through the same weight-loss program more than one time. Weight loss occurred more slowly a second time compared to the first, on the identical diet.

These data are consistent with what little survey research exists[20] and with anecdotal reports from dieters that weight loss becomes more difficult after multiple diets. The best way to address this issue experimentally will be with prospective studies of athletes as they progress through careers with varying patterns of weight change.

NUTRIENT SELECTION. There is evidence from both animal and human studies that weight cycling alters the selection of nutrients in the diet. Two animal studies[21,22] found that animals who cycled, selected more dietary fat when allowed to choose freely from fat, carbohydrate, and protein sources. Drewnowski and colleagues[23] had 61 obese and 31 lean men and women taste and rate 9 mixtures of sugar and fat solutions. Subjects with childhood-onset obesity and a history of weight cycling showed the highest preferences for sugar and fat. The issue has not been studied in athletes.

Diet composition, particularly the percentage of fat in the diet, could be important for athletes for several reasons. First is the general relationship between diet and health.[24] If weight cycling produces deleterious changes in the diet, health in athletes could be impaired during or after participation in the sport. In addition, diet can affect the performance of the athlete (see Chapters 5 and 19), so the very practice (dieting) used to enhance performance could impede the progress of the athlete.

EFFECTS ON METABOLISM

Dieting is known to reduce metabolic rate, but how long this endures and whether it is exacerbated by weight cycling is not known. The most pertinent evidence comes from two studies with wrestlers.[15,25] In one study with 27 elite high school wrestlers, subjects were classified as cyclers or noncyclers according to their weight history.[15] The groups were compared on resting energy expenditure (REE). The cyclers and noncyclers did not differ on age, height, weight, body surface area, lean body mass, or percent body fat, but the cyclers had a 14% lower value for REE.

In a study with collegiate wrestlers, 12 weight-cycling wrestlers were compared to 13 weight-stable nonwrestlers.[25] At the beginning of the study, the wrestlers had significantly higher resting metabolic rate (RMR) values than controls. At midseason, the RMR in the wrestlers dropped but did not fall below the level for controls. After the season, RMR values for the wrestlers had returned to preseason levels and were significantly higher than for the controls.

Without further research, it is difficult to reconcile the differences between these two studies, one showing lower energy requirements among cycling wrestlers[15] and the other showing no such effect.[25] The study with high school wrestlers was correlational, whereas the study with college wrestlers was longitudinal. The high school study had noncycling wrestlers as controls; the college study had nonwrestlers as controls. Whether weight cycling lowers energy requirements must be considered an open question at this point.

EFFECTS ON HEALTH

There is ample reason to be concerned about the health effects of weight cycling. As an example of the animal literature, rats exposed to cycles of weight loss and gain had increased blood pressure.[26] Human epidemiologic studies have found a link between body weight variability and risk for both cardiovascular disease and all-cause mortality.[27-29] These types of health effects of weight cycling have not been studied in athletes. Given the serious nature of the health effects suggested by animal and human epidemiology studies, the issue deserves further attention.

One area of potential importance relates to growth and development. In young athletes, restrictive diets and weight fluctuation occur during periods of rapid growth and development. In wrestling, for example, there is speculation about whether smaller individuals choose the sport or whether the practices of the sport itself inhibit growth. One researcher observed identical twins who were accomplished athletes; one was a wrestler, the other a gymnast.[30] At the time of collegiate competition, the wrestler was 2 inches shorter than his gymnast brother. This implicates wrestling as a causative factor in slowing growth, but this observation is not an empirical test. This is an area needing further study.

EFFECTS ON ATHLETIC PERFORMANCE

There is a pressing need for research on cycling and athletic performance, for both scientific and practical reasons. On the scientific side, the relationships between dieting practices, body weight changes, and human performance are not well understood. On the practical side, coaches and athletes may choose to ignore warnings about weight loss practices for health and metabolic reasons, as long as performance is thought to improve.

☐ RESEARCH QUESTIONS

Time and time again we have underscored the need for more research on weight cycling in athletes. The study of weight cycling in general is relatively new, but work with athletes has just begun.

Table 11-2 provides a list of the research questions we consider most pressing in this area. Many of the necessary studies are descriptive and show the need for documenting weight change patterns in (1) different groups of athletes, (2) the same athletes over time, and (3) long-term studies in which weight and the associated physiological and psychological factors are tracked over the course of several seasons. Several health areas are noted, including reproductive and menstrual function and growth and development. Our hope is that these areas will receive more research attention, and that the information will be helpful in maximizing the health and performance of the athlete.

☐ SUMMARY

Coaches, parents, and athletic officials are becoming increasingly concerned over the weight and dietary patterns of athletes in some sports. In sports such as wrestling, in which weight fluctuations are rapid, fre-

TABLE 11–2. RESEARCH NEEDS PERTAINING TO WEIGHT CYCLING PATTERNS IN ATHLETES

1. To document patterns of weight change in elite, nonelite, and recreational athletes
2. To document and distinguish different patterns of weight change in athletes. Examples are in-season vs. off-season differences (e.g., football and basketball players) and weight change within seasons due to weight standards for the sports (e.g., rowing, wrestling, and horse racing)
3. To conduct longitudinal studies to examine weight changes over time in different groups of athletes
4. To determine whether the effects of weight cycling endure beyond participation in sports. This would involve the study of former athletes, or the study of athletes as they stop active participation in the sport
5. To examine the health effects of weight cycling in athletes. Because there are different patterns of weight change in athletes, this would involve studies of different sports
6. To evaluate the effects of weight cycling on growth and other developmental factors in young athletes. In sports such as wrestling, in which some participants are smaller than age-matched peers, it is not known whether the sport inhibits growth or whether smaller individuals choose the sport
7. To study the effects of weight cycling on menstrual and reproductive issues. Females in general are under extreme pressure to be thin, and much of the dieting in female athletes comes during early reproductive development. The effects on menstrual function and later reproductive capacity merit investigation
8. To study the effects of weight cycling on athletic performance. This would include investigation of both the physical and psychological aspects of performance
9. To study the psychological effects of weight cycling and repeated dieting in athletes. It will be important to evaluate psychological factors before, during, and after such cycles and to evaluate these factors during the season and in the off season. Of particular interest are factors such as preoccupation with food, binge eating and purging, perceived degree of deprivation, eating disorders, body image, and mood changes related to dieting.

quent, and severe, the concern has spread to national organizations such as the American Medical Association[3] and the American College of Sports Medicine.[2]

Little is known about weight cycling, except in wrestlers. We believe, however, that the issue is relevant to many sports. Athletes cycle because of the demands of their sport, weigh-ins required by coaches, or their own concerns about weight and appearance. With increasingly intense pressure to perform (see Chapter 18), weight is one of the fronts on which many athletes prepare for competition. Some athletes cycle between seasons, and others cycle many times within a season. One of the pressing needs, therefore, is to document the nature of cycling patterns across sports and to evaluate the effects on performance, behavior, metabolism, and health.

Too little is known about weight cycling in athletes to issue stern warnings. The only exception might be wrestling, in which considerable data are available on negative physiological effects of severe weight loss. Data from both human and animal studies however, which have examined effects of weight cycling on behavior, metabolism, and health, are sufficiently suggestive to take the issue seriously. This argues for a sensible, data-based approach to choosing an ideal performance weight, or perhaps a minimum competition weight, for an athlete (see Chapters 6 and 20).

☐ REFERENCES

1. Brownell, K.D., Steen, S.N., and Wilmore, J.H.: Weight regulation practices in athletes: Analysis of metabolic and health effects. Med. Sci. Sports Exerc., *19*:546, 1987.
2. American College of Sports Medicine: Position stand on weight loss in wrestlers. Med. Sci. Sports Exerc., *8*:xi, 1976.
3. American Medical Association, Committee on the Medical Aspects of Sports: Wrestling and weight control. JAMA, *201*:541, 1967.
4. Wilmore, J.H., and Costill, D.L.: Training for Sport and Activity: The Physiological Basis of the Conditioning Process. Dubuque, IA, Brown, 1988.
5. Tipton, C.M., and Tcheng, T.K.: Iowa Wrestling Study: Weight loss in high school students. JAMA, *214*:1269, 1970.
6. Hursch, L.M.: Food and water restriction in wrestlers. JAMA, *241*:915, 1979.
7. Ribisl, P.M.: Rapid weight reduction in wrestling. J. Sports Med., *3*:55, 1975.
8. Steen, S.N., and Brownell, K.D.: Patterns of weight loss and regain in wrestlers: Has the tradition changed? Med. Sci. Sports Exerc., *22*:762, 1990.
9. Tuttle, W.W.: The effect of weight loss by dehydration and the withholding of food on the physiologic responses of wrestlers. Res. Q. *15*:158, 1943.
10. Doscher, N.: The effects of rapid weight loss upon the performance of wrestlers and boxers, and upon the physical proficiency of college students. Res. Q., *15*:317, 1944.
11. Tipton, C.M., Tcheng, T.K., and Paul, W.D.: Evaluation of the Hall method for determining minimum wrestling weights. J. Iowa Med. Soc., *59*:571, 1969.
12. Tcheng, T.K., and Tipton, C.M.: Iowa Wrestling Study: Anthropometric measurements and the prediction of a minimal body weight for high school wrestlers. Med. Sci. Sports, *5*:1, 1973.
13. Zambraski, E.J. et al.: Iowa Wrestling Study: Weight loss and urinary profiles of collegiate wrestlers. Med. Sci. Sports Exerc., *8*:105, 1976.
14. Strauss, R.H., Lanese, R.R., and Malarky, W.B.: Weight loss in amateur wrestlers and its effect on serum testosterone levels. JAMA, *254*:3337, 1985.
15. Steen, S.N., Oppliger, R.A., and Brownell, K.D.: Metabolic effects of repeated weight loss and regain in adolescent wrestlers. JAMA, *260*:47, 1988.
16. Short, S.H., and Short, W.R.: Four-year study of athletes' dietary intake. J. Amer. Dietet. Assoc., *82*:632, 1983.
17. Steen, S.N., and Brownell, K.D.: Nutrition, weight control practices, and pre-event meal of high school wrestlers. Paper presented at the American Dietetic Association Annual Meeting, October, 1988, San Francisco.
18. Brownell, K.D., Greenwood, M.R.C., Stellar, E., and Shrager, E.E.: The effects of weight loss and regain cycles in rats. Physiol. Behav., *38*:459, 1986.
19. Blackburn, G.L., et al.: Weight cycling: The experience of human dieters. Am. J. Clin. Nutr., *49*:1105, 1989.
20. Brownell, K.D., Rodin, J., and Wilmore, J.H.: Eat, drink and be worried? Runner's World, *23*:28, 1988.
21. Reed, D., et al.: Weight cycling in female rats increases dietary fat selection and adiposity. Physiol. Behav., *42*:389, 1988.
22. Gerardo-Gettens, T., et al.: Exercise decreases fat selection in female rats during weight cycling. Am. J. Physiol. *260*:R518, 1991.

23. Drewnowski, A., Kurth, C.L., and Rahaim, J.E.: Taste preferences in human obesity: Environmental and familial factors. Am. J. Clin. Nutr., in press.

24. U.S. Department of Health and Human Services: Surgeon General's Report on Nutrition and Health. Washington, DC, U.S. Government Printing Office, DHHS Pub. No. 88-50210, 1988.

25. Melby, C.L., Schmidt, W.D., and Corrigan, D.: Resting metabolic rate in weight cycling collegiate wrestlers compared with physically active, noncycling control subjects. Am. J. Clin. Nutr., 52:409, 1990.

26. Ernsberger, P., and Nelson, D.O.: Refeeding hypertension in dietary obesity. Am. J. Physiol. 254:R47, 1988.

27. Hamm, P.B., Shekelle, R.B., and Stamler, J.: Large fluctuations in body weight during young adulthood and 25-year risk of coronary death in men. Am. J. Epidemiol., 129:312, 1989.

28. Lissner, L., et al.: Variability in body weight and health outcomes in the Framingham population. N. Engl. J. Med., 324:1839, 1991.

29. Lissner, L., and Brownell, K.D.: Weight cycling, mortality, and cardiovascular disease: A review of epidemiologic findings. In Obesity. Edited by P. Bjorntorp and B. Brodoff. Philadelphia, Lippincott, 1991.

30. Smith, N.J.: Weight control in the athlete. Clin. Sports Med., 3:693, 1984.

C H A P T E R

12

EATING DISORDERS IN MALES: A SPECIAL CASE?

Arnold E. Andersen

Eating disorders have a long and checkered history regarding their classification, causes, mechanism, and treatment. Since the first widely accepted reports in the English language by Morton,[1] they have been identified as primary disorders of eating behavior, often having close ties to athletics, especially in males. Three major questions to be discussed in this chapter are the following:

1. Are eating disorders a special case of psychiatric illness, or are they simply one manifestation of another more fundamental illness such as obsessive-compulsive disorder, depression, anxiety states, or a personality disorder?
2. Are males with eating disorders a special case of fitness out of control, constituting merely one part of a spectrum of athleticism, or are they truly different from male athletes in general?
3. Are males with eating disorders a special case of gender-related illness, or are they similar to females with eating disorders?

☐ ARE EATING DISORDERS A SPECIAL FORM OF ILLNESS?

Between the time of Morton and the first modern case series by Gull in 1874,[2] eating disorders were a rare but recognized form of medical abnormality of speculative cause. The implication of possible physical causes of anorexia nervosa (bulimia nervosa was not formally defined until much later) was continued throughout the latter part of the nineteenth century and was only put to rest when postpartum pituitary necrosis was recognized as a medical disorder separate from anorexia nervosa.

The pendulum swung to the opposite direction during the second through the sixth decades of the twentieth century, when anorexia nervosa was essentially dismissed as a separate illness. It was seen instead as a psychodynamically understandable outcome of certain psychological conflicts, specifically the fear of oral impregnation and the confusion between sexuality and eating. The disorder was hypothesized to represent a symbolic outcome of age-old conflicts in maturation rather than a separate disease of any kind. Since that time, anorexia nervosa, and more recently bulimia nervosa, have been suggested to be disguised forms of several more basic psychiatric disorders. But with the passage of each half decade or so, it has been suggested to be a disguised form of a different underlying major psychiatric disorder.

Several decades ago, for example, anorexia nervosa was widely agreed to be an expression of an underlying schizophrenic illness, a view now rejected. Crisp and colleagues[3] have long viewed anorexia nervosa as a phobic avoidance of maturation, a "last ditch" stance provoked by fears of development. This phobic aspect of anorexia nervosa has been further described by Russell as a morbid fear of fatness that is out of all proportion to reality.[4] Studies by Cantwell et al.[5] began to make links between anorexia nervosa and depressive illness, finding in the families of anorectic patients a substantial increase in the presence of mood disorders.

The next step in implied cause shifted to an emphasis on eating disorders as an expression of an abnormal or a vulnerable personality. Piran and others[6] have documented the increased probability of a personality disorder being present in patients with eating disorders. More recently, and usually with imprecise definitions, eating disorders have been hypothesized to be a form of "addictive disorder." Many programs for eating disorders have been modeled on the 12 step approach originally applied to alcoholism and drug problems, and sometimes to obesity. The vague phrase "addiction to binge eating" or "addiction to starvation" ignores the many dissimilarities between true drug addiction and eating disorders, including the impossibility of applying an abstinence approach to food. More recently, investigators have begun to see the links between eating disorders and obsessive-compulsive disorder.[7] They share features of intrusive thoughts recognized to be alien and compulsive urges that are resisted but cause intolerable anxiety if not practiced.

Studies by Margolis et al.[8] have demonstrated, using the Lifetime Schedule of Affective Disorders and Schizophrenia, a thorough diagnostic interview, that anorexia nervosa and bulimia nervosa generally have from 2 to 4 associated psychiatric disorders of different types. In practical terms, this means that eating disorders almost always have companion psychiatric syndromes that are integral to the predisposition, onset, or maintenance of these disorders but are not the same as the eating disorders themselves.

Therefore, though eating disorders have many multiple psychiatric companions, they are not psychopathologically reducible to any single other disorder. In fact, they are disorders of motivated behavior, and once launched, they have a life of their own. These are syndromes that can be clearly defined as separate diagnostic entities and studied throughout their natural history without seeing them transmutate into other more basic underlying disorders. It is still a mystery how normal behavior, such as dieting behavior, makes a transition to an eating disorder that then becomes self-sustaining. The basic mechanisms underlying this process are not yet understood.

There is, however, a regular stepwise progression through sequential stages of illness that characterizes both anorexia nervosa and bulimia nervosa. Table 12–1 describes the stages of progression in anorexia nervosa, and Table 12–2 the pattern for bulimia nervosa. The initial stage of dieting behavior, with secondary, compensatory overeating, is not abnormal. By stage 2, however, these behaviors meet criteria for the formal definition of these eating disorders, manifesting now the shared central psychopathology of a morbid fear of fatness and the associated, defining, persisting behaviors, either of self-starvation for anorexia nervosa or binge behavior for bulimia nervosa. Finally, in the third stage, these disorders become autonomous, and ultimately confer a sense of professional identity to the individual.[9]

In summary, anorexia nervosa has a rich and complicated definitional history, of being viewed as a neurological disorder, as a nondisorder, and as a specialized form of almost every other major psychiatric entity. It even has been suggested to be a form of seizure disorder,[10] but almost certainly the electroencephalographic abnormalities noted in bulimic patients are the medical consequences of the disorder which have been confused with primary causes.

TABLE 12–1. STAGES OF DEVELOPMENT OF ANOREXIA NERVOSA

Stage 1. A normal behavior
Normal, voluntary dieting behavior
Stage 2. A diagnosable disorder
Dieting not under personal control and/or dieting has serious medical, social, psychological consequences. Characterized by morbid fear of fatness. DSM-III-R criteria met
Stage 3A. Autonomous behavior
The disorder does not resolve even if conditions promoting its origin have resolved. Behavior not susceptible to any degree of personal control. Secondary biological mechanisms frequently present
Stage 3B. Illness becomes an identity
The patient identifies with *being* the illness, not only having the illness (I *am* anorectic). Prospect of loss of illness leads to existential fears of loss of identity and inability to cope

---

TABLE 12–2. STAGES OF DEVELOPMENT OF BULIMIA NERVOSA

Stage 1A. Normal dieting behavior takes place. Similar to anorexia nervosa, stage 1
Stage 1B. Dieting behavior and weight loss lead to **INVOLUNTARY BINGE BE-HAVIOR,** based on a normal, motivated behavioral response to intense hunger
Stage 2. A diagnosable disorder. The trigger for binge behavior generalizes from hunger to a variety of uncomfortable mood states such as anxiety or depression. Marked fear of fatness is present. Meets DSM-III-R criteria. Can have serious medical, social, and psychological consequences
Stage 3A. Autonomous behavior. Binges autonomous, frequent, large. Secondary biological mechanisms are often present
Stage 3B. Illness becomes an identity. The thought of living without bulimic behavior provokes fear of losing a sense of identity and fear of inability to cope

---

☐ ARE MALES WITH EATING DISORDERS A SPECIAL CLASS OF ILLNESS, OR ARE THEY A FORM OF ATHLETICISM OUT OF CONTROL?

FEATURES SHARED BY MALE ATHLETES AND MALES WITH EATING DISORDERS

Research studies support the finding of many similarities between male athletes and males with eating disorders including the over-valued preoccupation with body size and shape in males with eating disorders.[11] Bob's case illustrates how an eating disorder can originate in an athlete's desire to change body shape.

CASE HISTORY. Bob, a 15-year-old student in tenth grade, was referred for treatment of anorexia nervosa and depression. Just after he turned 15 he felt a bit overweight despite being only 146 lb at 5 ft 9 in. tall, but mostly he felt flabby and out of shape, attempting to lose weight in order to increase the amount of lean muscle mass. He reduced to 122 lb in order to qualify for a lower weight in wrestling and to be more attractive to girls. He achieved his target of a lower weight through increased exercise and restricted food intake. When he reached 122 lb, however, he felt weak and experienced difficulty in mental concentration, but he was fearful of eating, specifically fearing loss of control and becoming fat. He demonstrated perceptual distortion, thinking that he was larger than he was. He exercised up to 3 h a day with a driven, compulsive quality. Bob came from a family with a history of depression, suicide, and alcoholism.

On mental status examination, Bob was a sad and anxious, thin young man with low mood and suicidal thoughts. He had fear of fatness and perceptual distortion, meeting criteria for anorexia nervosa, restricting subtype, as well as for major depressive illness. Although he was too young for a formal diagnosis of a personality disorder, he manifested personality vulnerabilities including obsessional, dependent, anxious, and self-critical features. He did well in hospital, restoring weight with nutritional rehabilitation and benefitting from psychotherapy and antidepressants. In addition, he gained confidence in his fitness by following a guided program of exercise, allowing him to increase to 150 lb at his current height of 6 ft along with attaining good muscular definition.

Comment. Bob illustrates a case of anorexia nervosa in a young athlete who was not overweight but was dissatisfied with his body shape. He dieted primarily to change his body shape rather than to reach a lower weight, evidenced by dissatisfaction at reaching a low weight. His illness developed an autonomous quality, however, and he met diagnostic criteria for anorexia nervosa. Exercise played a role in restoring his weight and in allowing him to achieve a fit, athletic appearance as well as in the initial progression of his illness.

Athletes, like eating-disordered patients, make a tremendous psychological and physical investment in their body form and function in order to accomplish important goals. In both cases, the body is the essential vehicle for achieving something important of high and personal value. The body is the source of glory or dishonor, of self-satisfaction or self-rejection, and carries in many ways, even if inappropriately, the burden of the male's whole sense of self-esteem and worthwhileness.

There are similar medical consequences for male marathon runners and males with anorexia nervosa.[12] MacConnie and colleagues concluded that highly trained male athletes have a deficiency of hypothalamic gonadotropin-releasing hormone. Male athletes and males with eating disorders both might abuse substances in the service of achieving impossible goals of body weight or muscular definition. Pope and Katz[13] and Brower et al.[14] have documented the severe physical and psychological consequences of anabolic androgenic steroids in male athletes. Males with eating disorders frequently abuse laxatives, diuretics, diet pills, ipecac, and other substances. In both cases, the end is thought to justify the means, despite the possibility of serious medical complications or death.

In regard to their observable behaviors, a potential for abusive exercise is therefore a common shared vulnerability for athletes and males with eating disorders. Additionally, there are few sports in which participants completely disregard the amount of food taken in. Most male athletes are either bulking up for sports such as football, slimming down for wrestling, or carbohydrate-loading for long-distance running. Third, in addition to sharing behaviors of exercise and alteration in dietary intake, athletes and males with eating disorders both intensely scrutinize their bodies in regard to appearance and performance, weighing themselves and at times measuring muscle size and strength. They are both at times vulnerable to fads and superstitions, even when intellectually aware of the lack of rational basis for these behaviors and beliefs.

Fourth, in personality, there are many common features. Anorexia nervosa in many ways represents a commitment equal to or greater in intensity than any professional vocation or athletic endeavor. Drivenness, perseverance, compulsivity, and perfectionism are all associated with "success" in both sports and eating disorders, especially anorexia nervosa.

The features common to the bulimic subgroup of males with eating disorders and male athletes represent other aspects of successful sports performance, namely impulsivity, risk-taking, and self-dramatizing features, which are valued in many sports. Dick's story illustrates how the drive by an impulsive athlete to get on a team led to a case of bulimia nervosa.

CASE HISTORY. Dick was overweight in high school, weighing 220 lb at 5 ft 7 in. He felt rejected by young women he wanted to date because of his weight and was not fast enough for a position on the football squad. He was also rejected for water polo because of his weight. He decided to exercise strenuously and restricted his food intake, going down to 145 lb. He further reduced for a short while to 115 lb., but he quickly became dissatisfied with extreme thinness. On the positive side, his self-esteem improved as he initially lost weight. Girls did begin to notice him more, and he was finally accepted on the water polo team. On the negative side, however, he began to experience binge eating followed by self-induced vomiting. He also started to use alcohol excessively and to smoke marijuana. He compensated for the increased appetite from smoking marijuana by using amphetamine to cut down his appetite. In hospital, his binge-purge pattern was interrupted and he began to identify triggers for binge eating, substituting healthy behaviors. He came to terms with his perfectionistic and impulsive personality traits. He began to develop his own identity and career instead of imitating his successful older brother. He was ashamed of his diagnosis of bulimia nervosa but gradually came to see it as an illness. He committed himself to an alcohol- and drug-free life.

Comment. Dick illustrates the pre-illness weight pattern of bulimic males who are frequently overweight prior to their illness. He also illustrates the common pattern of dissatisfaction with being overweight followed by unhappiness with being very thin. His brief flirtation with anorexia nervosa at 115 lb made him dissatisfied with thinness and led him to try to achieve a moderate weight with good muscular definition, but at a weight he was able to maintain without binges and purges. Finally, he exemplifies the increased tendency of males with eating disorders to abuse drugs.

Regarding the personal sense of identity, both eating disorders and athletics confer a way of life, a professional identity, and a set of privileges and burdens as well as requirements for a daily life. Woodall et al.[9] have correlated the chronicity and severity of eating disorder with the degree to which the person makes an identification with the eating disorder as a professional way of life.

Finally, athletes and individuals with eating disorders share many sociocultural subgroup identifications. Clearly, in such groups as jockeys, wrestlers, divers, skaters, and runners, the mixture of athletic commitment and eating disorders can overlap. Males more than females are involved in athletics, and they seek alteration of body shape more than body weight,[15] but these patterns are open to change and might not represent true gender-related differences.

CRITICAL DIFFERENCES BETWEEN ATHLETES AND MALES WITH EATING DISORDERS

The fundamental qualitative difference between male athletes and patients with eating disorders is the presence of the defining psychopathology in the eating-disordered individual—a morbid fear of fatness, associated with an inappropriate pursuit of thinness, a distortion of body image, and an inability to perceive the body accurately. Neither anorexia nervosa nor bulimia nervosa can be confidently diagnosed unless the characteristic psychopathology is present. Although the degree of dedication and drivenness that goes into athletics, often at a level that appears to be self-abusive, could be judged abnormal by others less committed to sports, mere attitudes and behaviors do not formally constitute eating disorders unless they have the associated characteristic psychopathology. When reports in the medical literature describing medical conditions misdiagnosed as eating disorders are carefully scrutinized, in fact, the characteristic psychopathology for defining the eating disorder is usually not present. So, first and foremost, for an individual to have an eating disorder, he must manifest the characteristic overvalued idea of an abnormal fear of fatness constituting the essential psychopathology.[16]

Certain characteristic behaviors can always be considered abnormal when present. Severe abuse of laxatives and diuretics, leading to lowered body potassium, is clearly abnormal and dangerous. The use of stomach tubes to empty the stomach after meals would be a similar example. When normal athletic behavior such as running is taken to an extreme, or performed in conditions that are dangerous to health, then it becomes a clinical judgment as to when it expresses a symptom of illness.

In the midst of training for a sports event, it might not be clear who has an eating disorder and who is simply a committed athlete, on the basis of analysis of the man or boy's behaviors. A cardinal way to differentiate between them, however, is to see what happens to the individual's behavior and thinking when the environment changes—the sports event or season is concluded—and the opportunity is present for eating and behaving normally. In contrast to individuals starved voluntarily (e.g., for sports) or from involuntary imprisonment, who eat in a normal way, gradually or rapidly increasing caloric intake after the reason for their deprivation is ended, individuals with anorexia nervosa do not partake of the amount of food necessary to restore the body to a healthy point even when adequate nutritional resources become available. Likewise, persons with bulimia nervosa do not stop binge-eating or purging themselves, as many wrestlers do, after the athletic season is over; instead they continue their behaviors in a way that indicates a true lack of ability to change. What this means is that a longitudinal evaluation of the individual's thinking and behavior can be an important supplement to the cross-sectional diagnostic evaluation in making a diagnosis and in differentiating athleticism from an eating disorder. Andy's case shows how difficult it can be to distinguish between true eating disorders and atypical forms. His symptoms should have improved but didn't.

CASE HISTORY. Andy, an 18-year-old college student, was referred to the Eating and Weight Disorders Clinic for weight loss and vomiting. His chief complaint was: "I wrestled for 5 years. I would only let myself eat if I was very hungry. I'd like to eat more, but I can't." Andy began wrestling as a freshman in high school, eating extra food to get his weight up from 90 to 93 lb so he could make the 98 lb class. He gained weight to 126 lb during the later years in high school and then began to starve himself because "I knew I could be better if I wrestled at a lower weight." With his coach's encouragement he decreased in weight to 110 lb, achieving a measurement of 5% body fat. He would only eat enough food until he was "the slightest bit full." After recently retiring from wrestling, he had become dissatisfied with his chronically low weight and wished to be 140 lb at 5 ft 9 in., but he could not eat enough food to gain this weight. He was dissatisfied with his legs, which he felt were too thin, and wanted broader shoulders and thicker forearms. His appetite was diminished, however, and if he forced himself to eat to gain the desired weight, he would vomit spontaneously. He exercised from 1 to 4 hours a day but denied being compulsively driven. On mental status examination, Andy was thin but not emaciated, with good muscular definition. He was discouraged but not formally depressed, without symptoms of mood disorder, and specifically without fear of fatness, binge eating, or self-induced vomiting. He had since childhood a "picky appetite" but no desire to lose additional weight. He showed perfectionist and compulsive personality features. Finally, he felt hopeless about learning to eat normally.

    Comment. Andy did not meet criteria for anorexia nervosa or bulimia nervosa but had an abnormal eating pattern that had developed a "life of its own." It began in the context of 5 years of repeated weight loss in order to meet lower weight classes for wrestling. When he was too thin as a freshman in high school, however, he first tried to increase his weight. Although he did not have anorexia nervosa or bulimia nervosa, his eating pattern was clearly abnormal, not self-correcting, and interfered substantially with his self-esteem, his ability to gain desired weight, and with being able to eat normally in restaurants. His Eating Attitudes Test was elevated, but his Eating Disorders Inventory was low on drive for thinness or bulimia.

Finally, patients with eating disorders appear to have a substantial increase in associated psychiatric conditions. The most common associated disorders, as noted previously, are mood disorders, anxiety disorders, personality disorders, and abuse of substances including illicit drugs (besides androgenic steroids) and alcohol.

In summary, male athletes and males with eating disorders share many features. The fact of being male in general increases the probability that the individual will be concerned with body shape, will be involved in athletics, and will have increased probability of abuse of substances. Male athletes and males with eating disorders have many similarities in their values and goals, their behaviors, their personality, their identity, and their participation in various subgroups in society. However, they differ in the important characteristics of the defining psychopathology of eating disorders, certain behaviors which are always abnormal, the presence of additional psychiatric diagnosis, and importantly, the lack of return to normal when the incentive for extremes in weight or shape change are no longer present. Chipman and colleagues[17] have described the diagnostic dilemma caused by excessive weight loss in the athletic adolescent.

☐ ARE MALES WITH EATING DISORDERS A SPECIAL CASE COMPARED WITH FEMALES WITH EATING DISORDERS?

Although the first two cases of eating disorders reported by Morton in the English language included a male, and the first large series of cases by Gull in 1874 included mention of males, the syndrome of anorexia nervosa in males was lost sight of or neglected during the last part of the nineteenth century and the first half of the twentieth century. A number of theoretical conceptualizations of anorexia nervosa required the presence of "fear of oral impregnation," a psychodynamic characteristic less likely to occur in males. Other diagnostic criteria for a diagnosis of anorexia nervosa[18] included amenorrhea, another sex-biased requirement. The stereotype of the disorder, that it was present only in young, white, adolescent, upper-middle-class girls, became fixed in the public mind, and too often, as well, in the mind of physicians and psychologists. The fact that eating disorders occur in matrons, in minorities, and males has only more recently been confidently reasserted.[19]

SIMILARITIES BETWEEN MALES AND FEMALES WITH EATING DISORDERS

The criteria for anorexia nervosa have changed over the years, different committees requiring different degrees of weight loss. Fundamentally, however, the central psychopathology has not varied. Russell[4] has summarized the essential characteristics as self-induced starvation, an irrational fear of becoming fat that is out of proportion to reality, and an abnormality of reproductive hormone functioning. In practice, when patients, male or female, have substantial weight loss, usually 15% or more below a healthy body weight, associated with the morbid fear of fatness, anorexia nervosa can be considered to be present. The abnormal reproductive hormone functioning can simply be a consequence of the amount of weight lost.

Both males and females with eating disorders have a high probability of coming from families with affective disorders and having personal histories of mood disorders and personality disorders. The rule for both males and females is that there are few "lone rangers," and most individuals carry from two to four additional psychiatric diagnoses besides the eating disorder.

The biological response to self-starvation or binge-purge behavior is similar, especially when extreme, and is independent of sex. The severely starved individual manifests low blood pressure, slow pulse, decreased muscle mass, and almost nonexistent fat stores and shows all the compensatory metabolic changes that the body is capable of in responding to starvation. Binge behavior itself causes much gastrointestinal distress, but purging is more uniformly dangerous because of its systemic effects when practiced frequently. Self-induced vomiting and laxative or diuretic abuse can lead to lowered body potassium, with consequences of cardiac arrhythmias, seizures, and potential kidney damage as well as generalized weakness. The use of ipecac to induce vomiting, with its potentially toxic ingredient emetine, adds the additional danger of cardiomyopathy, sometimes confused with postviral endocarditis or myocarditis. Starved individuals of either sex appear bony, lacking in differentiating personality characteristics, and are often either slowed-down or hyperactive. Treatment of severe starvation is fairly uniform.[20] When self-starvation is reversed, and patients reach about 90% of their ideal body weight and their metabolic abnormalities are corrected, the individual and the sex-related differences become more apparent.

Both males and females with eating disorders tend to belong to subgroups within society that encourage change in body weight and shape. Although general sociocultural reinforcements for thinness are especially directed toward women, as has been demonstrated in a number of studies,[21] men who develop anorexia nervosa often are members of subgroups that emphasizes weight loss. Whether it is the macrocosm of general society as with females, or the microcosm of a vocational or avocational group as with males, or even a particular family that exaggerates societal norms, these disorders do not begin "out of the blue," but originate in response to definable reinforcements promoting dieting or shape-changing behavior, and in a dose-response proportionality.

Individuals who develop an eating disorder share the probability of having the eating disorder become an important source of identity. These disorders usually develop in adolescence, when the challenge of developing a confident and age-appropriate identity is the paramount task, as described by Erikson.[22] Crisp[23] has persuasively described anorexia nervosa as a way of coping with developmental issues.

DIFFERENCES BETWEEN MALES AND FEMALES WITH EATING DISORDERS

Natural History of the Eating Disorder

Males with eating disorders have a higher probability of having been obese, especially if they meet criteria for bulimia nervosa rather than anorexia.[24] Although females in our society have experienced a distressingly high incidence of sexual abuse, males with eating disorders appear to have more difficulties in the area of sexual identity and gender identity rather than abuse prior to their eating disorder. Burns and Crisp have described the asexual or uncertain sexual identity of males who go on to develop anorexia nervosa.[25] Drewnowski and Yee documented an almost parallel dissatisfaction with body weight in both men and women of college age but with the significant difference that men are almost evenly split between those who wish to lose weight (40%) and those who wish to gain weight (45%), whereas women uniformly wish to lose weight.[26]

There is no sharp "on-off" endocrinological change in men comparable to the loss of periods in women. Instead, men experience, along with a gradual decrease in testosterone, an accompanying gradual change in libido and sexual performance.

We have found an increasing incidence of HIV-positive bulimic males not paralleled in a much larger number of female admissions.[27] Males are statistically more likely to be sexually active and have a higher probability of homosexual orientation.[28] This combination, in addition to the presence of frequent hypomanic features[29] and impulsive personality, leads to increased probability of HIV infection.

Eating disorders can be conceptualized to begin as a result of a "critical cluster" of risk factors that are present prior to the actual behavior of dieting. Bulimia nervosa, although behaviorally different from anorexia nervosa, also grows out of prior dieting behavior virtually all of the time. Because males have been documented to carry fewer of certain risk factors that females have (prior sexual abuse and less general sociocultural pressure toward thinness), the question can be asked: where do the risk factors of those males that develop eating disorders come from? We speculate that males have comparable severity in sexual distress, but the distress is more related to issues of sexual identity than prior sexual abuse. Also, we hypothesize that males have more extremes of personality vulnerabilities, namely obsessional features prior to onset of anorexia nervosa and more extremes of impulsive features prior to onset of bulimia nervosa. There is currently no evidence that they need fewer or less-severe risk factors to develop their eating disorders because of their sex, or that they are less vulnerable to eating disorders as a consequence of the biological differences that result from the XY chromosomal pattern instead of the XX.

Reasons for Dieting

There are, in our experience, at least four reasons for dieting more likely to be found in men compared to women presenting to an Eating and Weight Disorders Clinic. There is a higher probability, as noted above, of actual past obesity in males. This past history, in association with a sensitive personality, might lead males who go on to develop anorexia nervosa or bulimia nervosa to vow never again to be teased or criticized for their weight. Second, on the basis of cases in our clinic population, more males than females dieted in relationship to sports activities. As noted before, they diet to increase their performance by decreasing body weight and body fat, thereby increasing the percentage of lean body mass. This finding might not apply to the general population. Males also might occasionally diet defensively to prevent weight increases that they fear will occur after an injury resulting from sports. Knowing that decreased activity level can lead to increased weight, they might diminish food intake out of proportion to the situation. Chuck's case is an example of defensive dieting to avoid weight gain after an athletic injury.

CASE HISTORY. Chuck, a 35-year-old administrator, was referred to the Johns Hopkins Hospital Eating Disorders Program at 85 lb for treatment of low weight, compulsive exercise, and binge-purge behavior. Ten years prior to admission, after an injury to his knee during compulsive exercising, he feared gaining weight because of decreased ability to exercise. He restricted his food intake and, in addition, went back to compulsive exercising despite the injury, losing weight gradually until he weighed only 85 lb. As his body weight was decreased he began to experience binge episodes, which provoked fears of becoming fat and led to self-induced vomiting. He became preoccupied with food and with his general health. He required several hospitalizations for hypokalemia and for reduced body temperature. On mental status examination, Chuck was an emaciated white male with peripheral acrocyanosis. He reported low energy, low mood, and a self-critical attitude but no suicidal ideation. He described ritualized behavior regarding grooming, checking things around the house, and his eating pattern. Despite his knee injury, he felt compelled to exercise every day, provoking further physical debilitation. He denied being fat, but then resisted eating and finally said he would indeed have difficulty accepting a body weight of even 120 lb. He left hospital prematurely but with some benefit in weight and improved mood.

    Comment. Chuck illustrates a defensive attempt to cut down on food intake after athletic injury in order to not gain weight, followed by a pattern of compulsive exercise combined with food restriction that led him into a severe case of anorexia nervosa. He illustrates also how chronic the illness can be and how men with this disorder tend to resist treatment, having developed an identity that requires the continuation of a starved state.

In our series of patients we have found a number of males who dieted in order to become more attractive to homosexual partners. No females in our series exhibited this behavior. A number of male patients we have seen dieted in order to avoid medical illnesses they had seen develop in their families that might have been related to weight, such as heart disease, diabetes, and high blood pressure. They are more sensitive than same-age females to these problems even when the concerns are completely inappropriate to them. For example, thin 14-year-old boys who diet in order to avoid becoming hypertensive like their fathers usually have strong, obsessive-compulsive features as well as lack of psychological separation from the parent involved.

Response to Treatment

The more ill the patient, the less the patient's gender makes a difference in the treatment. As patients achieve about 90% of their target weight and their medical complications are decreased, their sex and their role in society become increasingly important in further treatment. Males, we feel, need to come to terms with the social disapproval existing toward the expression of their emotions[30] and with the often-felt need to demonstrate a sense of bravado or daring. Their personality strengths might be hidden because of the social stereotype they feel they have to follow. This is especially true in those who have an "external locus of control," those males who are sensitive to pleasing the audiences around them.

Males also need to deal with the excessive emphasis on attaining a stereotyped masculine physique, typified by the "inverted triangle," emphasizing development of the chest and shoulder. Finally, for those males who find change in general difficult, the changing and sometimes confusing male role in our society can lead to a perception of a lack of role models on which to pattern their development and to a personal state of confusion.

In a series of 10 patients at Johns Hopkins followed for up to 6 years after treatment[31] and in larger studies by Crisp and Burns,[32] no deaths have been reported in males treated for an eating disorder. They also appear to have at least no worse a prognosis than females do but show greater incidence of drug and alcohol abuse. Vomiting in males has been found in one series to have a positive rather than negative correlation with outcome.[33] Overall, outcome in males has been closely related to adequacy of early family relationships and degree of sexual maturity prior to their illness.[34]

Osteoporosis has become recognized increasingly as a medical complication of eating disorders in women,[35] with some amelioration of the osteoporosis if the women were athletes. Although males do not have the risk factor of decreased estrogen, and, have been thought to be less vulnerable to osteoporosis, we have found that a substantial proportion of males with eating disorders also suffer from deficiencies in bone mineral density.[36]

☐ SUMMARY

The preponderance of available evidence suggests that anorexia nervosa and bulimia nervosa are separate and specific diagnostic entities, not reducible to the status of subsets of other psychiatric or medical disorders. They "breed true" and recur in a stereotyped fashion in those who develop chronic illness. The data also suggest that male athletes with eating disorders are a special case even when compared with other male athletes. Although both groups place a high value on changing body weight and shape as means of achieving athletic goals and many in both groups demonstrate compulsive and perfectionist personality traits, only the males with eating disorders can be characterized as having a distinctive and diagnosable psychopathology. Also, males with eating disorders tend to continue in a self-sustaining way in their abnormal thinking and behavior even when the environment changes, whereas many male athletes have temporary, situation-related symptoms that improve when the incentive for weight loss disappears, such as after the wrestling season. Although wrestlers, as one example of a vulnerable group of male athletes, have frequent and large cycles of weight loss that can have enduring medical consequences, many tend to normalize these behaviors when not in training. Eating-disorder patients and male athletes can therefore share a continued conflict between biology and psychology that occurs when body weight is pushed substantially below the "set point" at which the body self-regulates, leading to a constant struggle between the desire to eat and the desire to stay too lean or thin, between the inbuilt, neuroendocrine based, motivated behavior and the psychologically based, learned desire to attain a non-physiological weight goal.

Some male athletes, however, do not recover from their temporary form of eating-disorder-like symptoms when training is over but go on to develop true, lasting illness, as described earlier in Andy's case. The evidence is not sufficient at this point to state clearly whether participation in athletics, by itself, increases the risk for developing an eating disorder. We believe that the critical factor in promoting an eating disorder is the demand to change in body weight, body shape, or body composition, in a person vulnerable to carrying the process of body change to excess for a variety of reasons, including personality factors, past life experiences, mood disorders, and family dynamics.

Finally, males and females on the whole share more features than they have dissimilar features in regard to their eating disorders. Nonetheless, males are distinctive in their increased probability of a past history of obesity, dieting in relationship to sports, homosexual orientation (2- to 5-fold increase above the general population but still a minority of patients), and dieting defensively to avoid medical illness even when this is completely inappropriate. On follow-up, males seem to have at least as good a prognosis as females.

Because diagnosis of many psychiatric disorders depends on the mental status examination and finding the characteristic defining psychiatric symptoms, it follows that thorough, careful questioning is essential. Diagnoses by this method remain less reliable, however, as in the case of eating disorders, than in medical conditions in which a laboratory examination can lead to a specific diagnostic test result. Nonetheless, the role of the laboratory and other technical studies in medicine can be easily overemphasized. Many diagnoses in medicine still depend primarily on history and examination. For example, migraine headaches, temporal lobe epilepsy, and myocardial ischemia (angina) are among the common medical symptoms in which a good history is the primary means of diagnosis.

The question whether males with eating disorders represent a special case of psychiatric disorder also highlights the distinction between categories and dimensions in psychiatry, between qualitatively distinct disorders vs. states that are only abnormal because of their extremeness of a normal dimension. We present a final case history to provoke thought about just what constitutes an eating disorder in an athlete.

CASE HISTORY. Ed, a 22-year-old man, was referred for treatment of binge eating. As a child he suffered from encephalitis, which left him with mild difficulty in coordination. When he was 15 years old, he hit his head against another player while playing rugby and was unconscious for several minutes. A CT scan revealed hydrocephalus. He was told he had to stop playing rugby or he would risk permanent or severe brain damage. As a result of stopping rugby he gained weight, making him feel fat. In addition, because of his restrictions in athletic activities, the only thing he looked forward to was eating. Finally, he found that binge eating helped his episodes of low mood. Occasionally he experienced brief hypomanic episodes. Because he was worried about gaining too much weight from binge eating, he began to induce vomiting. As a result he was able to bring his weight down to 185 from 210 lb and also found a job involving physical activity of a kind that was not restricted. On mental status examination, Ed was a tall, fit young man with a slight speech problem and mild physical incoordination. He had difficulty in learning new information but was able to remember clearly things he had previously learned. His mood was low and he felt demoralized and inadequate. He denied fear of fatness or pursuit of thinness. He feared he would not be able to cope with episodes of depression if he stopped binge eating.

    Comment. Ed illustrates the difficulty of placing certain patients in a strict diagnostic category. He clearly had abnormal binge eating not under his own control, but he did not have the characteristic morbid fear of fatness or pursuit of thinness required for diagnosis of an eating disorder or distortion of body perception. He had a realistic fear of becoming obese if he kept on eating excessively without being able to exercise. He showed also how a young man who was confident in athletics, and then had to restrict his sports activities, can suffer lowered self-esteem and loss of a sense of identity. His diagnoses included an atypical eating disorder, bipolar mood disorder, possibly secondary to brain injury, self-critical personality traits, and history of encephalitis with mild brain damage. He had a partial bulimic syndrome, not meeting full criteria for an eating disorder, because of the lack of defining psychopathology.

☐ REFERENCES

1. Morton, R.: Phthisiologica: Or a treatise of consumptions. London, S. Smith and B. Walford, 1694.
2. Gull, W.W.: Anorexia nervosa. Trans. Clin. Soc. London, 7:22, 1874.
3. Crisp, A.H.: *Anorexia Nervosa: Let Me Be*. New York, Grune and Stratton, 1980.
4. Russell, G.F.M.: Anorexia Nervosa. *In* Textbook of Medicine. Edited by P.B. Beeson, and W. McDermott. Philadelphia, W.B. Saunders, 1975, pp. 1386–1389.
5. Cantwell, D.P., et al.: Anorexia nervosa. Arch. Gen. Psychiatry, 34:1087, 1977.
6. Piran, N., et al.: Personality disorder in anorexic patients. Int. J. Eating Disorders, 7:589, 1988.
7. Hollander, E., and Walsh, B.T.: Eating disorders and obsessive compulsive disorder. Symposium presented at meeting of American Psychological Association, New York, May 12–17, 1990.
8. Margolis, R., Spencer, W., Simpson, S., et al.: Co-morbid psychiatric conditions in eating disorder patients: A quantitative analysis by eating disorder subtype. Unpublished manuscript.
9. Woodall, C., DiDomenico, L. and Andersen, A.E.: Anorexia nervosa as a professional career identity: Quantitative study and response to treatment. Abstract presented at International Conference on Eating Disorders, New York, April 27–29, 1990.
10. Green, R.S., and Rau, J.H.: Treatment of compulsive eating disturbances with anticonvulsant medication. Am. J. Psychiatry, 131:428, 1974.
11. Thornton, J.S.: Feast or famine: Eating disorders in athletes. Physician Sports Med., 18:116, 1990.
12. MacConnie, S.E., et al.: Decreased hypothalamic gonadotropin-releasing hormone secretion in male marathon runners. N. Engl. J. Med., 315:411, 1986.
13. Pope, H.G., Jr., and Katz, D.L.: Homicide and near-homicide by anabolic steroid users. J. Clin. Psychiatry, 51:28, 1990.
14. Brower, K.J., et al.: Evidence for physical and psychological dependence on anabolic androgenic steroids in eight weight lifters. Am. J. Psychiatry, 147:510, 1990.
15. Andersen, A.E. and DiDomenico, L.: Diet vs. shape content of popular male and female magazines: A dose-response relationship to the incidence of eating disorders? Int. J. Eating Disorders, in press.
16. McKenna, P.J.: Disorders with overvalued ideas. Br. J. Psychiatry, 145:579, 1984.
17. Chipman, J.J., et al.: Excessive weight loss in the athletic adolescent: A diagnostic dilemma. J. Adolesc. Health Care, 3:247, 1983.
18. Scott, D.W.: Anorexia nervosa in the male: A review of clinical, epidemiological and biological findings. Int. J. Eating Disorders, 5:799, 1986.
19. Andersen, A.E. (ed.): Males with Eating Disorders. New York, Brunner/Mazel, 1990.
20. Andersen, A.E.: Practical Comprehensive Treatment of Anorexia Nervosa and Bulimia. Baltimore, Johns Hopkins University Press, 1985.

21. Garner, D., and Garfinkel, P.: Cultural expectations of thinness in women. Psychol. Rep., *47*:483, 1980.
22. Erikson, E.H.: Childhood and Society. 2nd Ed. New York, W.W. Norton, 1963.
23. Crisp, A.H.: Anorexia nervosa. Br. Med. J., *287*:855, 1983.
24. Andersen, A.E.: Anorexia nervosa and bulimia nervosa in males. *In* Diagnostic Issues in Anorexia Nervosa and Bulimia Nervosa. Edited by P. Garfinkel and D. Garner. New York, Brunner/Mazel, 1988, pp. 166–207.
25. Burns, T., and Crisp, A.H.: Outcome of anorexia nervosa in males. Br. J. Psychiatry, *145*:319, 1984.
26. Drewnowski, A., and Yee, D.K.: Men and body image: Are males satisfied with their body weight? Psychosom. Med., *49*:626, 1987.
27. Andersen, A.E.: HIV positive bulimic males: Tip of an iceberg? Abstract presentation at International Conference on Eating Disorders, New York, April 27–29, 1990.
28. Herzog, D.M., Norman, D.K., Gordon, C., and Pepose, M.: Sexual conflict and eating disorders in 27 males. Am. J. Psychiatry, *141*:989, 1984.
29. Simpson, S.G., DePaulo, J.R., and Andersen, A.E.: Bipolar II affective disorder in bulimic inpatients. Abstract presentation at meeting of American Psychological Association, Montreal, May 7–12, 1988.
30. Kearney-Cooke, A., and Steichen-Asch, P.: Men, body image, and eating disorders. *In* Males with Eating Disorders. Edited by A.E. Andersen. New York, Brunner/Mazel, 1990, pp. 54–74.
31. Andersen, A.E., and Mickalide, A.D.: Anorexia nervosa in the male: An underdiagnosed disorder. Psychosomatics, *24*:1066, 1985.
32. Crisp, A.H., and Burns, T.: Primary anorexia nervosa in the male and female: A comparison of clinical features and prognosis. *In* Males with Eating Disorders. Edited by A.E. Andersen. New York, Brunner/Mazel, 1990, pp. 77–99.
33. Crisp, A.H., Burns, T., and Bhat, A.V.: Primary anorexia nervosa in the male and female: A comparison of clinical features and prognosis. Br. J. Med. Psychol., *59*:123, 1986.
34. Burns, T., and Crisp, A.H.: Factors affecting prognosis in male anorexics. J. Psychiatr. Res., *19*:323, 1985.
35. Rigotti, N.A., Nussbaum, S.R., Herzog, D.B., and Neer, R.M.: Osteoporosis in women with anorexia nervosa. N. Engl. J. Med., *311*:1601, 1984.
36. Andersen, A.E.: Osteoporosis in males with eating disorders. Abstract presentation at International Conference on Eating Disorders, New York, April 27–29, 1990.

EFFECTS OF EATING AND WEIGHT PROBLEMS ON THE ATHLETE

GENERAL HEALTH ISSUES OF LOW BODY WEIGHT AND UNDEREATING IN ATHLETES

E. Randy Eichner

To a coach or team physician, the boundary between undereating and a bona fide eating disorder is vague. Whenever an athlete loses weight too fast or drops below a reasonable body weight, concerns arise about health and performance. Indeed, these practical concerns arise irrespective of the more academic concern as to whether the athlete has, by strict definition, a full-blown classical eating disorder.

This chapter covers the general health concerns that arise in the face of low body weight and undereating in athletes. The six case reports serve to illustrate such concerns. Not all six of these athletes meet the diagnostic criteria for anorexia nervosa or bulimia, yet all six case reports pose general health concerns.

Case 1. A 17-year-old girl, a distance runner, entered college on a track and cross-country scholarship. She had run 50 miles a week for 3 years and had lifted weights for 2 years. Five feet, nine inches tall, she weighed 128 lb, considered herself muscular but not fat, and had a zest for life. In college, she was told that elite athletes her height tend to weigh about 112 lb. She ran long distances and dieted rigidly, "weighing in" daily and quickly losing weight. She also studied hard and made good grades in honors classes. Within 3 months, approaching the "ideal" weight of 112 lb, she began running poorly, had trouble with bronchitis, and fainted during a workout. She cut back and quickly gained weight. Over the next few months her weight and emotions cycled widely. At times the thought of running made her cry, and she could barely drag herself out of bed. At the end of the school year she withdrew from college.

Comment. This sad case raises concerns about fatigue, infection, fainting, and depression in the face of social pressures, undereating, and rapid weight loss in a college runner striving desperately to reach an idealized goal.

Case 2. A 19-year-old college sophomore went out for lightweight crew. He weighed 172 lb, with body fat gauged at 15%. He was told to lose 17 lb of body fat to meet the qualifying weight of 155 pounds. He was instructed on how to create a negative energy balance, designed to lose 2 pounds a week of body fat while eating at least 2000 kcal per day. In the first 2 weeks he lost 12 pounds; he was told to eat more. One week later he weighed 155 pounds; he was sent to a counselor and physician, who found no organic disease. During this time he rowed well, was popular, and made good grades, but he had times of depression and cried during counseling. He ate almost nothing but admitted that the pain of his hunger felt "sort of good." His aversion to food became extreme. When given a cake to enjoy, he sobbed and could hardly touch it. When pressured to eat 3 cookies, he ran 14 miles as penance. He dropped to 140 lb, losing 32 lb in 6 weeks. Seeing the physician frequently, he trained intensely and made the team. When he finally agreed to eat meals with 2 teammates, he soon increased to the desired 155 lb. One year later he weighed 182 pounds, continued to do well academically, and competed in openweight rowing.[1]

Comment. This case raises concerns about the mental and physical health of a young perfectionist who sets extremely high academic and athletic goals and will brook no failure. In a heroic but misguided struggle, food becomes the "opponent" he must crush.

Case 3. A 25-year-old man was referred to a hematologist because he was found to have mild anemia. He had been obese when young but had lost weight as an adult. He lacked an intense fear of becoming fat but based his self-confidence on athletic ability. In fact, he was on a quest for "perfect physical fitness." For 2 years he had exercised frenetically, going from 158 lb to 118 lb. Every day he cycled 10 or 20 miles or ran 6 miles, lifted weights, did 300 sit-ups, 96 dips, and 75 push-ups. He became anxious when he did not exercise. He counted calories and weighed himself daily. He claimed, however, to eat 3 balanced meals a day and denied vomiting or the use of diuretics or laxatives. In the past 6 months, he had left training for the priesthood, worked as a waiter, worked in an auto parts store, sought work as an accountant, and worked as a landscaper. He had pressure sores, from sit-ups, over his sacrum and posterior pelvic bones. His hemoglobin was 12.2 g/dL, but he was not deficient in iron, folic acid, or vitamin B_{12}. Besides the mild, nonspecific anemia, he also had mild neutropenia and reticulocytopenia; the bone marrow was hypocellular with fat atrophy and gelatinous background. In other words, his bone marrow seemed to be "undernourished" and consequently was making too few red cells and white cells. His serum chemistries were normal, as was his stool fat. His caloric intake, based on an 8-day recording, was 1900 kcal per day.[2]

Comment. This case raises concerns about blood changes, anemia, and risk of infection in an "obligatory athlete" who is undereating. Is this man a dedicated athlete or merely a neurotic, compulsive exerciser?

Case 4. A 15-year-old boy who played competitive sports was seen by a physician because of austere dieting for 6 weeks and vomiting for 3 days. During this time he avoided friends and began to run 5 miles a day. He said he was dieting to attain a weight ideal for a distance runner. His diet was based on his misinterpretation of the recommendations in a popular book on running. His caloric intake was 1500 kcal per day, about half of his estimated energy needs. He was 5 ft 8½ in. tall and weighed 114.4 lb (40th percentile), having lost 12.5 lb in 6 weeks. Two months later he weighed 105.5 lb (20th percentile); he was hospitalized because of vomiting. He had a dilated stomach, but fortunately his blood potassium level was normal and his gastric function soon improved. Over the next 3 months he ran 5 miles almost daily. It was unclear whether he was a runner with a misguided diet or had anorexia nervosa with running as a symptom. On further study he had low testosterone and gonadotropin levels, suggesting sluggish pituitary and gonadal function. On exercise testing, his maximal oxygen uptake was slightly subnormal for his age and his maximal heart rate was relatively slow, at 165 beats per minute. He displayed a distorted body image, depression, and a general sense of inadequacy. During 12 weeks of psychotherapy, he gained 14.7 pounds and his hormonal levels, maximal heart rate, and maximal oxygen uptake all returned to normal.[3]

Comment. This case raises concerns about gastrointestinal function, blood electrolyte levels, heart function, exercise capacity, and hormonal function in an undereating athlete. It also illustrates how difficult and tentative it can be to differentiate an athletic patient with anorexia nervosa from an athlete who is obsessed with, and harmed by, losing too much weight too fast.

Case 5. A 29-year-old woman marathoner saw a physician because of leg swelling for 2 weeks. She also had amenorrhea for 2 years and mild fatigue for 2 months. Every day she ran 1 hour and then biked, swam, and instructed in a fitness center. She admitted to a low dietary intake. She was 5 ft 3 in. tall and weighed 91 lb (76% of ideal). She was pale and gaunt and seemed older than her stated age. She had lanugo, preadolescent sexual features, and pitting edema to the knees. Her serum albumin was normal, but she had iron deficiency anemia, with a hemoglobin of 8.2 g/dL and a serum ferritin under 5 ng/mL. When told to substitute walking for her rugged running program, she merely added the walking to her regimen. She also resisted dietary advice and refused to see a psychiatrist. At follow-up, her weight had dropped to 84 lb and her prognosis was uncertain.[4]

Comment. This case raises concern about edema, fatigue, and anemia, as well as about anorexia nervosa masquerading as "super fitness." Excessive physical activity can be one of the earliest signs of anorexia nervosa, even predating notable weight loss. The family physician's working diagnosis here is, in fact, anorexia nervosa.

Case 6. A 29-year-old woman physician volunteered to participate in clinical research that involved providing blood and urine samples. She had no symptoms and took no medicines. She ran up to 6 miles a day. Her weight was 116.6 lb and her height was 5 ft 2½ in, and she was concerned about her body image. Her serum potassium was 3.2 mmol/L (low) and serum bicarbonate was 29.3 mmol/L (high). She had a mild metabolic alkalosis (pH 7.48), and her urine was high in sodium and potassium but low in chloride. She emphatically denied vomiting.[5]

Comment. This case raises concerns about electrolyte abnormalities owing to surreptitious vomiting as a means of weight control.

Of the 6 athletes here, probably only cases 4 and 5 have bona fide anorexia nervosa; case 6 might have bulimia. The point, however, is that all 6 are undereating and losing weight. Regardless of the precise medical diagnoses here, no doubt each athlete has an eating disorder, and each case raises concerns about health. Taken together, the concerns here span the general health issues among low-weight, undereating athletes.

◻ FATIGUE

As suggested by cases 1 and 5, an eating disorder, or the combination of undereating and rapid weight loss, can contribute to chronic fatigue in an athlete. As detailed elsewhere in this book, pathogenic weight-control behavior is distressingly common in "low-weight" athletes, e.g., runners, gymnasts, wrestlers, dancers, and skaters.[6] Such athletes, in misguided attempts to lose fat fast, can also lose muscle and strength.

As nutritionist Nancy Clark has said, for these athletes, food is not fuel, but a "fattening enemy" that thwarts their desire to be thin. Their goal is thinness at any price—often a price of mental anguish, physical fatigue, and impaired athletic performance. To wit, one runner failed to connect her inability to finish track workouts with her "1 banana a day diet." She thought she fell asleep in classes because she got insufficient sleep, not because she was underfed.[7]

Indeed, in allusion to cases 1 and 4, in a survey of 182 collegiate women athletes, 1 in 3 went beyond dieting to self-induced vomiting or binging, or the taking of laxatives, diet pills, and/or diuretics.[8] Then, too, a survey of 93 adult, elite, American women distance runners found that 60% ate no more than 2000 kcal per day, even though their estimated daily need, considering their average daily run of 10 miles, was 2600 kcal.[7] Similarly, a survey from South Africa found that 18 (14%) of 125 women distance runners had abnormal eating attitudes similar to those of anorexia nervosa, although only 1 runner (0.8%) had been treated for anorexia nervosa.[9]

Consider also that, especially during the early weeks of endurance training, a runner, for example, compared with a sedentary counterpart, needs more protein, to replace and build muscle. To be sure, the body preferentially catabolizes carbohydrate and fat for energy, but if these are in short supply, it will instead burn protein. Indeed, although this area is controversial, consensus seems to hold that, depending largely on intensity and duration, aerobic exercise always burns some protein. For example, it has been said that, depending on energy supply and level of training, during a hard 2-hour run, up to 5 or 10% of the energy can come from protein.

Protein requirements seem to be higher yet if total caloric intake is low. Ponder again case 1. An impressionable young woman charges into intense endurance training and, under pressure from coaches and peers, also diets harshly to lose weight fast. Is it farfetched to assume that her fatigue and declining race performance were related, at least in part, to loss of muscle and strength?

Finally, recent research suggests that some athletes who overtrain suffer chronic fatigue because they eat too little carbohydrate to meet their energy demands. To wit, 12 male collegiate swimmers doubled, for 10 days, their usual daily distance. Four of the 12 could not tolerate this sudden doubling in training load; these 4, compared with the other 8, had low muscle glycogen stores because of low carbohydrate intake.[10]

☐ INFECTION

Are undereating, low-weight athletes prone to infection? Common sense would suggest so. After all, case 1 developed bronchitis and case 3 had a low white blood cell count. And epidemiologic surveys have suggested more frequent upper respiratory infections in hard-training Danish orienteers and in marathoners in South Africa and Los Angeles.

The problem, however, is that, logical as it seems, there is yet no proof that eating disorders, at least in the early stages, predispose the athlete to infection. In fact, even in frank anorexia nervosa, there is little evidence for increased infections, except in the most advanced stages.

Leukopenia, for example, occurs in up to 50% of patients with anorexia nervosa. Compared with normal controls, patients with anorexia nervosa have substantially lower total leukocyte counts and lower absolute neutrophil, lymphocyte, and monocyte counts. Yet, as one representative study of leukopenia and infections in 68 patients reflects, the incidence of infection in such patients is not clearly increased above normal.[11]

Similarly, patients with anorexia nervosa can have decreased serum levels of immunoglobulins and complement components[12] and even impaired cellular immunity,[13] but generally such changes are modest until the stage of extreme malnutrition and emaciation. To be sure, infection is a cause of death in anorexia nervosa, but it remains unclear whether the typical athlete with an eating disorder is necessarily at special risk of infection.

It seems reasonable to propose, however, that as undereating and weight loss lead to ever increasing malnutrition in the athlete with a serious eating disorder, immune defense will suffer in concert. Surely, at some point, the risk of infection will rise.

☐ ANEMIA

As shown by cases 3 and 5, anemia can occur in athletes with eating disorders. How common it is in such athletes we do not know, but it occurs in about 30% of patients with anorexia nervosa.

The anemia is usually mild, in the range of 10 to 12 g/dL. Sometimes, as in case 3, it is normocytic, normochromic, and not from iron deficiency or vitamin deficiency. In frank anorexia nervosa, anemia can be associated with pancytopenia and acanthocytes, or spurred red cells. In such cases, as in case 3, the bone marrow is hypoplastic, with fat largely replaced by a gelatinous ground substance consisting of an acid mucopolysaccharide. This unique bone marrow picture reflects that the critical deficiency in anorexia nervosa is carbohydrate and calories, the main source of marrow fat.[14]

In women athletes with mild eating disorders, however, the most common anemia is iron deficiency anemia, as shown by case 5. As I have stated elsewhere,[15] women athletes as a group are not uniquely prone to iron deficiency anemia. In contrast, women athletes who diet stringently and/or eat mainly vegetarian diets are prone to iron deficiency anemia. Although the new Recommended Dietary Allowance for iron for women is 15 mg per day (the old RDA was 18 mg), many elite women runners, for example, consume no more than 2000 kcal per day, for 12 mg of iron.

Also, because many women athletes, with eating disorders or not, are modified vegetarians, much of their dietary iron is not easily absorbed. Research shows that women runners who follow a modified vegetarian diet are at higher risk of iron deficiency that runners who eat some red meat.[16] And in general, low-weight women athletes, because they starve themselves, are those athletes most likely to develop iron deficiency anemia. Simply put, they eat insufficient iron to match their menstrual and training losses.

Anemia, of course, causes fatigue in athletes, but mild anemia causes fatigue only during all-out exertion, such as during racing, when the athlete notes undue breathlessness, heavy sweating, and, from buildup of lactic acid, heavy, "burning" muscles, "tying up," and even retching. At rest, no fatigue is noted, but cold intolerance can occur.

☐ CARDIOVASCULAR CHANGES

Great concern arises as to possible cardiovascular changes in undereating athletes. Yet the cardiovascular changes, if any, are subtle and mixed from athlete to athlete, and it is difficult to predict who will have problems. For example, the athletes in cases 1 and 4 had mild complications that might have been in part cardiovascular, i.e., fainting and impaired all-out performance, but those in cases 2 and 3 had no clear-cut cardiovascular symptoms despite harsh regimens. In fact, the athlete in case 2 thrived in his rowing despite rapid weight loss.

Arguing by analogy from anorexia nervosa and from the liquid protein diet fiasco of the 1970s, however, one worries about potential cardiovascular changes in any athlete who undereats and loses weight rapidly, especially in the face of potential electrolyte abnormalities from purging.

The cardiovascular changes of anorexia nervosa, detailed in the following chapter, comprise bradycardia, low blood pressure, orthostatic hypotension with syncope (fainting), a decrease in heart chamber size and wall thickness, and electrocardiographic abnormalities, e.g., low voltage, T-wave inversion, and ST-segment depression.[17-20] The decrease in left ventricular size can cause mitral valve prolapse that reverts to normal with weight gain.[21] Most studies agree that, in anorexia nervosa, maximal exercise heart rate and maximal exercise capacity are reduced.[22,23]

Most ominous in anorexia nervosa is the rare occurrence of ventricular tachyarrhythmias, associated with electrocardiographic Q-T prolongation, that can cause sudden death.[24] Such arrhythmias resemble those that, in the 1970s, killed 58 people on the liquid-protein, modified-fast diets. The cause of such arrhythmias in anorexia nervosa is debated, but it is likely to include wasting of heart muscle, changes in autonomic nervous tone, and/or abnormalities in electrolytes, especially calcium, magnesium, and potassium.

All considered, then, are the fainting and decline in athletic performance seen in the case studies here related, at least in part, to subtle cardiovascular changes from undereating and rapid weight loss? Perhaps so; perhaps not. Similarly, the edema in case 5 is nonspecific. Edema is common in anorexia nervosa, but its cause is unclear. As in case 5, the serum albumin is usually normal; probably the anemia contributed to the edema here.

In fact, edema in anorexia nervosa seems to be most common during refeeding, as part of a syndrome of temporary congestive heart failure. Refeeding rapidly increases plasma volume, cardiac output, and metabolic rate—all faster than the shrunken left ventricle can re-expand. The result is volume overload, cardiac decompensation, and edema.[25] It is unclear how much, if any, refeeding stresses the heart of an undereating, low-weight athlete who does not have full-blown anorexia nervosa.

☐ DEPRESSION

As shown by cases 1, 2, and 4, athletes who undereat can be depressed. Whether depression is the horse or the cart, however, is sometimes unclear. Another confounder is that, especially in adolescents, athletic "burnout" or staleness can merge into depression.[26]

Every adolescent feels blue at certain trying times; such a response is quite normal. A rigid diet and training regimen can, of course, worsen the problem. The normal athlete should, however, "snap out of it" within 2 weeks. If not, he or she could be suffering from depression.

The incidence of depression in the United States is increasing, especially among the young and among women. Girls as young as 12 are more prone to depression than boys, and a prime factor is their preoccupation with their appearance. Some see themselves as ugly or fat when objectively that is not the case.

The higher rate of depression among girls persists through adolescence and into adulthood, at which point women are twice as likely as men to be diagnosed as depressed. Among the signs of depression, these tend to be more common in girls: body image distortion; loss of appetite and weight; and lack of satisfaction with home, school, and social life. To what extent such thoughts plagued the athlete in case 1 is unknown, but experiences at the University of Texas[27] and elsewhere suggest that many women athletes, not to mention their coaches, alas, are culturally destined to focus unduly on body image.

In contrast, these signs of depression tend to be more common in boys: irritability; social withdrawal (as occurred in case 4); and drop in school performance.

Parents, coaches, and physicians should know how to recognize clinical depression in undereating athletes, because therapy, i.e., counseling and/or medication, can cure up to 90%. In contrast, without therapy, the result can be tragic. Depression should be considered if an athlete has, for more than 2 weeks, 4 or more of the symptoms listed in Table 13–1.

☐ ENDOCRINE ABNORMALITIES

Amenorrhea, osteoporosis, and stress fractures are cardinal features of eating disorders in women athletes, of course, but these are covered in another chapter. Suffice it to say here that the mental and physical stresses of undereating, low body fat, and rigorous training and competition can combine to suppress the hypothalmic-pituitary-gonadal axis in some women athletes.

A similar suppression can occur in hard-driving male athletes. That is, exhaustive endurance training can suppress testicular function. For example, when 6 endurance athletes doubled the duration of their cycling for 2 weeks, all developed general fatigue and reported a decline in sex drive and sexual activity. Their plasma testosterone fell 17%, and

TABLE 13–1. SYMPTOMS THAT CAN INDICATE DEPRESSION

Change in appetite
Major weight loss or gain without obvious dieting
Change in sleep pattern: Too much or too little
Waking in the morning 2 or more hours early
Feeling sad and moving slowly
Loss of interest in or pleasure from activities formerly enjoyed
Fatigue or loss of energy
Feeling worthless or inappropriately guilty
Inability to concentrate, decide, or think
Irritability
Thoughts of death or suicide

Adapted from Eichner, E.R.: Chronic fatigue in adolescent athletes. Your Patient and Fitness, 1:8, 1989.

their sperm counts also tended to fall.[28] Whether undereating plays any role here is unknown.

Undereating can also affect the thyroid gland. Like illness itself, severe undereating and/or strenuous exercise, perhaps in part by releasing cortisol, can inhibit the peripheral conversion of thyroxine (T_4) to triiodothyronine (T_3), thereby creating the "euthyroid sick syndrome." The relative lack of T_3, the body's most potent thyroid hormone, lowers the body's metabolic rate.[18] Teleologically, this unique form of mild hypothyroidism seems to be "adaptive," i.e., seems designed to conserve energy and otherwise combat the ravages of mental and physical stress.

The euthyroid sick syndrome occurs in anorexia nervosa, of course, but to what extent it occurs in the milder degrees of undereating in low-weight athletes is uncertain. It does seem, however, to be part of the syndrome of "overtraining" or staleness in endurance athletes.

Certain elite athletes have tried to reverse the euthyroid sick syndrome by taking increasing doses of thyroxine. Unfortunately, they ended up doing more harm than good, e.g., suffering a decline in maximal oxygen uptake and undue racing of the heart during all-out effort. The best way to treat the euthyroid sick syndrome is to exercise less and eat more.

METABOLIC AND MISCELLANEOUS ABNORMALITIES

Electrolyte abnormalities can be a clue to bulimia. As case 6 shows, a metabolic alkalosis with a low blood potassium suggests surreptitious vomiting. A low potassium can raise the risk of cardiac arrhythmias in an athlete and can also cause muscular fatigue. Other clues to hidden bulimia are covered elsewhere.

The most common renal abnormality in the face of an eating disorder is an increase in the blood urea nitrogen, usually the result of dehydration. Dehydration probably occurs most often in the face of vomiting, purging, or the use of diuretics. In general, kidney function is normal in the eating disorders.

Some undereating athletes have mild elevations in the blood "liver chemistries," most likely as a result of mild fatty change of the liver, which can occur as a result of malnutrition.[17,18,20]

Vitamin deficiencies, fortunately, are not common in the eating disorders, but abnormal bleeding because of vitamin K deficiency has been reported in a young woman with bulimia.[29]

Gastrointestinal problems can range from constipation and abdominal pain, especially in anorexia nervosa, to diarrhea from the surreptitious taking of laxatives. Dilatation of the stomach, with delayed emptying, can occur, as in case 4. Rarely, persistent vomiting can cause more serious gastrointestinal problems;[19] these are covered in Chapter 14.

Paradoxically, severe undereating, as seen in anorexia nervosa at least, can increase blood levels of low-density lipoprotein cholesterol. In theory, this metabolic change, if long-lasting, would boost the risk of coronary heart disease. The pathophysiologic mechanism is unknown. Fortunately, with weight gain, the cholesterol falls to normal. We need more research on how undereating affects the blood cholesterol profile in low-weight athletes.[30]

☐ REFERENCES

1. Smith, N.J.: Excessive weight loss and food aversion in athletes simulating anorexia nervosa. Pediatrics, 66:139, 1980.
2. Liberman, R.B., and Palek, J.: Hematologic abnormalities simulating anorexia nervosa in an obligatory athlete. Am. J. Med., 76:950, 1984.
3. Chipman, J.J., et al.: Excessive weight loss in the athletic adolescent: A diagnostic dilemma. J. Adolesc. Health Care, 3:247, 1983.
4. Eichner, E.R.: 36th annual meeting of the American College of Sports Medicine: Clinical highlights and perspective. IM—Int. Med. Specialist, 10:99, 1989.
5. Kamel, K.S., Ethier, J., Levin, A., and Halperin, M.L.: Hypokalemia in the "beautiful people." Am. J. Med., 88:534, 1990.
6. Brownell, K.D., Steen, S.N., and Wilmore, J.H.: Weight regulation practices in athletes: Analysis of metabolic and health effects. Med. Sci. Sports Exerc., 19:546, 1987.
7. Clark, N., Nelson, M., and Evans, W.: Nutrition education for elite female runners. Phys. Sportsmed., 16:124, 1988.
8. Rosen, L.W., McKeag, D.B., Hough, D.O., and Curley, V.: Pathogenic weight-control behavior in female athletes. Phys. Sportsmed., 14:79, 1986.
9. Weight, L.M., and Noakes, T.D.: Is running an analog of anorexia? A survey of the incidence of eating disorders in female distance runners. Med. Sci. Sports Exerc., 19:213, 1987.
10. Costill, D.L., et al.: Effects of repeated days of intensified training on muscle glycogen and swimming performance. Med. Sci. Sports Exerc., 20:249, 1988.
11. Bowers, T.K., and Eckert, E.: Leukopenia in anorexia nervosa: Lack of increased risk of infection. Arch. Intern. Med., 138:1520, 1978.
12. Wyatt, R.J., et al.: Reduced alternative complement pathway control protein levels in

anorexia nervosa: Response to parenteral alimentation. Am. J. Clin. Nutr., *35:*973, 1982.
13. Pertschuk, M.J., Crosby, L.O., Barot, L., and Mullen, J.L.: Immunocompetency in anorexia nervosa. Am. J. Clin. Nutr., *35:*968, 1982.
14. Amreain, P.C.: Friedman, R., Kosinski, K., and Ellman, L.: Hematologic changes in anorexia nervosa. JAMA, *241:*2190, 1979.
15. Eichner, E.R.: Anemia in female athletes. Your Patient Fitness, *3:*3, 1989.
16. Synder, A.C., Dvorak, L.L., and Roepke, J.B.: Influence of dietary iron source on measures of iron status among female runners. Med. Sci. Sports Exerc., *21:*7, 1989.
17. Herzog, D.B., and Copeland, P.M.: Eating disorders. N. Engl. J. Med., *313:*295, 1985.
18. Brotman, A.W., Rigotti, N., and Herzog, D.B.: Medical complications of eating disorders: Outpatient evaluation and management. Compr Psychiatry, *26:*258, 1985.
19. Mitchell, J.E., Seim, II.C., Colon, E., and Pomeroy, C.: Medical complications and medical management of bulimia. Ann. Intern. Med., *107:*71, 1987.
20. Palla, B., and Litt, I.F.: Medical complications of eating disorders in adolescents. Pediatrics, *81:*613, 1988.
21. Myers, D.G., Starke, H., Pearson, P.H., and Wilken, M.K.: Mitral valve prolapse in anorexia nervosa. Ann. Intern. Med., *105:*384, 1986.
22. Moodie, D.S., and Salcedo, E.: Cardiac function in adolescents and young adults with anorexia nervosa. J. Adolesc. Health Care, *4:*9, 1983.
23. Nudel, D.B., Gootman, N., Nussbaum, M.P., and Shenker, I.R.: Altered exercise performance and abnormal sympathetic responses to exercise in patients with anorexia nervosa. J. Pediatr., *105:*34, 1984.
24. Isner, J.M., Roberts, W.C., Heymsfield, S.B., and Yager, J.: Anorexia nervosa and sudden death. Ann. Intern. Med., *102:*49, 1985.
25. Powers, P.S.: Heart failure during treatment of anorexia nervosa. Am. J. Psychiatry, *139:*1167, 1982.
26. Eichner, E.R.: Chronic fatigue in adolescent adults. Your Patient Fitness, *1:*3, 1989.
27. Thornton, J.S.: Feast or famine: Eating disorders in athletes. Phys. Sportsmed., *18:*116, 1990.
28. Griffith, R.D., Dressendorfer, R.H., Fullbright, C.D., and Wade, C.E.: Testicular function during exhaustive endurance training. Phys. Sportsmed., *18:*54, 1990.
29. Niiya, K., et al.: Bulimia nervosa complicated by deficiency of vitamin K-dependent coagulation factors. JAMA, *250:*792, 1983.
30. Mordasini, R., Klose, G., and Greten, H.: Secondary type II hyperlipoproteinemia in patients with anorexia nervosa. Metabolism, *27:*71, 1978.

MEDICAL ISSUES IN THE EATING DISORDERS

Claire Pomeroy and James E. Mitchell

Our society values winning, and all too often the motto becomes "success at any cost." Athletes—from the weekend jogger to the professional—are particularly subject to such pressures. As has been discussed in previous chapters, the athlete frequently responds to pressures to improve performance by losing weight and can be at risk of developing an eating disorder such as anorexia nervosa or bulimia nervosa. Tragically, the eating disorder can result in serious medical problems[1-5] and even death.[6,7]

Coaches, teachers, trainers, parents, team physicians, and the athletes themselves must be aware of the potential medical complications of eating disorders in athletes and the appropriate approach to medical management. Early diagnosis and referral for treatment are essential to protecting the health of athletes. All too often signs and symptoms of eating disorders are ignored or trivialized until serious medical damage has occurred.

☐ MISUSE OF LAXATIVES, DIET PILLS, IPECAC, AND DIURETICS

Athletes have long used and abused drugs to control their weight. For example, among male jockeys, one study found that food avoidance, use of saunas, laxative abuse, diuretic abuse, and the use of appetite suppressants were commonly used to control weight.[8] Some high school wrestlers use dieting, binging and vomiting, sweating and fluid restriction for weight control.[9] The use of laxatives and diuretics for weight control also is frequent in female athletes, including gymnasts, ballet dancers, and swimmers. It is not known how many of the athletes who abuse these substances meet criteria for a diagnosis of an eating disorder.[10] Nevertheless, it is clear that many of these behaviors exist on a continuum and may present health hazards for the athlete.

The abuse of these substances has been better studied in people with a diagnosed eating disorder. Individuals with eating disorders, especially those with bulimia nervosa, might misuse certain drugs in an attempt to promote weight loss, suppress appetite, minimize food absorption, or induce vomiting. Several classes of drugs can be misused by these patients, including diet pills, diuretics, laxatives, and the drug ipecac, which is used to induce vomiting.[11] In one survey of 275 bulimic women, 60.6% had used laxatives for weight control, 50.2% had used diet pills, and 33.9% had used diuretics.[12]

LAXATIVES

Laxatives are probably the type of drug most commonly abused by individuals with bulimia.[13] The reported prevalence of laxative misuse and abuse by bulimics has ranged from 18 to 75%. The misuse of laxatives among bulimic women usually involves ingestion of amounts of the drug many times in excess of the amount recommended by the manufacturer. Stimulant-type laxatives are most frequently used, especially Ex-Lax and Correctol.[13] Abuse of laxatives is an ineffective method of weight loss, because the weight loss that occurs is due to temporary fluid loss rather than prevention of caloric absorption.[13]

Several of the commonly available stimulant laxatives that are abused by bulimics are listed in Table 14–1. All of these laxatives contain at least one stimulant compound, the most common ones being a dyphenyl-methane derivative, phenolphthalein, and an anthraquinone, cascara sagrada. Docusate sodium, a stool softener, is also included in several of the products. The dyphenylmethane derivatives act directly on the colon by increasing colonic motility, as does cascara sagrada, a product obtained from the bark of the cascara buckthorn tree.[11]

DIET PILLS

Although many persons with bulimia nervosa use diet pills, long-term, high-dose abuse is uncommon, possibly because of the side effects of these drugs or their relative lack of efficacy in promoting weight loss.[11] A few bulimics, however, do use large amounts, occasionally in conjunction with amphetamines, and such patients are at high risk of health problems. Data on several commonly available over-the-counter diet pills are summarized in Table 14–2. All of these drugs contain phenylpropanolamine as an active ingredient.

TABLE 14–1. COMMONLY AVAILABLE OVER-THE-COUNTER LAXATIVES

BRAND	ACTIVE INGREDIENT	RECOMMENDED AMOUNT (mg)	RECOMMENDED DOSAGE/DAY*	NUMBER IN PACKAGE
Correctol	Tablets—yellow phenolphthalein and docusate sodium	65 100	1 or 2	15, 30, 60, 90
Ex-Lax	Liquid—yellow phenolphthalein Yellow phenolphthalein	65 90	tblsp 1 or 2	8, 16 fl oz 6, 18, 48, 71 (chocolate) 8, 30, 60 (unflavored) 24, 48 (extra gentle)
Feen-a-Mint gum	Yellow phenolphthalein	97.2	1 or 2	5, 16, 40
Feen-a-Mint pills	Yellow phenolphthalein and docusate sodium	65 100	1 or 2	15, 30, 60
Nature's Remedy	Casara sagrada Aloe	150 100	2	12, 30, 60

* Recommended dosing as listed on package.
From: Mitchell, J.E., Pomeroy, C., and Huber, M.: A clinician's guide to the eating disorders medicine cabinet. Int. J. Eating Disorders, 7:211, 1988.

TABLE 14–2. COMMONLY AVAILABLE OVER-THE-COUNTER DIET PILLS

BRAND	ACTIVE APPETITE SUPPRESSER	RECOMMENDED AMOUNT (mg)	RECOMMENDED DOSAGE/ DAY†	RECOMMENDED NUMBER IN PACKAGE
Acutrim 16 Hour	Phenylpropanolamine HCL	75	1	20, 40
Acutrim II Max. Duration	Phenylpropanolamine HCL	75	1	20, 40
Appendrine Max. Strength	Phenylpropanolamine HCL	25	3	30, 60
Control Max. Strength	Phenylpropanolamine HCL	75	1	14, 28, 56
Dexatrim	Phenylpropanolamine HCL	50	1	28, 56
Dexatrim Extra Strength*	Phenylpropanolamine HCL	75	1	16, 26, 32, 40
Dexatrim 15	Phenylpropanolamine HCL	75	1	20, 40
Dietac	Phenylpropanolamine HCL	75	1	20, 40
Prolamine Max. Strength	Phenylpropanolamine HCL	37.5	2	20, 50
Super Odrinex	Phenylpropanolamine HCL	25	3	50, 110

* Two formulations available: Extra strength with Vitamin C (20, 40) and Caffeine-Free Extra Strength (16, 32).
† Recommended package dosing schedule.
From Mitchell, J.E., Pomeroy, C., and Huber, M.: A clinician's guide to the eating disorders medicine cabinet. Int. J. Eating Disorders, 7:211, 1988.

These compounds have been the source of considerable debate among clinicians and researchers relative to both their efficacy and safety. There is a large, mostly anecdotal medical literature reporting side effects and toxicities for these drugs. These have included elevated blood pressure, renal failure, seizures, and a variety of adverse central nervous system effects, including agitation, anxiety, memory loss, transient neurological deficits, and intracranial hemorrhages.[11] The precise effects of these drugs in athletes, most of whom are not overweight, have yet to be investigated.

IPECAC

Some persons with eating disorders abuse ipecac syrup as a way of inducing vomiting. In one series, 28% of bulimics reported having used the drug. One bulimic who had used over 2000 doses of ipecac developed a severe myopathy.[11]

Ipecac syrup is dispensed in bottles containing 30 mL of the syrup, which is the equivalent of 21 mg of emetine base. Emetine is apparently responsible for the serious cardiomyopathy and skeletal muscle myopathy that can develop. Despite several case reports of fatal ipecac-induced cardiomyopathies, ipecac remains available as a nonprescription drug.

DIURETICS

Because diuretics are available in a wide variety of over-the-counter formulations as well as by prescription, the exact prevalence of diuretic use among athletes, or among persons with eating disorders, remains unknown. Three to four percent of females in high school and college populations report having used diuretics, and in one study 33.9% of bulimic women reported diuretic use specifically for weight-control purposes.[12]

Over-the-counter diuretic preparations are used most commonly by women in the general population for control of "idiopathic edema" and control of symptoms associated with the "premenstrual syndrome," particularly the attendant weight gain. The pathogenesis of idiopathic edema is unknown, and some research has suggested that it might actually be secondary to diuretic use. The normal fluctuation in weight during the menstrual cycle can lead to initiation of diuretic use, which is followed by stimulation of the renin-angiotensin-aldosterone system because of the fluid loss. When the diuretic is discontinued, reflex fluid retention results.[11] Instead of allowing the system to readjust and weight to return to baseline, the patient resumes diuretic use believing that continued diuretic use is required to control the edema. Clearly not all people who use diuretics for idiopathic edema or relief of symptoms associated with premenstrual syndrome abuse the drug, and not all women who abuse diuretics have bulimia nervosa or other eating disorders. The link might be common, however, and it is probably unrecognized in many cases.

Several types of prescription diuretic drugs are available. The major groups and their mechanisms of action and side effects are summarized in Table 14–3. Abuse of thiazide diuretics or loop diuretics is associated with hypokalemia and metabolic alkalosis, which place the patient at risk for cardiac conduction defects, arrhythmias, hypokalemic nephropathy, and hypokalemic cardiomyopathy.

In our experience, most but not all bulimics who misuse or abuse diuretics actually use over-the-counter preparations, which are summarized in Table 14–4. Most of the over-the-counter diuretics contain pamabrom, ammonium chloride, or caffeine as the diuretic ingredient.[11] The effects of these over-the-counter diuretics in individuals with eating disorders who might use excessive amounts of these drugs and who might have associated electrolyte abnormalities is unknown.

TABLE 14–3. MECHANISM OF ACTION AND MAJOR SIDE EFFECTS OF COMMONLY USED PRESCRIPTION DIURETICS

CLASS OF DIURETICS	EXAMPLES	MECHANISM OF ACTION	MAJOR SIDE EFFECTS
Thiazide diuretics	Chlorothiazide Hydrochlorothiazide	Inhibit Na^+ reabsorption in distal tubules	Decreased extracellular fluid volume with 2° hyperaldosteronism Potassium depletion and metabolic alkalosis Hyponatremia Hyperglycemia, hyperuricemia, and hyperlipidemia Zinc and magnesium depletion Hypercalcemia
Loop diuretics	Furosemide Ethacrynic acid	Inhibit Na^+ reabsorption in thick ascending limb of loop of Henle	Decreased extracellular fluid volume with 2° hyperaldosteronism Potassium depletion and metabolic alkalosis Magnesium depletion Hypocalcemia Hyponatremia Hyperuricemia Ototoxicity, cross-reaction in sulfa-allergic patients
Potassium-sparing diuretics	Spironolactone	Competitive inhibition of the effect of aldosterone on the distal tubule	Hyperkalemia and metabolic acidosis
	Triameterene	Direct inhibition of Na^+ transport in the distal tubule	Hyperkalemia and metabolic acidosis Triameterene nephrolithiasis Acute renal failure (with indomethacin)
Carbonic anhydrase inhibitors	Acetazolamide	Inhibits carbonic anhydrase and thus proximal bicarbonate reabsorption	Mild hyperchloremic metabolic acidosis with potassium depletion

From Mitchell, J.E., Pomeroy, C., and Huber, M.: A clinician's guide to the eating disorders medicine cabinet. Int. J. Eating Disorders, 7:211, 1988.

TABLE 14–4. COMMONLY AVAILABLE OVER-THE-COUNTER DIURETICS*

BRAND	ACTIVE DIURETIC INGREDIENT	AMOUNT (mg)	RECOMMENDED DOSAGE/DAY	NUMBER IN PACKAGE
Premesyn-PMS	Pamabrom (with 15 mg pyrilamine maleate)	25	8/d	20, 40
Sunril Premenstrual Capsules	Pamabrom (with 25 mg pyrilamine maleate)	50	4/d	100
Midol-PMS	Pamabrom (with 15 mg pyrilamine maleate)	25	8/d	32
Odrinil	Pamabrom	25	8/d	60
Diurex-MPR	Pamabrom	25	8/d (no more than 10 consecutive d/mo except by physician's recommendation)	28
Pamprin Menstrual Relief	Pamabrom (with 15 mg pyrilamine maleate)	25	8/d	24, 48 tabs 16, 21 caps
Aqua-Ban	Ammonium chloride	325	6/d	60
	Caffeine	100	(no more than 6 d per mo)	
Maximum Strength Aqua-Ban Plus	Ammonium chloride	650	3/d	30
	Caffeine	200	(no more than 6 d per mo)	
Odrinil Natural Diuretic	Caffeine (with herbal extracts)	Not specified	4/d	—
Diurex	Caffeine (with uva ursi, buchu)†	Not specified	4/d	42

* Preparations containing merely a small amount of caffeine and therefore having limited diuretic effects are not included in this table.

† Extract buchu and extract uva ursi have been classified as Category II (not generally recognized as safe and effective or misbranded) for menstrual symptoms by the Food and Drug Administration.

From Mitchell, J.E., Pomeroy, C., Seppala, M., and Huber, M.: Pseudo-Bartter's syndrome, diuretic abuse, idiopathic edema and eating disorders. Int. J. Eating Disorders, 7:225, 1988.

☐ SPECIFIC MEDICAL COMPLICATIONS OF EATING DISORDERS

Anorexia nervosa and bulimia nervosa can cause serious, at times fatal, medical complications.[14] The mortality in anorexia nervosa has been reported to be as high as 19%, death is usually attributable to inanition, fluid and electrolyte abnormalities, or suicide.[7] Mortality in bulimia nervosa is less well studied but deaths do occur, usually secondary to the complications of binge-eating or purging or the complications of laxative, ipecac, diet pill, or diuretic abuse. The major medical complications of anorexia nervosa are summarized in Table 14–5, and the major medical complications of bulimia nervosa are summarized in Table 14–6.

RENAL AND ELECTROLYTES

Electrolyte problems, and of particular concern hypokalemia (low serum and total body potassium levels) are common in persons with eating disorders.[15,16] Many of the deaths attributable to eating disorders are due to electrolyte abnormalities. Decreased intake can exacerbate the problem, and significant potassium loss can occur secondary to diuretic abuse or laxative-induced diarrhea. In addition, diuretic abuse and vomiting often result in a severe contraction alkalosis that makes correction of potassium levels difficult.[17] Many persons with low potassium levels are asymptomatic, and it is impossible to predict when a life-threatening cardiac arrhythmia will occur.

Elevated serum blood urea nitrogen (BUN) levels are found in both anorectics and bulimics, usually attributable to fluid restriction or fluid losses. Decreased glomerular rates are common, and decreased urinary concentrating ability might explain the polyuria experienced by some such patients.[18] Stimulation of the renin-angiotensin-aldosterone system can result in pseudo-Bartter's syndrome.[17]

CARDIOVASCULAR

The most serious manifestations of hypokalemia are usually cardiac. Arrhythmias can be asymptomatic, cause palpitations, or result in inadequate cardiac output and death.[6] Normalization of potassium values is a critical aspect of care for the eating-disordered individual.

Cardiac arrhythmias are most commonly seen in patients with hypokalemia but can occur in the absence of electrolyte abnormalities.[19] Bradycardia is common, and a variety of non-specific ST–T wave abnormalities can be observed on the electrocardiogram. Of more concern, serious conduction defects and ventricular arrhythmias can occur.

Other cardiac complications of eating disorders are less common. Refeeding cardiomyopathy is a possible consequence of overly aggressive refeeding in anorexia nervosa. Bulimics who abuse ipecac can develop a different form of cardiomyopathy.[20] In addition, an association be-

TABLE 14–5. MEDICAL COMPLICATIONS OF ANOREXIA NERVOSA

ORGAN SYSTEM	COMPLICATION
Cardiovascular	Bradycardia
	Orthostasis/hypotension
	Congestive heart failure
	EKG abnormalities
	Mitral valve prolapse
	Refeeding edema
	Refeeding cardiomyopathy
	Sudden cardiac death
Endocrine	Growth retardation
	Delayed onset of puberty
	Elevated growth hormone levels
	Abnormal hypothalamic-pituitary-gonadal axis:
	Amenorrhea
	Low plasma LH, FSH levels
	Low plasma estradiol levels
	Low progesterone levels
	Lack of LH, FSH response to gonadotropin-releasing hormone
	Decrease urinary excretion of pituitary gonadotropins and estrogens
	Abnormal hypothalamic-pituitary-thyroid axis:
	Depressed T_3 formation from T_4 leading to low T_3 levels
	Preferential deiodination to "reverse T_3" (with normal T_4 levels)
	Abnormal hypothalamic-pituitary-adrenal axis:
	Increased plasma cortisol levels
	Loss of normal diurnal variation of plasma cortisol levels
	Nonsuppression on DST (dexamethasone suppression test)
	Elevated CSF levels of CRF
	Decreased endogenous opioids (?)
Gastrointestinal	Delayed gastric emptying
	Superior mesentery artery syndrome
	Gastric dilatation and rupture
	Refeeding pancreatitis
	Increased incidence of elevated liver enzyme tests (?)
Pulmonary	Subcutaneous emphysema
Dermatologic	Hair loss
	Lanugo-like hair growth on face and trunk
	Dry skin, brittle hair and nails
	Petechiae, purpura (2° to thrombocytopenia)
Renal	Decreased glomerular filtration rate
Neurological	Enlarged external CSF-spaces on head CT scans
	Caudate hypermetabolism on PET scans (?)
Metabolic	Zinc deficiency (rare)
	Other trace mineral deficiencies (rare)
	Hypovitaminosis A (rare)
	Other vitamin deficiencies, incl. pellagra and scurvy (all rare)
	Osteoporosis
	Osteopenia
	Increased plasma cholesterol
	Increased plasma carotene
Hematological	Anemia
	Leukopenia with relative lymphocytosis
	Thrombocytopenia
	Low erythrocyte sedimentation rates
Impaired thermoregulation	

From Pomeroy, C., and Mitchell, J.E.: Medical complications and management of eating disorders. Psychiatr. Ann., *19*:488, 1989.

TABLE 14–6. MEDICAL COMPLICATIONS OF BULIMIA NERVOSA

ORGAN SYSTEM	COMPLICATION
Cardiovascular	Bradycardia
	Orthostasis, hypotension
	EKG abnormalities
	Arrhythmias (usually secondary to hypokalemia)
	Congestive heart failure
	Myocarditis (secondary to ipecac abuse)
	Hypokalemic cardiomyopathy
	Cardiomyopathy secondary to ipecac abuse
	Sudden cardiac death
	Idiopathic edema (secondary to diuretic abuse?)
	Increased incidence of mitral valve prolapse (?)
Endocrine	Nonsuppression on dexamethasone suppression test
	Irregular menses
	Abnormal serotonin metabolism
	Hypoglycemia
	Blunting of TSH response to TRH (?)
	Blunting of GH response to TRH (?)
	Elevated fasting prolactin levels (?)
	Failure of GH to suppress in response to oral glucose (?)
	Low estradiol levels, abnormal luteal phase, low progesterone levels (?)
Salivary/parotid gland hypertrophy	
Gastrointestinal	Hyperamylasemia
	Pancreatitis
	Esophageal perforation
	Esophagitis
	Mallory-Weiss tears
	Delayed gastric emptying
	Gastric dilatation and rupture
	Constipation
	Cathartic colon
	Melanosis coli
	Hypokalemic ileus
	Steatorrhea and protein-losing gastroenteropathy (secondary to laxative abuse)
	Abnormal liver enzymes
Pulmonary	Aspiration pneumonitis (secondary to self-induced vomiting)
	Pneumomediastinum
Dermatologic	Russell's sign (finger calluses and abrasions)
Fluid and electrolytes	Dehydration
	Hypokalemia
	Hypochloremia
	Metabolic alkalosis
	Hyponatremia
	Hypocalcemia (rare)
	Hypophosphatemia (rare)
	Hypomagnesemia
Renal	Reduced glomerular filtration rate
	Tubular dysfunction
	Kaliopenic nephropathy
	Elevation of BUN
	Pyuria, hematuria
	Proteinuria
	Polydipsia, polyuria
Neurological	EEG abnormalities (?)
Dental	Enamel erosion
	Periodontal disease
Disordered thermoregulation	

From Pomeroy, C., and Mitchell, J.E.: Medical complications and management of eating disorders. Psychiatr. Ann., *19*:488, 1989.

tween mitral valve prolapse with both anorexia nervosa and bulimia nervosa has been reported.[21,22]

Finally, both anorexia nervosa and bulimia nervosa are associated with dehydration, orthostatic blood pressure changes, and hypotension. In anorexia nervosa, this is primarily due to restriction of fluid intake, whereas in bulimia nervosa, self-induced vomiting and abuse of laxatives and diuretics usually are implicated.

ENDOCRINE

The endocrine abnormalities associated with anorexia nervosa have been extensively studied. Recent research on endocrine abnormalities in bulimia nervosa has suggested more subtle endocrine system abnormalities, which in some cases have been difficult to consistently confirm. Menstrual irregularities, including amenorrhea, are among the most prominent symptoms of eating disorders in women.[23] The influences of healthy exercise and frank eating disorders on menstrual function are discussed in Chapter 15.

Women with anorexia nervosa often have low levels of plasma estradiol, luteinizing hormone (LH), and follicle-stimulating hormone (FSH). An "immature" response (resembling that of premenarchal girls) of LH and FSH to gonadotropin-releasing hormones can be seen. Amenorrhea is often accompanied by growth retardation and delayed onset of puberty. Many women with bulimia nervosa experience irregular menses, but frank amenorrhea is uncommon.[23]

Although amenorrhea or irregular menses are hallmarks of eating disorders, many questions about their causes still remain. Originally amenorrhea was presumed to be attributable solely to weight loss or weight fluctuations, because similar abnormalities occur in other forms of starvation. Some evidence suggests, however, that there might be primary dysfunction of the hypothalamic-pituitary function in a subgroup of individuals with eating disorders. First, amenorrhea in anorexia nervosa has been shown to often precede or coincide with the onset of food refusal, and resumption of menses does not always correlate with weight restoration. Second, bulimics who are of normal weight also have an increased incidence of irregular menses. One recent study found fewer LH secretory spikes and blunted LH responses to estradiol in both anorectic and bulimic subjects compared to controls.[24] Stimulation with gonadotropin-releasing hormone produced exaggerated LH responses in bulimic subjects but blunted responses in anorectic subjects.[24] The authors concluded that abnormalities of the hypothalamic-pituitary-gondal axis could not be attributed solely to emaciation.

Abnormal thyroid function tests are frequently found in people with anorexia nervosa.[25] The "low T_3 syndrome" is due to decreased peripheral conversion of T_4 to T_3 and reflects the state of semistarvation. There is preferential deiodination to "reverse T_3," a less-active form of the hormone. Thus symptoms such as fatigue, constipation, and hypothermia can be caused by thyroid abnormalities despite normal T_4 levels.

Extensive abnormalities of the hypothalamic-pituitary-adrenal system have been described in anorexia nervosa.[26-28] Sustained hypercortisolism is one of the best characterized neuroendocrine abnormalities in anorexia nervosa.[26] Both plasma and cerebrospinal levels of free cortisol are elevated, plasma ACTH levels are generally normal, and cerebrospinal fluid ACTH levels are low.[27] Elevated plasma cortisol levels are caused both by increased production and by slowed metabolism.[29] Thus nonsuppression of cortisol by dexamethasone is common in anorectic patients, and the dexamethasone suppression test must be interpreted with caution.

The hypothalamic-pituitary-adrenal system has been less extensively evaluated in patients with bulimia nervosa. Some studies have found that plasma cortisol and ACTH levels in bulimics were similar to those in controls,[26] whereas a more recent study found that bulimic women have elevated plasma cortisol and ACTH levels with a blunted response to corticotropin releasing hormone (CRH).[30] The authors of the latter study suggested that these abnormalities might be due to central activation of CRH because they occurred in the absence of weight disturbances.[30] Nonsuppression on the dexamethasone test occurs in 20 to 67% of bulimic subjects.[31]

Other endocrine abnormalities in bulimia nervosa are less well studied. Acute hypoglycemia has been reported anecdotally. Although some studies have reported elevated prolactin levels and abnormal responses of growth hormone and thyroid stimulating hormone to provocative stimuli,[32] the abnormalities occur in a small percentage of subjects and have not been confirmed in other studies. Studies of endocrine abnormalities in bulimia nervosa are an important area of ongoing research.[33]

METABOLIC

New advances in our ability to quantitate bone loss have facilitated the documentation of osteopenia and osteoporosis in many patients with anorexia nervosa.[34,35] This is not surprising because conditions associated with low estrogen levels are often complicated by the development of osteoporosis. These abnormalities result in an increased propensity for fractures. Both hypogonadism (low estradiol levels) and hypercortisolemia might contribute to the development of osteoporosis in patients with anorexia nervosa.[34,36] In contrast, recent study found that bone density was similar in bulimic subjects and controls.[36] More information on osteoporosis is presented in Chapter 16.

Serum cholesterol elevations have been frequently reported in persons with anorexia nervosa.[15] Elevated serum carotene levels are found in up to 72% of persons with anorexia nervosa and are sometimes associated with frank carotenodermia.[37] Hypercarotenemia is primarily a result of elevation of vitamin A active carotenoids, especially B-carotene.[25] Zinc and other trace metal deficiencies are rare complications. Vitamin deficiencies, including pellagra and scurvy, are rare.

PAROTID AND SALIVARY GLANDS

Swelling of the parotid or submandibular glands or both is a classical finding in persons with bulimia nervosa and often is one of the few physical examination clues to the diagnosis of an eating disorder in bulimics.[38] Resolution of salivary gland hypertrophy after successful treatment of the eating disorder is the norm, although this can take several months.

GASTROINTESTINAL

Gastrointestinal complications are a major source of morbidity for persons with eating disorders.[39] The impaired gastric emptying described in patients with both anorexia nervosa and bulimia nervosa can contribute to feelings of "bloating" and early satiety.[40] Abdominal pain is frequent. Often no serious pathology can be identified and symptoms must be attributed to altered gastrointestinal motility. In anorexia nervosa, abdominal pain also can be due to vascular compression of the third portion of the duodenum—the so-called "superior mesenteric artery syndrome."

In bulimics and anorectics who vomit, recurrent vomiting of acidic stomach contents can result in painful esophagitis and esophageal strictures. Forceful vomiting also can cause tears in the esophagus (Mallory-Weiss tears) with bleeding.[41]

As discussed above, laxative abuse is a common practice among bulimic women and causes a wide variety of medical problems. Chronic use can result in the loss of normal colonic peristalsis. Cathartic colon (loss of normal colon function) can become severe and can even necessitate colonic resection. Chronic recurrent use of stimulant-type laxatives results in gastrointestinal bleeding, ranging from occult to frank blood loss. Stimulant-type laxatives promote fluid loss through the intestine. This can result in volume depletion and lead to a secondary hyperaldosteronism, causing reflex peripheral edema, which becomes particularly problematic during laxative withdrawal. Laxative-induced diarrhea markedly elevates the electrolyte content of the feces and can result in hypokalemia and acidosis. Other medical complications of laxative abuse include the development of steatorrhea and protein-losing gastroenteropathy, pancreatic dysfunction, osteomalacia, pseudofractures, hypocalcemia, and hypomagnesemia.[13]

Abdominal pain in patients with an eating disorder can herald other, potentially life-threatening, complications. Gastric dilatation after a binge-eating episode can proceed to potentially fatal gastric necrosis and rupture, requiring immediate surgical intervention.[42] Esophageal rupture must also be treated as an emergency. Mallory-Weiss tears and gastrointestinal bleeding require aggressive medical or surgical management.

Finally, a recent report describes five patients who relapsed during therapy for hyperlipidemic pancreatitis and were diagnosed with an eating disorder.[43] One of these patients died following an episode of acute pancreatitis. These cases emphasize the need for establishing the diagnosis of an eating disorder and providing appropriate therapy.

DERMATOLOGIC

Dermatologic complications of eating disorders have recently been extensively reviewed.[37] Complications can be divided into four major groups: those associated with starvation and malnutrition, those associated with self-induced vomiting, those associated with drugs consumed to promote weight loss, and those associated with concomitant psychiatric illnesses.[37] In the first group, hair loss and development of lanugo-like hair occur in up to 29% of anorectics and are often particularly distressing to the patient. Dry skin and brittle nails are often found in anorexia nervosa. In the second group, calluses on the dorsum of the hand, called "Russell's sign," are a good clue to the diagnosis of bulimia nervosa. Erosions and calluses on the hands result from damage to the skin by the teeth during attempts to induce vomiting. In the third group, fixed drug eruptions secondary to phenolphthalein-containing laxatives and photosensitivity due to thiazide diuretics have been reported. Finally, self-inflicted dermatoses can be diagnosed in eating disorders patients with concomitant psychiatric illnesses.[37]

PULMONARY

Spontaneous pneumomediastinum and subcutaneous emphysema can occur in persons with anorexia nervosa and bulimia nervosa.[4] The mechanism is poorly understood. Although it seems logical that vomiting could be responsible by raising intrathoracic pressures, this complication has been described in patients who do not vomit. In addition, chemical pneumonitis from aspiration of acidic stomach contents or bacterial aspiration pneumonia can also complicate bulimia nervosa.

HEMATOLOGIC

Leukopenia, anemia, and thrombocytopenia all have been reported in persons with anorexia nervosa. If starvation is severe, frank marrow cell necrosis can occur.[44] Although leukopenia with a relative lymphocytosis is seen in anorexia nervosa, there is no good evidence of increased risk of bacterial infections.[45] Hematologic abnormalities have not been described with bulimia nervosa.

Coagulopathy due to a deficiency of vitamin-K-dependent factors has been reported but apparently is quite rare.[46]

NEUROLOGIC

Because many of the basic control systems for feeding behavior are located in the central nervous system, examination of the neurological system has been an area of significant research. Enlarged ventricles and sulci on computed tomography (CT) scans have been described in patients with anorexia nervosa and bulimia nervosa.[47-49] These abnormalities have been termed "pseudoatrophy" of the brain. In addition, abnormalities in brain glucose metabolism, specifically hypermetabolism in the caudate region, can be detected by positron emission tomography (PET) scans.[50] These findings again raise the possibility of a primary hypothalamic dysfunction in patients with eating disorders, but this remains speculative. Further research is necessary to establish the pathophysiology and significance of these abnormalities.

Several reports have suggested that persons with anorexia nervosa have abnormal EEG patterns, especially fragmentation of sleep continuity and reduction of rapid eye movement (REM) sleep, but these studies have been difficult to consistently replicate.[3] A more recent study found that the subset of eating-disordered patients with "pseudoatrophy" on CT scan had decreased REM sleep and that this correlated with high cortisol levels and low T_3 levels.[51] Further research into these areas might provide more clues about the basic causes of eating disorders.

DENTAL

Dental abnormalities generally occur only in the subset of people with eating disorders who engage in self-induced vomiting. Decalcification of the lingual, palatal, and posterior occlusal surfaces of the teeth is commonly seen, indicating that the acid is coming from the back of the mouth.[52,53] Because amalgams are resistant to acid, they become much more obvious due to the erosion of enamel. Some researchers have found an increased incidence of caries, but several recent reports have failed to show this association.

TEMPERATURE REGULATION

Disordered thermoregulation might contribute to the cold intolerance experienced by many persons with eating disorders. Persons with anorexia nervosa often demonstrate exaggerated fluctuations in core body temperature when exposed to extremes of environmental temperature. Many persons with eating disorders also complain of Raynaud's phenomenon in the cold and easy vasodilatation and swelling of the hands and feet in warm temperatures. These symptoms can be quite disabling, but unfortunately little is known about the pathogenesis of these phenomena and no specific therapy is available.

☐ RECOGNITION OF EATING DISORDERS

Excessive weight loss is the most prominent clue to the recognition of anorexia nervosa and is often quite obvious. In contrast, the athlete with bulimia nervosa can appear physically healthy and recognition of the disorder might only occur with discovery of the associated behaviors of purging and laxative or diuretic abuse.

Individuals with anorexia nervosa usually will not complain of weight loss. In fact, they view themselves as normal or overweight, and unfortunately this misperception can be encouraged by others who believe that further weight loss might be beneficial to athletic performance.

Bulimia nervosa patients are often successful in hiding their illness from others. Binge-eating and purging are most often done in private. Abuse of diet pills, laxatives, diuretics, or ipecac is often done in secret and can escape detection or be denied by the athlete. If the bulimic does present for medical care with nonspecific complaints of lethargy, feeling "bloated," constipation, or swelling of the hands and feet, the diagnosis can be missed if the physician misses these subtle clues. Even patients might not realize that their symptoms are manifestations of the eating disorder. As with anorexia nervosa, the recognition of bulimia nervosa requires a high awareness that athletes are at risk for these eating disorders and a willingness to address the problem.

☐ ROLE OF THE PHYSICIAN

When an athlete is recognized as having a possible eating disorder, referral to a physician for a complete history and physical examination is essential. Referral to a family practitioner or general internist is often the first step toward adequately identifying and treating an eating disorder. The physician should assess whether the patient does indeed have an eating disorder, determine the presence of medical complications, and arrange for appropriate treatment of the eating disorder itself and the medical complications.

Other patients might enter the health care delivery system by attending a clinic specializing in treatment of eating disorders. Such clinics are present in many larger cities and are usually staffed by a variety of health care professionals who can attend to the psychiatric, physical, and social needs of the patient. Still other patients might wish to see a psychiatrist or psychologist who is experienced in treating patients with eating disorders. Unfortunately a few patients still enter the system through the hospital emergency room with life-threatening medical problems.

Whatever route is chosen, the most important thing is for these individuals to get help. Eating disorders can be successfully treated. It is up to the athlete, his or her teammates, parents, coach, teacher, and physician to make sure that warning signs are not ignored.

At the initial visit, the physician should take a careful medical history in a nonjudgmental and caring atmosphere.[14] The most common symptoms are summarized in Table 14–7. Inquiries about dietary habits and weight history should be routine. Menstrual irregularities are an important clue to the presence of an eating disorder. Particular attention should be paid to a history of use of diuretics, ipecac, diet pills, or

TABLE 14–7. COMMON SYMPTOMS AND SIGNS OF EATING DISORDERS

ANOREXIA NERVOSA	BULIMIA NERVOSA
Symptoms	Symptoms
Amenorrhea	Irregular menses
Constipation	Abdominal pain
Abdominal pain	Lethargy
Cold intolerance	Fatigue, headaches
Lethargy	Depression
Anxious energy	Swelling of hands/feet
Fatigue, headaches	Bloating
Signs	Signs
Hypotension	Russell's sign
Hypothermia	Parotid gland enlargement
Dry skin	Dental: enamel erosion
Lanugo-like hair	Often appear healthy
Bradycardia	
Edema	
Inanition	

laxatives.[3] Next, a thorough physical examination should be performed. The history will provide clues to areas that should be emphasized in the physical examination, but careful attention should always be paid to the degree of inanition, state of hydration, dental abnormalities, and the cardiac and gastrointestinal systems.[14] The most common physical examination signs of eating disorders are summarized in Table 14–7.

Choice of laboratory tests should be guided by the results of the history and physical examination.[14] Most patients with eating disorders should have a complete blood count, (BUN), creatinine, electrolytes, blood glucose, thyroid function tests, and a stool guaiac test for occult blood. Liver enzymes, muscle enzymes (creatine phosphokinase and aldolase), amylase, cholesterol, calcium, and magnesium tests are also frequently indicated. An electrocardiogram with rhythm strip is desirable for some patients. Specific complaints or abnormalities on physical examination might necessitate a chest radiograph, electromyography, or abdominal radiographic or endoscopic evaluation. Finally, if diuretic or laxative abuse is suspected but denied by the patient, urine samples to detect the surreptitious use of such agents can be ordered.[14]

☐ MANAGEMENT OF THE MEDICAL COMPLICATIONS OF EATING DISORDERS

Correction of body weight in anorexia nervosa poses a challenge to both the clinician and the patient. Although there is no absolute weight below which patients should be hospitalized to achieve weight gain, the physician should consider degree of inanition, likelihood of compliance with outpatient care, and presence of medical complications in making the choice between outpatient and inpatient refeeding. Gradual restitution of caloric intake is the most desirable approach. In severe cases, liquid supplements can be used initially. Total parenteral nutrition (TPN) should be reserved for the unusual case in which other methods have failed and the risks of TPN can be justified. Forced refeeding should be avoided if at all possible due to the obvious deleterious psychological effects. Careful attention to cardiac and electrolyte monitoring should be maintained, especially during the initial high-risk period.

Correction of electrolyte abnormalities is essential. In cases in which hypokalemia is significant, consideration should be given to oral potassium supplementation. Unfortunately, the efficacy of oral potassium can be abrogated by the presence of contraction metabolic alkalosis, which must be corrected before the serum potassium level can be normalized. This usually involves the cessation of vomiting, and the patient must understand the importance of not vomiting. In the presence of marked alkalosis, dehydration, or hypokalemia, hospitalization for intravenous fluid and electrolyte management needs to be considered.

Attention also must be given to interrupting the associated behaviors of laxative, ipecac, and diuretic abuse. Patients who stop laxatives often suffer from transient constipation. The use of stimulant laxatives should be avoided, and bulk-type laxatives, roughage, regular exercise, and hydration should be encouraged. Discontinuation of diuretics can result in reflex edema formation, which is often quite troublesome to the patient and can interfere with successful therapy. Mild sodium restriction during the first few days following discontinuation of diuretics and reassurance that fluid balance will soon normalize are useful.

Dental consultation for bulimic patients who have been vomiting frequently is strongly recommended.[52] The use of bicarbonate rinses can curtail future enamel erosion.

☐ SUMMARY

Athletes are at risk of developing an eating disorder and can develop serious medical complications. Those working with athletes must not encourage unhealthy weight restriction and must teach athletes to avoid the use of substances such as laxatives, diet pills, and diuretics to promote weight loss. If an athlete is diagnosed as having an eating disorder, it is essential that he or she be referred for treatment of the eating disorder itself and any medical complications. Preserving the health of the athlete must be the ultimate goal.

☐ REFERENCES

1. Harris, R.T., et al.: Eating disorders: Diagnosis and management by the internist. South. Med. J., 79:871, 1986.

2. Jacobs, M.B., and Schneider, J.A.: Medical complications of bulimia: A prospective evaluation. Q.J. Med., *54*:177, 1985.
3. Mitchell, J.E.: Medical complications of anorexia nervosa and bulimia. Psych. Med., *1*:229, 1983.
4. Mitchell, J.E., Seim, H.C., Colon, E., and Pomeroy, C.: Medical complications and medical management of bulimia. Ann. Intern. Med., *107*:71, 1987.
5. Palla, B., and Litt, I.F.: Medical complications of eating disorders in adolescents. Pediatrics, *81*:613, 1988.
6. Isner, J.M., Roberts, W.C., Heymsfield, S.B., and Yager, J.: Anorexia nervosa and sudden death. Ann. Intern. Med., *102*:49, 1985.
7. Patton, G.C.: Mortality in eating disorders. Psych. Med., *18*:947, 1988.
8. King, M.B., and Mezey, G.: Eating behavior of male racing jockeys. Psychol. Med., *17*:249, 1987.
9. Woods, E.R., Wilson, C.D., and Masland, R.P.: Weight control methods in high school wrestlers. J. Adolesc. Health Care, *9*:394, 1988.
10. American Psychiatric Association: Diagnostic and Statistical Manual of Mental Disorders. 3rd Edition. Revised. Washington, DC, American Psychiatric Association, 1987.
11. Mitchell, J.E., Pomeroy, C., and Huber, M.: A clinician's guide to the eating disorders medicine cabinet. Int. J. Eating Disorders, *7*:211, 1988.
12. Mitchell, J.E., Hatsukami, D., Eckert, E.D., and Pyle, R.L.: Characteristics of 275 patients with bulimia. Am. J. Psychiatry, *142*:482, 1985.
13. Mitchell, J.E., and Boutacoff, L.I.: Laxative abuse complicating bulimia: Medical and treatment implications. Int. J. Eating Disorders, *5*:325, 1986.
14. Pomeroy, C., and Mitchell, J.E.: Medical complications and management of eating disorders. Psychiatr. Ann., *19*:488, 1989.
15. Mira, M., Stewart, P.M., Vizzard, J., and Abraham, S.: Biochemical abnormalities in anorexia nervosa and bulimia. Ann. Clin. Biochem., *24*:29, 1987.
16. Mitchell, J.E., et al.: Electrolyte and other physiological abnormalities in patients with bulimia. Psychiatr. Med., *13*:273, 1983.
17. Mitchell, J.E., Pomeroy, C., Seppala, M., and Huber, M.: Pseudo-Bartter's syndrome, diuretic abuse, idiopathic edema and eating disorders. Int. J. Eating Disorders, *7*:225, 1988.
18. Boag, F., et al.: Diminished creatinine clearance in anorexia nervosa. Reversal with weight gain. J. Clin. Pathol., *38*:60, 1985.
19. Schocken, D.D., Holloway, J.D., and Powers, P.S.: Weight loss and the heart. Arch. Intern. Med., *149*:877, 1989.
20. Palmer, E.P., and Guay, A.T.: Reversible myopathy secondary to abuse of ipecac in patients with major eating disorders. N. Engl. J. Med., *313*:1457, 1985.
21. Meyers, D.G., Starke, H., Pearson, P.H., and Wilken, M.K.: Mitral valve prolapse in patients with anorexia nervosa. Ann. Intern. Med., *105*:384, 1986.
22. Johnson, G.L., et al.: Mitral valve prolapse in patients with anorexia nervosa and bulimia. Arch. Intern. Med., *146*:1525, 1986.
23. Pirke, K.M., Fichter, M.M., Chlond, C., and Doerr, P.: Disturbances of the menstrual cycle in bulimia nervosa. Clin. Endocrinol., *27*:245, 1987.
24. Devlin, M.J., et al.: Hypothalamic-pituitary-gonadal function in anorexia nervosa and bulimia. Psychiatr. Res., *28*:11, 1989.
25. Curran-Celentano, J., Erdman, J.W., Nelson, R.A., and Grater, S.J.E.: Alterations in vitamin A and thyroid hormone status in anorexia nervosa and associated disorders. Am. J. Clin. Nutr., *42*:1183, 1985.
26. Gold, P.W., et al.: Abnormal hypothalamic-pituitary-adrenal function in anorexia nervosa. N. Engl. J. Med., *314*:1334, 1986.
27. Gwirtsman, H.E., et al.: Central and peripheral ACTH and cortisol levels in anorexia nervosa and bulimia. Arch. Gen. Psychiatry, *46*:61, 1989.

28. Hudson, J., et al.: Hypothalamic-pituitary-adrenal axis hyperactivity in bulimia. Psychiatr. Res., *8:*111, 1983.
29. Boyar, R.M., et al.: Cortisol secretion and metabolism in anorexia nervosa. N. Engl. J. Med., *296:*190, 1977.
30. Mortola, J.F., Rasmussen, D.D., and Yen, S.S.C.: Alterations of the adrenocorticotropin-cortisol axis in normal weight bulimic women: Evidence for a central mechanism. J. Clin. Endocrinol. Metab., *68:*517, 1989.
31. Mitchell, J.E., Pyle, R.L., Hatsukami, K., and Boutacoff, L.I.: The dexamethasone suppression test in patients with bulimia. J. Clin. Psychiatry, *45:*508, 1984.
32. Kiriike, N., et al.: Thyrotropin, prolactin and growth hormone responses to thyrotropin-releasing hormone in anorexia nervosa and bulimia. Biol. Psychiatry, *22:*167, 1987.
33. Levy, A.B.: Neuroendocrine profile in bulimia nervosa. Biol. Psychiatry, *25:*98, 1989.
34. Biller, B.M.K., et al.: Mechanisms of osteoporosis in adult and adolescent women with anorexia nervosa. J. Clin. Endocrinol. Metab., *68:*548, 1989.
35. Rigotti, N.A., Nussbaum, S.R., Herzog, D.B., and Neer, R.M.: Osteoporosis in women with anorexia nervosa. N. Engl. J. Med., *311:*1601, 1984.
36. Newman, M.M., and Halmi, K.A.: Relationship of bone density to estradiol and cortisol in anorexia nervosa and bulimia. Psychiatr. Res., *29:*105, 1989.
37. Gupta, M.A., Gupta, A.K., and Haberman, H.F.: Dermatologic signs in anorexia nervosa and bulimia nervosa. Arch. Dermatol., *123:*1386, 1987.
38. Ogren, F.P., et al.: Transient salivary gland hypertrophy in bulimics. Laryngoscope, *97:*951, 1987.
39. Ceuller, R.E., and VanThiel, D.H.: Gastrointestinal consequences of the eating disorders. Anorexia nervosa and bulimia. Am. J. Gastroenterol., *81:*1113, 1986.
40. Shih, W-J, et al.: Tc-99m labeled triethelene tetraamine polysterene resin gastric emptying studies in bulimia patients. Eur. J. Nucl. Med., *13:*192, 1987.
41. Ceullar, R., et al.: Upper gastrointestinal tract dysfunction in bulimia. Dig. Dis. Sci., *33:*1549, 1988.
42. Abdu, R.A., Garritano, D., and Culver, O.: Acute gastric necrosis in anorexia nervosa and bulimia. Arch. Surg., *122:*830, 1987.
43. Gavish, D., et al.: Bulimia: An underlying behavioral disorder in hyperlipidemic pancreatitis: A prospective multidisciplinary approach. Arch. Intern. Med., *147:*705, 1987.
44. Smith, R.R.L., and Spivak, J.L.: Marrow cell necrosis in anorexia nervosa and involuntary starvation. Br. J. Haematol., *60:*525, 1985.
45. Bowers, T.K., and Eckert, E.: Leukopenia in anorexia nervosa: Lack of increased risk of infection. Arch. Intern. Med., *138:*1520, 1978.
46. Niya, K., Kitagawa, T., and Fumishita, M.: Bulimia nervosa complicated by deficiency of vitamin K dependent coagulation factors. JAMA, *250:*792, 1983.
47. Krieg, J-C., Backmund, H., and Pirkem, K-M: Cranial computed tomography findings in bulimia. Acta Psychiatr. Scand., *75:*144, 1987.
48. Krieg, J-C, et al.: Brain morphology and regional cerebral blood flow in anorexia nervosa. Biol. Psychiatry, *25:*1041, 1989.
49. Krieg, J-C., Pirke, K-M., Lauer, C., and Backmund, H.: Endocrine, metabolic, and cranial computed tomography findings in anorexia nervosa. Biol. Psychiatry, *23:*377, 1988.
50. Herholz, K., et al.: Regional cerebral glucose metabolism in anorexia nervosa measured by positron emission tomography. Biol. Psychiatry, *22:*43, 1987.
51. Lauer, C., et al.: The effect of neuroendocrine secretion on brain morphology and EEG sleep in patients with eating disorders. Eur. Arch. Psychiatr. Neurol. Sci., *238:*208, 1989.
52. Simmons, M.S., Grayden, S.K., and Mitchell, J.E.: The need for psychiatric-dental liaison in the treatment of bulimia. Am. J. Psychiatry, *143:*783, 1986.
53. Roberts, M.W., and Li, S-H.: Oral findings in anorexia nervosa and bulimia nervosa: a study of 47 cases. J. Am. Dent. Assoc., *115:*407, 1987.

EATING, BODY WEIGHT, AND MENSTRUAL FUNCTION

Michelle P. Warren

Eating behavior and body weight appear to profoundly influence women's reproductive cycles. The effects of nutrition on fertility have been appreciated since the time of Darwin,[1] who observed that reproductive function was impaired under conditions of inadequate nutritional intake. This phenomenon has also been appreciated by anthropologists such as Vande Walt et al.,[2] who noted decreased fertility during the dry season in the hunter-gatherer !Kung people of the Kalahari desert when food supplies were short. Inadequate nutrition can have profound effects on different aspects of menstrual function, including delayed menarche, inadequate luteal phases, and infertility. Athletic activity appears to compound the effects of inadequate nutrition and low body weight.[3] Studies on athletes have shown that the exercise-induced reproductive dysfunction is difficult to induce with exercise alone,[3] and physical activity alone without other predisposing factors has been increasingly questioned as a cause of reproductive dysfunction. Some of the predisposing factors have included low body weight or body fat stores, changes in nutrition, eating disorders, weight loss and a history of late menarche or previous menstrual irregularity.[3-8] The quantity and quality of the diet might be involved, as well as the perceived stress of the activity and the loss of body fat.[7-10]

☐ DELAYED MENARCHE

Poor nutrition, dietary behavior, low weight, and a high exercise load with athletic training can have profound effects at puberty, when the hypothalamic-pituitary axis is immature. All of these factors are seen in young ballet dancers studying for entry into professional schools. The necessity to conform to a body type considered ideal for their art often forces dancers to weigh less than 10 to 20% below accepted standards. Associated with this thin body type, pubertal development can be profoundly delayed, the first period on the average occurring at 15 years in contrast to the normal 12.9 (Figure. 15–1).[4] One study showed that the first period in dancers was related to degree of leanness, whereas

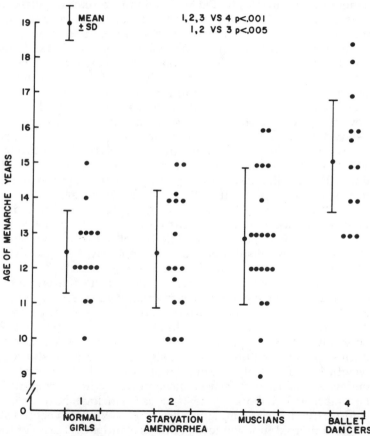

FIG. 15–1. Ages of menarche in ballet dancers compared with those in three groups. 1, 2, 3 vs. 4, P < 0.01; 1, 2 vs. 3, P < 0.05. From Warren, M.P.: The effects of exercise on pubertal progression and reproductive function in girls. J. Clin. Endocrinol. Metab., *51*:1150, 1980.

in a control group it was correlated (as expected) to the mother's reported age of menarche.[11] Thus this environmental influence overrides the genetic effects. In a group of swimmers, each year of training prior to menarche was reported to be associated with a 4-month delay in the first period.[10] Aside from dancers[12] and swimmers, this delay is also seen in gymnasts and figure skaters, in whom low body weight is desirable and whose adolescent training is intensive.[3-5]

The mechanism for the suppression of puberty is not well understood, but it undoubtedly involves suppression of luteinizing hormone (LH) pulsatile secretion in the pituitary by a lack of normal stimulatory activity in the hypothalamus in the brain. Normal puberty is heralded by pulses of gonadotropin-releasing hormone (GnRH), which in turn stimulate LH. How GnRH is suppressed is not completely understood, but it is thought to be due to altered activities of signals driving the GnRH pulse generator—neurons situated in the arcurate nucleus of the hypothalamus. Attempts at isolating specific metabolic substrates that might cause this problem have been unsuccessful. LH suppression can be reproduced by food restriction in rats, sheep, and monkeys.[13] Over the last few decades, some investigators have suggested that a threshold of body weight, later refined to percent body fat, is critical to the initiation of puberty. This simplified hypothesis is attractive because it associates much demographic data showing later maturation with poor nutrition. Low body weight and low body fat are undoubtedly associated with delayed menarche. It is unlikely, however, that body weight or body composition triggers or delays puberty. Metabolic cues are probably associated with low body weight, however, but these have yet to be identified. Recent literature also suggests that the reproductive alterations represent an adaptive effect that conserves energy.[14]

Delayed menarche is impressive in some cases. Some dancers have their first period as late as the early twenties, and 5 to 40% report some delay in the first period. Growth is not affected, distinguishing this syndrome from constitutional delay of puberty, but growth can be compromised if an eating disorder is present as well.[15]

Evaluation of delayed menarche in the setting of exercise should focus on the usual workup for primary amenorrhea; history of growth and development is important; breast and pubic hair appearance, weight loss and diet, somatic abnormalities, and exercise training should also be examined. Some patients deny weight loss, but continued growth during puberty without an increase in weight constitutes a relative weight loss. Physical examination should evaluate weight, height, secondary sexual characteristics, and a pelvic or rectal examination should be performed. Laboratory tests usually include hormonal studies including LH, follicle-stimulating hormone (FSH), prolactin, estradiol levels, and thyroid function tests; bone age and a CAT scan of the pituitary are done only if indicated. The usual pattern of tests reveals a low estrogen, normal prolactin, and low to normal LH and FSH levels. Treatment depends on whether growth has been completed (usually confirmed by a bone age assay) and presence of complications, if any.

Athletes, in particular, might report stress fractures. The feasibility of decreasing activity or gaining weight, or both, should be addressed because these changes often resolve the problem.

☐ SECONDARY AMENORRHEA

Secondary amenorrhea, or cycles without ovulation, is another menstrual problem seen with exercise training and weight loss. The prevalence varies but has been reported to be 2 to 20% in runners (50% in elite runners) and 30 to 50% in professional dancers.[3-9] Abnormal menstrual cycles occur more frequently in competitive athletes and are related to the amount of exercise; they are more common in women with delayed menarche, in vegetarians, in sports in which it is advantageous to be underweight, and in women with previously irregular cycles.[3-10] One study showed that amenorrheic runners can become more energy efficient by lowering their metabolic rate and their thermic response to food,[14] although other studies have not confirmed this.[16] Others have speculated that dieting and intense exercise deplete energy stores, stimulating the body to increase food efficiency.[17]

A popular theory has maintained that low body fat is the cause of amenorrhea. Twenty-two percent body fat is thought to be necessary for maintenance of regular cycles.[18] This variable has been increasingly challenged as a causal mechanism, however. Regular cycles are seen in athletes with less than 17% body fat, and amenorrheic and eumenorrheic runners have been found to have similar percentages of body fat.[19,20] Thus the fact that reproductive dysfunction is not commonly seen in athletes who have a high percent body fat probably reflects metabolic parameters other than weight or body fat. Loss in weight can profoundly affect cycles in athletes (Fig. 15–2). Recent research on specific fat stores suggests that fat stores are gender-specific; depletion of regional fat stores that accumulate below the waist in the mature female can signal inadequate reserves for pregnancy and lactation. This might in turn affect GnRH function.[17]

The decrease in pulse frequency of LH secretion that is seen in delayed menarche is also apparent with secondary amenorrhea (Fig. 15–3).[21,22] Similar alterations of the GnRH pulse generator in the hypothalamus are probably causing these problems. A definite dampening of LH pulses occurs in this kind of menstrual dysfunction, and occasionally a reversion to pubertal and prepubertal types of LH secretion occurs with spiking of LH pulses at night. A variety of hormonal changes occurs with exercise,[4] but studies on exercise-related amenorrhea continue to be hampered by the inability to control for stress, the use of different exercise protocols, the lack of longitudinal studies and of a precise definition of the "amenorrhea" with detailed hormonal and reproductive endocrine classification. Multiple hormonal changes occur with exercise,[23,24] but it is unclear whether the hormonal adaptation to endurance training is connected with the development of menstrual cycle abnor-

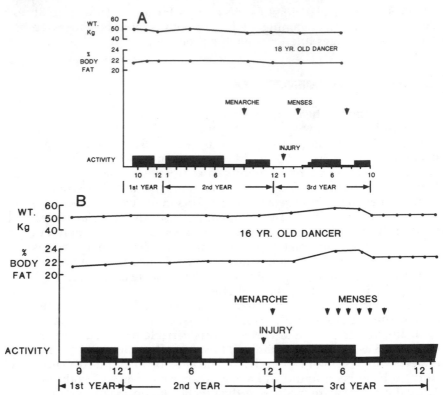

FIG. 15–2. Relationships among menses, exercise, weights, and calculated body fat values in two young ballet dancers. From Warren, M.P.: The effects of exercise on pubertal progression and reproductive function in girls. J. Clin. Endocrinol. Metab., *51*:1150, 1980.

malities. Menstrual cycle dysfunction has been difficult to induce by training of normal women, particularly without weight loss,[25–30] although minor abnormalities are frequent. Recent work has focused on the importance of β-endorphins, which are known to rise with exercise[31] and depress LH pulsations. When measured in peripheral plasma, however, β-endorphins are thought to reflect ACTH levels. Most of the effects of β-endorphins occur in the central nervous system, where their receptors are; thus peripheral measurements might not reflect the direct central nervous system effect that results from in situ secretion. Experiments with nalaxone (a β-endorphin antagonist) restored pulsations in some but not all trained amenorrheic athletes.[31]

There is also a marked interrelationship between the hypothalamic-pituitary-gonadal axis and the hypothalamic-pituitary-adrenal axis.[22] Corticotropin-releasing factor (CRF) secreted in the hypothalamus has been shown to affect GnRH pulsations in monkeys.[32] Glucocorticoids

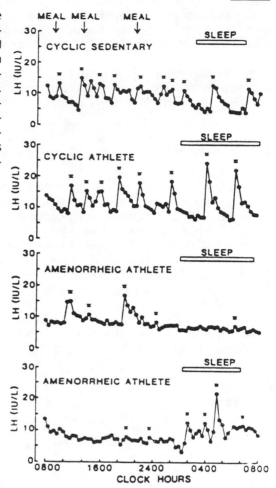

FIG. 15–3. Different LH pulse patterns in menstruating controls, athletic controls, and amenorrheic athletes. Plasma LH concentrations were obtained every 20 min for 24 h. From Loucks, A.B., et al.: Alterations in the hypothalamic-pituitary-ovarian and the hypothalamic-pituitary-adrenal axes in athletic women. J. Clin. Endocrinol. Metab., 68:402, 1989.

and other adrenal steroids that are increased in response to stress and exercise and chronic undernutrition.[33–36] might inhibit gonadotropin secretion. Corticotropin-releasing factor can also affect gonadotropin production,[32–37] either directly or indirectly through stimulation of opioid production. Trained women, particularly amenorrheics, develop mild hypercortisonism despite normal ACTH levels, whereas the ACTH response to CRF is blunted.[22]

☐ INADEQUATE LUTEAL PHASE

Inadequate luteal phases and subtle exercise-related menstrual dysfunction occur frequently without overt changes in the menstrual cycle. Women frequently report a shortening of the interval between menstrual cycles and occasionally report a lengthening of the cycle. These patterns have been reproduced by training in normal women, particularly in association with weight loss. The follicular phase of the cycle might be prolonged with a delay in ovulation, or the luteal phase might be shortened; the latter in particular can lead to infertility problems. This problem usually resolves with a decrease in training.[25,38,39] This can be a significant problem in women who are attempting to conceive.

☐ MENSTRUAL DYSFUNCTION AND EATING DISORDERS

Recent literature has begun to examine the frequency with which eating disorders occur in the athletic population. Eating disorders have recently been recognized as a contributing cause of the so-called "athletic amenorrhea," which is classified as a hypothalamic amenorrhea—i.e., the dysfunction occurs at the level of the hypothalamus (Fig. 15–4). Eating disorders, particularly anorexia nervosa, have been considered the prototype of the so-called "hypothalamic amenorrhea." In this syndrome, a classic triad occurs with amenorrhea, weight loss, and a psychiatric disturbance. The latter includes a disturbance of perception with a distorted view of the body, generally with an unreasonable concern about being "too fat." These subjects are often hyperactive and might engage in strenuous sports such as long-distance running. There are diverse

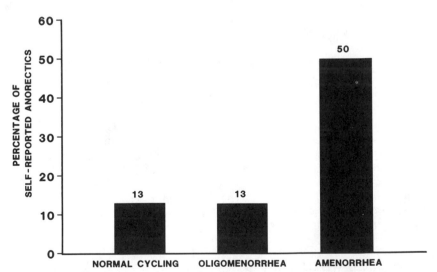

FIG. 15–4. Percentages of dancers with and without menstrual irregularities who reported anorexia nervosa. From Brooks-Gunn, J., Warren, M.P., and Hamilton, L.H.: The relationship of eating problems to amenorrhea in ballet dancers. Med. Sci. Sports Exerc., *19:*41, 1987.

TABLE 15–1. SYMPTOMS AND SIGNS OF ANOREXIA NERVOSA

	TOTAL NO.	%	REPORTED IN STARVATION
Amenorrhea (22 postpubertal girls)	22/22	100	Yes
Constipation	26/42	61.9	Yes
Preoccupation with food	19/42	45.2	Yes
Abdominal pain	8/42	19	Yes
Intolerance to cold	8/42	19	Yes
Vomiting	5/42	4.9	No
Hypotension	36/42	85.7	Yes
Hypothermia	27/42	64.3	Yes
Dry skin	26/42	61.9	Yes
Lanugo-type hair	22/42	52.4	Yes
Bradycardia	11/42	26.2	Yes
Edema	11/42	26.2	Yes
Systolic murmur	6/42	14.3	No
Petechiae	4/42	9.5	Yes

Modified from Warren, M.P., and Vande Wiele, R.L.: Clinical and metabolic features of anorexia nervosa. Am. J. Obstet. Gynecol., *117*:435, 1973.

physical changes, which are generally thought to be due to a physical and metabolic adaptation to the semistarved state. Common signs are listed in Table 15–1. LH patterns are often prepubertal or pubertal, these juvenile patterns showing decreased and low-amplitude pulsations. The pattern of LH secretion can be artificially made to return to the normal pattern by the pulsatile administration of exogenous GnRH; follicular maturation, and even menstruation, can be induced in these severely hypoestrogenic patients (Fig. 15–5). A number of other abnormalities in addition to reproductive changes have been described in anorexia nervosa that suggest hypothalamic dysfunction. There is a deficiency in handling a water load thought to result from mild diabetes insipidus, abnormal thermoregulatory responses, and lack of shivering. Cortisol secretion appears to be altered, with a higher 24-h set point and occasionally a mild decrease in thyroid hormone T_3; Thyroxine (T_4) is metabolized differently in this state, away from the formation of the active T_3 to the production of reverse T_3, an inactive metabolite.[38]

Bulimics can also present with menstrual irregularities, but reproductive dysfunction is not as severe, and these patients can be anovulatory with adequate estrogen secretion. Because bulimic behavior is often secretive and weight can remain within a normal range, a careful history and associated physical findings are important for the diagnosis. These include swollen parotid glands, tooth decay, cramps of the hands and feet (due to development of a metabolic alkalosis secondary to vomiting), and a decrease in ionized calcium that can lead to tetanic seizures.[40]

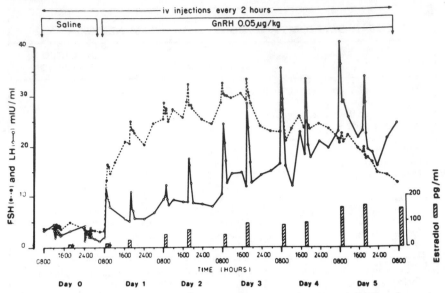

FIG. 15–5. Plasma FSH (closed circles), LH (open circles), and estradiol responses to GnRH (0.05 µg/kg) every 2 h in Patient 1. The arrow indicates values below the sensitivity of the estradiol assay. From Marshall, J.C., and Kelch, R.P.: Low dose pulsatile gonadotropin-releasing hormone in anorexia nervosa: A model of human pubertal development. *J. Clin. Endocrinol. Metab., 49*:712, 1986.

Another nutritional pattern of interest in young women is the trend toward vegetarian diets.[41–44] This pattern is seen particularly in endurance athletes and in girls with highly restrictive diets.[41–46] It is seen in patients with anorexia nervosa who have definite food preferences, the most frequent being vegetarianism.[45] This pattern is important because vegetarianism has recently been associated with a variety of hormonal abnormalities,[46–48] and in general the American vegetarian diet has been found to be more nutrient- and calorie-deficient than nonvegetarian diets.[49] The combination of vegetarian diets, overly restrictive dietary patterns, and compulsive athletic activity can be a sign of poor psychological health that bears investigation.

☐ COMPLICATIONS AND TREATMENT

Evaluation of the patient with secondary amenorrhea includes a detailed exercise and weight loss history and proceeds along the outline of that done for primary amenorrhea. These patients may be given medroxyprogesterone (Provera) 10 mg for 5 days as a test of endogenous estrogen secretion after a β-HCG level has been obtained to rule out pregnancy. Eating disorders should also be looked for; if a disorder is suspected, the patient's weight should not be allowed to decline without psychiatric intervention. Anovulatory patients are not necessarily hypoestrogenic. If hypoestrogenism is present, treatment depends on the length of time the problem has been present and the feasibility of increasing weight or decreasing exercise. A history of fractures can also influence the decision to give replacement hormones.

Osteoporosis and skeletal problems have been reported in hypoestrogenic amenorrheic athletes (see Chapter 16).[25,50-53] In adolescents, scoliosis has been reported in ballet dancers.[54] Osteopenia, particularly of trabecular bone, is common, and the rate of bone loss is similar to that associated with menopause of 5% per year.[50,55] Injuries such as stress fractures and femoral head collapse can be due to exposure of weakened bone to the impact of exercise, particularly with overuse syndromes.[56] Young patients also might not be attaining their peak mass. Bone mass accumulation can continue until the early 30s, but this process might not progress normally in the absence of estrogen.[57,58] Stress or other fractures in an athlete who has hypoestrogenic amenorrhea can be an indication for treatment, particularly when a change in lifestyle (such as weight gain or a decrease in exercise) is not feasible or is rejected by the patient. Estrogen is given cyclically in combination with a progestin. Premarin or its equivalent is given in doses of 0.625 mg for 25 days, with Provera, 10 mg, added on days 17 to 25. A week without therapy follows. This dose is thought to be protective for the bones. A patient might not have cyclic bleeding. If periods are desired, the patient might need to take 1.25 to 2.5 mg of Premarin or its equivalent per day. Patients who have been hypoestrogenic for long periods (greater than a year) will need 5 mg of Premarin per day to stimulate an underactive endometrium.

Subjects who have not completed their growth should not receive hormones because this therapy can cause epiphyseal closure. Growth potential can be determined by a bone age study.

Exercise has also been recommended to preserve or increase bone mass. The effect is small, but exercise appears to be beneficial, particularly in the postmenopausal population. Recent data suggest, however, that young hypoestrogenic ballet dancers do not accumulate bone in response to mechanical stress. This is in contrast to mature postmenopausal women, in whom exercise will offset the loss seen with hypoestrogenism; some postmenopausal women experience an increase over baseline.

Review of the data on weight loss and eating in young women suggests that reproductive function is sensitive to changes in nutrition and caloric demands. The mechanisms that alter reproductive cyclicity are not completely understood but appear to occur at the level of the hypothalamus. These mechanisms delay puberty, suppress ovulation, and favor reproductive economy. Amenorrhea in athletes occurs more frequently in those who report a delayed menarche, whether or not they have trained in adolescence. Thus athletes with amenorrhea might be genetically predisposed to a suppression of reproductive function that appears appropriate in the face of a large energy output and marginal nutritional intake. Much research on this interesting syndrome is still needed.

▢ REFERENCES

1. Darwin, C.: On the origin of species by means of natural selection. London, John Murray, 1859.
2. Vande Walt, L.A., Wilmsen, E.N., and Jenkins, T.: Unusual sex hormone patterns among desert dwelling hunter gatherers. J. Clin. Endocrinol. Metab., 46:658, 1978.
3. Warren, M.P.: The effects of undernutrition on reproductive function in the human. Endocr. Rev., 4:363, 1983.
4. Neinstein, L.S.: Menstrual dysfunction in pathophysiologic states (clinical review). West. J. Med., 143:476, 1985.
5. Warren, M.P.: The effects of exercise on pubertal progression and reproductive function in girls. J. Clin. Endocrinol. Metab., 51:1150, 1980.
6. Abraham, S.F., et al.: Body weight, exercise and menstrual status among ballet dancers in training. Br. J. Obstet. Gynecol., 89:507, 1982.
7. Feicht, C.B., et al.: Secondary amenorrhea in athletes. Lancet, 2:1145, 1978.
8. Schwartz, B., et al.: Exercise-associated amenorrhea: A distinct entity? Am. J. Obstet. Gynecol., 141:662, 1981.
9. Deuster, P.A., et al.: Nutritional intakes and status of highly trained amenorrheic and eumenorrheic women runners. Fertil. Steril., 46:636, 1986.
10. Nelson, M.E., et al.: Diet and bone status in amenorrheic runners. Am. J. Clin. Nutr., 43:910, 1986.
11. Warren, M.P., and Brooks-Gunn, J.: Delayed menarche in athletes: The role of low energy intake and eating disorders and their relation to bone density. In Hormones and Sport. Edited by Z. Laron and A. Rogol. New York, Raven Press, 1989.
12. Frisch, R.E., et al.: Delayed menarche and amenorrhea of college athletes in relation to age of onset of training. JAMA, 246:1559, 1981.
13. Warren, M.P.: Weight control. In Seminars in Reproductive Endocrinology. Interactions Between Lifestyles, Environment, and the Reproductive Systems. Edited by L. Speroff. New York, Thieme, 1990, pp. 25–30.
14. Myerson, M., et al.: Resting metabolic rate and energy balance in amenorrheic and eumenorrheic runners. Med. Sci. Sports Exerc., 23:15, 1991.
15. Brooks-Gunn, J., Warren, M.P., and Hamilton, L.H.: The relationship of eating disorders to amenorrhea in ballet dancers. Med. Sci. Sports Exerc., 19:41, 1987.
16. Wilmore, J.H., et al.: Energy efficiency in eumenorrheic and amenorrheic distance runners. Submitted for publication.
17. Brownell, K.D., Steen, S.N., and Wilmore, J.H.: Weight regulation practices in athletes: Analysis of metabolic and health effects. Med. Sci. Sports Exec., 19:546, 1987.
18. Frisch, R., and McArthur, J.: Menstrual cycles: Fatness as a determinant of minimum weight for height necessary for their maintenance or onset. Science, 185:949, 1974.
19. De Souza, M.J., et al.: Body compositions of eumenorrheic, oligomenorrheic, and amenorrheic runners. J. Appl. Sport Sci. Res., 2:13, 1987.
20. Sanborn, C.F., Albrecht, B.H., and Wagner, W.W., Jr.: Athletic amenorrhea: Lack of association with body fat. Med. Sci. Sports Exerc., 19:207, 1987.
21. Cumming, D.C., et al.: The effect of acute exercise on pulsatile release of luteinizing hormone in women runners. Am. J. Obstet. Gynecol., 153:482, 1985.
22. Loucks, A.B., et al.: Alterations in the hypothalamic-pituitary-ovarian and the hy-

pothalamic-pituitary-adrenal axes in athletic women. J. Clin. Endocrinol. Metab., *68*:1, 1989.

23. Keizer, H.A., and Rogol, A.D.: Physical exercise and menstrual cycle alterations: What are the mechanisms? Sports Med., *10*:218, 1990.
24. Highet, R.: Athletic amenorrhoea: An update on aetiology, complications and management. Sports Med., *7*:82, 1989.
25. Bullen, B.A., et al.: Induction of menstrual disorders by strenuous exercise in untrained women. N. Engl. J. Med., *312*:1349, 1985.
26. Boyden, T.W., et al.: Prolactin responses, menstrual cycles and body composition of women runners. J. Clin. Endocrinol. Metab., *54*:711, 1982.
27. Boyden, T.W., et al.: Sex steroids and endurance running in women. Fertil. Steril., *39*:629, 1983.
28. Boyden, T.W., et al.: Impaired gonadotropin responses to gonadotropin-releasing hormone stimulation in endurance-trained women. Fertil. Steril., *41*:359, 1984.
29. Ronkainen, H.: Depressed follicle-stimulating hormone, luteinizing hormone, and prolactin responses to the luteinizing releasing hormone, thyrotropin-releasing hormone. Fertil. Steril., *44*:755, 1985.
30. Ronkainen, H., Pakarinen, A., Kirkinen, P., and Kauppila, A.: Physical exercise–induced changes and season-associated differences in the pituitary-ovarian function of runners and joggers. J. Clin. Endocrinol. Metab., *60*:416, 1985.
31. Ruffin, M.T., Hunter, R.E., and Arendt, E.A.: Exercise and secondary amenorrhoea linked through endogenous opioids. Sports Med., *10*:65, 1990.
32. Olster, D.H., and Ferin, M.: Corticotropin-releasing hormone inhibits gonadotropin secretion in the ovariectomized rhesus monkey. J. Clin. Endocrinol. Metab., *65*:262, 1987.
33. Bronson, F.H.: Effect of food manipulation on the gonadotropin releasing hormone–luteinizing hormone–estradiol axis of the young female rat. Am. J. Physiol., *254*:R616, 1988.
34. Villanueva, A.L., et al.: Increased cortisol production in women runners. J. Clin. Endocrinol. Metab., *63*:133, 1986.
35. Loucks, A.B., and Horvath, S.M.: Exercise-induced stress responses of amenorrheic and eumenorrheic runners. J. Clin. Endocrinol. Metab., *59*:1109, 1984.
36. Boyar, R.M., et al.: Cortisol secretion and metabolism in anorexia nervosa. N. Engl. J. Med., *296*:190, 1977.
37. Rivier, C., and Vale, W.: Influence of corticotropin-releasing factor on reproductive functions in the rat. Endocrinol., *114*:914, 1984.
38. Prior, J.C., et al.: Menstrual cycle changes with marathon training: Anovulation and short luteal phase. Can. J. Appl. Sport Sci., *7*:173, 1982.
39. Prior, J.C., et al.: Reversible luteal phase changes and infertility associated with marathon training. Lancet, *2*:269, 1982.
40. Warren, M.P.: Anorexia nervosa and eating disorders. *In* Textbook of Internal Medicine. Edited by W.N. Kelley. Philadelphia, Lippincott, 1989.
41. Brooks, S.M., Sanborn, C.F., Albrecht, B.H., and Wagner, W.W.: Diet in athletic amenorrhea. Lancet, *10*:559, 1984.
42. Slavin, J., Lutter, J., and Cushman, S.: Amenorrhea in vegetarian athletes. Lancet, *1*:1474, 1984.
43. Zierath, J., Kaiserauer, S., and Snyder, A.C.: Dietary patterns of amenorrheic and regulatory menstruating runners. Med. Sci. Sports Exerc., *18*:S55, 1986.
44. Cohen, J.L., Potosnak, L., Frank, O., and Baker, H.: A nutritional and hematological assessment of elite ballet dancers. Phys. Sportsmed., *13*:43, 1985.
45. Huse, D.M., and Lucas, A.R.: Dietary patterns in anorexia nervosa. Am. J. Clin. Nutr., *40*:251, 1984.

46. Hill, P.B., Garbaczewski, L., Daynes, G., and Gaire, K.S.: Gonadotropin release and meat consumption in vegetarian women. Am. J. Clin. Nutr., 43:37, 1986.
47. Hill, P.B., Garbaczewski, L., Haley, N., and Wynder, W.L.: Diet and follicular development. Am. J. Clin. Nutr., 39:771, 1984.
48. Pirke, K.M., et al.: Dieting influences the menstrual cycle: Vegetarian versus non-vegetarian diet. Fertil. Steril., 46:1083, 1986.
49. Sanders, T.A.B.: The health and nutritional status of vegetarians. Plant Foods Manag. 2:181, 1978.
50. Drinkwater, B.L., et al.: Bone mineral content of amenorrheic and eumenorrheic athletes. N. Engl. J. Med., 311:277, 1984.
51. Lindberg, J.S., et al.: Exercise-induced amenorrhea and bone density. Ann. Intern. Med., 101:647, 1984.
52. Marcus, R., et al.: Menstrual function and bone mass in elite women distance runners. Ann. Intern. Med., 102:158, 1985.
53. Lloyd, T., et al.: Interrelationships of diet, athletic activity, menstrual status and bone density in collegiate women. Am. J. Clin. Nutr., 46:681, 1987.
54. Warren, M.P., et al.: Scoliosis and fractures in young ballet dancers: Relation to delayed menarche and secondary amenorrhea. N. Engl. J. Med., 314:1348, 1986.
55. Cann, C.E., et al.: Decreased spinal mineral content in amenorrheic women. JAMA, 251:626, 1984.
56. Frusztajer, N.T., et al.: Nutrition and the incidence of stress fractures in ballet dancers. Am. J. Clin. Nutr., 51:779, 1990.
57. Dhuper, S., Warren, M.P., Brooks-Gunn, J., and Fox, R.P.: Effects of hormonal status on bone density in adolescent girls. J. Clin. Endocrinol. Metab., 71:1083, 1990.
58. Warren, M.P., et al.: Lack of bone accretion and amenorrhea: Evidence for a relative osteopenia in weight bearing bones. J. Clin. Endocrinol. Metab., 72:847, 1991.

CHAPTER

16

AMENORRHEA, BODY WEIGHT, AND OSTEOPOROSIS

Barbara L. Drinkwater

When the sports world opened up for women in the early 1970s, little was known about how women responded to training, what type of training programs were most effective for women, and what problems— if any—would result from training and competing at a high level. As more and more women took advantage of their new opportunities and performance expectations for women increased, training regimens became more demanding. Evidence from a number of studies indicated that women responded to training just as men did with better performance, improved cardiovascular fitness, greater muscular strength and endurance, increased flexibility, and a better balance between body fat and lean tissue mass. Then came the early reports that some female endurance athletes were experiencing irregular menses or no periods at all. The initial concern of the athletes and their physicians was focused on the future reproductive health of these women. As anecdotal evidence accumulated that this type of menstrual dysfunction was reversible, however, and that former amenorrheic athletes were bearing healthy infants, the concern evaporated. For many women the absence of monthly periods was a welcome consequence of their training program. This lighthearted attitude changed with the first report of decreases in vertebral bone density in amenorrheic female athletes similar to those observed in some postmenopausal women.

☐ THE "POSTMENOPAUSAL" YOUNG ATHLETE

Cann et al.[1] were the first to report that active young women with hypothalamic amenorrhea might be at risk for premature bone loss. Their results were received with some skepticism. No evidence was presented that the amenorrhea experienced by their subjects was directly related to strenuous physical training. No matched control group was included in the study, and no hormonal or nutritional data were provided. There had also been a number of studies showing that athletes had better than average bone mass[2–5] and that exercise had been found to increase bone mineral density (BMD) in postmenopausal women.[6,7] The decrease in endogenous estrogen production at menopause is associated with an accelerated bone loss;[8] exercise programs for postmenopausal women apparently reversed that loss. Was it possible that young amenorrheic female athletes, exercising much more vigorously, could be at risk for bone loss?

Other investigators[9–12] designed studies taking a number of confounding factors into account and found the same result—both amenorrheic and oligomenorrheic athletes have significantly lower vertebral bone density than regularly cycling athletes matched for age, weight, sport, and training (Fig. 16–1). The evidence strongly suggests that these athletes do indeed face the risk of premature bone loss. The reason for the lower bone mass appears to be hormonal. During amenorrheic periods these young women have estrogen levels similar to those found in postmenopausal women (range = 8.6 to 46 pg/mL).[1,9,11,12] As far as their bones are concerned, these athletes *are* postmenopausal women.

☐ TECHNIQUES OF MEASURING BONE MASS

A number of noninvasive techniques are available for measurement of bone mineral density. With each new technology the precision and accuracy of the measurements are improved, and the number of skeletal sites that can be scanned increases. These devices provide the athlete and her physician with the means to evaluate her current bone status in order to make informed decisions about treatment. For example, an athlete whose lumbar density is only slightly below average has time to experiment with adjustments in training, nutrition, and lifestyle to encourage resumption of a normal menstrual cycle. On the other hand, an athlete whose BMD is equivalent to that of a woman in her eighties and who has experienced several stress fractures cannot afford to lose more bone and should be advised to consider some form of intervention immediately.

The appropriate measurement technique is one that allows evaluation of vertebral BMD as well as BMD of other skeletal sites. Single-photon absorptiometry (SPA) is useful for other populations, but it does not measure BMD at the spine. Because the lumbar region is the area where

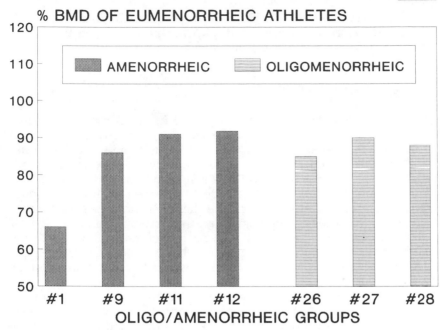

FIG. 16–1. Lumbar BMD of amenorrheic and oligomenorrheic athletes shown as a percent of values for eumenorrheic athletes. Data from Cann, C.E., Martin, M.C., Genant, H.K., and Jaffe, R.B.: Decreased spinal mineral content in amenorrheic women. JAMA, *251*:626, 1984; Drinkwater, B.L., Nilson, K., Chesnut, C.H. III, et al.: Bone mineral content of amenorrheic and eumenorrheic athletes. New Engl. J. Med., *311*:277, 1984; Marcus R., et al.: Menstrual function and bone mass in elite women distance runners. Ann. Int. Med., *102*:158, 1985; Nelson, M.E., Fisher, E.C., Catsos, P.D., et al.: Diet and bone status in amenorrheic runners. J. Clin. Nutr., *43*:910, 1986; Baker, E., and Demers, L.: Menstrual status in female athletes: Correlation with reproductive hormones and bone density. Obstet. Gynecol., *72*:683, 1988; Cook, S.D., Harding, A.F., Thomas, K.A., et al.: Trabecular bone density and menstrual function in women runners. Am. J. Sports Med., *15*:503, 1987; and Lloyd, T., Myers, C., Buchanan, J.R., and Demers, L.M.: Collegiate women athletes with irregular menses during adolescence have decreased bone density. Obstet. Gynecol., *72*:639, 1988.

low bone mass has been reported for amenorrheic athletes, it must be included in any evaluation of their bone status. The most widely used techniques include dual-photon absorptiometry (DPA), computed tomography (CT), and dual-energy X-ray absorptiometry (DXA). Both DPA and DXA have lower levels of radiation (<5 mREM) than CT (100 to 300 mREM). CT provides the capability of isolating trabecular bone, however, and DXA and DPA measure the integral of cortical and trabecular bone. DXA is the newest addition to bone densitometer technology. It has the fastest scanning speed and excellent precision (0.5 to

1.3%) and accuracy (3 to 5%). Both DPA and DXA can do a whole-body scan as well as regional scans, but DXA has now come on the market with a technique for a lateral scan as well.

◻ SKELETAL AREAS AT RISK

The skeleton is composed of two types of bone. Cortical or compact bone is the dense outer portion—for example, the shaft of long bones of the legs and arms. Trabecular or cancellous bone is the lattice-like structure found primarily in the vertebrae, pelvis, flat bones, and ends of long bones. Bone is not static. It is a metabolically active tissue, constantly renewing itself through a process of bone resorption and bone formation. In the healthy young adult these two processes are coupled so that each balances the other and bone mass remains constant. If these two events become "uncoupled" and the rate of resorption exceeds formation, bone mass decreases. Trabecular bone, which has a more rapid remodeling rate than cortical bone, is most apt to reflect early changes in bone homeostasis.

It is an area with a high proportion of trabecular bone, the lumbar vertebrae, that the BMD of amenorrheic athletes is significantly lower than that of athletes with normal menses. The apparent preferential loss in this area might be related to its trabecular content, or it might reflect the fact that most reports to date have used measurement techniques that scanned either the vertebrae or the radius. As the measurement instruments become more sophisticated, additional skeletal areas will no doubt be included in the study protocols.

Only one study[10] has reported a lower radial shaft density in amenorrheic athletes. It appears, however, that this difference was due more to the higher than average density for the control group rather than a low density for the amenorrheic athletes. The distal site chosen in the same study, 2 cm distal to the styloid process, contains more trabecular bone than the distal areas selected in other studies of the radius, and differences here are likely to represent a real difference between groups.

Amenorrhea associated with anorexia nervosa has even more severe consequences on bone. Women with this disorder not only have premature bone loss at the spine but also in the proximal femur and the radius and ulna.[13,14] Bone loss is so severe in this group that fractures of the hip and multiple crush fractures of the spine have been documented.[14,15] It is assumed that the malnutrition typical of this condition, in addition to estrogen deficiency, is responsible for the greater bone loss in anorexia than in the amenorrhea associated with exercise. Nevertheless, many athletes also strive for a low body weight in hopes of improving their performance. Although they do not fit the psychiatric profile of the anorexic, low-weight amenorrheic athletes are more at risk for low lumbar BMD than amenorrheic women of average weight (Fig. 16–2).

Our data (unpublished) also suggest that athletes with very low ver-

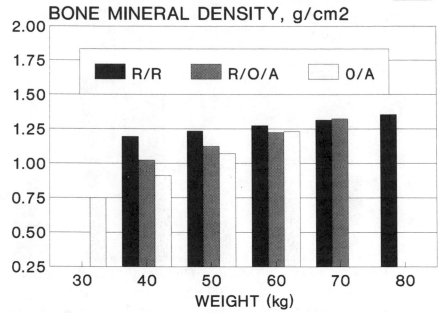

FIG. 16–2. Lumbar BMD of athletes who have always had regular menses (R/R), regular cycles interspersed with irregular or absent menses (R/O/A), and of women who have been oligomenorrheic or amenorrheic since menarche plotted against body weight (kg). Data were calculated at 10-kg intervals from regression equations for each menstrual group. From Drinkwater, B.L.: Amenorrheic athletes: At risk for premature osteoporosis? *In* Proceedings, First International Olympic Committee World Congress on Sport Sciences, Colorado Springs, Oct. 28–Nov. 3, 1989. IOC, 1989, pp. 151–155.

tebral density have low BMD at other sites as well. One young dancer, age 21, with a spinal bone density equivalent to that of a woman in her 90s, has an average BMD at 5 other sites that is 75% of normal for her age (Fig. 16–3). A 28-year-old runner has a 70-year-old spine and an average BMD 80% of normal at the other 5 sites. The dancer had been amenorrheic 6 years; the runner, 5 years. Losses in cortical bone might take longer to develop, but it does not appear that amenorrheic athletes are immune to bone loss in those areas.

□ FACTORS DETERMINING THE EXTENT OF BONE LOSS

Intuitively one would assume that bone mass would be lowest in women who had been amenorrheic the longest. For women with anorexia nervosa, hyperprolactinemia and premature ovarian failure bone mass have indeed been correlated with the length of the amenorrheic period.[14,16,17] The total months a woman has been amenorrheic correlates with her

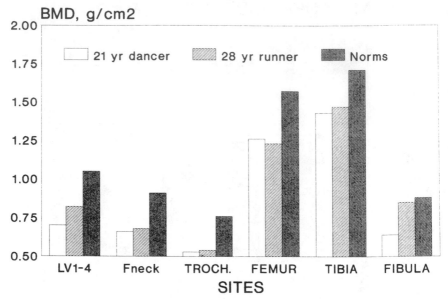

FIG. 16–3. Bone mineral density of an amenorrheic 21-year-old dancer and a 28-year-old runner compared to mean values at 6 sites for eumenorrheic athletes, mean age 26 years.

age, however, and in two of the studies[14,17] bone mass also decreased with age. Was the lower BMD related to the length of the amenorrheic period, to age, or to the combination of aging plus low estrogen levels?

There are several reasons why the duration of amenorrhea might not predict current BMD accurately. Among the women in our group, a 27-year-old athlete, amenorrheic 11 years, has a vertebral BMD of 0.88 g/cm^2; a 33-year-old runner, amenorrheic 5 years, has a vertebral density of 0.76 g/cm^2; and a 19-year-old dancer, also amenorrheic for 5 years, has a spinal BMD of 0.86 g/cm.^{2} Has aging added to the bone loss in the older athlete? Has bone mass failed to develop in the youngest woman? Or do the different densities reflect the effect of the amenorrheic period superimposed on individual genetic potential for bone mass? Finally, it should be remembered that postmenopausal women often lose bone rapidly in the first 3 or 4 years after menopause and then more slowly during the following years. If the same pattern holds true for amenorrheic athletes, there will not be a linear relationship between bone loss and the length of amenorrhea. Only 2 studies have analyzed this relationship for amenorrheic athletes.[1,18] Neither found a significant relationship.

Another possible factor is the effect of mechanical stress on specific skeletal sites. Athletes in different sports have different BMD profiles. For example, when runners, dancers, and weight lifters were matched

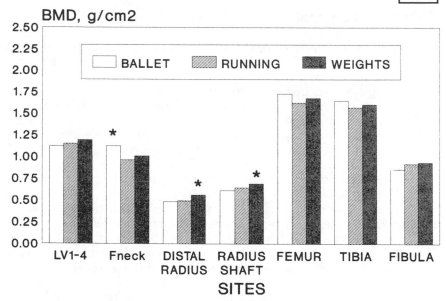

BMD, g/cm2

FIG. 16–4. Comparison of BMD at 7 sites for ballet dancers (n = 14), runners (n = 14), and runners who also train with weights (n = 14). Asterisks indicate P ≤0.05.

on age, height, weight, and menstrual history, bone density varied according to the demands of the sport (Fig. 16–4). It might be that the effect of amenorrhea will also differ depending on the athlete's event. In one study the vertebral BMD of light-weight oarswomen who were amenorrheic did not differ significantly from that of rowers with normal menses although the BMD of the four amenorrheic rowers was 9% lower than that of cyclic rowers.[19] The lack of significance was most likely due to the small number of subjects, although there might have been some positive effect from the mechanical stress placed on the spine during rowing. More data are needed to determine whether mechanical stress and weightbearing exercise can effectively prevent or attenuate bone loss at specific skeletal sites.

There is some evidence to suggest that sedentary amenorrheic women lose more bone than those who are active. When anorectics were divided into highly active and less-active groups, the active women were found to have normal levels of radial BMD and those of the less-active women were significantly lower.[14] Amenorrheic athletes in another study also had normal BMD at the predominantly cortical site on the radius whereas women with nonexercise-related amenorrhea had significantly lower densities at the same location.[16] In other words, both exercise and normal estrogen levels are important in maintaining bone mass. Active women with normal menses have the best chance of achieving their potential peak bone mass during their early adult years.

☐ POTENTIAL PROBLEMS

The amenorrheic athlete has reason to be concerned about the effect of decreased bone density. As a young adult, she should be doing everything possible to maximize her bone mass as one way of reducing her risk for osteoporosis in the future; instead, she is losing bone. Theoretically, if a woman has a larger bone mass when the age-related decline in BMD starts, osteoporotic fractures can be delayed or even prevented. If amenorrheic women reach the age of peak skeletal density with a BMD that is below average, will they be at risk for premature osteoporosis? The answer to that question will have to wait a few years, but there is some evidence already that the risk of stress fractures is higher among young athletes with irregular or absent menses.

At least four studies[10,11,20,21] have found a higher incidence of bone injuries among amenorrheic and oligomenorrheic athletes than those with regular cycles, a 39% and a 16% incidence respectively. Whether these injuries were actually related to lower bone density is uncertain. Two of the studies[20,21] used questionnaires and did not actually measure BMD. Even when bone density is measured, it is difficult to explain why fractures are more frequent at sites such as the tibia, fibula, and femur, where low BMD has not been reported in amenorrheic women. In these instances, group data can be misleading; BMD should be reported for the injured athlete, not the group. For example, a 28-year-old runner who had a nontraumatic fracture of the femur 20 yards from the finish of a half-marathon had bone densities at four sites that were below average for both eumenorrheic and amenorrheic athletes (Fig. 16–5).

The results in three of the four studies are also confounded by the fact that the injured women ran more miles per week than the uninjured runners. Were the fractures an overuse injury or a result of diminished bone mass? Prospective studies that carefully control the many other factors implicated in stress fractures and that document the diagnoses with appropriate tests will be necessary to determine if amenorrheic athletes are already experiencing the detrimental effect of low bone mass.

☐ CAN LOST BONE BE REGAINED?

Age-related decreases in bone mass result when there is an uncoupling of the balance between bone formation and resorption with a resultant increase in resorption. Because this uncoupling is presumed to be irreversible in older women, there is concern that the same might be true for the amenorrheic athlete.

Fortunately, there is evidence that some bone can be regained if the athlete resumes normal menses. Two studies[22,23] have reported that female athletes who resumed menses after an extended period of amenorrhea had an average increase of about 6% in vertebral BMD over a period of 14 months. The use of exogenous estrogen does not appear

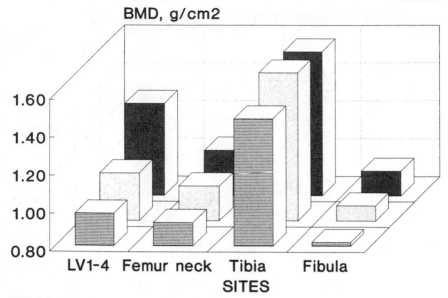

FIG. 16–5. Bone density of the lumbar vertebrae (LV1-4), neck of the femur, tibia, and fibula of a runner with a history of oligo/amenorrhea who suffered a nontraumatic fracture of the femur while running a half-marathon (horizontal lines) compared to mean values for eumenorrheic athletes (dark stippled) and amenorrheic athletes (light stippled).

to be as effective. The effect of hormone replacement therapy on the lumbar BMD of a small group of amenorrheic women (n = 4) was the same as that reported for postmenopausal women; bone loss stopped but little or no bone was regained (Fig. 16–6). Even the beneficial effect of resuming menses might be finite:

> Recent observations in our laboratory have suggested that this gain may indeed be limited, raising the question of whether extended periods of menstrual irregularity may exert a prolonged effect on bone mineral density. The increase in bone density (6.3%) observed during our previous study slowed to 3% the following year and then ceased during the next two years (unpublished data). Lumbar bone density for these women remains well below the average for their age group four years after resumption of normal menses.[18]

There are now two studies[18,24] that suggest some of the bone loss is irreversible. When 97 active young women, average age 27.6 years, were grouped according to their present and past menstrual patterns, lumbar bone density was highest in women who had always had regular men-

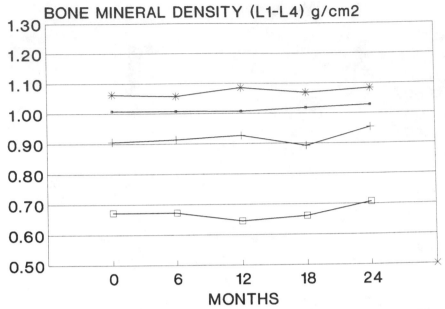

FIG. 16–6. Changes in lumbar BMD over 24 mo in 4 amenorrheic women on hormone replacement therapy (cyclic 0.625 Premarin, 10 mg Provera).

strual cycles (1.28 g/cm²), lower in women who had experienced episodes of amenorrhea or oligomenorrhea interspersed with periods of regularity (1.18 g/cm²), and lowest in those who were currently amenorrheic and had had previous episodes of amenorrhea or oligomenorrhea (1.05 g/cm²). Menstrual history was a significant predictor of current lumbar density, a relationship confirmed by Cann et al.[24] If amenorrheic women are likely to experience an irreversible loss of bone, some type of intervention must be considered early in the course of the amenorrhea.

☐ TREATMENT

The treatment of choice, of course, is resumption of normal menses. The precise cause of exercise-associated amenorrhea has not been determined, but most women regain normal cycles within 2 or 3 months when they decrease their training programs slightly and gain a few pounds. If cessation of menses is an indication of overtraining, performance might actually improve by changes in the training regimen, better nutrition, and addition of more lean body mass.

A more perplexing question is what can be done to halt or reverse bone loss in women who do not resume menses? What is the most effective way to protect them from further bone loss? The logical step is to replace the inadequate endogenous estrogen with an appropriate source of exogenous estrogen. One might presume the regimens found effective for postmenopausal women would be equally effective for the amenorrheic athlete, but there have been no controlled studies demonstrating that this is the case. There is also resistance on the part of many female athletes to this type of intervention; they do not want to have menstrual periods, which they find inconvenient and uncomfortable. Interestingly, the aversion to hormone treatment per se does not carry over to oral contraceptives, and some physicians are prescribing oral contraceptives in hopes that their estrogen component will prevent bone loss. At this time the appropriate formulation and dose of estrogen, · frequency of use, potential side effects, and effect on bone are unknown for these young athletes.

It has been suggested that an increase in calcium intake can also be of some benefit in preventing or slowing bone loss in amenorrheic women. Because less calcium is absorbed and retained when estrogen levels are low, calcium balance in postmenopausal women can be maintained only by increasing the daily intake of calcium to 1500 mg/day.[25] Would additional calcium benefit the amenorrheic athlete?

In a recent study (unpublished data) we increased the daily calcium intake of young amenorrheic athletes to 1500–1800 mg/day for a 24-month period. At the end of that time there was a significant increase in tibial BMD of the high-calcium group, whereas amenorrheic athletes on a lower calcium intake (800 to 1000 mg/day) had no increase. Vertebral density continued to decrease during the first 6 months and then slowly returned to original levels for both the high and normal calcium groups. The tibia, of course, receives most of the impact stress of weight-bearing exercises such as running, dancing, and aerobics. We concluded that increasing calcium intake to 1500 mg/day can have a positive effect on the cortical bone of amenorrheic women at sites subjected to an exercise stimulus. Similar changes in the vertebrae for both groups suggest that some factor other than calcium intake is responsible for those changes (perhaps fluctuations in endogenous estrogen levels).

☐ COMMENT

An editorial by Heath (1985) in the *Annals of Internal Medicine* suggests that "there are unique aspects of female biology that impose definite constraints on women's athletic achievements and expose them to special hazards." Marcus et al.[11] concluded that it would be "judicious for most women who participate in endurance activity not to train to the degree that menstrual function is compromised." This advice is reminiscent of the days when women were excluded from physically demanding sports on the assumption that they were physiologically incapable of handling the physical stress. It is unlikely to be heeded by competitive or professional female athlete. Concern for the future bone health of these athletes is justified, but a blanket prescription for decreased activity is not the answer. Research efforts must be continued to find the cause of menstrual irregularities as well as the safest and most effective way of protecting women from premature bone loss during their amenorrheic periods.

☐ REFERENCES

1. Cann, C.E., Martin, M.C., Genant, H.K., and Jaffe, R.B.: Decreased spinal mineral content in amenorrheic women. JAMA, 251:626, 1984.
2. Dalen, N., and Olsson, K.E.: Bone mineral content and physical activity. Acta Orthop. Scand., 45:170, 1974.
3. Jacobsen, P.C., Beaver, W., Grubb, S.A., et al.: Bone density in women: College athletes and older athletic women. J. Orthop. Res., 2:328, 1984.
4. Kirk, S., Sharp, C.F., Elbaum, N., et al.: Effect of long-distance running on bone mass in women. J. Bone Min. Res., 4:515, 1989.
5. Nilsson, B.E., and Westlin, N.E.: Bone density in athletes. Clin. Orthop., 77:179, 1971.
6. Chow, R.K., Harrison, J.E., Brown, C.F., and Hajek, V.: Physical fitness effect on bone mass in postmenopausal women. Arch. Phys. Med. Rehabil., 67:231, 1986.
7. Dalsky, G., Stocke, K.S., Eshani, A.A., et al.: Weight-bearing exercise training and lumbar bone mineral content in postmenopausal women. Ann. Intern. Med., 108:824, 1988.
8. Riggs, B.L., and Melton, L.J.: Involutional osteoporosis. N. Engl. J. Med., 314:1676, 1986.
9. Drinkwater, B.L., Nilson, K., Chesnut, C.H., III, et al.: Bone mineral content of amenorrheic and eumenorrheic athletes. New. Engl. J. Med., 311:277, 1984.
10. Lindberg, J.S., et al.: Exercise-induced amenorrhea and bone density. Ann. Int. Med., 101:647, 1984.
11. Marcus, R., et al.: Menstrual function and bone mass in elite women distance runners. Ann. Int. Med., 102:158, 1985.
12. Nelson, M.E., Fisher, E.C., Catsos, P.D., et al.: Diet and bone status in amenorrheic runners. J. Clin. Nutr., 43:910, 1986.
13. Treasure, J.L., Russell, G.F.M., Fogelman, I., and Murby, B.: Reversible bone loss in anorexia nervosa. Brit. Med., J., 295:474, 1987.
14. Rigotti, N.A., Nussbaum, S.R., Herzog, D.B., and Neer, R.M.: Osteoporosis in women with anorexia nervosa. N. Engl. J. Med., 311:1601, 1984.
15. Kaplan, F.S., Pertschuk, M., Fallson, M., and Haddad, J.: Osteoporosis and hip fracture in a young woman with anorexia nervosa. Clin. Orthop., 21:250, 1986.
16. Jones, K.P., Ravnikar, V.A., Tulchinsky, D., and Schiff, I.: Comparison of bone density in amenorrheic women due to athletics, weight loss, and premature menopause. Obstet. Gynecol., 66:5, 1985.
17. Koppelman, M.C.S., et al.: Vertical body bone mineral content in hyperprolactinemic women. J. Clin. Endocrinol. Metab., 59:1050, 1984.
18. Drinkwater, B.L., Bruemmer, B., and Chesnut, C.H. III: Menstrual history as a determinant of current bone density in young athletes. JAMA, 263:545, 1990.
19. Snyder, A.C., Wenderoth, M.P., Johnston, C.C., and Hui, S.L.: Bone mineral content of elite lightweight amenorrheic oarswomen. Hum. Biol., 58:863, 1986.
20. Barrow, G.W., and Saha, S.: Menstrual irregularity and stress fractures in collegiate female distance runners. Am. J. Sports Med., 16:209, 1988.
21. Lloyd, T., Triantafgllou, S.J., Baker, E.R., et al.: Women athletes with menstrual irregularity have increased musculoskeletal injuries. Med. Sci. Sports Exerc., 18:374, 1986.

22. Drinkwater, B.L., Nilson, K., Ott, S., and Chesnut, C.H. III: Bone mineral density after resumption of menses in amenorrheic women. JAMA, 256:380, 1986.
23. Lindberg, J.S., Powell, M.R., Hunt, M.M., et al.: Increased vertebral bone mineral in response to reduced exercise in amenorrheic runners. West. J. Med., 146:39, 1986.
24. Cann, C.E., Cavanaugh, D.J., Schnurpfiel, K., and Martin, M.C.: Menstrual history is the primary determinant of trabecular bone density in women. Med. Sci. Sports Exerc., 20:S59, 1988.
25. Heaney, R.P., Recker, R.R., and Saville, P.D.: Menopausal changes in calcium balance performance. J. Lab. Clin. Med., 92:953, 1978.
26. Baker, E., and Demers, L.: Menstrual status in female athletes: Correlation with reproductive hormones and bone density. Obstet. Gynecol., 72:683, 1988.
27. Cook, S.D., Harding, A.F., Thomas, K.A., et al.: Trabecular bone density and menstrual function in women runners. Am. J. Sports Med., 15:503, 1987.
28. Lloyd, T., Myers, C., Buchanan, J.R., and Demers, L.M.: Collegiate women athletes with irregular menses during adolescence have decreased bone density. Obstet. Gynecol., 72:639, 1988.
29. Drinkwater, B.L.: Amenorrheic athletes: At risk for premature osteoporosis? In Proceedings, First International Olympic Committee World Congress on Sport Sciences, Colorado Springs, Oct. 28–Nov. 3, 1989. IOC. 1989, pp. 151–155.

PHYSIOLOGICAL AND PSYCHOLOGICAL EFFECTS OF OVERTRAINING

Rod K. Dishman

Nontraumatic pathological adaptations to exercise training historically have been termed as overtraining[1,2] or staleness.[3] Discussions of these problems appeared in the literatures of athletic training and sports medicine during the 1920s,[4-6] and in the 1960s the American Medical Association included signs and symptoms of staleness in its *Standard Nomenclature of Athletic Injuries.*[7] Modern research on overtraining and staleness has paralleled renewed interest by top-level athletes and by the United States Olympic Committee, who recognize that maladaptive training responses are major barriers to health and performance. Morgan et al.[8] have argued that overtraining should be viewed as the process by which a quantifiable exercise stimulus is applied, whereas staleness represents the signs and symptoms of pathological adaptations to overtraining. Overtraining is not synonomous with staleness, because an overload of the exercise stimulus is common in the traditions of athletic

Appreciation is extended to Frank J. Landy, Russell R. Pate, and Andrea L. Dunn for contributing to the sections on psychological models,[76] physiological monitoring, and HPA disruption,[59] respectively. Thanks go to Donna Smith for preparing the manuscript and Marlee Stewart for adapting the graphs.

conditioning for many endurance sports, but only a portion of athletes show signs or symptoms of staleness.

The sequelae and the syndrome of staleness are not understood well enough to permit standardized criteria for diagnosis or guidelines for prevention. Physicians, physiologists, and psychologists have concurred for many years, however, on a number of clinical features and precipitating conditions. A representative definition was provided by Moore[9] over 20 years ago:

> Staleness may be defined as a condition in which an individual not only seems to be learning at a slow rate but also appears to have lost much of the ability already acquired. Physical staleness may be due to overwork . . . . Loss of weight and lack of desire for food are indications of staleness. Others are irritability, depression, and loss of skill (p. 105).

Earlier the physician/physiologist Brouha[10] concluded that

> regardless of the physical capacity of a given subject, there is a level of exercise which frequently repeated will lead to chronic fatigue and "staleness." This state is characterized, among other factors, by higher heart rates and lactic acid concentrations for a standard exercise than we previously observed during the training program (p. 415).

Although the incidence, prevalence, and causes of staleness due to overtraining are not yet established according to epidemiological or medical traditions, the monitoring of physiological and psychological changes that accompany chronic training has shown promise for detecting risk. The determination and monitoring of risk factors for staleness are important for prevention because they would permit training to be reduced or tapered before the clinical onset of staleness. There is professional consensus that the only cure for staleness is extended rest, and this can interfere with competitive schedules. Thus prevention of staleness is a preeminent goal for sports medicine, athletes, and coaches. Prevention first requires that predictors of staleness be identified.

For a marker or predictor of risk for staleness due to overtraining to be useful for athletes and coaches, it must be a variable that changes predictably to periods of increases and decreases in an athlete's normal training in a manner that is both *sensitive* (i.e., most athletes who become stale show changes in the marker; false-negative predictions are minimized) and *specific* (i.e., the changes are due only to the overtraining stimulus; false-positive predictions are minimized), and it must be measurable by practical methods. Variables that are not measurable by practical means might, however, be scientifically important for understanding how and when practical markers predict staleness. The existing scientific literature suggests that several physiological, neuroendocrine, immunological, and psychological variables might be useful risk factors for staleness. Most of what is known, however, comes from anecdotes, from cross-sectional comparisons of selected groups of athletes, or from the training studies of small groups without the experimental control necessary to confirm the cause-and-effect nature of the results. Because the scientific understanding of overtraining and staleness is not fully mature, the goal of this chapter is to summarize and evaluate what is known, what appears practically useful at the present, and what deserves continued research and consideration.

☐ THE PROBLEM

Mathematical models of time-and-distance relationships for top-level athletes in several endurance sports show that world endurance records are far below the limits of human physiology and provide evidence that increased performance requires a training volume that places athletes in these sports at risk for pathological adaptations. The analysis of record-setting amateur performances from 1924 through 1972 shown in Figure 17–1 shows nearly linear rates of acceleration, ranging from 5% to 15%, at all distances.[11] Of more importance for staleness is not the increase in speed, but the increase across distances of what has been termed *specific endurance* (the ability to sustain work requiring high power output.) For example, the 1988 marathon record of Belaine Densimo was run at 331.2 m/min. This is not only faster than the 326.3-m/min pace of Great Britain's Charles Lawes when he established the mile record in 1864, but the 26.2-m distance of the marathon means that Densimo had a specific endurance that was 26.2 times that of Lawes. For the trends projected by these data to hold true across the next 35 yrs (e.g., by the year 2028 the 10,000 m would be run in 24 min 31 and the marathon in 1 h 53 min 13 s), specific endurance will generally need to be doubled from the 1972 values. In other words, to reach the record pace of 408 m/min predicted for the 10,000 m, an athlete would need to be capable of sustaining the 360 m/min pace of the 1972 world record for a distance of 20,000 m. Currently top male 10,000-m runners train for endurance at a pace no faster than 300 m/min.

A more recent analysis, illustrated by Figure 17–2, shows a similar picture. A time-vs.-distance plot of world running records prior to the 1980 Summer Olympic Games in Moscow predicted that for a world-class male runner to gain 1% in speed at any distance, he must be able to travel 13% farther at his previous top speed.[12]

Similar analyses of recent records have not been done to verify these early predictions, but they seem reasonable by today's standards. Norway's Ingrid Kristiansen, the 1990 women's world record holder in the marathon at just over 2 h 21 min, illustrates the challenge of endurance training. She lowered the women's top marathon time of the mid-1960s

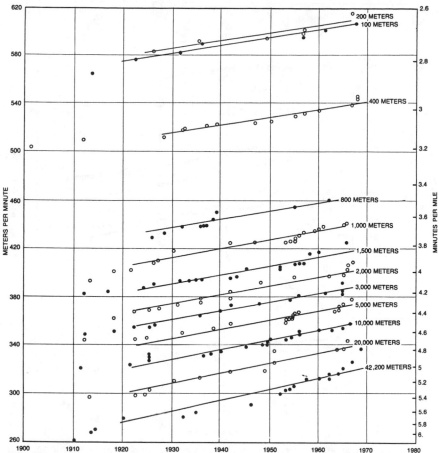

FIG. 17–1. Linear increases in human performance derived from linear mathematical modeling of world running records from 1910 to 1968. From Ryder, H.W., Carr, H.J., and Herget, P.: Future performance in footracing. Sci. Am., *234*:109, 1976.

(3½ h) by more than one-third. If the concept of *specific endurance* is valid, Kristiansen first had to be capable of running at the 1960s record-setting pace for more than 4 times the distance.

These calculations indicate that speed cannot increase until endurance is increased. Based on current knowledge, increased endurance cannot reliably occur without overtraining. Thus physiological adaptability appears subordinate to motivational and medical barriers of staleness following overtraining. The endurance athlete is therefore confronted with two problems of adaptation. Biological changes must accommodate the increasing metabolic requirements of longer training at a faster pace, but motivation and health must be maintained to permit these changes

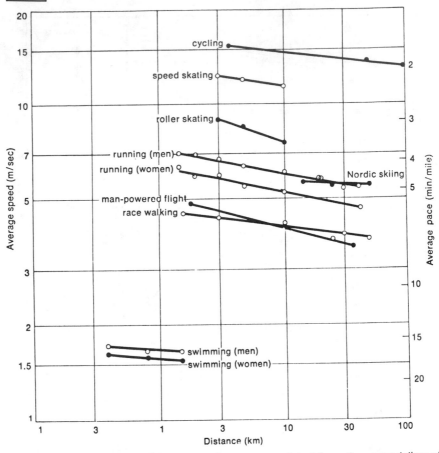

FIG. 17–2. Linear levels of human performance predicted from linear modeling of world record performances from 1968 to 1980. From Riegel, P.S.: Athletic records and human performance. Am. Scientist, 69:281, 1981.

to occur. Staleness results when motivation and health are not maintained during overtraining.

☐ PHYSIOLOGICAL MONITORING OF OVERTRAINING

The existing scientific and clinical literatures in sports medicine suggest that several physiological and psychological variables might be valuable markers of risk for staleness during overtraining in endurance athletes. Increased morning resting heart rate and T-wave changes in the electrocardiogram (ECG) have been associated with overtraining.[13,14] $\dot{V}_{O_{2max}}$, $\dot{V}_{O_2}$ during standard submaximal exercise, oxygen pulse (HR/

$\dot{V}O_2$), rating of perceived exertion during standard exercise, and blood lactate responses to submaximal and maximal exercise are widely used measures of training status. Each has been suggested as a potential predictor of staleness.[1,2,14,15–17] Muscular strength and power can decrease in staleness,[14,18,19] and muscle soreness can increase.[1,2,20] Concentrations in the blood of several hormones and enzymes also have been implicated as markers of staleness. These include serum creatine phosphokinase (CPK), which is generally regarded as an indicator of microinjury to skeletal muscle,[21,22] and plasma interleukin-1 (IL-1).[23,24] Interleukin-1 is produced by macrophages and damaged cells, and it has multiple effects, including immunostimulation,[25] initiation of the acute-phase response to infection by the liver,[25] fever,[24] induction of slow-wave sleep,[26] muscle pain and the breakdown of muscle tissue,[27] and decreased sensitivity to pain.[25] It is biologically plausible that each of these responses could be sensitive and specific to overtraining in a predictable dose-response manner. Recent research[28] has suggested that somatosensory evoked potentials (e.g., tendon reflexes) that can be assessed by electromyography might be alterable by overtraining.

It is also known that the body's response to physical or psychological stress or both involves interactions among the central nervous, endocrine, and immune systems.[29,30] It has been suggested that many of the symptoms of staleness due to overtraining result from altered function of these systems.[31–37] There are a number of reports of the effects of strenuous exercise on blood concentrations of endogenous opiates (B-endorphin and enkephalin),[38,39] ACTH and cortisol,[34,37,39,40] and various markers of immune function[36,41–44] at rest and in response to acute exercise. It is biologically plausible that overtraining could affect immune responses because of the immunoactivating effects of body heating, the immunosuppressive effects of norepinephrine and cortisol on T-lymphocytes, and the inhibitory influence of blood β-endorphin on the suppression of lymphocyte number and function by catecholamines and glucocorticoids like cortisol. There are anecdotes and some cross-sectional research reports of increased incidence of upper respiratory infections among overtrained athletes in endurance sports.

Measures of the status and function of endocrine and immune systems could be useful as markers of overtraining. One problem is their low reliability within an individual. That is, many blood-borne biochemical variables, including β-endorphin and CPK, can fluctuate greatly day-to-day without obvious cause. These fluctuations make it difficult to determine their sensitivity and specificity as markers of staleness due to overtraining. Also, many of these measures are elevated or depressed during normal levels of high-intensity exercise training without reports of staleness.

☐ PSYCHOLOGICAL MONITORING OF OVERTRAINING

Although adaptations to training involve complex physiological processes, alterations in psychological variables have long been recognized as important features of overtraining and staleness. Psychological factors have been implicated both as symptoms of staleness and as moderators of risk for staleness during overtraining. Kereszty[1] summarized clinical observations on staleness from the 1920s through 1952 and described a distinct cluster of psychological symptoms and behavioral signs:

> This group is earmarked by emotional and motivational imbalance, giving way either to an unusual irritability that might make a person become quarrelsome, even provocative, or else to apathy, sluggishness, and drowsiness. Self-confidence seems to be lost; the subject definitely endeavors to spare his energies, seeks to avoid situations that require greater effort, and has an aversion to training and a developing antipathy for sports grounds or other places of training (p 219).

Irritability, apathy, lack of appetite, and sleep disturbances have been associated with overtraining.[1,2,3,8,20,35] The work of Morgan and his students[8,20,40] indicates that mood disturbance might be an indicator of overtraining and staleness. In a series of cross-sectional and prospective studies with endurance athletes (runners, wrestlers, rowers, and swimmers), Morgan and colleagues have repeatedly found that successful athletes (defined by Olympic and national team selection or consensus elite status) show profiles of mood states (POMS) that indicate positive mental health. At the outset of training or the team selection process, athletes who will eventually be successful show less tension, depression, anger, fatigue, and confusion but more vigor than do unsuccessful athletes or the average nonathlete of the same age. Morgan has coined this the "iceberg profile" (see Fig. 17–3) because the negative moods are lower than for the average person, i.e., below the "surface," whereas the positive mood of vigor is well above average and is analogous to the tip of an iceberg.

Observations of U.S. Olympic male speedskaters shown in Figures 17–3 and 17–4 suggest that the "iceberg profile" is sensitive to overtraining.[45] Skaters were monitored 6 mo prior to the trials for the 1980 Winter Games, at the end of summer conditioning, and immediately before and after the trials. Athletes subsequently selected for the team demonstrated decreasing depression and increasing vigor across the training period, peaking at the trials. By comparison, the athletes not selected showed more variation in mood and showed a sustained reduction in vigor from pretraining levels. These results suggest that the athletes not selected for the national team were at higher risk for staleness based on their POMS profiles. Similarly, athletes on the U.S. Alpine ski team who were dropped from the team were more likely to score high on self-rated depression at the outset of the ski season than were those not dropped from the team, and poor initial psychological well-being predicted health problems later in the year.[46]

Mood disturbance is associated with level of training (see Fig. 17–5), and it increases with decreased performance and increased muscle sore-

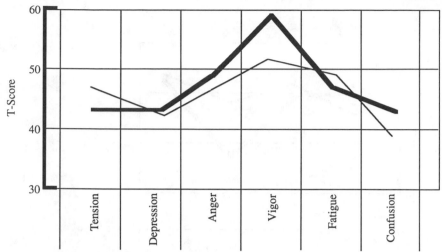

FIG. 17–3. Profile of mood states (POMS) for male contenders for the 1980 U.S. Olympic speedskating team. T1 (heavy line) represents the average pretraining baseline. T2 (thin line) represents the average responses following 5 mo of summer training on land and ice. Results show less-positive moods following training. Adapted from Guttmann, M.L., et al.: Training stress in Olympic speedskaters: A psychological perspective. Phys. Sportsmed., *12*:45, 1984.

ness among collegiate swimmers across the season. Conversely, as training volume decreases with tapering, mood disturbance lessens. It is common for initial iceberg profiles to invert for male and female college swimmers who present to a university health service complaining of symptoms of staleness.

Personality can play a role in psychological adaptation to training. For male and female candidates for the 1984 U.S. Olympic speedskating team, those who scored high on a psychometric test of self-motivation[47] showed less mood disturbance and missed fewer training sessions across the training period.[48] Similar findings were recently seen during training for a women's collegiate crew team.[49]

The POMS appears to be a useful and practical marker of pathological responses during training. Self-reports of total mood disturbance on the POMS have repeatedly been shown to be sensitive to chronic increases[8,20,40] and decreases[50] in an exercise training stimulus. Psychological monitoring can help prevent staleness, because an athlete's response to overtraining can be compared to a known clinical range based on population norms and to the athlete's own typical response established in the absence of overtraining. These comparisons can detect psychological changes that might be able to predict staleness before physiological (e.g., heart rate or body weight changes) and performance markers of staleness appear.

Studies of overtraining are needed that combine assessments of psy-

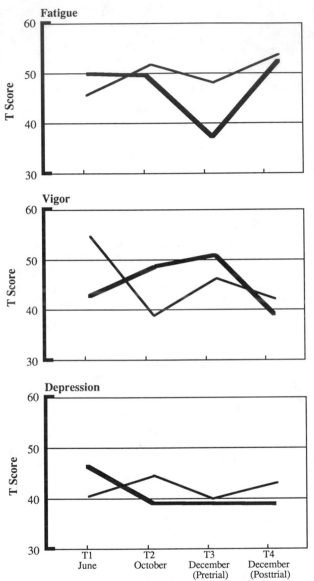

FIG. 17–4. Profile of mood states (POMS) for male contenders for the 1980 U.S. Olympic speedskating team. Results show increased fatigue and depression with decreased vigor for contenders who were eventually not selected for the U.S. team. Thick line, Olympians; thin line, non-Olympians. Adapted from Guttmann, M.L., et al.: Training stress in Olympic speedskaters: A psychological perspective. Phys. Sportsmed., *12*:45, 1984.

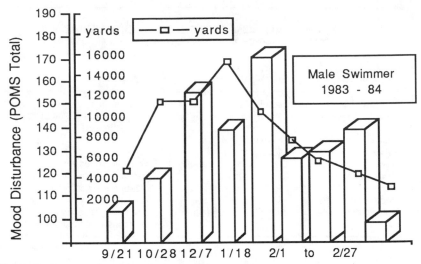

FIG. 17–5. Case study of a collegiate swimmer during the competitive season. The results show that mood disturbance is sensitive to overtraining and tapering of the exercise training stimulus. Adapted from Morgan, W.P., et al.: Psychological monitoring of overtraining and staleness. Br. J. Sports Med., 21:107, 1987.

chological, neuroendocrine, and immune responses in order to establish dose-response relationships. Stress emotions related to mood disturbance have been linked with immunocompetence[51] and lymphocyte cytotoxicity.[41] In addition, evidence from psychoneuroimmunology suggests that stress hormones[52–54] mediate psychological influences on immune responses. The relationships between psychological traits and states, stress hormones, and immune function have not been studied during exercise training,[55] but it is likely their interactions can explain important aspects of the causes of the clinical features of staleness.

☐ THE NEED FOR THEORY

Much more research must be done to develop standardized signs and symptoms of staleness and the volume of overtraining, including aspects of the training environment, that will reliably predict staleness. The physiological and psychological literatures on overtraining and staleness have lacked theoretical direction. This absence of theory, coupled with nonuniform methods used to study diverse and often uncomparable samples of athletes, has impeded the resolution of conflicting findings and beliefs about the causes and cures for staleness. For example, paradoxical signs of staleness have been reported, including dominance of the sympathetic nervous system marked by *increased* heart rate, blood pressure, and resting metabolic rate, as well as a presumed shift to

TABLE 17–1. PHYSIOLOGICAL EFFECTS OF OVERTRAINING FOR ATHLETES FROM GERMANY AND THE USSR

PARAMETER	WOLF ($N = 50$)	MOSCOW INSTITUTE ($N = 50$)
Pulse frequency	High in 47	Unchanged
Blood pressure	Elevated in 47	Depressed in 10, all others unchanged
Vital capacity	Decreased in 12	Unchanged
White blood cells	Mostly increased	Unchanged
Blood sugar level	Elevated in 27, lower in 4	Mostly decreased
Basal metabolism	Increased in 42	Mostly increased
Nitrogen balance	Mostly negative	Data are lacking
Body weight	Mostly lower	Mostly lower
Autonomous tone	Sympathetic dominance	Relative predominance of the parasympathetic side

Data from Wolf, W.: A contribution to the question of overtraining. In Health and Fitness in the Modern World. North Palm Beach, FL, Athletic Institute, 1961, pp. 291–301; and from Kereszty, A.: Overtraining. In Encyclopedia of Sports Science and Medicine. Edited by L.A. Larson and D.E. Hermann. New York, Macmillan, 1971, pp. 218–222.

parasympathetic dominance leading to *reduced* heart rate and blood pressure.[14] Both depressed and elevated adrenal function have been implicated. Table 17–1 shows early reports that conflicted over these responses. These measures and their changes are representative of most research. The cause or meaning of the conflicting results cannot be determined because of unstandardized definitions of overtraining and staleness, the comparison of selected groups of athletes rather than comparing experimental and control conditions, and the absence of biologically coherent conceptual models for predicting and explaining the effects reported.

CROSS-DISCIPLINARY HUMAN PERFORMANCE MODEL

Because most studies on overtraining and staleness have lacked a conceptual basis, the results have not been clearly plausible. In other words, it has been difficult to explain the causes of most of the findings reported. It will not be possible to implement practical means for reducing the risk of staleness until causes for the signs and symptoms that accompany overtraining are known. The lack of theory has also made it difficult to reconcile physiological results that do not agree.

Recent work by Costill and colleagues[15,18,20,56] illustrates the necessity of using cross-disciplinary approaches to resolving this problem. These investigators have employed a sports medicine team approach to research, combining traditions from physiology, nutrition, and psychology. Their recent reports that objectively defined staleness (decreased performance and coaches' ratings) is accompanied by *lower* blood lactate during exercise is in conflict with the long-held view that stale athletes show *high* blood lactate. The stale athletes in the Costill et al. research also had low muscle glycogen and low carbohydrate intake in their diets, however. The unavailability of glycogen substrate during exercise would explain low blood lactate, and a link between poor diet, low glycogen stores in muscle, and the resulting decrease in performance offers a biologically explainable contributing factor to staleness. The stale athletes in these studies also reported more mood disturbance (see Fig. 17–6) and muscle soreness than did swimmers who showed no performance decrease.[20] Whether the mood disturbance represented an independent marker of staleness, a response to diet, or led to diet changes is unclear. Studies that have altered dietary composition during chronic exercise training show mixed effects on mood,[57,58] so the relationship between diet, substrate availability, mood, and performance during overtraining warrants more study.

PSYCHONEUROENDOCRINE MODEL

Another conceptual model for understanding adaptations to overtraining that lead to staleness involves the hypothalamic-pituitary-adrenal (HPA) axis. Stale athletes, and patients who are anxious and depressed for reasons not due to athletic training, all show signs and symptoms of a disrupted HPA axis at rest and during challenge. These signs and symptoms include disturbances of mood, appetite, sleep, motivated behavior, and several indexes of autonomic, endocrine and immune status.[59] A common thread that binds these signs and symptoms is hypercortisolism, i.e., abnormally high secretion of cortisol.[60] One of the major functions of cortisol is to maintain blood sugar levels during stress through the liberation and use of stored fat and glycogen and amino acids from muscle cells.[61] In normal physiological concentrations, cortisol helps the body combat stress. In very high concentrations, however, cortisol suppresses immune responses to infection and can inhibit healing. To understand the role of hypercortisolism in overtraining and staleness, it is necessary to understand the role of cortisol in the regulation of the HPA axis and how the HPA axis can be disrupted.

The HPA axis consists of a number of neuroendocrine structures and functions[62,63] (see Fig. 17–7). After neural stimulation by higher brain centers, the hypothalamus releases corticotropin-releasing factor (CRF) into the anterior pituitary. The anterior pituitary then releases adrenocorticotropin hormone (ACTH) and β-endorphin. ACTH causes increased synthesis and secretion of cortisol from the cortex of the adrenal gland.

As blood concentrations of ACTH and cortisol rise, they also inhibit further CRF production and/or release at the level of the hypothalamus or higher in the CNS. This inhibition provides a natural negative feedback so that a normally functioning HPA axis can self-limit its activity (e.g., ACTH, cortisol, and β-endorphin return to resting levels) when

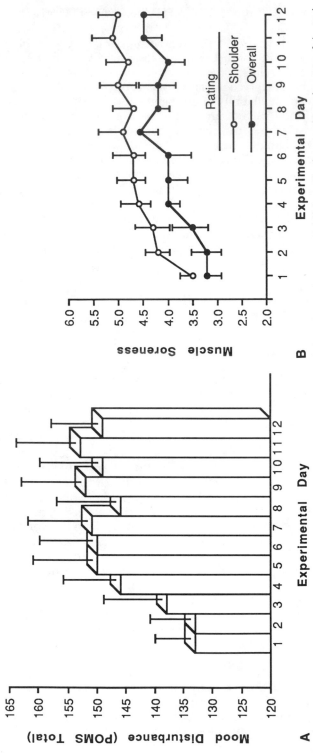

FIG. 17–6. Overtraining is accompanied by increased mood disturbance (*A*) and muscle soreness (*B*) in collegiate male swimmers. Adapted from Morgan, W.P., et al.: Mood disturbance following increased training in swimmers. Med. Sci. Sports Exerc., 20:408, 1988.

FIG. 17–7. Model of the hypothalamic-pituitary-adrenal axis and its major regulatory pathways. From Dunn, A.L., and Dishman, R.K.: Exercise and the neurobiology of depression. Exerc. Sport Sci. Rev., in press.

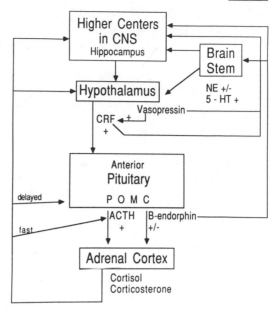

the need for a stress response subsides. Neurotransmitters such as dopamine (DA), norepinephrine (NE), serotonin (5-HT), and β-endorphin can also stimulate or inhibit the secretion of hypothalamic releasing hormones.

After chronic exposure to excessive stress, the HPA axis can lose some of its ability to turn on or off when acute stress is encountered. A characteristic sign of some types of depressive and anxiety disorders is hypercortisolism or the failure to suppress pituitary ACTH after infusion of cortisol or CRF.[64,65] Hypersecretion of cortisol can be explained by a disruption at any of several sites in the HPA axis.[66] These include but are not limited to (1) hypersensitivity of the adrenal gland to ACTH, (2) hyposensitivity of the pituitary gland to cortisol, (3) hypersensitivity of the pituitary to CRF, (4) hypersecretion of CRF by the hypothalamus, and (5) resistance to neural feedback.

Although daily cortisol levels provide a practical marker of HPA disruption, the many sites for regulating the HPA axis explain why studies have not always agreed over the autonomic and endocrine responses that accompany overtraining. Conflicting results can occur because of differences in the regulatory status of the HPA axis. Also, concentrations of HPA hormones under resting conditions might not be as sensitive or specific to overtraining as are hormone responses to challenge tests of the HPA axis.

A recent study.[67] reported a decreased resting ACTH and cortisol response to CRF among highly trained runners compared with sedentary and moderately trained runners. This response was consistent with sustained hypercortisolism in the highly trained group. It occurred despite comparable increases for all groups in ACTH and cortisol during exercise. However, the cross-sectional design of the study prevents the conclusion that overtraining rather than other intrinsic HPA differences explained the results. Self-selection biases can cloud results in these types of studies. This is illustrated by another cross-sectional comparison between highly trained endurance athletes and sedentary individuals that found no differences in plasma DA and NE responses to nonexertional stressors including a reaction-time shock avoidance task and the cold presser test.[68]

Uncontrolled prospective studies of overtraining also report mixed results. Increased salivary cortisol and mood disturbance have been reported after overtraining in female collegiate swimmers,[40] (see Fig. 17–8) and these results are consistent with a hypercortisolism marker of staleness. Another study of "stale" endurance athletes, however, showed lower than expected plasma cortisol, ACTH, growth hormone, and prolactin response to insulin-induced hypoglycemia, and the responses returned to normal following 4 weeks of rest.[34] These results were interpreted as evidence for inhibition of the normal responsiveness by the hypothalamus as a result of overtraining.

These two studies show that cortisol responses of stale athletes can differ between resting conditions and tests that challenge functions of the HPA axis. They also suggest that the response seen must be judged against a biologically appropriate index of normal HPA function.

Related to hypercortisolism is the disruption of circadian rhythms.[69,70] In major depression, disruption of these rhythms is reflected by an atypical pattern of cortisol secretion and abnormalities of nighttime sleep. For example, a shortened latency of rapid-eye-movement (REM) sleep, the period between sleep onset and the first period of dreaming, is a consistent finding among depressed patients. Other abnormalities of sleep have also been noted in depression. These include an absence of slow-wave sleep (SWS) (stages 3 and 4) and an increased number of spontaneous awakenings.

Scientific studies of sleep during overtraining or sleep problems reported by stale athletes have not been done. Incompletely controlled experimental studies[71–75] of normal subjects have shown that acute exercise is followed by increased SWS during the evening following the exercise. High-intensity (50 to 70% $\dot{V}O_2$ peak) exercise to exhaustion leads to increased SWS early in the sleep period and a decrease in REM sleep. These effects have been seen most often when trained athletes are studied, but comparisons of fit and unfit individuals indicate that sleep differences do not depend on daily exercise. Although this implies that a training effect is necessary for sleep effects, selection bias (i.e., personal attributes other than fitness) is another explanation. Convincing prospective studies of initially low fit persons have not been reported. Prospective studies have not been conducted to see if exercise training alters sleep in individuals with sleep disorders, and no studies have been conducted with depressed patients to see if exercise causes

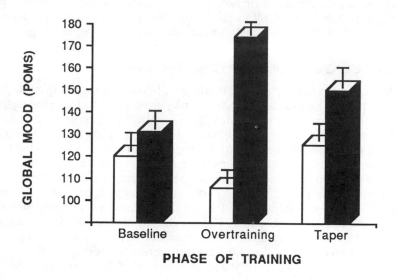

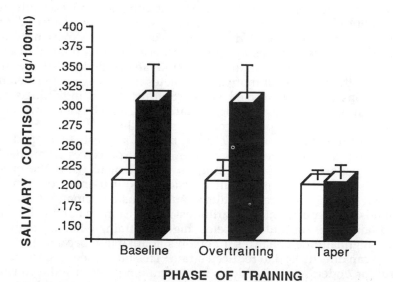

FIG. 17–8. Changes in mood disturbance (A) and salivary cortisol (B) following overtraining and tapering in female collegiate swimmers. Adapted from O'Connor, P.J., et al.: Mood state and salivary cortisol levels following overtraining in female swimmers. Psychoneuroendocrinol., *14:*303, 1989.

REM latency to lengthen or whether SWS increases in depressed patients. Similarly, it is not known if objective changes in sleep patterns can be used as markers of risk for staleness during overtraining.

PSYCHOLOGICAL MODELS FOR OVERTRAINING

Studies of exercise overtraining could also benefit from attention to prevailing psychological models of work stress.[76] Modern theoretical models that consider how athletes appraise the environmental demands of their sports and their confidence in ability and personal control over training and competitive decisions might help explain some aspects of the chronic stress that accompanies training for endurance sports.

In the most popular models of work stress, environmental events that accompany exercise training are not viewed as uniform stressors that affect all athletes equally. Their impact depends on perceptions or evaluations made by the individual. These evaluations are not only estimates of the demands stemming from the environment but also estimates by the individual of personal ability and motivation to meet those demands. One popular model of work stress proposes that two protective mechanisms combat stress: social support and ego defense. If these mechanisms do not function, stresses will develop into strains that can lead to impaired performance, psychosomatic disorders, and dissatisfaction.

This model provides an interesting perspective on the traditional models of athletic overtraining, because it considers how an athlete's personality can moderate staleness. For example, self-motivated candidates for the 1984 U.S. Olympic speedskating team experienced less mood disturbance and missed fewer practice sessions than did candidates with low self-motivation.[47] Self-motivated individuals have high ego-strength.[48] Thus, self-motivated athletes might have better defense mechanisms against perceived stress. Self-motivated individuals also score high on a test of psychological hardiness, which is a known moderator of the relationship between stress and illness.[77]

A recent modification of work stress models suggests that equally or more important than the stress that an athlete perceives from the demands of sport or the sport setting is the extent to which he or she perceives control over important decisions about training or competition. For this model, stress results from various combinations of sport demands and constraints or latitudes in decision making. High demand–low decision latitude yields highest strain, whereas high demand–high latitude enhances a person's adaptability because personal actions can directly lead to reduced strain. This model seems particularly useful for understanding athletes in overtraining, because the constant biological requirements of athletic conditioning make it difficult for athletes to adjust perceived abilities or motives to an extent that will offset the physical demands of their sports. Because the physical demands of training that are placed on athletes are constant, perceived control over training decisions offers more room for change and might enhance an athlete's ability to cope with the stress of overtraining.

Each of these work stress models offers testable hypotheses regarding the psychology of adaptations to overtraining among athletes. They can add an important dimension to the predominantly physiological approaches taken to overtraining and staleness, because they recognize that how an athlete evaluates the stress of training can affect health and motivation during overtraining in ways that are independent of the physiological strain of overtraining.

☐ OVERTRAINING, EATING, AND BODY WEIGHT

Moderate exercise has several potentially healthful benefits. There are few scientific studies of its possible negative effects. This is particularly true for psychological outcomes.[78] Clinical parallels have been drawn between excessively committed runners and patients diagnosed as suffering from anorexia nervosa. Those problems are discussed in detail in Chapters 8 and 9. It is believed that the disciplined training and social milieu in sports that place a high premium on a lean body composition and dietary restriction can promote the development of eating problems or add to existing problems.

It remains unclear, however, if these circumstances describing sports training and eating disorders reveal a common cause, if they are motivated by common goals or incentives, or if each represents compulsions with similar surface behaviors but with different origins, underlying processes, and medical outcomes. These are important questions to resolve because case studies have reported that running psychotherapy can aid the treatment of anorexia and because exercise is an alternative to restrictive dieting among weight-conscious females. It is clear that regular exercise can assist weight loss and weight management for many people. Although the link between exercise and body weight appears to offer healthful benefits for many, pathological extremes might be present as well: instances in which obsessions with weight loss might parallel excessive commitment to exercise and physical fitness.

Although concern over excessive exercise and risk for eating disorders appears to have some basis, results from other studies reveal that the issues are complex. Anorectics are commonly reported to augment food restriction by hyperactivity, but their aerobic fitness ($\dot{V}O_{2peak}$ is well below average, whereas that of habitual runners and overtrained athletes is well above average. In addition, cross-sectional studies have not revealed a common psychopathology between obligatory (i.e., excessively committed) runners and anorectic patients.[78,79]

Scientific findings that are available do not yet permit clear conclusions. Previous studies lack generalizability and standardization of sampling and method. Small selected groups of athletes from different sports, regions, levels of competition, and socioeconomic backgrounds have been sampled. This makes it difficult to compare risks between types of sport when other influences on eating behaviors such as family history, personality, and socioeconomic status might differ between samples. Similarly, athletes' risk profiles have not been evaluated against those for nonathlete matched controls from the same academic, socioeconomic, and psychological background. Furthermore, standardized measures of eating attitudes and behaviors have not been uniformly used with athlete samples. Thus it is difficult to compare study outcomes because different dependent measures have been used. Studies that have compared habitual exercisers from a community or population base with anorectic patients have not quantified the exercise behavior of either sample to verify the similarities or differences in physical activity assumed to exist between the two groups. This prevents conclusions that differences of similarities in eating behaviors or attitudes seen in athletes and anorectics are due to involvement in sport or exercise rather than to attributes that existed prior to self-selection into the anorectic and exerciser groups.

There are case reports, however, of excessive involvement or dependence with exercise training. Morgan[80] described eight cases of "running addiction" in which commitment to running exceeded prior commitments to work, family, social relations, and medical advice. Similar cases have been labeled as positive addiction, runner's gluttony, fitness fanaticism, athlete's neurosis, obligatory running, and exercise abuse.[78] Little is understood, however, about the origins, diagnostic validity, or the mental health impact of abusive exercise. For most people, the benefits of exercise exceed the risks of exercise abuse; sedentariness represents a more prevalent public health problem.

On the other hand, the inability or unwillingness to interrupt or reduce one's involvement in an exercise training program or to replace a preferred form of exercise with an alternative, when this decision is indicated by medical reasons or vocational or social responsibilities, might reveal an emotional disturbance of clinical meaning. The few studies that show psychopathology in habitual runners indicate that exaggerated emphasis on exercise roles or fitness abilities can reflect a pre-existing proneness to problems of a self-concept that is insecure and overly restricted to exercise and fitness goals.

Because endurance exercise continues to be promoted as a health behavior, it is important to accurately identify overall risks, and individuals at risk, for eating disorders that might accompany an exercise training regimen. The randomized clinical trials needed to answer these questions for the population of North American exercisers are costly, however, and they are not justified until compelled by convincing cross-sectional and correlational studies. In two recent controlled experimental studies of risks,[81,82] we have not observed the negative health consequences we expected based on earlier cross-sectional studies. Healthy inactive women showed no pathological signs of eating disorders or mental health problems following a 6-month overtraining period during which weekly running mileage was increased from less than 10 to more than 60 miles per week. We have also observed increased muscular strength and cardiorespiratory endurance following 12 weeks of training in males diagnosed as seropositive for the HIV-1 human immunodeficiency virus and symptomatic for AIDS or AIDS-related complex. The increased fitness occurred with no change in T-lymphocyte indicators of immune status or in clinical diagnosis of health status. In both studies, overtraining was gradual according to the guidelines of the American College of Sports Medicine.[83] Thus our results show that the amount of overtraining that will reliably increase risk for staleness is unknown and might vary widely from person to person.

Despite the importance of issues over disorders of eating and body weight that can accompany overtraining, much more systematic research is needed that follows the traditions of epidemiology and the clinical sciences of psychology and psychiatry. It is now unclear whether overtraining is a risk factor for disorders of eating and body weight or whether these disorders can lead to staleness.

☐ SUMMARY

Table 17–2 depicts the physiological and psychological effects of overtraining that have been implicated as potential indicators of staleness in the sports medicine literature. I have rated these effects according to their potential usefulness by athletes and coaches as practical risk factors for staleness, their established sensitivity and specificity as risk factors or indicators of staleness, and on the quantity and quality of the scientific evidence implicating them for overtraining and staleness. On the basis of current research, none of these effects satisfies medical or epidemiological standards as a sign or symptom of staleness with established sensitivity and specificity for predicting or explaining staleness adaptations to overtraining. Part of this uncertainty is due to the absence of uniform standards in past research for defining the overtraining stimulus in terms relative to an athlete's individual tolerance for chronic exercise and for defining staleness. When a lasting performance decrement is not clearly shown in all studies, it is difficult to regard "staleness" signs and symptoms as emanating from the same course. Even when staleness is not defined or produced, it is important to determine which signs and symptoms show sensitive and specific dose-response changes with overtraining and with periods of detraining.

Experimentally controlled clinical studies of athletes while they overtrain are needed to determine the causes and consequences of staleness. Most studies of overtraining and staleness have used case reports, cross-sectional comparisons of selected groups of athletes, or uncontrolled descriptions of responses during overtraining. A number of potentially useful markers of risk for staleness have been suggested by these studies. The absence of scientific control limits our confidence in the predictive validity of the responses seen, however, because other factors besides overtraining could have caused the responses.

Prospective studies of athletes undergoing systematic periods of overtraining and decreased training, contrasted with comparable athletes who do not overtrain or with a truly randomized control group, are

TABLE 17–2. POTENTIAL MARKERS OF RISK FOR STALENESS DURING OVERTRAINING

MARKER	CHANGE	SENSITIVE/ SPECIFIC	STRENGTH OF EVIDENCE*	PRACTICAL
Signs				
Resting HR[13,14]	↑ or ↓ ?	Yes/No	A,B	Yes
T-wave of ECG[13,14]	abnormal	No/No	A,B	No
VO_{2peak}[1,2,14,16]	↓	No/No	A,B	?
VO_2 at standard work rate[1,2,14]	↑	No/No	A	?
HR/VO_2 (oxygen pulse)[1,2]	↑	No/No	A,B	?
Blood lactate[1,2,14,17,56]	↑ or ↓ ?	No/No	A,B; D	Yes
Body weight[1,3,14,35]	↓	No/No	A,B	Yes
Muscle strength and power[18]	↓	Yes/No	C,D	Yes
Muscle glycogen[19]	↓	Yes/No	D	No; diet records, yes
Blood CPK[1,2,21,22]	↑	No/No	B,C	Yes
Blood and salivary cortisol[34,37,40]	↑	Yes/?	B,C	Yes
Blood testosterone[37]	↓	Yes/?	B	Yes
Blood β-endorphin and ACTH[38,39]	↑	?/No	Not studied	No
Blood IL-1[23,24]	↑	?/No	Not studied	No
Blood T-cell Lympho-cytes[31,32,36,42,55]	↑ or ↓ ?	?/No	B	No
Somatosensory reflexes[26]	?	?/?	C	No
Symptoms				
Mood Disturbance (POMS total)[8,20,40,55]	↑	Yes/No	C,D	Yes
Anxiety[1,3]	↑	?/No	A	?
Self-confidence[1,2,3]	↓	?/No	A	?
Depression[8,51,52]	↑	?/No	A,C	?
Hostility[1,3]	↑	?/No	A	?
Apathy[1,3]	↑	?/No	A	?
Appetite[1,3]	↓	?/No	A,B	Yes; reliable?
Sleep disturbance[3,20]	↑	?/?	A,B,C	Yes; reliable?
Perceived exertion[1,2,35]	↑	Yes/?	A,B,C	Yes
Muscle soreness[1,20]	↑	?/Yes	A,B,C	Yes
Chronic fatigue[1,3,45]	↑	Yes/No	A,B,C	Yes

* A, anecdotal support, generalizability unknown; B, clinical studies with poor scientific control, predictive validity and generalizability unknown; C, controlled, nonrandomized prospective studies, cause and effect not established; D, experimental support, predictive validity and generalizability must be determined by replication.

necessary before the sensitivity, specificity, and predictive validity of staleness risk factors can be identified. Randomized experiments will also permit understanding of the physiological and psychological mechanisms responsible for staleness adaptations. Epidemiological studies with large representative samples are also needed to establish the prevalence and incidence of staleness, and its risk factors, among populations of athletes from sports in which overtraining and staleness are believed to be problems.

For both types of research, it will be important to have guidance from the theoretical models so that the physiological and psychological plausibility of the presumed causes, signs, and symptoms of staleness can be determined. Plausibility and practicality will be the ultimate standards against which effective guidelines and principles for monitoring overtraining responses and for the primary and secondary prevention of staleness will be judged by athletes, coaches, and sports medicine specialists.

☐ REFERENCES

1. Kereszty, A.: Overtraining. In Encyclopedia of Sports Science and Medicine. Edited by L.A. Larson and D.E. Hermann. New York, Macmillan, 1971, pp. 218–222.
2. Mellerowicz, H., and Barron, D.K.: Overtraining. In Encyclopedia of Sports Science and Medicine. Edited by L.A. Larson and D.E. Hermann. New York, Macmillan, 1971, pp. 1310–1312.
3. Wolf, J.G.: Staleness. In Encyclopedia of Sport Sciences and Medicine. Edited by L.A. Larson. New York, Macmillan, 1971, pp. 1048–1051.
4. Brustmann, W., and Horske, G.: Zur diagnostik und Therapie des Ubertrainings. Muenchener Medizineische Wochenschrift, 251:1834, 1928.
5. Griffith, C.R.: Psychology of Coaching. New York, Scribner, 1926.
6. Parmenter, D.C.: Some medical aspects of training of college athletes. Boston Med. Surg. J., 189:49, 1923.
7. American Medical Association: Standard Nomenclature of Athletic Injuries. Chicago, American Medical Association, 1966.
8. Morgan, W.P., et al.: Psychological monitoring of overtraining and staleness. Br. J. Sports Med., 21:107, 1987.
9. Moore, J.W.: The psychology of athletic coaching. Minneapolis, Burgess, 1970.
10. Brouha, L.: Training. In Science and Medicine Exercise and Sports. Edited by W.R. Johnson. New York, Harper & Brothers, 1960, pp. 403–416.
11. Ryder, H.W., Carr, H.J., and Herget, P.: Future performance in footracing. Sci. Am., 234:109, 1976.
12. Riegel, P.S.: Athletic records and human performance. Am. Scientist, 69:281, 1981.
13. Dressendorfer, R.H., Wade, C.E., and Scaff, J.H., Jr.: Increased morning heart rate in runners: A valid sign of overtraining? Phys. Sportsmed., 13:77, 1985.
14. Wolf, W.: A contribution to the question of overtraining. In Health and Fitness in the Modern World. North Palm Beach, FL, Athletic Institute, 1961, pp. 291–301.
15. Costill, D.L., et al.: Metabolic characteristics of skeletal muscle during detraining from competitive swimming. Med. Sci. Sports Exerc., 17:339, 1985.
16. Hickson, RC., and Rosenkoetter, M.A.: Reduced training frequencies and maintenance of increased aerobic power. Med. Sci. Sports Exerc., 13:13, 1981.

17. Maron, M.B., Horvath, S.M., and Wilkerson, J.E.: Blood biochemical alterations during recovery from competitive marathon running. Eur. J. Appl. Phys., 38:231, 1977.
18. Costill, D.L., et al.: Effects of reduced training on muscular power in swimmers. Phys. Sports Med., 13:95, 1985.
19. Costill, D.L., et al.: Effects of repeated days of intensified training on muscle glycogen and swimming performance. Med. Sci. Sports Exerc., 20:249, 1988.
20. Morgan, W.P., et al.: Mood disturbance following increased training swimmers. Med. Sci. Sports Exerc., 20:408, 1988.
21. Houston, M.E., Bentzen, H., and Larsen, H.: Interrelationships between skeletal muscle adaptations and performance as studied by detraining and retraining. Acta Phys. Scand., 105:163, 1979.
22. Burke, E.R., et al.: Creatine kinase levels in competitive swimmers during a season of training. Scand. J. Sports Sci., 4:1, 1982.
23. Cannon, J.G., et al.: Physiologic mechanisms contributing to increased interleukin-1 secretion. J. Appl. Phys., 61:1869, 1986.
24. Cannon, J.G., and Kluger, M.J.: Endogenous pyrogen activity in human plasma after exercise. Science, 236:617, 1983.
25. Oppenheim, J.J., and Shevach, E.M.: Immunophysiologic role of interleukin-1. In Immunophysiology. Edited by J.J. Oppenheim and E.M. Shevach. Oxford, Oxford University Press, 1989, p. 219.
26. Kreuger, J.M., et al.: Sleep-promoting effects of endogenous pyrogens (interleukin-1). Am. J. Phys., 246:R994, 1984.
27. Baracos, V., et al.: Stimulation of muscle protein degradation and prostoglandin E2 release by leukocytic pyrogen (interleukin-1). N. Eng. J. Med., 308:553, 558, 1983.
28. Koceja, D.M., and Kamen, G.: Conditioned patellar tendon reflexes in sprint- and endurance-trained athletes. Med. Sci. Sports Exerc., 20:172, 1988.
29. Bateman, A., et al.: The immune-hypothalamic-pituitary-adrenal axis. Endocr. Rev., 10:92–112, 1989.
30. Rabin, B., Cunnick, J.E., and Lysle, D.T.: Stress-induced alternation of immune function. Prog. Neuroendocrin. Immumol., 3:116, 1990.
31. Mackinnon, L.T., et al.: The effects of exercise on secretory and natural immunity. Adv. Exp. Med. Biol., 216A:869, 1988.
32. Peters, E., and Bateman, E.: Ultramarathon running and upper respiratory tract infections. S. Afr. Med. J., 64:582, 1983.
33. Ayers, W.J.T., Komesu, Y., Romani, T., and Ansbacker, R.: Anthropomorphic, hormonal, and psychologic correlates of semen quality in endurance-trained male athletes. Fertil. Steril., 19:1155, 1984.
34. Barron, J.L., et al.: Hypothalamic dysfunction in overtrained athletes. J. Clin. Endocrin. Metabl, 60:803, 1985.
35. Ryan, A.J., et al.: Overtraining in athletes: A round table. Phys. Sportsmed., 11:92, 1983.
36. Tomasi, T.B., et al.: Immune parameters in athletes before and after strenuous exercise. J. Clin. Immunol. 2:173, 1982.
37. Stray-Gundersen, J., Videman, T., and Snell, P.G.: Changes in selected objective parameters during overtraining. Med. Sci. Sports Exerc., 18(Suppl. 2):54, 1986.
38. Davis, J.M., et al.: Opioid modulation of feeding behavior following repeated exposure to forced swimming exercise in male rats. Pharmacol. Biochem. Behav. 23:709, 1985.
39. Harber, V.J., and Sutton, J.R.: Endorphins and exercise. Sports Med., 1:154, 1984.
40. O'Connor, P.J., et al.: Mood state and salivary cortisol levels following overtraining in female swimmers. Psychoneuroendocrinol. 14:303, 1989.
41. Eskola, J., et al.: Effect of sport stress on lymphocyte transformation and antibody formation. Clin. Exp. Immunol., 32:339, 1978.

42. Hanson, P.G., and Falherty, D.K.: Immunological responses to training conditioned runners. Clin. Sci., 60:225, 1981.
43. Hedfors, E., Holm, G., and Ohnell, B.: Variations of blood lymphocytes during work studied by cell surface markers, DNA synthesis and cytotoxicity. Clin. Exp. Immunol., 24:328, 1976.
44. Watson, R.R., et al.: Modification of cellular immune function in humans by endurance exercise training during β-adrenergic blockade with atenolol or propranolol. Med. Sci. Sports Exerc., 18:95, 1986.
45. Guttmann, M.L., et al.: Training stress in Olympic speedskaters: A psychological perspective. Phys. Sportsmed., 12:45, 1984.
46. May, J.R., and Veach, T., et al.: A psychological study of health, injury, and performance in athletes on the U.S. Alpine Ski Team. Phys. Sportsmed., 13:111, 1985.
47. Dishman, R.K., and Ickes, W.: Self-motivation and adherence to therapeutic exercise. J. Behav. Med., 4:421, 1981.
48. Knapp, D., et al.: Self-motivation among 1984 Olympic speedskating hopefuls and emotional response and adherence to training (abstr.). Med. Sci. Sports Exerc. 16:114, 1984.
49. Raglin, J.S., Morgan, W.P., and Luchsinger, A.E.: Mood and self-motivation in successful and unsuccessful female rowers. Med. Sci. Sports Exerc., 22:849, 1990.
50. Wittig, A.F., Houmard, J.A., and Costill, D.L.: Psychological effects during reduced training in distance runners. Int. J. Sports Med., 10:97, 1989.
51. Kiecolt-Glaser, J.K., and Glaser, R.: Psychosocial moderators of immune function. Ann. Behav. Med., 9:16, 1987.
52. Bateman, A., et al.: The immune-hypothalamic-pituitary-adrenal axis. Endocr. Rev., 10:92, 1989.
53. Rabin, B.S., Cunnick, J.E., and Lysle, D.T.: Stress-induced alteration of immune function. Progr. Neuroendocrin. Immunol., 3:116, 1990.
54. Shavit, Y., and Martin, F.C.: Opiates, stress, and immunity: Animal studies. Ann. Behav. Med., 91:11, 1987.
55. Keast, D., Cameron, K., and Morton, A.R.: Exercise and the immune response. Sports Med., 5:248, 1988.
56. Kirwin, J.P., et al.: Physiological responses to successive days of intensive training in competitive swimmers. Med. Sci. Sports Exerc., 20:255, 1988.
57. Morgan, W.P., et al.: Influence of increased training and diet on mood states. Med. Sci. Sports Exerc., 20:S95, 1988.
58. Prusaczyk, W.K., Dishman, R.K., and Cureton, K.C.: Effects of glycogen depleting exercise and altered diet composition on mood state of young adult males. Med. Sci. Sports Exerc., in press.
59. Dunn, A.L., and Dishman, R.K.: Exercise and the neurobiology of depression. Exerc. Sport Sci. Rev., in press.
60. Sachar, E.J., et al.: Recent studies in the neuroendocrinology of major depressive disorders. Psychiatr. Clin. North Am., 3:3113, 1980.
61. Galbo, H., et al.: Discussion: Hormonal adaptation to physical activity. In Exercise, Fitness and Health: A Consensus of Current Knowledge. Edited by C. Bouchard, R.J. Shepard, T. Stephens, J.R. Sutton, and B.D. McPherson. Champaign, IL, Human Kinetics, 1990, pp. 259–263.
62. Bennett, G.W., and Whitehead, S.A.: Mammalian Neuroendocrinology. New York, Oxford, 1983.
63. Jones, M.T., and Gillham, B.: Factors involved in the regulation of adrenocorticotropic hormone/B-lipotropic hormone. Physiol. Rev. 68:743, 1988.
64. Gold, P.W., Goodwin, F.K., and Chrousos, G.P.: Clinical and biochemical manifestations of depression. Relation to the neurobiology of stress (first of two parts). N. Eng. J. Med., 319:348, 1988.

65. Gold, P.W., Goodwin, F.K., and Chrousos, G.P.: Clinical and biochemical manifestations of depression. Relation to the neurobiology of stress (second of two parts). N. Eng. J. Med., 319:413, 1988.
66. Sapolsky, R.M., and Plotsky, P.M.: Hypercortisolism and its possible neural bases. Biol. Psychiatry, 27:937, 1990.
67. Luger, A., et al.: Acute hypothalamic-pituitary-adrenal responses to the stress of treadmill exercise: Physiologic adaptations to physical training. N. Eng. J. Med., 316:1309, 1987.
68. Claytor, R.P., et al.: Aerobic power and cardiovascular response to stress. J. Appl. Physiol., 65:1416, 1988.
69. Krieger, D.T.: Rhythms in CRFT, ACTH, and corticosteroids. In Endocrine Rhythms. Edited by D.T. Krieger. New York, Raven Press, 1979, pp. 123–142.
70. Meltzer, H.Y., and Lowy, M.T.: Neuroendocrinine function in psychiatric disorders and behavior. In American Handbook of Psychiatry. 2nd ed. Edited by S. Arieti. Vol. 8. Biol. Psychiatry. Edited by P.A. Berger and H.K.H. Brodie. New York, Basic Books, 1986, pp. 111–150.
71. Horne, J.A.: The effects of exercise upon sleep: A critical review. Biol. Psychol., 12:241, 1981.
72. Horne, J.A., and Moore, V.J.: Sleep EEG effects of exercise with and without additional body cooling. Electroencephalogr. Clin. Neurophysiol., 60:33, 1985.
73. Kupfer, D.J., et al.: Exercise and subsequent sleep in male runners: Failure to support the slow wave sleep-mood-exercise hypothesis. Neuropsychobiol., 14:5, 1985.
74. Torsvall, A., Akerstedt, T., and Lindbeck, G.: Effects of sleep stages and EEG power density of different degrees of exercise in fit subjects. Electroencephalogr. Clin. Neurophysiol., 57:347, 1984.
75. Trinder, J., et al.: Endurance as opposed to power training: Their effect on sleep. Psychophysiology, 22:668, 1985.
76. Dishman, R.K., and Landy, F.J.: Psychological factors and prolonged exercise. In Perspectives in Exercise Science and Sports Medicine, Vol. 1, Prolonged Exercise. Indianapolis, Benchmark Press, 1988, pp. 140–167.
77. Kobasa, S.C., et al.: Effectiveness of hardiness, exercise, and social support as resources against illness. J. Psychosom. Res., 29:525, 1985.
78. Dishman, R.K.: Medical psychology in exercise and sport. Med. Clin. North Am., 69:123, 1985.
79. Blumenthal, J.A., Rose, S., and Chang, J.L.: Anorexia nervosa and exercise. Sports Med., 2:237, 1985.
80. Morgan, W.P.: Negative addiction in runners. Phys. Sportsmed., 7:57, 1979.
81. Dishman, R.K., et al.: Psychological and behavioral effects of overtraining in healthy women: No evidence of health risk. Unpublished manuscript.
82. Rigsby, L. et al.: The effects of exercise training on males seropositive for the human immunodeficiency virus-1. Unpublished manuscript.
83. American College of Sports Medicine: The recommended quantity and quality of exercise for developing and maintaining cardiorespiratory and muscular fitness in healthy adults. Med. Sci. Sports Exerc., 22:265, 1990.

P A R T

V

APPLIED ISSUES

CHAPTER

18

MODERN ATHLETICS: THE PRESSURE TO PERFORM

Donna A. Lopiano and Connee Zotos

Participation in competitive sport has always involved a component of courage and risk-taking: trying out for a team, competing in front of family and friends, and making quick decisions followed by quick actions that often determine the outcome of the athletic contest.[1] Athletes place their ego "at risk" through every step of the process. Sport has always been an exciting stimulus or stressor with positive and negative possibilities, and athletes have always faced and had to overcome self-imposed and externally generated pressures to succeed. The pressure on an athlete to perform is not limited, however, to the contest or training environment.

Dealing with the consequences of athletic participation cannot be separated from the athlete as a youth going through stages of normal adolescent development and his or her concomitant at-risk periods. Further, it should come as no surprise that the majority of dysfunctional responses to athletic participation appear in our post-secondary school programs. Unique to sport in the United States is the fact that the vast majority of amateur athletics programs are sponsored and conducted by educational institutions. Pinkerton, et al.[2] maintain that college student-athletes are particularly at risk for experiencing various forms of developmental crises and psychological distress because the normal stage of adolescent development they face involves major transitions that are not easily accomplished. They contend that college-age youth must master the challenges of "separating from family and assuming independence, consolidating an identity and a mature sexuality, learning to manage feelings of intimacy, establishing a set of values, and solidifying career goals."[2] Academic demands, long hours of practice and training, time-consuming trips to athletic events, and often separate living quarters are just a few of the many factors that can lead to ways of "crystallizing identities that are narrowly restricted and interpersonally isolated. For those who master this period successfully, the rewards can be substantial. For those less fortunate, it can become a potentially crippling personal experience."[2]

Today's elite athletes, like other adolescents, face increased stress from more external sources than ever before. Compared to athletes who competed just a short 20 years ago, they are more likely to come from a single-parent family or one that has been fractured by separation or divorce of spouses. Their immediate family is more likely to be geographically separated. The more investigative, aggressive, and news-hungry media are apt to reveal their problems as well as successes. The games they play have grown into a major sports institution and one NCAA postseason basketball game nets $250,000. A dropped pass or missed free throw in the culminating seconds of such contests is perceived by the public as the failure of the highest magnitude. Accomplished athletes in many sports are aware of the possibility of multi-million dollar professional sport incomes for those few who are good enough to be the very best. Thus the pressure of being the best has taken on new meaning. Female athletes have arrived in large numbers on the elite sport scene, and though societal views concerning the acceptability of participation for women appear to have changed significantly, there is still considerable dissonance involved in the female athlete role.

Sport has changed from an imprecise to a precise science. The explosion of knowledge about training techniques and sports performance reflects the financial commitment of nations, colleges, and universities to attract the finest coaches and involve the best researchers in training the elite athlete. This more sophisticated approach to sport has created a large number of athletes who are capable of competing at the highest levels. These fine athletes are all seeking the extra edge—the small mechanical change, the better show or sports implement, the superior diet, the performance-enhancing drug, vitamin, or herb, or the sophisticated weight-training machine or program. The sport environment, only a short time ago brash, exuberant, enthusiastic, and fun-filled, is now steeped in deadly serious perfectionism with an increasing dependence on technology and knowledge.

One must examine the factors contributing to eating and weight problems in athletes within this complex and pressure-filled context. The purpose of this chapter is to expand the reader's view of the source and nature of stress confronted by the athlete participating in modern athletics.

☐ PERFORMANCE PRESSURE

In order to understand and appreciate competitive performance pressure, one must understand the concept of stress. Psychologists have experienced great difficulty in formulating a specific and useful definition of stress. Some psychologists choose to define stress in a way that would be consistent with the typical definition used in engineering, namely "the application of sufficient force to an object or system to distort or deform it."[3] When adjusting this definition to a psychological context, Benson, as cited in Woolfolk and Richardson, defined stress as "environmental demands that require behavioral adjustment."[3] Woolfolk and Richardson contend that environmental demands are neutral events, and stress is more precisely an individual's perception that a behavioral adjustment is needed due to these demands. The demands also "call into question the degree to which the individual believes he can respond with success and comfort."[3] A person might become complacent, aroused, anxious, or fearful depending on the perceived threat or discomfort of the situation. An anxious response to a situation is known as "state anxiety."[4] Within the athletic environment, variables related to an actual contest (e.g., perceived skill level of participants, importance of event, number and demeanor of fans all affect the level of state anxiety experienced by each athlete.

Spielberger[4] introduced a second form of anxiety known as trait anxiety. Trait anxiety is a relatively stable personality disposition. It can be learned or inherited. An athlete scoring high on trait anxiety will have a tendency to perceive a wider spectrum of situations to be more threatening and will therefore have a higher level of state anxiety in any given situation than an athlete who scores lower on trait anxiety.

Singer[5] maintains that an understanding of each athlete's trait anxiety levels coupled with the contest variables that might affect state anxiety can help the coach and the athlete predict performance levels. The ability to perform under pressure is not contingent on eliminating anxiety but on controlling it as the contest variables change. An optimal level of anxiety brings about ideal performance.[5] That level will change depending on complexity of task, the athlete's disposition, and the situational demands. Thus "the relationship between stress and sports performance is an extremely complex one and involves the interaction between the nature of the stressor, the cognitive demands of the task being performed and the psychological characteristics of the individuals performing it."[6]

When one thinks of the pressure of competitive performance, images of actual contest events are easily conjured in the mind. Imagine shooting a free throw with 2 seconds on the clock and the game tied or positioning yourself in the starting blocks with an American record-holder in an adjacent lane. Both of these are situations that increase the state anxiety of an athlete. But several other performance-related pressures occur during the athlete's training program and throughout the competitive season that require understanding.

The nature of training for athletic competition instills the belief in athletes that more is better. If practicing a forehand 100 times is better than 50 times, wouldn't 500 repetitions be better? If eating more carbohydrates than fat or protein produces more fuel for physical activity, wouldn't eating all carbohydrates and no fat or protein be best? These simplistic and often compulsive attitudes, commonly held by coaches and athletes preoccupied with achieving superior sport performance, often result in overuse injuries, overtraining, and constant fatigue and dysfunctional behaviors.

The nature of competitive sport also plays into the doubts of those with low self-esteem or self-image who have to constantly prove to others and themselves that they are competent and worthy of respect. Sport is repetitious. Day after day, the athlete does the same thing. Contest after contest the athlete seeks to prove himself or herself better than opponents. Even after a win, the joy is short-lived, and the focus goes to the next contest. When athletes really know how good they are, the contest and the outcome of the contest become less important. The important performance issue is whether the athlete has fulfilled his or her potential or improved on a previous performance rather than beating a new opponent or validating self as a "winner."

Morgan[7] maintains that athletic scholarships, media attention, and other forms of pressure to compete at intense levels result in greater incidence of fear of failure and high-level anxiety about sport performance. When an athlete believes that he or she is experiencing lowered performance, whether actual or imagined, the result is usually some form of emotional distress. Even if the performance deficit is a symptom of some other psychological problem the impact can be the same, "a reverberating cycle of lowered efficiency accompanied by a reduction in self-esteem."[7] Deykin et al.[8] report that depression is one of the most common emotional problems among elite athletes, and depression, particularly in the young, correlates positively with many forms of substance abuse and behavioral disorders. Couple these responses with the strong possibility that the athlete is undereducated and emotionally underdeveloped due to an overprotective and privileged environment, and the susceptibility for substance abuse to increase performance or self-esteem increases dramatically.[7]

□ COACH-ATHLETE RELATIONSHIP

The standard roles that characterize leader and subordinate often invoke a love-hate relationship between the athlete and the coach. Several studies using the IPC scale, which measures locus of control, found that athletes perceive coaches as "powerful others" who play a significant role in their lives as collegiate athletes.[9] The athlete admires, respects, and is eager to receive the benefits of the coach's sport expertise. The coach is perceived as having the key that will unlock the secret to successful athletic performance. On the other hand, the coach is responsible for guiding, and often pushing, athletes through barriers that limit athletic performance. The techniques used to help athletes achieve new heights of skill and performance can be positive or negative, benign or intensely damaging. Although the coach's intent is frequently admirable, his or her choice of method might be questionable. As in any situation in which motivation is required, a variety of techniques is important. The variety of techniques at the coach's disposal happen to be increased as a result of the athlete's unquestioning obedience and fear that failure to comply with the coach's wishes will result in withdrawal of attention and performance failure.

Telander[10] takes a much more critical view. He maintains that coaches are "experts at brainwashing" who attempt to keep their players subservient and thankful for the simplest of rewards. In his critique of big-time football, Telander contends that coaches are out of touch with reality:

> Put simply, a coach lives in a world that has little relationship to the real world, and his actions in his coach's world are performed to please him alone without regard to the feelings or development of those below him. . . . Far from socializing their players, coaches all too often shape them into young men with warped perspectives on obedience, morality and competition. These young men are often unable to function appropriately in the real world—that is, any world without football at its epicenter—until they learn new methods of behavior and thought.[10]

Blinde[11] also reports that coaches use manipulation and exclusion as techniques to control athletes. Athletes are ignored if their performances do not live up to coaches' expectations, and athletic scholarships are used as a means to manipulate and control athletes. The NCAA national study on intercollegiate athletics[12] also suggests that some coaches use physical abuse as a means of control. The study reported that 20% of football and basketball athletes have experienced at least one incident of physical abuse by their coaches. The athlete appears to be particularly at risk when the coach is perceived as ineffective in nonathletic areas.

Blinde[11] suggests that the female athlete is subject to unique forms of psychological rather than physical exploitation as a result of frequently and increasingly being under the supervision of male coaches. Currently over half of all the coaches of women's teams are male, and the diminution of numbers of female coaches is a demonstrable 15-year trend. "Patterns of interactions between male coaches and female athletes may sometimes parallel the dominant-subordinate roles usually accorded males and females respectively in a patriarchal society."[11]

The dysfunctional consequences of coaches who try to control their player's behavior through strict rules, psychological manipulation, creation of dependencies, or physical abuse are considerable. Bruno Bettleheim, the noted child psychologist, writes:

> To be disciplined requires self-control. To be controlled by others and to accept living by their rules or orders makes it superfluous to control oneself. When the more important aspects of a child's actions and behavior are controlled by, say, his parents or teachers, he will see no need to learn to control himself; others do it for him.[13]

☐ VALUE INCONGRUENCY

Values taught in sport can be incongruent with the values necessary to achieve in society outside of sport. There are those who contend that coaches and other personnel associated with the sport program are educating athletes in a dysfunctional manner. Messengale and Frey, as cited in Telander, believe that the things players are taught are not what they need:

> Selected actions, behaviors, and traits are often taught, reinforced, and then rewarded, although these actions do not reflect desirable social values. For example: How often is blind obedience taught in place of the courage of conviction? How often is intimidation taught under the guise of tenacity? How often is manipulation and deliberate rule violation taught as strategy? How often is composure and sportsmanship mistaken for lack of effort? . . . This list could go on forever.[10]

Telander[10] concurs that coaches and athletics personnel produce so much contradictory information that a player who absorbs it all can find himself or herself almost frozen with indecision:

> I think of all the times my teammates and I were told to play with "reckless abandon" and then a moment later to be "under control." We were told to "have fun out there" and to "get serious," to "knock their heads off" and to be "gentlemen." I remember making a mistake on a coverage one day and my secondary coach asking me what I was doing. "When the flanker blocks down, I thought . . . " "Don't think!" yelled the coach. "Goddammit, react."[10]

Athletes faced with these inconsistencies and contradictory requirements also see their coaches berate referees, ignore or intentionally break the rules of the game, chastise poor players, make exceptions for star players, and leave whenever a better job offer comes along.[10] Athletes process all of this information and eventually realize that many of the things they are being taught are fraudulent. Sometimes, probably too often, the athlete comes to the realization that his or her educational and athletic development is not a priority concern. Winning the game takes precedent. Such value incongruency creates considerable doubt and stress. The athlete might begin to question the validity of his or her own sport participation.

☐ ATHLETE-TEAM RELATIONSHIP

Teams are complex groups that generate their own expectations, pressures, and concerns. The sport team is frequently composed of young people of the same age, each member struggling through his or her own reactions to the same stage of normal physiological and psychological development. Add the pressures associated with sport participation discussed above and the fact that teammates are often opponents with whom the athlete is competing for a starting role, the coach's attention, or an athletic scholarship, and the notion of teammates playing a supporting role "bites the dust." Interactions among teammates competing against each other is another element of real pressure confronting the student-athlete.

☐ VISIBILITY OF PARTICIPATION

The visibility of athletic participation is greater than ever before because of the advent of local cable systems and the explosive development of regional sports cable networks offering 24-hour sports programming. The largest department of the daily newspaper with regard to numbers of employees is the sports department. Investigative reporters regularly appear at practice as well as games and camp out on the doorstep of athletics departments in hopes of uncovering the scoop or scandal from a disgruntled student-athlete, employee, or loose-tongued coach. The individual performances of student-athletes are scrutinized, and mistakes are identified by an immense fan base, all of whom think they understand the highly objective and exacting criterion for success—winning.[14] The athletes of today have thousands of parents and coaches who create the pressure of an expectation of consistently good performances.

The female athlete faces these and an additional set of problems. The print and electronic media depict women's sports differently than men's sports. Ambivalent messages combine positive portrayal of strength, skill, or expertise along with negative suggestions that trivialize the efforts of female athletes or imply that they are weak, inferior, incapable, or in some other way unsuited to sport or that the sport in which they are participating is not a *true* sport.[15] Duncan and Hasbrook,[15] in a research study that examined the visual images and commentary of women's sports television programs, concluded that "visuals fragmented and objectified women by presenting them in a highly sexualized way, focusing on certain body parts and depicting women in mostly passive poses.[15] The positive portrayal of the woman athlete by the program commentator was consistently undermined by the visual implication that women were decorative sex objects, unsuited to any endeavor as active and demanding as sports, which created a deeply ambivalent representation of female athletes. These researchers concluded that

> one of society's most influential mass media, television, symbolically denies power to women by its exclusionary and denigrating tactics. It excludes women by its brute neglect of women's sport, the failure to televise women's team sports for example. When women are allowed inside TV's hallowed arena, it denigrates them by conjoining images of female strength with images of female weakness.[15]

Thus, the pressures created by public visibility can be very different for male and female athletes.

☐ TIME DEMANDS AND SOCIAL ISOLATION

Erikson and Funkenstein[16] contend that strenuous demands on the athlete's time and lack of organizational skills to meet these time demands lead to the athlete being frustrated over his or her inability to manage athletic and academic responsibilities. The dysfunctional effects of time demands are not limited to the athletic and academic life of a student-athlete, however. The athletes are more likely to sacrifice their social life and friendships as a result of their college sport participation.

Pinkerton et al.[2] contend that time dedicated to sport training, travel, and competition and lack of identity in roles other than that of an athlete cause social isolation. Nonathlete students are more likely to resolve their identity crises in more realistic ways and to develop vocational identities more consistent with their capabilities than student-athletes. Athletes engaged in time-intensive training programs become isolated from their peers. This social isolation is further aggravated if the athlete spends the remainder of his or her limited time as a serious student studying alone. Adler and Adler,[17] however, note that social isolation of student-athletes from the rest of the student body can lead to the development of a peer subculture that is often anti-intellectual and anti-academic.

Many athletes are further isolated from the rest of the student body by being forced to live in athletic dormitories or placed in athlete-only sections of dormitories and eating at training tables restricted to athletes. A survey of 388 athletes at one institution found that more than two-thirds of the athletes "felt isolated from the student body" and would prefer not to live in athletic dorms.[18] Golden[19] maintains that special housing for athletes does not serve a purpose beyond that of control and confinement:

> It is a life-limiting experience to be surrounded by actual and proclaimed "super jocks" for twenty-four hours a day. Conversation is often salty and shallow, and psychosocial development is frequently limited to other team members who have neither the desire nor the capacity to discuss anything except sports. Special housing also pampers the athlete in a manner that is neither mature nor meaningful in light of the pressures to be faced in later years.[19]

Athletes can also become socially and emotionally isolated due to poor performance or improper management of successful performance. An athlete's inability to manage his or her success or failure can be accentuated by a growing perception of social and emotional isolation, the development of guilt feelings about assertion or overt aggression, the use of habitual rationalization to reduce the reality of facing true physical potential, unconscious feelings of resentment over external demands of parents, coaches, friends, media, and the public for excellence, and unconscious fear with regard to supporting the emotional weight of success or being the record holder.[20]

Another factor contributing to the social isolation of the athlete is resentment by the university community.[18] Athletes are likely to pursue the safety of an athlete peer group when faced with overt criticism of their privileges and special treatment by faculty and fellow students. They walk a narrow line between the admiration of those who appreciate winning and excellent sport performance and those who believe that such achievements are not sufficient to justify the athlete's special status.

☐ FATIGUE-RELATED STRESS

An important consideration in ability to cope with various stresses is the athlete's level of physical and mental fatigue. The NCAA national study on intercollegiate athletics[12] reported that 45% of football and basketball players and 36% of players in other sports were bothered by extreme tiredness and exhaustion. This is not only the result of long practices and actual competition, but it also stems from extensive travel, changes in diet and sleep habits, time changes, and waiting in airports.[21] In the revenue-producing men's sports of football and basketball, athletes are also required to spend extra time with coaches viewing films, learning playbook material, and attending position meetings between classes and during evening hours.

☐ INJURY

The NCAA national study on intercollegiate athletics[12] revealed that 56% of football and basketball players have injuries in a given year, and 70% felt extreme pressure to ignore injuries. In other sports, 48% had injuries and 50% felt pressure to ignore them. When athletes are injured and unable to perform, they often are in a position of losing their primary means of self-expression. If their coaches withdraw contact and support from those who cannot train or compete, the athletes isolated in this way also suffer from loss of attention from one of the most significant people in their lives. Under such circumstances one can better understand an athlete's unwillingness to comply with the decisions and instructions of those charged with the responsibility for medical treatment and rehabilitation. The athlete's return to competition eliminates considerable psychological stress.

Physical injury is an accepted risk of athletic participation; yet when an injury manifests itself, it is as mentally debilitating for an athlete as it is physically disabling. Ryan[22] maintains that athletes are highly susceptible to depression and compulsive behaviors during injury rehabilitation. Such susceptibility can be attributed to loss of self-esteem and identity formerly generated from their ability to perform.

Rotella and Heyman[23] contend that the athlete's reaction to injury parallels the classic response to the death of a loved one. Initially the injured athlete feels anger, shock, and disbelief. Then comes depression, followed by acceptance and resignation with the hope of eventually returning to training and competition. Initially the athlete might exaggerate the importance of the injury, deny its existence, or even believe that competing again will not be possible. Such a response can intensify feelings of anxiety, guilt, or depression.

☐ ACADEMIC PRESSURES

Student-athletes must deal with the pressure of academic performance standards as a condition of their participation. In high school these conditions range from prohibiting participation if the student-athlete has one failing grade to more complex grade-averaging systems developed to represent minimal expectations of academic effort. Colleges have been more indirect in their approach to academic eligibility rules. They show a preference for denying freshman eligibility on the basis of high school grades and college entrance examination scores rather than on college academic work. Once the athlete passes the freshman eligibility barrier, maintaining eligibility involves being enrolled in a full-time course load and passing 24 hours of course work per year applicable toward any degree plan. In his recent book, *The Character of American Higher Education and Intercollegiate Sport*, Chu reveals how the system can easily exploit the athlete:

> . . . neophyte intercollegiate athletes who too often are ill-prepared for university level work, have typically followed a particular eligibility strategy; by avoiding core courses required for graduation, athletes may skirt some of the more difficult courses in the university. By so doing, they also maintain the flexibility to change majors often. Changing majors ensures that upper-level junior and senior-level courses may be avoided. In addition, athletes may take every kind of physical education activity course and "gut" courses in other departments, where good grades are much more likely. Athletes, of course, share knowledge of these sorts of courses. Never mind that all these courses do not amount to a meaningful course load, one necessary for graduation and career after college.[24]

Athletes do not figure out this system on their own. In many cases they are assisted by coaches and counselors whose primary motivation is to keep athletes eligible for competition. Whether the athletes graduate is a secondary consideration. So much time is spent participating in athletic-related activities that all too often maximizing the student-athlete's academic potential is a meaningless promise heard only during the recruitment process. Rhatigan,[21] in a study of division I basketball schedules, revealed that student-athletes miss approximately 26% of their classes during the basketball season. That figure inflates to 30% if the team is involved in postseason competition. The NCAA, in its national study of intercollegiate athletics,[12] determined that collegiate football and basketball players spend more time in their sport during the season than the combination of time spent in class and studying. Approximately 20% of athletes in the NCAA study felt it was "much harder" as an athlete to keep up with course work and make academics their priority compared to 10% of a sample of students who participate in other types of extracurricular activities. Further, the NCAA study reported that 23 to 30% of student-athletes, depending on sport and competition level, found many courses "too difficult" compared to 19% of nonathlete students participating in extracurricular activities.

Blinde[11] synthesized several research studies which included survey data involving close to 2000 division I college athletes and 25 in-depth interviews of division I student-athletes, concluding that there was "evidence of academic exploitation." Athletes indicated that during the sport season they were forced to enroll in a fewer number of credit hours, and their grades suffered. Consequently the number of semesters needed to graduate increased, despite the fact that their athletic scholarship was usually limited to 4 years.

This conflict between participation and academic achievement places pressure on the athlete in a number of ways. High school and college eligibility rules create circumstances in which the academic inadequacies of the student-athlete are made public. Faced with the prospect of public humiliation, taking the easy way out by signing up for courses in which the prospect of failure is minimized becomes an acceptable alternative.

Though able to avoid the overt label of failure, the student-athlete is still faced with internalized knowledge of academic inadequacy. When coaches and advisors encourage academically capable young people to follow this safe route toward maintaining eligibility, these student-athletes know that their intellectual ability has been compromised and devalued.

The athlete must not only deal with the personal guilt associated with underutilization of his or her intellectual ability but must face society's often warranted stereotypic views. The media, general public, and members of the faculty often believe the student-athlete is an irresponsible, privileged, intellectually lazy, benefit-pampered, body preoccupied egotist more concerned with the development of muscle tissue than gray matter. The inordinate amount of financial support and attention afforded athletics compared to academic programs reinforces the faculty perception that big-time athletics is the antithesis of basic academic values. Thus it comes as no surprise to find that the NCAA national study on intercollegiate athletics[12] reported that athletes were over 10 times more likely than students participating in nonathletic extracurricular activities to indicate that it was "much harder" to be regarded as a serious student by professors.

The academic support system, designed to help the student-athlete succeed in the classroom, also has the unintended effect of breeding dependence. Elite collegiate athletes do not have to undergo the rigors of registration for classes because of registration priorities afforded them in order to free up adequate practice time. Many division I student-athletes receive free tutoring in plush academic department study facilities. Many athletes have academic decisions made for them by athletic department counselors rather than work with academic department advisors to make those decisions themselves. Dormitory accommodations and roommates are preselected. Most people in higher education would agree that athletes are more dependent on their athletic department support systems and less independent as individuals than other students. Over the long run, this dependence is stress-creating rather than stress-relieving. Pinkerton et al. maintain that the student-athlete's developmental struggles to become autonomous while reluctantly giving up the dependence of early developmental stages are amplified:

> The "macho male" and "all-American woman" stereotypes reinforce denial of problems and mitigate against seeking help. Also, since athletic departments often provide an array of support services, such as departmental advisors and tutors, student-athletes may develop dependence on these to the exclusion of other student services. Within the student-athlete peer system it may be more socially acceptable to allow dependence on athletic department supports than on external ones, particularly counseling and psychological services.[2]

Athletic departments often provide special privileges to student-athletes with the best of intentions: to ensure that they miss fewer classes, to reduce the pressure of living with nonathlete roommates who do not understand or share the athlete's extraordinary time demands or pressures, and to offset the dysfunctional consequences of athletic participation by ensuring access to classes and tutors. Such treatment often has latent consequences, however, including delayed maturation and a different set of pressures and adjustment problems.

☐ RACIAL STEREOTYPING AND DISCRIMINATION

No pressures are more intense and less understood than those faced by black athletes. Social stereotypes of black people assign expectations of intellectual inferiority, physical and sexual prowess, and lack of work ethic. One would expect educational institutions, in the search for truth, to be less accepting of such antiquated beliefs, but many researchers have found that schools serve as reinforcing agents for these age-old myths. Rosenthal[25] claimed that systematic degradation of blacks was nowhere more apparent than in public schools. Leach and Connors[18] say the sport environment reinforces this degradation by allowing the lure of athletic success and the exploitive nature of the coach to remove all expectations of academic success or social maturity. They maintain that black athletes learn to expect little of themselves outside the sport experience, and these attitudes are gradually incorporated into their self-concepts. If a black athlete enters a college program that does set academic and social expectations, it is like entering a game with new rules.[18]

Another source of pressure for the black athlete stems from the fact that the most highly visible and competitive division I programs are sponsored by universities with predominantly white student bodies. Minority student-athletes struggle for identity among predominantly white and middle-class peers with few or no systems for support. The NCAA national study on intercollegiate athletics[26] carefully examined the plight of black football and basketball players on predominantly white campuses. Compared to black student-athletes on predominantly black campuses, they are more likely to feel that they are (1) different from other students, (2) not in control of their lives, (3) isolated from other students, (4) racially isolated, and (5) racially discriminated against. Overall, 51% of the NCAA black football and basketball player sample reported racial isolation and 33% reported racial discrimination.[26] Black athletes on predominantly white campuses reported greater anxiety and depression. In a predominantly white student body with predominantly white coaching and support staffs, black athletes are more likely not to share these feelings and to withhold information. Black student-athletes find it more difficult to get to know other students and to be liked by others for just being themselves than black nonathletes. After their family and black-athlete friends, their primary support system is other teammates.

Although blacks are not the only student-athletes exploited, Edwards[27] maintains that the abuses usually happen to them first and have a greater impact. He contends that black student-athletes are especially vulnerable to victimization due to the stereotypic beliefs that blacks are innately superior athletes, and they have easy access to professional sports. Couple those beliefs with the tenuous life circumstances of the black student-athlete which are characteristic of lower socioeconomic status, and exploitation is an easily understood phenomenon.

The educational system's lower academic expectation for blacks has resulted in an entire generation of black student-athletes having to deal with the stress of being academically unprepared to confront the daily classroom demands of higher education. The NCAA national study of intercollegiate athletics[26] reports that the mean SAT score for black football and basketball players is 740 and the mean ACT score is 14; the mean SAT score for nonblack football and basketball players is 890 and the mean ACT is 19. Nationally, the general student body has an average SAT of 900.[28] Black football and basketball players are twice as likely as nonblack players to report high school grade-point averages in the bottom half of the distribution obtained from the national study (e.g., B- and below). At the other end of the distribution, nonblack football and basketball players are three times as likely to report high school grade-point averages in the upper quartile (e.g., A- and above). Differences like these in high school grade-point averages and test scores support the premise that black student-athletes have not been similarly prepared as non-black student-athletes to deal with the pressures of college academics. Further, this common knowledge of inadequate academic preparation creates a situation in which black student-athletes are regarded differently by coaches, counselors, and instructors once they are enrolled.

When the black student-athlete arrives on the college campus, he or she is more likely to be immediately labeled as "academically at-risk" and segregated from other athletes to participate in special athletic department academic-support programs. This labeling as inferior and further accentuation of difference unintentionally support the racially stereotypic view of blacks and further distances the black student-athlete from nonblack student counterparts.

Often the black student-athlete feels that his or her only opportunity to enhance self-esteem is through demonstration of sport skill competence. Under such circumstances, success in sport becomes inordinately important. Even on the playing field, however, the black student-athlete is faced with discriminatory treatment by a predominantly white coaching staff. Bolstered by acceptance of the stereotypic view of blacks, coaches practice positional discrimination. The thinking positions— quarterback, guard, catcher, and pitcher—are often closed to the black student-athlete.[29] The borderline black athlete is more likely than his or her white counterpart to get cut from the team than to be kept to sit on the bench. The pressure of having to deal with such exploitation and discrimination is significant indeed.

☐ GENDER STEREOTYPES AND DISCRIMINATION

Unequal treatment and trivialization of sport participation place a special burden of stress on the female athlete. Title IX of the 1972 Education Amendments Act and the 1988 Civil Rights Restoration Act prohibit discrimination on the basis of sex in all educational institutions that receive federal aid. Despite the fact that these legislative acts have lowered the barrier to sport participation for women, other forms of discrimination continue to haunt the female athlete. Males are still perceived as better than females within the athletics context though no head-to-head competition exists. Kane and Snyder[30] contend that women's sports have been stereotyped and trivialized due to the "sport typing"—emphasizing and supporting only those men's sports that "exaggerate the dimension of physicality/power." This preference for men's sports "reproduces the ideology of male supremacy because it acts as a constant and glorified reminder that males are biologically, and thus inherently, superior to females."[30] In the past, women were denied the opportunity to play because society wished to protect a physically and psychologically weaker gender. Now the female athlete must deal with the significant pressure of trivialization or minimalization of her skills and efforts.

Although participation barriers have been lowered, they have not been eliminated. Twice as many men as women receive athletic participation opportunities, and male sports still receive better funding and more benefits. This institutional preference for taking care of male athletes is perceived by the female athlete as a devaluation of her participation and worth. Also, discrimination against women is not limited to the sport experience. The NCAA national study of intercollegiate athletics[28] revealed that 13% of women basketball players and 8% of women with athletic scholarships in other sports reported at least 6 experiences of sexual discrimination since enrolling in college.

The plight of the female athlete is even more complicated in that gender stereotypes still dominate the culture. Fulfilling society's expectation of the perfect female body and developing muscular strength and power are competing demands that can create considerable stress. On the playing field, she is expected to express traditionally male attitudes and behaviors; off the field, she is required to display traditionally female patterns. "Retaining her athletic presence off the field may lead others to speculate that she is a lesbian. Retaining traditionally feminine qualities during competition would be unacceptable to teammates."[2] Anthrop and Allison[31] maintain that lowered self-esteem and self-image are the result of this stereotypic and dichotomous view of behavior. This source of dissonance for the female athlete is accentuated by the absence of female role models in many sports and the lack of early direction and focus on dealing with these issues.

The male athlete is also at risk. Androgynous or more gentle male athletes who discover that their personalities conflict with macho sport stereotypes are susceptible to homophobia. Pinkerton et al.[2] maintain that many male athletes find themselves trying to overcompensate for "feminine" characteristics they might possess. Male athletes who are sensitive, compassionate, interested in the arts, or inclined toward intimacy can find themselves suffering from the same dissonance experienced by the female athlete attempting to cope with the competing demands of her culture. Macho males can find a homosexual teammate threatening. The homosexual male athlete is faced with the problem of integrating his sexual preference into what he, his peers, and society have defined as a macho identity and must deal with ostracism by his teammates.[2] Pinkerton et al. reveal additional complexities of sex role differences for athletes:

> Unlike males who become homosexual, females may find attributes that are more traditionally associated with being a male—aggressiveness, physical strength, competitiveness, masculinity—less dissonant with their concepts of the ideal. . . . Even heterosexually oriented student-athletes may have difficulty integrating culturally defined opposite-sex traits into their personalities. For male student-athletes, this difficulty may mean protecting the macho identity. Expressions of dependency, intimacy, tenderness, and compassion may be personally experienced or viewed by others as incongruent with being a male athlete. Often tender feelings must be denied or sublimated to such an extent that the macho image is not compromised.[2]

Social support of the macho image of sport, as reflected by expectations of athletes and financial support for physicality/power sports dominated by male athletes, appears incongruent with the expectations of modern society. Technological advances have reduced the need for physicality and power in most jobs. Educational systems have been redesigned to focus on preparing people for work in people-service industries in which traditionally feminine qualities of cooperation, compassion, and understanding are most important. Gender stereotypes are slowly becoming more adrogynous. Yet we rely on highly competitive sport to teach young people how to work on teams, and in so doing increase the stress of dealing with conflicting messages that imply what personal attributes are required for success.

◻ CONCLUSIONS

Exploring one's physical competencies and pursuing excellence in skill acquisition and athletic competition has its place in school and amateur sport systems. Elimination of environmental stress surrounding the competitive sport experience is not the aim. Stress occurs whenever a person is faced with new circumstances and challenges. Indeed, the human organism becomes stronger and more resilient as it confronts and adapts to these pressures, For the individual prone to or suffering from eating disorders, however, these pressures reinforce dysfunctional behaviors to control weight and increase the individual's preoccupation with using exercise as an important method of weight control.

Programs must be designed to (1) educate coaches and athletes on the sources of stress in the education-based amateur sport system, (2) minimize or eliminate unnecessary or dysfunctional forms of stress, and (3) teach student-athletes various strategies for dealing with the inevitable pressures encountered during sport participation. Most important, coaches and athletics administrators must fully recognize the powerful role they play in the athlete's life and the critical role they play in dealing with student-athletes with eating disorders. These professional sport educations must be held accountable for establishing a sport environment that is physically, emotionally, and socially supportive and rewarding for each individual athlete.

☐ REFERENCES

1. Hemery, D.: The Pursuit of Sporting Excellence: A Study of Sport's Highest Achievers. Champaign, IL, Human Kinetics, 1986.
2. Pinkerton, R., Hinz, L., and Barrow, J.: The college student-athlete: Psychological considerations and interventions. J. Am. Coll. Health, 37:218, March 1989.
3. Woolfolk, R.L., and Richardson, F.C.: Stress, Sanity, and Survival. New York, Simon and Schuster, 1978.
4. Spielberger, C.: Trait-state anxiety and motor behavior. J. Motor Behav., 3:265, 1971.
5. Singer, R.N.: Myths and Truths in Sports Psychology. New York, Harper and Row, 1975.
6. Jones, J.C., and Hardy L.: Stress and cognitive functioning in sport. J. Sports Sci., 7:41, 1989.
7. Morgan, W.P.: Selected psychological factors limiting performance: A mental health model. Champaign, IL, Human Kinetics, 1985, pp. 70–80.
8. Deykin, E.Y., Levy, T.C., and Wells, V.: Adolescent depression, alcohol and drug abuse. Am. J. Public Health, 77:178, 1987.
9. LeUnes, A.D., and Nation, J.R.: Sport Psychology: An Introduction. Chicago, Nelson Hall, 1989.
10. Telander, R.: Something must be done. Sports Illustr., p. 92, Oct. 2, 1989.
11. Blinde, E.: Unequal exchange and exploitation in college sport: The case of the female athlete. Arena Rev. 13:77, 1989.
12. American Institute for Research: Summary Results from the 1987–88 National Study of Intercollegiate Athletics (Report No. 1). Palo Alto, Center for the Study of Athletics, American Institute for Research, November 1988.
13. Telander, R.: Something must be done. Sports Illustr., p. 100, Oct. 2, 1989.
14. Straub, B.: Stress: Relieving anxiety in college athletes. Coll. Athlet. Management, 2:38, 1990.
15. Duncan, M.C., and Hasbrook, C.A.: Denial of power in televised women's sports. Socio. Sport J., 5:1, 1988.
16. Erikson, E.H., and Funkenstein, D.J.: The student and mental health: An international view. New York, World Federation for Mental Health, 1959.

17. Adler, P., and Adler, P.A.: Role conflict and identity salience: College athletics and the academic role. Soc. Sci. J., 24:443, 1984.

18. Leach, B., and Connors, B.: Pygmalion on the gridiron: The black student-athlete in a white university. *In* Rethinking Services for College Athletes. New Directions for Student Services, Vol. 28. Edited by A. Shriberg and F.R. Brodzinski. San Francisco, Jossey Bass, 1984, pp. 31–50.

19. Golden, D.C.: Supervising college athletics: The roles of the chief student affairs officer. *In* Rethinking Services for College Athletes. New Directions for Student Services, Vol. 28. Edited by A. Shriberg and F.R. Brodzinski. San Francisco, Jossey Bass, 1984, pp. 59–70.

20. Ogilvie, B.C., and Tutko, T.A.: Security. *In* Encyclopedia of Sport Sciences and Medicine. Edited by L. Larsen. New York, Macmillan, 1971, pp. 910–913.

21. Rhatigan, J.J.: Serving two masters: The plight of the college student-athlete. *In* Rethinking Services for College Athletes. New Directions for Student Services, Vol. 28. Edited by A. Shriberg and F.R. Brodzinski. San Francisco, Jossey Bass, 1984, pp. 5–11.

22. Ryan, R.: Mental health services for elite female student-athletes at the University of Texas at Austin. Perform. Team Newsletter, 2:3, 1989.

23. Rotella, R.J., and Heyman, S.R.: Stress injury and the psychological rehabilitation of athletes. *In* Applied Sport Psychology: Personal Growth to Peak Performance. Edited by J.M. Williams. Palo Alto, Mayfield, 1986, pp. 343–364.

24. Chu, D.: The Character of American Higher Education and Intercollegiate Sport. Albany, State University of New York Press, 1989, p. 109.

25. Rosenthal, R.: Pygmalion in the Classroom. New York, Holt, Rinehart, and Winston, 1968.

26. The Experiences of Black Intercollegiate Athletes at NCAA Division I Institutions (Report No. 3). Palo Alto, CA, Center for the Study of Athletics, American Institute for Research, 1989.

27. Edwards, H.: Educating black athletes. Atlantic Monthly, p. 31, August 1983.

28. American Institute for Research: Women in Intercollegiate Athletics at NCAA Division I Institutions (Report No. 4). Palo, Alto, CA, Center for the Study of Athletics, 1989.

29. Lapchick, R.E.: The Promised Land, *In* Fractured Focus: Sport as a Reflection of Society. Edited by R.E. Lapchich. Lexington, MA, D.C. Heath, 1986, pp. 111–136.

30. Kane, M.J., and Snyder, E.: Sport typing: The social "containment" of women in sport. Arena Rev., 13:77, 1989.

31. Anthrop, J., and Allison, M.: Role conflict and the high school female athlete. Res. Q., 54:104, 1983.

C H A P T E R

19

SOUND NUTRITION FOR THE ATHLETE

Suzanne Nelson Steen and Jacqueline R. Berning

A number of factors contribute to being a successful athlete. Dedication and training techniques are still an athlete's most effective means of developing natural abilities, but nutrition is also an important component of the conditioning process. The purpose of this chapter is to provide practical information about optimum nutrition for peak performance. For a more detailed discussion about the underlying principles of nutrition for sport and exercise physiology please refer to Chapter 5.

How can nutrition help the athlete achieve top performance? To begin with, all athletes should adjust their diets to the energy requirement of their sport. An athlete's energy and nutrient requirements vary depending on weight, height, age, sex, and metabolic rate and on the type, intensity, frequency, and duration of training. The emotional and physical stress of training and competition combined with hectic travel schedules also affect intake. As a result, calories and nutrients must be carefully planned to meet nutritional requirements for training and health. Depending on the training regimen, athletes need to consume at least 50% but ideally 60 to 70% of total calories from carbohydrate. The remaining calories should be obtained from protein (10 to 15%) and fat (20 to 30%). Calories and nutrients should come from a variety of food on a daily basis. The four food groups, along with the number of recommended daily servings, are presented in Table 19–1.

TABLE 19–1. THE FOUR FOOD GROUPS—MINIMUM NUMBER OF SERVINGS: A GUIDE TO MAKING WISE FOOD CHOICES

FOOD GROUP	RECOMMENDED NUMBER OF SERVINGS			
	CHILD	TEENAGER	ADULT	TRAINING
Milk	3	4	2	*
Milk or yogurt, 1 cup				
Cheese, 1 oz				
Cottage cheese, ½ cup				
Ice cream, ½ cup				
Meat	2	2	2	*
Cooked lean meat, fish, or poultry, 2–3 oz				
Egg, 1				
Dried beans or peas, ½ cup				
Peanut butter, 2 tbsp				
Cheese, 2 oz				
Fruits and vegetables	4	4	4	8
Cooked or juice, ½ cup				
Raw, 1 cup				
Medium piece of fruit, 1				
Grains (whole grains, fortified, enriched)	4	4	4	8
Bread, 1 slice				
Cereal (ready to eat), 1 oz				
Pasta, ½ cup				

Adapted from National Dairy Council: Guide to Good Eating. 5th ed. Rosemont, IL, National Dairy Council, 1990; and Eating on the Road. In Sports Nutrition for the 90s. Edited by J.R. Berning and S.N. Steen. Gaithersburg, MD, 1991, p. 65.

☐ CARBOHYDRATES

With repeated bouts of training, carbohydrate intake on a regular basis is important to maintain glycogen stores. Only minimal glycogen synthesis occurs for athletes who consume a low-carbohydrate diet containing 300 to 350 g of carbohydrate.[1] On such a diet the athlete is susceptible to fatigue and premature exhaustion because muscle glycogen stores are easily depleted. On the other hand, a high-carbohydrate diet of 500 to 600 g carbohydrate per day provides near maximal repletion of muscle glycogen stores following strenuous training.[1] Consuming more than 600 g of carbohydrate per day does not result in proportionately greater amounts of muscle glycogen.[1] More important, excess carbohydrate will be stored as fat. For additional information on carbohydrate requirements for athletes please refer to Chapter 5.

For athletes who must meet a certain weight class (e.g., wrestlers) or maintain a low body weight for aesthetic reasons (e.g., ballet dancers), nutrient intake can be compromised.[2,3] Fasting, dieting, or chronically omitting carbohydrate-rich foods decreases muscle glycogen levels.[4] In addition, athletes who are in negative caloric balance limit their ability to synthesize glycogen.[4] If the athlete finds that normal exercise intensity is difficult to maintain, performance gradually deteriorates, or a sudden weight loss occurs, glycogen depletion is a probable cause. To prevent glycogen depletion, athletes must focus on consuming both adequate calories and a carbohydrate-rich diet daily. Examples of high-carbohydrate foods are listed in Table 19–2.

Periodic rest days are important to allow the muscles sufficient time to rebuild energy stores.

If the athlete has difficulty consuming ample amounts of carbohydrate due to a high energy expenditure, a high-carbohydrate nutritional supplement might be necessary. The products listed in Table 19–3 should not replace regular food but are designed to provide additional carbohydrate and calories.

TABLE 19–2. EXAMPLES OF HIGH-CARBOHYDRATE FOODS

FOOD	CALORIES	CARBOHYDRATE (g)
Apple	81	21
Applesauce (1 cup)	194	52
Bagel	163	31
Baked potato (large)	220	51
Banana (medium)	105	27
Bread (whole wheat) (2 slices)	122	22
Cereal (Cream of Wheat) (¾ cup)	115	24
Cereal (Golden Grahams) (¾ cup)	109	24
Corn (½ cup)	88	21
Grapes (1 cup)	58	16
Raisins (⅔ cup)	300	79
Rice (1 cup)	205	50
Spaghetti (with sauce) (1 cup)	260	37
Tortilla (flour)	85	15
Waffle (buttermilk) (2 waffles)	175	29
Yogurt (lowfat) (1 cup)	225	43

TABLE 19–3. COMMERCIAL HIGH-CARBOHYDRATE DRINKS PER 12-OUNCE SERVING

PRODUCT	CALORIES	CARBOHYDRATE (g)
Gatorlode	280	70
Carboplex	324	81
Exceed High Carbohydrate Source	356	89

TABLE 19–4. EXAMPLES OF HIGH-CARBOHYDRATE MEALS*

Breakfast

Orange juice	Cranberry juice
Waffles with syrup	Raisin bran or oatmeal
Bagel	Lowfat milk
Lowfat yogurt	Apple bran muffin
Banana	

Lunch

Turkey sandwich on whole wheat roll	Baked potato with chili
Apple slices with peanut butter	Cornmeal muffin
Frozen lowfat yogurt	Vanilla milkshake

Dinner

Minestrone soup	Thick-crust cheese, mushroom, and
Pasta with tomato sauce	green-pepper pizza
Salad with tomato, carrots, cucumbers,	Lowfat milk
and mushrooms	Fresh fruit
Italian bread	
Fresh fruit	
Lowfat milk	
Sherbet	

* Caloric needs depend on age, sex, and activity level. In order to determine individual requirements, consult a sports nutritionist.

The rate of muscle glycogen storage is increased during the 2 h after exercise.[5] This means that delaying the carbohydrate intake for too long after exercise reduces muscle glycogen storage and impairs recovery. Recent evidence suggests that an athlete should consume 100 g of carbohydrate (400 calories) within 15 to 30 min after exercise, to be followed by additional 100-g feedings every 2 to 4 h thereafter.[5] Because most athletes are not hungry after exercising, the most effective strategy might be to encourage the athlete to drink a high-carbohydrate beverage or fruit juice immediately after exercise, followed by a high-carbohydrate meal within 2 to 4 h. Examples of high-carbohydrate meals are presented in Table 19–4.

TYPES OF CARBOHYDRATES

There are two types of carbohydrates—simple and complex. Simple carbohydrates include glucose, fructose, sucrose (table sugar), and galactose (milk sugar). Examples of simple carbohydrates are candy, cake, soda, and jelly. Complex carbohydrates are made from chains of simple sugars and include foods such as pasta, bread, cereals, fruits, and vegetables. During the digestive process, simple and complex carbohydrates are broken down into glucose, which then circulates in the blood.

Which type of carbohydrate is recommended for the athlete? Both simple and complex carbohydrates are important components of the athlete's diet. The emphasis should be on consuming more complex carbohydrates, however, because they contain B-vitamins, minerals, fiber, and protein, which contribute to a nutritionally balanced diet. Sugar is a concentrated energy source but offers no other nutritional value.

In addition, complex carbohydrates are digested somewhat more slowly than simple carbohydrates. As a result, glucose is absorbed more evenly into the bloodstream and less insulin is released. When simple carbohydrates are eaten, the blood glucose level rises sharply. Consequently a large amount of insulin is released, which causes the blood glucose level to drop suddenly. The effect is a carbohydrate high followed by a rapid decline, which results in temporary low blood sugar and is characterized by a light-headed sensation. For the athlete, these erratic fluctuations in blood glucose levels can have a negative impact on training and performance. Athletes should be encouraged to consume simple carbohydrates in addition to rather than in place of complex carbohydrates to ensure adequate consumption of vitamins, minerals, and fiber.

PRE-EVENT NUTRITION

The pre-event meal serves two purposes. First, it keeps the athlete from feeling hungry before and during the event; second, it maintains optimal levels of blood glucose for the exercising muscles during training and competition.[6,7]

Athletes often train early in the morning without eating. This overnight fast lowers liver glycogen stores and can impair performance, particularly if the exercise regimen involves endurance training.

Carbohydrate feedings prior to exercise can help restore suboptimal liver glycogen stores, which might be called on during prolonged training and competition. Though allowing for personal preferences and psychological factors, the pre-event meal should be high in carbohydrates, nongreasy, and readily digested.[6,7] High-fat, high-protein foods such as steaks, hamburgers, eggs, and hot dogs should be avoided in the pre-event meal because fat slows gastric emptying time. Exercising with a full stomach also can cause indigestion, nausea, and possibly vomiting.

How much carbohydrate should the athlete consume in the pre-event meal? Current research suggests that 1 to 4 g of carbohydrate per kilogram of body weight should be consumed 1 to 4 h prior to exercise.[7] To avoid gastrointestinal distress, the carbohydrate content of the meal should be reduced the closer to the event or exercise period that it is consumed. For example, a carbohydrate feeding of 1 g/kg is appropriate immediately before the exercise, whereas 4 g/kg can be safely consumed 4 h before exercise.[7]

Liquid meals can be consumed closer to competition than solid meals because of their shorter gastric emptying time. This might help to avoid pre-competition nausea for those athletes who are tense and have an associated delay in gastric emptying.

When should the pre-event meal be eaten? In the past, athletes were warned not to eat large amounts of sugar prior to exercise. This advice was based on data that indicated that consuming 50 to 75 g of glucose 30 to 45 min prior to exercise reduced endurance by causing a hypoglycemic response.[8] Findings from a recent study showed that 75 g of glucose consumed 45 min prior to bicycling to exhaustion did not negatively affect exercise time.[9] These contradictory results suggest that individuals differ in their susceptibility to a lowering of blood glucose during exercise.[7]

Pre-exercise sugar consumption can benefit the endurance athlete by providing glucose to the exercising muscles when glycogen stores have dropped to low levels.[7] Although new evidence suggests that sugary foods can be consumed 30 to 45 min prior to exercise, this practice could harm performance of athletes who are sensitive to fluctuations in blood sugar. Athletes should be advised to evaluate whether they are sensitive to a lowering of blood glucose by trying various amounts of carbohydrate before exercise during training.[7] For information on carbohydrate loading refer to Chapter 5.

☐ FAT

Although maximal performance is impossible without muscle glycogen, fat also provides energy for exercise. Fat is the most concentrated source of food energy, supplying more than twice as many calories by weight than do protein or carbohydrate (9 calories per gram versus 4 calories per gram for both protein and carbohydrate). Fats provide essential fatty acids and are necessary for cell membranes, skin, hormones, and transporting fat-soluble vitamins. Whereas the body's total glycogen stores (in muscle and liver) comprise about 2500 calories, each pound of body fat supplies 3500 calories. This means that an athlete weighing 74 kg (163 lb) with 10% body fat has 16.3 lb of fat, which equals 57,000 calories!

Fat is the major if not the most important fuel for exercise of light to moderate intensity. Although fat is a valuable metabolic fuel for muscle activity during longer-term aerobic exercise and performs many important functions in the body, no attempt should be made to store fat (as one can store glycogen) because, as is evident from the previous example, more fat is stored than is ever needed. In addition, athletes who consume a high-fat diet typically eat fewer calories from carbohydrate.[10] Low-fat diets are also important for health reasons: a high intake of fat has been associated with cardiovascular disease, diabetes, and obesity, among other chronic diseases.[11]

Fats are categorized as either saturated or unsaturated (including polyunsaturated and monounsaturated), depending on their chemical structures. Saturated fat is solid at room temperature and is derived mainly from animal sources. Unsaturated fat is liquid at room temperature and is found mainly in plants. Palm and coconut oils are exceptions—they are highly saturated vegetable fats. To promote good health and fitness,

TABLE 19–5. LOWER FAT SUBSTITUTIONS

INSTEAD OF:	TRY:
Bacon	Canadian bacon
Cream	Evaporated skim milk
Creamed cottage cheese	Lowfat cottage cheese
Ground beef	Ground turkey
Ice cream	Ice milk
Mayonnaise	Lowfat yogurt
Cheese	Part skim, lowfat cheese
Oil-packed tuna	Water-packed tuna
Whole milk	Skim or lowfat milk
Fried meat, fish, or chicken	Prepare as broiled, baked, or stir-fried
Doughnut	Bagel, English muffin
Croissant	Muffin, scone
Pasta in cream sauce	Pasta with a red sauce
Creamed soups	Clear soups
Potato chips	Pretzels

one should use vegetable oils such as corn, safflower, soybean, and sunflower, which have high percentages of polyunsaturated fats, rather than those with high percentages of saturated fats such as butter.

Athletes also need to recognize the many sources of hidden fat in foods. Fat is present but not separately visible in dairy products such as cheese, ice cream and whole milk, and in bakery items, granola bars, french fries, avocados, chips, nuts, and many highly processed foods. The other dietary sources such as margarine, butter, mayonnaise, salad dressing, oil, and sour cream are more clearly visible.

Athletes should consume not more than 20 to 30% of their daily calories from fat. Limiting the consumption of dietary fat reduces excess calories, but not nutrients. Suggestions for reducing fat intake are listed in Table 19–5.

☐ PROTEIN

Protein is essential for the growth and development of almost all tissues in the body. Proteins are composed of amino acids and are found in both plant and animal sources. The body combines specific amino acids to create a particular protein. Eight (9 in children) of the 20 amino acids found in protein cannot be synthesized by the body and must be obtained from the diet. These are referred to as essential amino acids. Proteins from animal sources generally contain all the essential amino acids and are considered "complete." Protein from plant sources is "incomplete" in that one or more of the essential amino acids are missing.

Most athletes believe that they require increased amounts of protein to perform at an optimal level. Bodybuilders and strength athletes typically consume a high-protein diet and/or take protein supplements to increase strength and muscle mass.[12] Although stronger muscles can improve performance, consumption of large amounts of protein does not increase muscle size. In fact, the most important factor in increasing strength is not what the athlete eats but how the athlete trains. How much strength is gained depends on the intensity and type of weight training. Muscle size is also dictated by heredity.

Although protein is an important component of muscle, the athlete might be surprised to learn that the composition of muscle is 70% water and only 20 to 22% protein. One pound of muscle is 70 to 75% water, 15 to 20% protein, and 5 to 7% other material such as fat, glycogen, minerals, and enzymes. Therefore 1 lb of muscle contains 70 to 105 g protein. If the athlete could gain 1 lb of pure muscle in 2 weeks, this increase would require the consumption of only an additional 5 to 8 g of protein per day. There are approximately 10 g of protein in each of the following: 1 oz of meat, 1 egg, 8 oz of milk, 1 oz of cheese, and 4 slices of bread.

Daily protein requirements vary according to the type of sport (strength versus endurance), intensity of training, stage of training, and most important, the energy balance of the diet. For any given protein intake, increasing energy intake improves nitrogen balance. Recent evidence suggests that some athletes require 50 to 150% more protein than the RDA of 0.8 g/kg of body weight.[13] This means that athletes might need 1.2 g/kg and might benefit from up to 2 g/kg during periods of muscle-building or prolonged heavy endurance exercise.[13] Athletes who chronically restrict calories also require slightly higher intakes of protein (1.2 to 1.5 g/kg) to allow for adequate synthesis and repair of muscle tissue.[14]

An adequate protein intake is certainly important for increasing muscle strength and size, but most athletes consume far more protein than they require. Athletes should instead, as discussed earlier, concentrate on eating enough carbohydrate. If the body doesn't have sufficient carbohydrates for energy, protein will be used for energy instead of for maintaining or building muscle.

What about taking large amounts of protein or amino acid supplements? It is important to recognize that the body cannot store extra protein. If more protein is consumed than the body can use, the protein is broken down and part of it is either used for energy or stored as body fat. The other part, which is nitrogen, can be toxic to the body in excess amounts. Because excess protein does not turn into muscle, "bulking up" by consuming high levels of protein can lead to excess body fat and a less efficient athlete rather than a more muscular one. In addition, large amounts of protein can lead to dehydration and loss of urinary calcium and can stress the kidneys and liver.[15]

As stated earlier, amino acids are the individual units of protein that are consumed in various foods. Athletes buy amino acids because promoters claim that they stimulate an anabolic effect, stimulate growth,

TABLE 19–6. COMPLEMENTING PROTEINS TO MAKE COMPLETE PROTEINS*

Legumes and grains	Dairy products and grains
Lentil soup and wheat bread	Lowfat yogurt and a peanut butter sandwich
Barley soup with navy beans	Macaroni and cheese
Baked beans and brown rice	**Legumes and nuts and seeds**
Split pea soup and rye bread	Raisin nut sunflower seed snack

* For best results, these foods should be eaten at the same meal or within 2 to 3 h of each other.

and reduce body fat. Amino acids are often sold individually or in "special" combinations. Arginine and ornithine are sold as a "natural steroid," and arginine and lysine are touted as promoting weight loss. Unfortunately, these claims are unfounded and are not supported by any scientific studies.

The body cannot distinguish between the amino acids supplied by pills or powders or foods; they are all metabolized in the same way. Taking amino acids either singly or in combination can interfere with absorption of certain essential amino acids.[15] An additional concern is that substituting amino acid supplements for food can cause inadequate intake of other nutrients found in protein-rich foods, such as iron, niacin, and thiamine. Athletes and coaches need to realize that amino acid supplements taken in large doses have not been tested in humans, and no margin of safety is available.

Some athletes follow a vegetarian diet. Although animal products are an important source of protein and other minerals, a diet that derives its protein from vegetable sources can provide adequate protein, vitamins, and minerals as well as a high carbohydrate intake that athletes need to sustain heavy, prolonged workouts. A lacto-ovovegetarian diet or a semivegetarian diet should provide adequate high-quality protein from eggs and dairy products. Obtaining needed protein can be difficult on a strict vegetarian diet, however. Athletes who are strict vegetarians must be careful to complement their sources of protein to ensure consumption of all essential amino acids. How to complement proteins is presented in Table 19–6.

☐ FLUID NEEDS

WATER

Water is the most important nutrient for the athlete during any phase of training and competition. Water comprises approximately 60 to 70% of body weight and as little as a 2% decrease in body weight from fluid

---

TABLE 19–7. GUIDELINES FOR FLUID REPLACEMENT

Drink 1½ to 2½ c of cool fluid 10 to 20 min before activity
During exercise, drink an additional ½ to 1 c of cool fluid every 15 to 20 min
Weigh-in without clothes before and after exercise. Drink 2 c of cool fluid for every pound
  of body weight lost

American College of Sports Medicine: Position Stand on Prevention of Thermal Injury During Distance Running. Med. Sci. Sports Exerc., 16:ix–xiv, 1984.

---

loss can lead to a significant decrease in muscular strength and stamina.[16] This translates into a 2½-lb loss for a 125-lb (57 kg) female; or a 3½-lb loss for a 175-lb (79.5 kg) male.

Water is critical for the body's cooling system, and it also transports nutrients to tissues and maintains adequate blood volume. Dehydration causes the body to overheat. As an individual becomes dehydrated, heart rate increases, blood flow to the skin decreases, and body temperature can subsequently rise steadily to dangerous levels.[17,18] Exercise in a hot environment places a greater demand on the cardiovascular system and increases the need for adequate fluid.[17] Relative humidity can be a problem as well: athletes can lose large amounts of fluid and become dehydrated even at cooler temperatures when humidity is high, because the sweat cannot evaporate to cool the body.

Because a substantial level of dehydration can occur before the body ever feels "thirsty," athletes must make a conscious effort to consume fluids before, during, and after exercise. Guidelines to help ensure adequate fluid intake are presented in Table 19–7.

Fluid losses can be monitored by checking the color of the urine. A dark-gold color suggests dehydration, whereas a pale-yellow color indicates adequate hydration. Though this is a practical way for athletes to evaluate fluid loss, both caffeine and alcohol can mask dehydration. This is because both of these substances act as diuretics, promoting water loss and consequently diluting the urine. An individual can be dehydrated even though the urine is pale yellow.

SPORTS DRINKS

For exercise bouts lasting less than 60 min, water is recommended as a fluid replacement.[6] When the workout period exceeds 60 min, however, sports drinks can be beneficial because they supply energy and electrolytes, which are key ingredients for maximum fluid absorption.[6] Results of recent research by Davis and colleagues indicate that a 6% carbohydrate solution enters the bloodstream as rapidly as water.[19,20] The 6% beverage not only entered the blood as fast as water, but unlike water it was associated with improved endurance. Both drinks had the same favorable influence on cardiovascular and thermoregulatory function. Additional studies have shown that consumption of sports drinks between 6 and 8% carbohydrate maintain physiologic function as well as water and provide additional performance benefits exceeding those of water.[21,22]

Though it is apparent that carbohydrate feedings during exercise can improve exercise performance, with the vast array of sports drinks available, how does the athlete decide which one to use? First, although some beverages in the marketplace are touted as "sports drinks," not all measure up to sports science standards of an optimal fluid replacer. For example, carbonated beverages are not recommended because they usually have a high carbohydrate concentration of 10% or more, which slows absorption.[6,22] In addition, the carbonation can lead to a bloated feeling, abdominal cramps, and nausea.

When choosing a sports beverage, the source of carbohydrate is important to consider. Glucose, glucose polymers (maltodextrins), and sucrose all stimulate fluid absorption in the small intestine.[6,22] The effect of ingestion of these types of sugars on exercise performance is similar, and all result in similar cardiovascular and thermoregulatory responses.[23,24] Research shows, however, that beverages containing fructose as the sole carbohydrate source are absorbed more slowly than other sugars and do not stimulate as much fluid absorption.[25] In addition, gastrointestinal distress and osmotic diarrhea are common side effects of drinking fructose solutions during exercise.[25] Fructose ingestion during exercise has not been associated with performance improvement.[25]

The concentration of the sports beverage should be between 6 and 8% because such beverages are absorbed into the bloodstream as quickly as water.[20,21,25] Drinks under 5% probably do not provide enough energy to enhance performance, whereas stated earlier, those that exceed 10 to 12% can cause gastric upset and impair performance.[20,21,25] The amount of carbohydrate in 1 cup of sports drink should be between 14 and 19 g. Calories should fall between 50 and 80 per 8 oz.

Ultimately, if the sports beverage meets the above guidelines, personal preference becomes the deciding factor. The athlete must choose which product tastes the best and works well with the individual exercise regimen. The athlete should be encouraged to evaluate different products during training, not during competition.

☐ VITAMINS

Because athletes are often looking for an edge, something that will give them an advantage, many turn to supplements in the form of pills, powders, and liquids in an effort to make the body perform at its best. Unfortunately many self-proclaimed "experts" are eager to convince athletes that their product will improve athletic performance by improving muscle contractions, preventing fat gain, enhancing strength, or supplying energy, to name just a few. These "experts" might insist that the athletes' fatigue and muscle soreness are due to a vitamin or mineral deficiency. In fact, when there is a nutritional reason for fatigue, it is usually a lack of calories or carbohydrate or both.

Vitamins function as metabolic regulators that influence the processes of growth, maintenance, and repair. They are organic molecules, which the body cannot manufacture but requires in small amounts. Vitamins are divided into two groups—water-soluble and fat-soluble. A, D, E, and K are soluble in fat, whereas C and the B vitamins are soluble in water. Table 19–8 lists all of the vitamins, their physiological function, and major food sources.

Fat-soluble vitamins are stored in body fat, principally in the liver. Excess accumulation of fat-soluble vitamins, particularly vitamins A and D, can produce serious toxic effects. Although excesses of most water-soluble vitamins are typically excreted, some can pose toxicity problems. Large amounts of niacin, for example, can cause burning or tingling, skin rash, nausea, and diarrhea.[26] High doses of niacin also interfere with fat mobilization and increase glycogen depletion.[26]

Athletes need to understand that more is not always better. The National Academy of Sciences has established Recommended Daily Allowances (RDAs) for vitamins and minerals as a guide for determining nutritional needs.[27] The RDA is the daily amount of a nutrient recommended for practically all healthy individuals to promote optimal health. It is not a minimal amount needed to prevent disease symptoms—a large margin of safety is included. For example, the body needs approximately 10 mg of vitamin C per day to prevent the deficiency disease called scurvy. The RDA for vitamin C is set far above that level at 60 mg. It has been shown that a severely inadequate intake of certain vitamins can impair performance, but it is unusual for an athlete to have such deficiencies.[28] Even marginal deficiencies do not appear to markedly affect the ability to exercise efficiently.[28]

◻ MINERALS

Minerals perform a variety of functions in the body. Some are used to build tissue, such as calcium and phosphorus for bones and teeth, and others are important components of hormones, such as iodine in thyroxine. Iron is critical for the formation of hemoglobin, which carries oxygen within red blood cells. Minerals are also important for regulation of muscle contractions and body fluids, conduction of nerve impulses, and regulation of heart rhythm.

Minerals are divided into two groups. The first group, referred to as macrominerals, are needed in amounts from 100 mg to 1 g. These include calcium, phosphorus, magnesium, sodium, potassium, chloride, and sulfur. The other group, called trace minerals, are needed in far smaller amounts. These include iron, manganese, copper, iodine, zinc, cobalt, fluoride, and selenium. Food sources and the physiological functions for each mineral are listed in Table 19–9.

TABLE 19–8. VITAMINS

VITAMIN	MAIN FUNCTION	GOOD SOURCES
A	Maintenance of skin, bone growth, vision, and teeth	Eggs, cheese, margarine, milk, carrots, broccoli, squash, and spinach
D	Bone growth and maintenance of bones	Milk, egg yolk, tuna, and salmon
E	Prevents oxidation of polyunsaturated fats	Vegetable oils, whole-grain cereal, bread, dried beans, and green leafy vegetables
K	Blood clotting	Cabbage, green leafy vegetables, and milk
Thiamine (B_1)	Energy-releasing reactions	Pork, ham, oysters, breads, cereals, pasta, and green peas
Riboflavin (B_2)	Energy-releasing reactions	Milk, meat, cereals, pasta, mushrooms, and dark green vegetables
Niacin	Energy-releasing reactions	Poultry, meat, tuna, cereal, pasta, bread, nuts, and legumes
Pyridoxine (B_6)	Metabolism of fats and proteins and formation of red blood cells	Cereals, bread, spinach, avocados, green beans, and bananas
Cobalamin (B_{12})	Formation of red blood cells and functioning of nervous system	Meat, fish, eggs, and milk
Folacin	Assists in forming proteins and in formation of red blood cells	Dark-green leafy vegetables, wheat germ
Pantothenic acid	Metabolism of proteins, carbohydrates, and fats, formation of hormones	Bread, cereals, nuts, eggs, and dark green vegetables
Biotin	Formation of fatty acids and energy-releasing reactions	Egg yolk, leafy green vegetables, and egg yolk
C	Bones, teeth, blood vessels, and collagen	Citrus fruits, tomato, strawberries, melon, green pepper, and potato

IRON

The iron status of the athlete, particularly the female athlete, is of concern because indexes of low serum iron (ferritin, iron, and hematocrit) have been observed.[29,30] Reasons for these low levels can be inadequate dietary intake, low bioavailability of iron, or high rates of iron loss.[29] Females are at an increased risk for iron deficiency not only because of increased physiological needs, but because of lower caloric intakes and poor eating habits. In addition, many athletes, particularly females, are vegetarians. In one report, 42% of the female distance runners studied

TABLE 19–9. MINERALS

MINERAL	MAIN FUNCTION	GOOD SOURCES
Calcium	Formation of bones, teeth, nerve impulses, and blood clotting	Cheese, sardines, dark green vegetables, clams, and milk
Phosphorus	Formation of bones and teeth, acid-base balance	Milk, cheese, meat, fish, poultry, nuts, and grains
Magnesium	Activation of enzymes and protein synthesis	Nuts, meats, milk, whole-grain cereal, and green leafy vegetables
Sodium	Acid-base balance, body water balance, and nerve function	Most foods except fruit
Potassium	Acid-base balance reactions, body water balance, and nerve function	Meat, milk, many fruits, cereals, vegetables, and legumes
Chloride	Gastric juice formation and acid-base balance	Table salt, seafood, milk, meat, and eggs
Sulfur	Component of tissue, cartilage	Protein foods
Iron	Component of hemoglobin and enzymes	Meats, legumes, eggs, grains, and dark-green vegetables
Zinc	Component of enzymes, digestion	Milk, shellfish, and wheat bran
Iodine	Component of thyroid hormone	Fish, dairy products, vegetables, and iodized salt
Copper	Component of enzymes, digestion	Shellfish, grains, cherries, legumes, poultry, oysters, and nuts
Manganese	Component of enzymes, fat synthesis	Greens, blueberries, grains, legumes, and fruit
Fluoride	Maintenance of bone and teeth	Water, seafood, rice, soybeans, spinach, onions, and lettuce
Chromium	Glucose and energy metabolism	Fats, meats, clams, and cereals
Selenium	Functions with vitamin E	Fish, poultry, meats, grains, milk, and vegetables
Molybdenum	Component of enzymes	Legumes, cereals, dark-green leafy vegetables

followed modified vegetarian diets and consumed less than 200 g of meat per week.[31]

Dietary intake of iron is tied to caloric intake, but iron absorption depends on the bioavailability of the iron in foods. Meats contain heme-iron, which is highly bioavailable. Meats are therefore a superior source of iron. Heme iron also enhances the absorption of the nonheme iron found in leafy greens, legumes, cereals, whole grains, and enriched breads. Combining these foods with a source of vitamin C can significantly enhance the absorption of iron; for example, orange juice together with an iron-enriched cereal, pasta in combination with broccoli, or tomatoes and green peppers.

Regular monitoring of iron levels in athletes, including biochemical evaluations and dietary assessments, is recommended to ensure optimal training and performance. For individuals with iron-deficiency anemia, supplements are required because it is difficult to overcome this condition through dietary measures alone. Supplementation should not be given routinely to athletes without medical supervision, however. Taking excessive amounts of iron does not improve performance, and iron can be toxic when taken in large doses.

CALCIUM

Adequate consumption of calcium is also important, because low levels can lead to stress fractures and osteoporosis. These complications are most relevant for females because they have thinner bones and lose bone density at a faster rate after reaching maturity. In addition, many female athletes have amenorrhea.[32] Studies have shown that these women have decreased spinal bone mass, compared to both active and sedentary women who are menstruating. The cause of this decrease in bone mineral content is not clear because amenorrhea is associated with a number of variables including low body weight and low body fat, weight loss, low caloric and nutrient intake, physical stress, energy drain, and chronic hormonal alterations.[32,33]

Consumption of lowfat dairy products which are rich in calcium, such as yogurt, cheese, and milk, should be encouraged. If a supplement is necessary, calcium carbonate is the best choice because it supplies elemental calcium and is free from toxins such as those found in dolomite and bone meal. Calcium supplements can cause nausea and loss of appetite, however.

ELECTROLYTES

Salt tablets should not be taken because they can irritate the stomach lining, cause nausea, and increase the body's need for water. Sweat contains proportionately more water, sodium and potassium than does blood plasma. Therefore it is important to replace fluid losses first. Electrolytes can be replaced after training through dietary intake. The potential for a fluid and electrolyte imbalance does exist, however, for athletes who undergo prolonged repeated exposure to the heat, and during exercise lasting several hours. Hyponatremia (low blood sodium) has been reported in ultraendurance athletes, as a result of excess sodium loss through sweat.[34] Drinking solutions that contain small amounts of sodium can reduce the risk of this type of electrolyte disturbance.

Certainly, for the athlete who is chronically dieting, taking a one-a-day multivitamin and multimineral (100% of the RDA) is prudent to ensure adequate intake of micronutrients. For the athlete with a diagnosed deficiency, supplementation by a health professional is necessary. Most researchers agree that indiscriminate use of supplements does not guarantee a high level of performance. Overconsumption can lead to a false sense of security or to toxicity and can alter the utilization of other micronutrients. The bottom line is that megadoses of supplements will not make up for a lack of training or talent or give one the edge over the competition.

☐ ASSESSING DIETARY INTAKE

How does the health professional assess whether an athlete is consuming adequate amounts of calories, carbohydrate, protein, vitamins, and minerals? Evaluation of eating patterns and nutrient intake in athletes is a challenge. To obtain dietary information about an individual without influencing typical habits is difficult, because the report of food intake can depend on what the athlete believes the sports nutritionist wants to see or hear. The nutritionist needs both objectivity and skill to obtain an accurate description of nutrient intake and dietary patterns. Several assessment techniques can be used, depending on the information desired.

24-HOUR RECALL

To obtain a brief overview of what an athlete is consuming, a 24-hour recall can be used. The athlete is asked to recall foods and beverages consumed within the previous 24 hours. Because 1 day is not representative of the season, 24-hour recalls are most appropriate to characterize eating patterns for a specific day. For example, a recall can be taken on a group of runners the day of a race to characterize pre-event and post-event meal patterns.

FOOD FREQUENCY

Food frequency questionnaires provide information about the quality of the diet by having the individual indicate the number of times per day, week, or month an individual consumes particular foods and beverages. The food frequency questionnaire can either include questions about all foods or it can be selective for specific foods suspected of being adequate or excessive in the diet. For example, a food frequency questionnaire given to female athletes might focus on consumption of foods high in calcium and iron (Table 19–10). These questionnaires are useful for categorizing individuals and groups by food intake characteristics.

FOOD INTAKE RECORDS

A more complete picture of food intake can be obtained from a food record in which the athlete records all foods and beverages consumed during a specified length of time, usually 4 or 7 days. This allows for

TABLE 19–10. SELECTIVE FOOD FREQUENCY FORM FOR CALCIUM AND IRON

			FREQUENCY OF CONSUMPTION			
FOOD ITEM	DAILY	3–4 TIMES/WK	ONCE/ WK	EVERY 2 WK	ONCE/ MONTH	NEVER
Milk						
Whole						
Lowfat						
Skim						
Buttermilk						
Cheese						
American						
Cheddar						
Swiss						
Cottage						
Yogurt						
Plain						
Fruit						
Frozen						
Ice cream						
Ice cream						
Ice milk						
Sherbet						
Sardines						
Dark, leafy green vegetables						
Oysters						
Enriched cereals						
Dried beans						
Beef						
Pork						
Poultry						
Fish						
Eggs						
Supplements						
Calcium						
Iron						
Multimineral						

an evaluation of types of foods eaten, nutrient intake, and food patterns. In addition to asking the athlete to write down what he or she eats, the time, location, feelings, and any other information deemed important can also be recorded. Patterns emerge from keeping daily records that can provide important information about how often the athlete eats, where food is typically eaten, and during what time of day. On the basis of this information, strategies to promote optimal intake can be recommended. For example, the eating patterns of a female heavyweight collegiate rower are illustrated in Table 19–11. Because of early practice, this athlete was not consuming any food until noon because she had

TABLE 19-11. EATING PATTERNS OF A FEMALE HEAVYWEIGHT ROWER (1 DAY FROM A 5 DAY FOOD RECORD)

TIME	FOOD/ BEVERAGE	AMOUNT EATEN	PLACE EATEN	FEELINGS
6:30–8:30 A.M. (practice)				tired
9:00 A.M.– 12:00 P.M. (classes)				hungry
12:30 P.M.	rye bread	2 slices	cafeteria	rushed
	boiled ham	2 oz		
	swiss cheese	1 oz		
	mayonnaise	1 tsp		
	mustard	$\frac{1}{2}$ tsp		
	diet Coke	2 12-oz cans		
1:00–2:00 P.M. (class)				couldn't concentrate
2:00–3:00 P.M. (sleep)				
3:15 P.M.	Cheetos	1 $\frac{1}{4}$ oz	going to practice	
	apple juice (Very Fine)	8 oz		
5:00–6:30 P.M. (practice)				
7:00 P.M.	hamburger (broiled)	4 oz	cafeteria	exhausted
	hamburger roll	1		
	mayonnaise	1 tsp		
	ketchup	2 tbsp		
	salad with:			
	iceberg lettuce	2 cups		
	chopped tomatoes	$\frac{1}{2}$ cup		
	cauliflower	$\frac{1}{4}$ cup		
	French dressing	5 tbsp		
	carrot cake with icing	1 piece, 4 × 4 × 3		
9:00 P.M.	saltines	15 crackers	Sandy's	frustrated
	cheddar cheese (Kraft)	2 oz		
	diet Coke	12-oz can		
10:45 P.M.	popcorn (Pop-Secret Lite)	3 cups	home	my roommate made it!
	diet Coke	12-oz can		
11:45 P.M.	(SLEEP)			

From Steen, S.N., Mayer, K.M., and Brownell, K.D.: Dietary intake of female heavyweight rowers. Med. Sci. Sports Exerc., 22:S106, 1990.

classes immediately after practice (last recorded intake was at 10:45 P.M. the previous day). She consumed the majority of calories following late afternoon practice between 7:00 P.M. and 11:45 P.M. As is evident from her record, the rower complained of being tired and having difficulty concentrating. Both training and school work were affected.

Food records can also be used to screen for unusual or ritualistic patterns of food consumption that could indicate an eating disorder. Initiating a casual discussion of food preferences with an athlete can also provide insight into a potential problem.

Food records are the best method available for evaluating intake among athletes (aside from direct observation in a metabolic unit, which is impractical for this population), but there are limitations. For example, some individuals might have difficulty recording or remembering types and amounts of foods eaten or incorrectly estimate portion sizes, leading to an under- or overestimation of nutrient intake. Others might not be motivated to complete the records, and certain individuals might resist providing detailed information because of an eating problem. Despite these limitations, however, if individuals are given specific instructions on how to keep records by a trained professional and an incentive to do so, valuable information can be obtained.

□ EVALUATING DIETARY INTAKE

Two methods can be used to evaluate dietary intake for nutrient adequacy. The first method is a fast, rough estimate that involves estimating the number of servings from the food groups that were consumed during the day recorded, and comparing them to what is recommended (see Table 19–1). Low intakes of protein, iron, calcium, riboflavin, and vitamins A and C can be detected this way. In addition, the U.S. Dietary Goals can be used for a general evaluation of nutrients consumed in excess, such as fat, cholesterol, sugar, and sodium.

The second method is more precise and involves calculating the nutrients in every food and beverage consumed. This process can be done by hand with the use of USDA food composition books and information from manufacturers and food labels, or with a computerized nutrient data bank or computer software program. (The sources used for nutrient composition vary for computer programs, and the programs should be evaluated carefully before a choice is made for analysis.) In addition, not all foods have been analyzed for certain nutrients such as magnesium, vitamin B_6, vitamin B_{12}, limiting interpretation of results.

After determining the nutrient composition for each food, the nutrient composition of overall daily intake can be calculated. A comparison can be made to a desired standard such as the RDA. From food intake data, statements can be made regarding the adequacy of the diet for various nutrients as compared to the RDA. The assumption cannot be made, however, that if an individual has a low or inadequate intake of a certain nutrient, that he or she is deficient in that nutrient. In order to establish whether a deficiency exists, blood tests and a clinical examination must be performed.

After analysis of the food records is completed, a nutritionist is needed to translate computer output data into dietary advice. On the basis of the interpretation, recommendations can be made that consider the athlete's sport, position, training intensity and frequency, climate, age, and sex.

☐ SOURCES OF RELIABLE NUTRITION INFORMATION

Individuals at all levels of the sports community can have an impact on promoting sound nutrition for the athlete. Athletic directors can play a key role by supporting the efforts of health professionals to provide seminars and workshops on sports nutrition within the high school or university. Better still is having a sports nutritionist as part of the sports medicine team. Doing so can help athletes perform at their best and establish healthy eating habits that can last a lifetime.

Having the support and cooperation of the coaching staff is of utmost importance when educating a team or player about nutrition. The result can be enhanced rapport between nutritionist and athlete. Subsequently, the message conveyed to the athlete can be more readily received and put into practice. Aside from encouraging athletes to seek advice from a sports nutritionist, coaches can also help in the effort to combat misinformation by providing team members with handouts from credible resources. Finally, coaches can serve as role models by making healthy dietary changes themselves. This is particularly important for the young athlete. Parents are also important role models for the adolescent athlete and can have an impact on promoting positive dietary choices by providing nutritious food at home.

To consult a sports nutritionist in your area, contact Sports and Cardiovascular Nutritionists (SCAN),* which is a practice group of the American Dietetic Association (ADA). Members of this group are Registered Dietitians and have expertise in the area of nutrition and exercise.

The following publications are recommended for further information on nutrition and exercise:

Jackie R. Berning and Suzanne Nelson Steen (Eds.): *Sports Nutrition for the 90s: The Health Professional's Handbook*. Gaithersburg, MD, Aspen, 1991.

Nancy Clark: *Nancy Clark's Sports Nutrition Guidebook: Eating to Fuel Your Active Lifestyle*. Champaign, IL, Leisure Press, 1990.

Ellen Coleman: *Eating for Endurance*. Palo Alto, CA, Bull Publishing, 1988.

---

* Sports and Cardiovascular Nutritionists (SCAN) 216 West Jackson Street, Suite 800 Chicago, Illinois 60606. (1-800-877-1600).

Frank I. Katch and William D. McKardle: *Nutrition and Weight Control* Philadelphia, Lea & Febiger, 1988.

Marilyn Peterson and Keith Peterson: *Eat to Compete*. Chicago, Yearbook Medical Publishers, 1989.

Nathan J. Smith and Bonnie Worthington-Roberts: *Food for Sport*. Palo Alto, CA, Bull Publishing, 1989.

◻ REFERENCES

1. Costill, D.L., and Miller, J.M.: Nutrition for endurance sport: Carbohydrate and fluid balance. Int. J. Sports. Med., *1*:2, 1980.
2. Steen, S.N., and McKinney, S.M.: Nutrition assessment of college wrestlers. Phys. Sportsmed., *14*:100, 1986.
3. Calabrese, L.H., and Kirkendall, D.T.: Nutritional and medical considerations in dancers. Clin. Sports Med., *2*:539, 1983.
4. Costill, D.L.: Carbohydrates for exercise: Dietary demands for optimal performance. Int. J. Sports Med., *9*:1, 1988.
5. Ivy, J.L., Katz, A.L., Cutler, C.L., et al.: Muscle glycogen synthesis after exercise: Effect of time of carbohydrate ingestion. J. Appl. Physiol., *6*:1480, 1988.
6. Coleman, E.: Carbohydrates: The Master Fuel. *In* Sports Nutrition for the 90s: The Health Professional's Handbook. Edited by J.R. Berning and S.N. Steen. Gaithersburg, MD Aspen, 1991, pp. 31–52.
7. Sherman, W.M.: Pre-event nutrition. Gatorade Sports Science Exchange, *1*, February, 1989.
8. Costill, D.L., Coyle, E.F., Dalsky, G. et al.: Effects of elevated plasma FFA and insulin on muscle glycogen usage during exercise. J. Appl. Physiol. *43*:695, 1977.
9. Hargreaves, M., Costill, D.L., Fink, W.J., et al.: Effect of pre-exercise feedings on endurance cycling performance. Med. Sci. Sports Exerc., *19*:33, 1987.
10. Short, S.H., and Short, W.R.: Four-year study of university athletes' dietary intake. JADA, *82*:632, 1983.
11. Krause, M.E., and Mahan, L.K.: Food Nutrition and Diet Therapy. 7th Ed. Philadelphia, Saunders, 1984.
12. Steen, S.N.: Pre-contest strategies of a male bodybuilder. Int. J. Sport Nutr., *1*:69, 1991.
13. Lemon, P.: Influence of dietary protein and total energy intake on strength improvement. Gatorade Sports Science Exchange, *2*, April 1989.
14. Butterfield, G.: Amino acids and high protein diets. *In* Perspectives in Exercise Science and Sports Medicine. Vol. 4. Ergogenics-Enhancement of Exercise and Sports Performance. Edited by D.R. Lamb and M.H. Williams. Carmel, IN, Benchmark Press, 1991, pp. 87–122.
15. Slavin, J.: Protein needs for the athlete. *In* Sports Nutrition for the 90s: The Health Professional's Handbook. Edited by J.R. Berning and S. Nelson Steen. Gaithersburg, MD, Aspen, 1991. pp. 1–14.
16. Buskirk, E.R., Iampietro, P.F., and Bass, D.F.: Work performance after dehydration: Effects of physical conditioning and heat acclimatization. J. Appl. Physiol. *12*:189, 1958.
17. Rowell, L.B.: Human cardiovascular adjustment to exercise and thermal stress. Physiol. Rev., *54*:75, 1974.
18. Ekblom, B., Greenleaf, C.J., Greenleaf, J.E., and Hermansen L.: Temperature regulation during exercise dehydration in man. Acta Physiol. Scand., *79*:475, 1970.
19. Davis, J.M., Lamb, D.R., Burgess, W.A., and Bartoli, W.P.: Accumulation of deuter-

ium oxide in body fluids after ingestion of D20-labeled beverages. J. Appl. Physiol., 63:2060, 1987.

20. Davis, J.M., Lamb, D.R., Burgess, W.A., et al.: Effects of ingesting 6% and 12% glucose-electrolyte beverages during prolonged intermittent cycling exercise in the heat. Eur. J. Appl. Physiol., 57:563, 1988.

21. Lamb, D.R., and Brodowica, G.R.: Optimal use of fluids of varying formulation to minimize exercise-induced disturbances in homeostasis. Sports. Med., 3:247, 1986.

22. Murray, R.: The effects of consuming carbohydrate-electrolyte beverages on gastric emptying and fluid absorption during and following exercise. Sports. Med., 4:322, 1987.

23. Murray, R., Eddy D.E., Murray T., et al.: The effect of fluid and carbohydrate feedings during intermittent cycling exercise. Med. Sci. Sports Exerc., 19:597, 1987.

24. Owen, M.D., Kregel, K.C., Wall, P.T., and Gisolfi, C.V.: Effects of carbohydrate ingestion on thermoregulation, gastric emptying, and plasma volume during exercise in the heat. Med. Sci. Sports Exerc. 18:568, 1986.

25. Fruth, J.M., and Gisolfi, C.V.: Effects of carbohydrate consumption on endurance performance: Fructose vs. glucose. In Nutrient Utilization During Exercise. Edited by E.L. Fox. Columbus, OH, Ross Laboratories, 1983, pp. 68–77.

26. Krause, M.E., and Mahan, L.K.: Food Nutrition and Diet Therapy. 7th Ed. Philadelphia, Saunders, 1984.

27. National Research Council: Recommended Dietary Allowances. 10th Edition. Washington DC, National Academy Press, 1989.

28. Roe, D.A.: Vitamin requirements for increased physical activity. In Exercise, Nutrition, and Energy Metabolism. Edited by E.S. Horton and R.L. Terjung. New York, Macmillan, 1988, pp. 172–179.

29. Pate, R.R.: Sports anemia: A review of the current research literature. Phys. Sportsmed., 11:115, 1983.

30. Synder, A.C., Dvorak, L.L., and Roepke, J.B.: Influence of dietary iron on measures of iron status among female runners. Med. Sci. Sports Exerc., 21:7, 1989.

31. Brooks, S.M., Sanborn, C.F., Albrecht, B.H., and Wagner, W.W.: Diet in athletic amenorrhoea. Lancet, 1:559, 1984.

32. Loucks, A.B., and Horvath, S.M.: Athletic amenorrhea: A review. Med. Sci. Sports Exerc., 17:56, 1985.

33. Drinkwater, B.L., Nilson, K., Chesnut, C.H., et al.: Bone mineral content of amenorrheic and eumenorrheic athletes. N. Engl. J. Med., 311:277, 1984.

34. Frizzell, R.T., Lang, G.H., Lowance, D.C., and Lathan, S.R.: Hyponatremia and ultramarathon running. JAMA, 255:772, 1986.

C H A P T E R

20

BODY WEIGHT STANDARDS AND ATHLETIC PERFORMANCE

Jack H. Wilmore

Coaches and athletes today are acutely aware of the importance of achieving and maintaining optimal body weight for peak performance in their sport. This can be more of an issue in sports such as gymnastics, distance running, and diving than in sports such as golf, bowling, and archery. Yet few sports or athletes have escaped the fixation on weight that has driven the world of sport over the past 10 years. This focus on weight has led to a better understanding of the role body weight plays in specific sports or events within a sport. It has resulted in the establishment of weight standards that are widely used throughout sport. Though this has usually resulted in a more fit athlete, and an athlete who is better prepared for his or her sport, there have also been negative consequences for the improper use of these weight standards.

During spring training for professional baseball and preseason summer training camps for professional football, the sports pages of the daily newspapers provide the details of who is overweight and how much they are being fined per day for each pound overweight. In these instances, the athlete is forced to face a monetary punishment for exceeding the weight standard assigned to him. In other situations, the punishment for not meeting the weight standard can be more subtle. The college distance runner is not allowed to receive her uniform, the junior high school wrestler is held out of competition and not allowed to travel with the team, and the high school drill team will not even allow the entering freshman to "try out" because she has not met the team's strict weight standards.

Many might not see the above examples as "negatives," but merely as just punishment for unmet standards that top-level athletes are expected to meet. There are other considerations, however. How fair are the established standards? How are these standards determined, what is their scientific validity, and what consideration is given to individual differences and measurement error? A true story will vividly illustrate the serious potential for harm when standards are set that are neither fair nor scientifically justified.

A former major league baseball player, during the first few years in the majors, was making minimum salary. The early preseason polls had projected his team to finish the season at the bottom of their division. Much to the surprise of even the most knowledgeable baseball experts, this team ended up in the World Series. This player became one of the best at his position in the National League during that season, and once the World Series was over he asked management for a substantial increase in his salary (an increase of $75,000 in the mid-1970s). Management agreed to his salary demands, but made his increase in salary contingent on his loss of 25 pounds! The player refused to lose the weight, so the player and management were deadlocked.

The team physician suggested that management fly both the player and vice-president who was responsible for all salary negotiations to a major university where an accurate body composition assessment could be performed. All agreed with this suggestion, and a hydrostatic weighing was performed. The results showed that the player was less than 6% body fat, with only 11 lb of fat total! Because 3 to 4% body fat is necessary for the body to survive, this player had only 4 to 5 lb of fat to lose, and that loss was not advised because he was already at the lower level recommended for wrestlers, who are known for their rapid weight-loss techniques.[1] This player received his increase in salary, he did not have to lose weight, and management was satisfied.

There was a happy ending to this story, but how many other athletes have been given similar advice, followed it, and then found that their athletic ability had deteriorated as a result of substantial losses of lean or fat-free weight? This athlete's weight was well above the range of weights for his height, and he also had a peculiar gait when he walked and ran—a gait commonly referred to as a waddle. The combination of being overweight by the standard height-weight charts and a waddle led management to the suggestion of a 25-lb weight loss. Had the athlete followed this edict, he would more than likely have destroyed himself as a professional athlete. How many athletes have been faced with a similar situation? How many gave in?

This chapter looks at the whole issue of weight standards. First, the relationship of weight and body composition to physical performance is reviewed, to determine the validity of setting weight standards for sport. This is followed with a discussion of the inappropriate use of weight standards and the possible consequences of such practices. Next, guidelines on how to establish weight standards for sport are addressed, focusing on the importance of body composition in establishing these standards. The final section looks at the body composition of the elite athletic populations.

□ BODY COMPOSITION AND SPORTS PERFORMANCE

With an emphasis now on weight standards for most sports, it is important to look at the basis for justifying weight standards. Is there any evidence that an athlete will perform better at a lower body weight? Is the issue really one of body weight, or body composition? Do weight standards apply to all sports, or only to those in which body weight must be moved either horizontally or vertically through space? These and other issues are addressed in this section.

Over the past 50 years, scientists have been able to demonstrate a significant negative relationship between body weight, or body composition, and performance, where performance involves jumping for height or distance, or running for speed or endurance, i.e., the higher the body weight, the poorer the performance. Intuitively, it might seem like the amount of body fat rather than total body weight would be the single most important factor limiting performance.

For most activities, body fat, not body weight, is the most critical factor, although weight alone does present limitations. For example, an ideal body mass and composition for an offensive lineman in football would be ≥275 pounds and ≤10% body fat. Yet, this lean athlete would not be successful as a long-distance runner, long jumper, high jumper, or pole vaulter, because of his size alone. Even if he were to reduce his relative or absolute body fat to the level of the elite athletes in these events, he would still be seriously handicapped by his body size, i.e., predominantly his body weight.

Within a given sport, it is generally true that the leaner athlete performs better. One of the first studies to investigate the relationship between performance and body composition was published in 1947 by Kireillis and Cureton.[2] They determined the relationship between the sum of six skinfolds as an estimate of total body fat and various fitness tests, using a sample of 113 college-age males. Moderately high negative correlations were reported for mile run time ($r = 0.40$), 100-yard dash time ($r = -0.34$), and long jump ($r = -0.33$). Riendeau et al.[3] published one of the earliest studies of the relationship between weight, fat, and performance, where relative body fat was determined by hydrostatic weighing. Sixty-one young men on active duty in the military participated in a series of performance tests, the results of which were correlated against body weight and relative body fat. The resulting correlations for selected measures were as follows:

Performance Test	Relative Body Fat	Total Body Weight
Sit-ups	−0.29	−0.09
Standing long jump (Σ3 trials)	−0.61	−0.13
75-yard dash	−0.52	−0.22
220-yard dash	−0.68	−0.38

They also presented their results according to level of fatness by dividing their total sample into 3 groups of low, moderate, and high relative body fat. Their results further demonstrate the importance of leanness for optimal performance in these activities below:

Performance Test	Low (<10%)	Moderate (10–15%)	High (>15%)
220-yard dash, s	29.3	31.6	35.0
75-yard dash, s	9.8	10.1	10.7
Standing long jump, ft Σ3	23.8	22.7	20.2
Sit-ups in 2 min	43.4	41.6	36.2

This study clearly shows that relative body fat, but not body weight, has a substantial effect on running and jumping activities.

Ismail et al.[4]; conducted a study relating body composition, measured by ^{40}K, and various performance factors in a sample of 81 boys, 10 to 12 years old. Relative lean body mass, used as a measure of relative leanness as opposed to relative fatness, was found to have moderate correlations with vertical jump (r = 0.34), standing long jump (r = 0.44), and 50-yard dash (r = -0.55). A composite factor, "body fitness," was derived from tests of running, jumping, strength, balance, and agility. Relative lean body mass was the most significant factor in their factor analytic analysis of "body fitness." Similar results were reported by Cureton et al.[5] in a sample of 49 boys, 8 to 11 years of age. Total body density correlated r = -0.40 with 50-yard dash time and r = -0.47 with 600-yard dash time.

Further Boileau and Lohman,[6] in their study of 205 boys and girls, 7 to 12 years of age, found a substantial relationship between relative body fat and 600-yard and mile run times, with the slower running times associated with higher relative body fat. Finally, Pate et al.[7] reported significant negative correlations between the sum of two skinfolds and distance run performance (mile run or distance run in 9 min; data expressed as velocity in meters per second) in 2520 students 6 to 16 years of age. The correlations were statistically significant, although of lesser magnitude than those reported in the previous studies cited in this section. The lower correlations could be the result of using only the sum of two skinfolds to represent total body fat. Thus these studies have demonstrated that the effect of body composition on performance is present even at these relatively young ages.

In further studies on the adult population, Leedy et al.[8] investigated the relationship between performance on 19 physical performance items and body composition in 40 subjects 21 to 57 years of age. No measures of running performance were obtained, but standing long jump correlated 0.51 with relative lean body mass, the reciprocal of relative body fat. Katch et al.[9] investigated the relationship between relative body fat and endurance running performance in 36 college-age women. They found relative body fat to correlate r = -0.55 with a 12-min endurance run test. Body weight was not correlated with running performance, however (r = -0.05).

Cureton et al.[10] investigated the role of body fatness on selected physical performance tests using 55 men and 55 women college students. The men had significantly less body fat and performed significantly better than the females on the physical performance tests. By regression analysis, the authors were able to speculate that if the relative body fatness had been the same in the two groups, the differences between the man and women in performance on the various tasks would have been reduced substantially. Relative body fat was found to correlate r = -0.58 with the total distance covered in 12 min, r = 0.73 with the total time it took to run a 50-yard dash, and r = -0.67 with the total height jumped in a vertical jump test.

The levels of both absolute and relative body fat can have a profound influence on running endurance performance in highly trained distance runners, the lower levels equating to better performance.[11,12] Endurance athletes attempt to minimize their fat stores, because it has been clearly shown that excess weight negatively affects endurance performance. Cureton and Sparling subjected male and female runners to submaximal and maximal treadmill runs and to an all-out 12-min run.[11] Each male completed all testing under normal conditions and also while carrying external weight added to the trunk to simulate the relative body fat of the female to which he had been matched. With the added weights, the cost of submaximal exercise was increased and the maximal oxygen uptake was reduced. The relationships between the nonweighted trials (NW) for the men and women and the weighted trial (AW) for the men are illustrated in Figure 20–1.

Pate et al.[12] matched men and women runners on the basis of their performance times to complete a 15-mile road race. Normally, male runners have a much lower relative body fat when compared to female runners, and this is postulated to be one of the most important factors that accounts for the differences in running performance between elite men and women distance runners.[13] They found, however, no difference in the relative body fat values between the women and men (17.8%

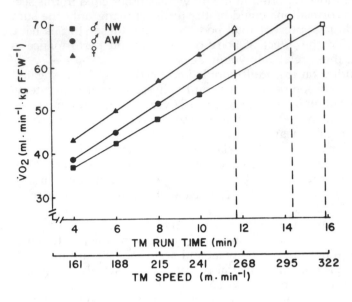

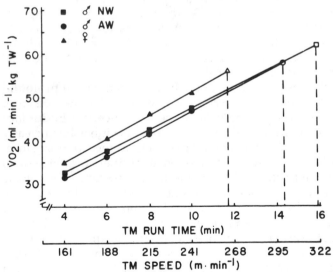

FIG. 20–1. Mean submaximal and maximal oxygen uptake expressed relative to both fat-free weight and total weight in men and women distance runners. The men completed the submaximal and maximal tests twice, once under normal conditions (NW) and once with weights attached to the trunk (AW). From Cureton, K.J., and Sparling, P.B.: Distance running performance and metabolic responses to running in men and women with excess weight experimentally equated. Med. Sci. Sports Exerc., *12*:288, 1980.

vs. 16.3% respectively). These data support the importance of relative body fat on endurance running performance.

Most of the data reported in this section have been obtained from non-athletic populations, with the exception of the last two studies using distance runners. There is a paucity of data on athletic populations. One major problem of using athletic populations is that they typically represent a homogeneous population with respect to body type (physique or somatotype) and training background. Gymnasts, distance runners, high jumpers, and wrestlers are good examples of this. With homogeneous populations, statistical techniques are unlikely to reveal subtle differences that might differentiate between the successful and unsuccessful athlete in that specific sport or activity. With this in mind, I present limited data on a group of professional and a group of university football players in which body composition and performance data had been collected.

During the summer of 1973, body composition by underwater weighing and 1.75-mile run performance data were obtained on a group of 39 professional football players who were participating in their second week of preseason summer training camp (J.H. Wilmore, unpublished data). Heights and weights varied from 69 to 78 in. and 163 to 260 lb respectively. Relative body fat ranged from 3 to 24%, fat-free weight from 150 to 216 lb, and fat weight from 5 to 61 lb. The time to complete the 1.75-mile run varied from 629 sec to 831 sec, or from an average of 6 min/mile to almost 8 min/mile. Correlations of run time with weight and body composition variables were as follows: weight, $r = 0.73$; fat-free weight, $r = 0.56$; fat weight, $r = 0.76$; and relative fat, $r = 0.71$. These relationships are illustrated in Figure 20–2. These data confirm the point made at the beginning of this section that total body weight can be a limiting factor for some types of performance. It should be noted, however, that while 1.75-mile run time is an acceptable estimate of cardiorespiratory endurance capacity, and endurance capacity is important for football players over the course of the four quarters of the game, 1.75-mile run time has little to do with skill and performance as a football player.

In a study of an entire football team at a major university, body composition estimated from skinfolds was correlated to speed in a 40-yard dash (A.S. Jackson, personal communication, 1976). The timing of the 40-yard dash was set up to provide the time to complete the first 5 yards (0 to 5 yards) and the last 20 yards (20 to 40 yards). Fat weight and relative fat was correlated $r = 0.50$ and $r = 0.45$ with 0- to 5-yard time, and $r = 0.65$ and $r = 0.58$ with 20- to 40-yard time.

There has been one notable exception to all of these studies cited in this section. Stager and Cordain[14] determined the relationship of body fatness, by underwater weighing, to swimming performance in 284 competitive female swimmers 12 to 17 years of age. Using the best time in their best event and the best time in the 100-yard freestyle, swim performance was found to be unrelated to relative body fat ($r = 0.18$, ns) but significantly related to fat-free, or lean, body mass ($r = -0.26$, p

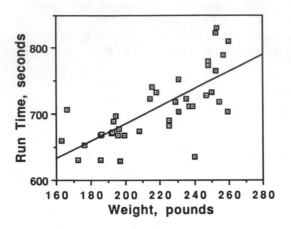

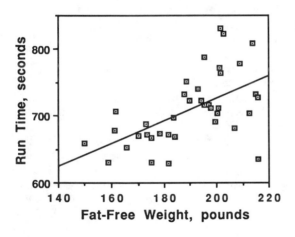

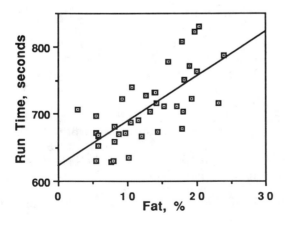

FIG. 20–2. Relationship of total body weight, fat-free weight, and relative fat to 1.75-mile run time for 39 professional football players.

≤0.001). Controlling for age by partial correlation, the relationship between lean body mass and 100-yard swim performance was no longer significant. In swimming, body fat might provide some advantages because it improves buoyancy and should reduce body drag in the water.[15]

☐ INAPPROPRIATE USE OF WEIGHT STANDARDS

Coaches and athletes alike are always looking for that winning edge. Once a coach or athlete hits on something that works and performances improve, it does not take long for the word to spread. The widespread use of anabolic steroids is a classic example of this principle. What started out in the late 1940s and early 1950s as "experimentation" among a small number of body builders and weight lifters has spread throughout the world of sport, to where the majority of the elite athletes in certain sports are habitual steroid users. A similar phenomenon has occurred with the emphasis on leanness in athletes. There has been a concern with body weight over many years in several sports. Over the past 10 to 15 years this concern has become more widespread, and now most sports have weight standards. Coaches have seen athletes' performances improve as body weight decreased. Unfortunately, some have adopted the philosophy that if small weight losses improve performance a little, major weight losses should be even better.

Coaches are not the only ones guilty of this. Athletes, and the parents of athletes, also get drawn into this philosophy. A woman university athlete, considered to be one of the best in the United States in her sport, had dieted and exercised herself down to such a low body weight that her relative body fat was less than 5%. If anyone joined the team who appeared to be leaner than her, she would work even harder to reduce her weight even more. This woman started to notice a deterioration in her performance as an athlete. Further, she started to develop injuries that never seemed to heal. Finally, she was diagnosed as an anoretic and is now receiving professional treatment.

It is extremely important to recognize that pushing body weight too low can have major repercussions. When weight drops below a certain optimal level, the athlete is likely to experience decrements in performance and increased incidence of both major and minor illnesses and injuries. The decrements in performance can be due to a number of factors. Chronic fatigue often accompanies major losses in weight. The sources of this fatigue have not been clearly established, but there are several likely candidates when this chronic fatigue occurs in athletes. The athlete who is chronically underweight, i.e., below optimal competitive weight, has symptoms that mimic those seen with overtraining. There are both neural and hormonal components to the phenomenon of overtraining. There appears to be a sympathetic inhibition and parasympathetic dominance of the autonomic nervous system. Further, there appears to be hypothalamic dysfunction. These lead to a cascade of symptoms, including chronic fatigue.[16,17]

This chronic fatigue could also be due to substrate depletion. Energy for almost all athletic activities is derived predominantly from carbohydrates. Carbohydrates also represent the smallest source of stored energy. The combined storage pools of muscle, liver, and extracellular fluid account for approximately 2000 kcal of stored energy. When athletes are training hard and are not eating an adequate diet, either in total calories or in total carbohydrate calories, the carbohydrate energy stores become depleted. This leads to a number of problems, but most important to the athlete are the decreases in liver and muscle glycogen and the subsequent reduction in blood glucose. Low blood glucose coupled with low liver and muscle glycogen stores can lead to chronic fatigue and considerable declines in performance.[18,19] Further, under these conditions the body also uses body protein stores as an energy substrate for exercise, which can lead to a gradual depletion of muscle protein over time.[20]

The constant attention given to either achieving or maintaining a prescribed weight goal, or both, particularly if the weight goal is inappropriately set, can lead to disordered eating. It is difficult to obtain accurate estimates of the prevalence of eating disorders in any population, but particularly in athletic populations. Nevertheless, a significant number of indicators suggest that the prevalence of eating disorders is very high in select athletic populations (see Chapter 9). On certain teams in several sports, at the elite or world-class level, the prevalence approaches or even exceeds 50%. The female athlete prone to an eating disorder is open to a triad of disorders that are more than likely intricately interrelated, i.e., anorexia nervosa or bulimia nervosa, menstrual dysfunction, and bone mineral disorders.

Menstrual dysfunction in athletes is a phenomenon whose occurrence is widely recognized, but whose pathophysiology is not well understood. High prevalences of oligomenorrhea, amenorrhea, and delayed menarche have been associated with sports in which there is an emphasis on low body weight or low body fat. Weight loss induced by calorie restriction and a vegetarian diet is associated with luteal phase deficiency and menstrual dysfunction.[21] This combination of caloric restriction and vegetarian diet is typical among women endurance athletes. There is a tight coupling between anorexia nervosa and menstrual dysfunction. A similar relationship has not been clearly established as yet with bulimia, but an increasing number of athletes are presenting as bulimic and amenorrheic. The physiological and emotional relationships between these two disorders have yet to be established. Refer to Chapter 15 for a detailed discussion of menstrual dysfunction in athletes.

The third member of this triad, bone mineral disorders, was first reported in 1984. It is now recognized as a potentially serious consequence associated with menstrual dysfunction,[22] and a number of scientists are researching the relationship between menstrual dysfunction in athletes and low bone mineral content or density. Although studies have suggested that bone density increases with the resumption of normal menses, more recent observations suggest that the regain of bone is limited and that bone density remains well below normal even with re-establishment of normal menstrual function.[22] The long-term consequences of these chronically low bone densities in an athletic population are not yet established. Refer to Chapter 16 for an extensive discussion of this topic.

To briefly summarize this section, pushing body weight too low can have serious health and performance consequences. Coaches, athletes, and parents, as well as the team physician and athletic trainer, must be aware of these consequences. Athletes who are attempting to lose weight, or those who are already at very low body weights, should be closely monitored. Chronic fatigue, decrements in performance, and changes in menstrual function should be used as possible signs of maladaptation to the stress of weight loss or the stress of attempting to maintain a body weight at a level below optimal.

☐ GUIDELINES IN ESTABLISHING WEIGHT STANDARDS

The potential for abuse of weight standards has been clearly established. If standards are not set appropriately, the potential exists for pushing athletes well below their optimal body weight. Thus the issue of how to properly set standards becomes of critical importance.

How are weight standards established? The reader is encouraged to review Chapter 6. In that chapter the point was made that body weight standards should be established on the basis of the athlete's body composition. Once a body composition determination has been made, the fat-free mass is used to estimate what the athlete should weigh at a specific relative body fat. If the goal is to get a woman distance runner down to 15% body fat, her weight at 15% body fat would be estimated by dividing her fat-free weight by 85% or 0.85, the fraction of her goal weight that is to be represented by her fat-free tissue. Thus the establishment of weight standards really translates into the establishment of standards of relative body fat for each sport. Because there are basic differences between males and females with respect to fat patterning, the established standards should be sex-specific.

What is the recommended relative body fat for an elite athlete in any given sport? There must be an optimal value, above which or below which the athlete's performance is negatively affected. This is an important question, but there is not an easy answer. First, it must be remembered (see Chapter 6) that there are inherent errors in the existing techniques for measuring body composition. Even with the better laboratory techniques there is a 1 to 3% error in the measurement of body density. Further, it is important to understand the concept of individual variability. Not every male distance runner will have his best performance at 6% body fat. Some will be able to achieve slightly lower values and improve performance, and others will find it impossible to get down to values this low and will have to compete at higher values.

I suggest that a range of values be set for males and females in each

TABLE 20–1. RANGES OF RELATIVE BODY FAT FOR MEN AND WOMEN ATHLETES IN VARIOUS SPORTS

SPORT	MEN	WOMEN
Baseball, softball	8–14	12–18
Basketball	6–12	10–16
Body building	5–8	6–12
Canoeing and Kayaking	6–12	10–16
Cycling	5–11	8–15
Fencing	8–12	10–16
Football	6–18	—
Golf	10–16	12–20
Gymnastics	5–12	8–16
Horse racing	6–12	10–16
Ice and field hockey	8–16	12–18
Orienteering	5–12	8–16
Pentathlon	—	8–15
Racketball	6–14	10–18
Rowing	6–14	8–16
Rugby	6–16	—
Skating	5–12	8–16
Skiing	7–15	10–18
Ski jumping	7–15	10–18
Soccer	6–14	10–18
Swimming	6–12	10–18
Synchronized swimming	—	10–18
Tennis	6–14	10–20
Track and field		
Running events	5–12	8–15
Field events	8–18	12–20
Triathlon	5–12	8–15
Volleyball	7–15	10–18
Weightlifting	5–12	10–18
Wrestling	5–16	—

sport, recognizing both individual variability and methodological error. To this end, Table 20–1 provides a summary of values of relative body fat for athletes in selected sports. In most cases, these values of relative body fat are representative of the elite athletes in those sports. When athletes exceed the upper end of the range for their sport, they should work toward achieving the upper end goal weight slowly, losing not more than 1 to 2 lb per week. This should be accomplished by modest reduction in the daily intake of calories combined with modest increases in energy expenditure. Weight reductions of more than 1 to 2 lb per week will lead to a loss in fat-free mass, which is usually not the outcome desired. Once the upper limit of the range has been reached, any further weight loss should be undertaken only with close supervision of the coach, athletic trainer, and team physician. This weight loss should be achieved at an even slower rate, i.e., less than 1 lb per week, and should be titrated against performance and medical symptoms.

☐ BODY COMPOSITION OF ELITE ATHLETIC POPULATIONS—A FINAL WARNING

Table 20–1 provides a range of relative body fat values for various sports for both males and females. As stated in the previous section, these ranges of values were established primarily from values obtained from elite athletes within a given sport. This strategy assumes that the elite athlete represents the ultimate level of conditioning for that sport or event. For years, researchers and clinicians have used the elite athlete as a template against which aspiring athletes can be compared in order to determine areas of strength and weakness. Though this has generally proven to be an acceptable and useful approach, it is important to recognize the limitations of this practice.

Figure 20–3 provides an excellent illustration of the limitations of these guidelines for determining ranges of relative body fat for athletes in various sports. This figure presents the relative body fat data for a number of the United States' top women track and field athletes from 1970 through 1975. Many of the distance runners were below 10% body fat. In fact, most of the best distance runners were below this level. The two

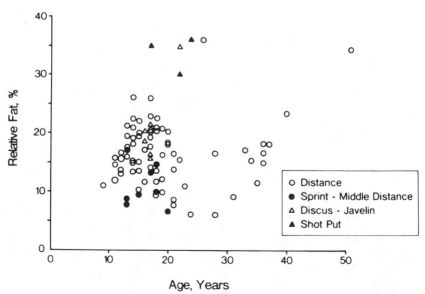

FIG. 20–3. Relative body fat values for female track and field athletes. From Wilmore, J.H., and Costill, D.L.: Training for Sport and Activity: The Physiological Basis of the Conditioning Process. 3rd Ed. Dubuque, IA, Wm. C. Brown, 1988, p. 322.

top distance runners at that time were ~6% body fat. One had won six consecutive international cross-country championships, and the other held the best time in the world for the marathon. It would be tempting from these data to suggest a range of relative fat values for women distance runners between 6 and 12%. Yet one of the best distance runners in the United States at that time, who was within 2 years of taking over the top spot, had a relative body fat of 17%. One woman had a relative body fat of 37%, and she set the best time in the world for the 50-mile run within 6 months of her evaluation. More than likely, it would not have been desirable to get either of these two women below 12% body fat.

☐ REFERENCES

1. American College of Sports Medicine: Position stand on weight loss in wrestlers. Med. Sci. Sports Exerc., 8:xi, 1976.
2. Kireilis, R.W., and Cureton, T.K.: The relationships of external fat to physical education activities and fitness tests. Res. Q., 18:123, 1947.
3. Riendeau, R.P., Welch, B.E., Crisp, C.E., et al.: Relationships of body fat to motor fitness test scores. Res. Q., 29:200, 1958.
4. Ismail, A.H., Christian, J.E., and Kessler, W.V.: Body composition relative to motor aptitude for preadolescent boys. Res. Q., 34:462, 1963.
5. Cureton, K.J., Boileau, R.A., and Lohman, T.G.: Relationship between body composition measures and AAHPER test performances in young boys. Res. Q., 46:218, 1975.
6. Boileau, R.A., and Lohman, T.G.: The measurement of human physique and its effect on physical performance. Orthop. Clin. North Am., 8:563, 1977.
7. Pate, R.R., Slentz, C.A., and Katz, D.P.: Relationships between skinfold thickness and performance of health related fitness test items. Res. Q. Exerc. Sport, 60:183, 1989.
8. Leedy, H.E., Ismail, A.H., Kessler, W.V., and Christian, J.E.: Relationships between physical performance items and body composition. Res. Q., 36:158, 1965.
9. Katch, F.I., McArdle, W.D., Czula, R., and Pechar, G.S.: Maximal oxygen uptake, endurance running performance, and body composition in college women. Res. Q., 44:301, 1973.
10. Cureton, K.J., Hensley, L.D., and Tiburzi, A.: Body fatness and performance differences between men and women. Res. Q., 50:333, 1979.
11. Cureton, K.J., and Sparling, P.B.: Distance running performance and metabolic responses to running in men and women with excess weight experimentally equated. Med. Sci. Sports Exerc., 12:288, 1980.
12. Pate, R.R., Barnes, C., and Miller, W.: A physiological comparison of performance-matched female and male distance runners. Res. Q. Exerc. Sport, 56:245, 1985.
13. Wilmore, J.H., Brown, C.H., and Davis, J.A.: Body physique and composition of the female distance runner. Ann. N.Y. Acad. Sci., 301:764, 1977.
14. Stager, J.M., and Cordain, L. Relationship of body composition to swimming performance in female swimmers. J. Swim. Res., 1:21, 1984.
15. Sinning, W.E.: Body composition and athletic performance. In Limits of Human Performance. Edited by D.H. Clarke and H.M. Eckert. Champaign, IL, Human Kinetics, 1985, pp. 45–56.
16. Kuipers, H., and Keizer, H.A.: Overtraining in elite athletes: Review and directions for the future. Sports Med., 6:79, 1988.

17. Barron, J.L., Noakes, T.D., Levy, W., et al.: Hypothalamic dysfunction in overtrained athletes. J. Clin. Endocrinol. Metab., *60*:803, 1985.
18. Wilmore, J.H., and Costill, D.L.: Training for Sport and Activity: The Physiological Basis of the Conditioning Process. 3rd Ed. Dubuque, IA, Wm. C. Brown, 1988.
19. Sherman, W.M.: Carbohydrate feedings before and after exercise. *In* Ergogenics—Enhancement of Performance in Exercise and Sport. Edited by D.R. Lamb and M.H. Williams. Dubuque, IA, Brown and Benchmark, 1991, pp. 1–27.
20. Butterfield, G.: Amino acids and high protein diets. *In* Ergogenics—Enhancement of Performance in Exercise and Sport. Edited by D.R. Lamb and M.H. Williams. Dubuque, IA, Brown and Benchmark, 1991, pp. 87–117.
21. Shangold, M., Rebar, R.W., Wentz, A.C., and Schiff, I.: Evaluation and management of menstrual dysfunction in athletes. JAMA, *263*:1665, 1990.
22. Drinkwater, B.L., Bruemner, B., and Chesnut, C.H.: Menstrual history as a determinant of current bone density in young athletes. JAMA, *263*:545, 1990.

CHAPTER

21

CLINICAL TREATMENT OF EATING DISORDERS

David L. Tobin, Craig L. Johnson, and Kevin Franke

This chapter provides an overview of what a comprehensive treatment program for eating disorders should provide patients. Though patients with anorexia nervosa and bulimia nervosa present with an easily identified, circumscribed pattern of eating symptoms, eating disorders often occur with a wide spectrum of concomitant symptoms that complicate the treatment process. It is important for eating disorders programs to offer a broad range of services that reflects the diversity of presentation within these patient populations.

Though the chapter is primarily oriented to the treatment considerations of general populations of women with eating disorders, the needs of the eating-disordered athlete are also considered. In addition to the social pressures to be thin that face all young women in our culture, athletes also have the additional burden of sporting activities that promote prolonged periods of exercise and dietary regimens that are risk factors and even symptoms of eating disorders. To the extent that athletes are pressured to lose weight and reduce body fat in order to increase their athletic performance they incur additional risk for developing an eating disorder (see Chapter 8). This risk can be mitigated by the proper attitude of coaches, parents, and peers.

☐ CLINICAL FEATURES

The clinical features of eating-disorder patients as described in DSM-III-R[1] include attempts to maintain a low body weight, binge eating in bulimic patients, and certain concomitant psychiatric symptoms.

ANOREXIA NERVOSA

Anorexia nervosa is characterized by attempts to maintain body weight 15% below what is normally expected for a given age and height. Despite successful efforts at remaining thin, anorectics have an intense fear of gaining weight or becoming fat, such that even the accumulation of a few pounds provokes tremendous anxiety. Perhaps most remarkable is the disturbance in body image: they believe they are fat even when they are emaciated. To be classified as anorectic under DSM-III-R criteria a woman must have been amenorrheic for at least 3 months.[1]

BULIMIA NERVOSA

Bulimia nervosa is characterized by recurrent episodes of binge eating (at least twice weekly) followed by purging behavior that may include self-induced vomiting, use of laxatives, diet pills, diuretics, or rigorous dieting. During the eating binges there is a feeling of lack of control over eating and a persistent overconcern with body shape and weight.[1]

PSYCHIATRIC SYMPTOMS

Eating disorders are often complicated by concomitant psychiatric symptoms that include but are not limited to affective disorders and personality disorders. Approximately half of our patients present with symptoms of affective and anxiety disorders, at least one-third being moderately to severely depressed.[2–4] Other clinics have reported significant chemical dependency problems in one-fourth of patients. Approximately 50% of patients demonstrated evidence of concomitant axis II diagnoses, usually from personality disorder cluster II.[2,3,5,6] Patients occasionally present with symptoms of schizophrenia. Though some investigators have hypothesized a causal pathway that is determined by the presence of either affective,[7,8] or anxiety[9,10] disorders, there is no correlation between severity of eating symptoms and level of depression, anxiety, or personality disturbance in tertiary clinic patients.[2,3]

Concomitant psychiatric diagnoses often determine the course of treatment. In a recent follow-up report of response to outpatient psychotherapy, Johnson and his colleagues[3] found that 90% of bulimia nervosa patients without personality disturbance or severe depression were able to achieve significant reductions in eating symptoms in an average of 30 sessions whereas fewer than half of patients with personality disorders or severe depression were able to achieve such reductions, even after receiving twice as much treatment (i.e., an average of 60 sessions). Fortunately, even the patients with affective and personality disturbance were able to remit symptomatic behavior when they had received 100 sessions of psychotherapy. Patients who present with both substance-abuse and eating-disorder symptoms are likely to need significantly more treatment than patients who present with circumscribed symptoms. It is therefore recommended that patients receive an initial evaluation that diagnoses the full range of difficulties found in eating-disorder patients. It is important to prepare patients for the extent and type of treatment they are likely to require.

◻ INITIAL EVALUATION

On the mistaken assumption that eating-disordered patients are homogeneous in their symptom presentation, some programs offer little more than an administrative screening for entry into standardized treatment protocols. This offers the patient a pretense of expertise that can result in treatment failure, and the patient is more likely to conclude that she is untreatable.

The intake interview is designed to be comprehensive in covering factors that have influenced the course of the disorder and that would affect the course of treatment.[11] It is important to acknowledge that some pathologic aspects of the eating patterns of athletes with eating disorders can be the result of self-discipline and long-term goals. Moreover, it might be necessary for athletes to continue with dietary regimens or intensive exercise programs that would automatically be targeted for elimination in other patients. For example, anorexic patients who perform excessive aerobic exercise (e.g., an hour or more) on a daily basis must be asked to stop. For most people, this level of excessive exercise goes beyond being health-conscious and probably interferes with normal daily living in a number of ways. For many athletes, however, aerobic exercise is often fundamental to remaining competitive. Sorting through what is healthy and what is pathological becomes complex in such cases, and this is explored in the following sections. But it is important for evaluators to acknowledge and align themselves with the part of the eating-disordered athlete that is healthy, not only to appreciate their strengths but also to reassure them that treatment will be in their best interest. The interview, which takes 1.5 to 2 hours, is divided into the following subsections: weight history, body image, dieting behavior, binge eating, purging behavior, medical issues, personality disorder, family characteristics, and general level of adaptive functioning.

WEIGHT HISTORY

The interview begins with questions about the patient's current, highest, lowest, and desired weight. This often provides a historical record of how weight preoccupations and fluctuations have affected the patient's self-esteem and life adjustment. For the athlete, it is important to consider and take into account the training demands of particular sporting events and how such demands might influence fluctuations in body weight.

BODY IMAGE

Body image perception ranges from mild distortion to severely delusional and can reflect the patient's overall adjustment. Though eating-disordered patients have traditionally been preoccupied with being thin as a way of managing interpersonal and intrapersonal difficulties, the athlete who trains in the search of other forms of physical perfection (e.g., large pectorals) can be just as pathological. Ideal body shape varies from individual to individual. Therefore, the evaluator must view the patient's body dissatisfaction and distortion of physical appearance from within the patient's vision of what is ideal.

DIETING BEHAVIOR

It is important to know at what age a patient began dieting, the frequency of dieting attempts, the degree of restriction, the use of fad dieting techniques, and the general pattern of dieting behavior. It is also important to consider the training demands of a patient's sport. Evaluators must look at the total context in which the patient has tried to lose or gain weight, including the patient's biological set point, the demands of a particular sporting event, and the feasibility of a particular training goal.

BINGE EATING

The assessment of binge eating behavior involves assessment of the major life circumstances surrounding the onset of the behavior as well as the assessment of the patient's daily routine and the specific pattern of binge eating episodes. One is interested in knowing the onset of such episodes, their precipitants, duration, and frequency, and the types of foods on which the patient binges. Again, it is important to appreciate training goals when labeling behavior as pathological.

PURGING BEHAVIOR

It is important to know the method or methods a patient employs to purge unwanted calories. Commonly used methods involve vomiting, laxatives, diuretics, diet pills, restrictive dieting, and excessive exercise. Unfortunately for the diagnostician, purging calories is commonly practiced in some sporting events, such as wrestling and long-distance running. When trying to assess whether purging is pathological, it is important to consider the context and pattern of purging behavior. Does the patient purge prior to meets in order to make weight, or does she engage in purging behavior at other times, perhaps to manage emotional tensions? The more circumscribed a particular pattern of purging, the less likely it is to reflect the presence of an eating disorder or other psychological concerns. A more pervasive pattern of purging suggests the presence of an eating disorder and emotional difficulties. Different purging behaviors can serve somewhat different adaptive functions. For example, restrictive dieting might give a patient a more anorectic presentation, whereas the use of laxatives frequently adds a self-punitive function to the purging behavior.

MEDICAL ISSUES

In addition to assessing the adaptive function of the binge-purge cycle, it is important to evaluate the patient's physical condition for medical complications of bulimia or anorexia (see Chapter 14). Patients should receive a complete physical examination on entering treatment. Excessive dieting, binge eating, and purging can influence endocrine function, disturb blood chemistry, destroy tooth enamel, irritate the esophagus, and disturb the gastrointestinal system. Severe medical complications make hospitalization the only treatment option.

PERSONALITY DISORDER

Assessment for personality disorder is perhaps the most important aspect of the initial evaluation, because the presence of such disorder forecasts a slow, difficult treatment.[2,3] It can be an even more important area of assessment for the eating-disordered athlete than for nonathlete patients because the disordered behaviors themselves, whether binge eating (e.g., to increase strength and power), dieting (e.g., to increase speed), vomiting or using laxatives (e.g., to make weight), or excessive exercise (e.g., to promote endurance), are likely to be part of a normal training regimen. Thus, when it is difficult to determine whether eating or exercise behaviors constitute excess or abuse, it is necessary to consider the patient's experience with the training regimen and to evaluate the extent to which the training regimen is serving as a defensive or compensatory function in the patient's life.

Some of this information can be gathered by history. Evidence of stormy, chaotic interpersonal relationships might suggest that training and disregulated patterns of eating are relied on as substitutes for close interpersonal relationships. Such evidence might indicate that a patient would have a difficult time engaging in a helping relationship. The patient's approach to the interview is also an important source of information in assessing personality. For example, excessive patient mistrust during the intake interview can suggest the presence of personality disturbance.

Other patterns of behavior also indicate personality disturbance. A history of self-injury or other self-destructive behavior is of great concern. For some athletes this takes the form of sports injuries that could have been avoided. Other patients might have stable relationships but have difficulty identifying and working toward long-term goals. These patients might appear relatively undisturbed because they can readily adapt to their external environment to meet the needs of others. They have difficulty, however, in meeting their own needs. These patients have been described as having a "false self" or narcissistic personality disorder.[12–14] Children or adolescents who are pushed into athletic competition by family can develop this kind of personality difficulty.

A more formal assessment battery composed of projective (e.g., Rorschach test, Thematic Apperception Test) and objective testing instruments (Minnesota Multiphase Personality Inventory, Millon Clinical Multiaxial Inventory) can be helpful in specifying the personality profile, but some preliminary decisions about level of personality disturbance must be made on the basis of the interviewer's impressions.

Identification of personality disorders and character pathology is crucial to the disposition process. In a sample of 55 clinic patients with bulimia, 21 were identified as having borderline personality disorder and 19 were diagnosed as being free from personality disorder.[3] Only 21% of the patients without personality disorder remained symptomatic at the end of 1 year, but 62% of the borderline patients continued to meet DSM-III-R criteria for bulimia. Patients without personality disorders can frequently benefit from brief therapy. Personality-disordered patients will probably not benefit from brief therapy; both clinic and patient must be prepared to make a long-term commitment to the treatment process.

FAMILY CHARACTERISTICS

Family history, family dynamics, and the patient's current level of family involvement play a crucial role in the onset and maintenance of eating disorder symptoms. It is important to rule out the extent to which symptomatic behavior is promoted by the family system and to elicit information about communication patterns within the family that could influence individual treatment.[15] It is also important to assess the family's cohesiveness, communication style, method of conflict resolution and behavior control, and the role of the patient's symptoms within the family system. It is important not only to assess the family's involvement with the eating difficulty, but also to determine the possibility of overinvolvement by the family in the patient's athletic accomplishments.

As in the assessment of personality disturbance, the interview provides two important sources of information: family history and the interview process itself. If the patient is an adolescent or young adult living at home, we insist that the parents come to the evaluation. When family members refuse to attend the evaluation, we can infer a limited amount of family support for the patient's attempts to change symptomatic behavior.

GENERAL LEVEL OF ADAPTIVE FUNCTIONING

Assessment of general level of adaptive functioning overlaps with level of personality disturbance. Even when there is no sign of personality disturbance it is important to assess the extent to which the patient is able to work, go to school, or engage in interpersonal relationships. Furthermore, it is important to examine the patient's capacity to be alone, and the extent to which time alone is overwhelming and provokes disregulated eating. The evaluator should also assess whether the patient is willing and motivated to change and the intellectual, emotional, and financial resources she can bring to treatment.

☐ CLINICAL INTERVENTION

At the end of the comprehensive intake interview, the evaluator offers the patient a formulation and a recommendation for treatment. Sometimes the patient needs to gather additional information (e.g., explore family support for treatment) or the evaluator feels the need to seek consultation with clinic staff. In proposing an initial treatment plan, the evaluator must weigh all the available information and attempt to match patient need with program activities. Sometimes the fit between a given patient and a particular program is not good, and a referral to a program that more adequately meets the patient's needs must be made (e.g., a patient with both eating and substance difficulties who might benefit from a 12-step program). The treatment interventions that are necessary for this patient population are quite varied, and it is difficult for a program to excel in every area.

One of the first issues likely to arise in treating an athlete who has been diagnosed with an eating disorder is the question of how the treatment plan will affect the athlete's training and performance schedule. By the time the eating-disordered athlete gets to a clinic for an evaluation, athletic skill and performance might already have been adversely influenced by the gradual progression of symptoms. At this point the athlete is more likely to view the therapy plan as a potential aid in returning to a previous level of athletic ability. Clinical intervention is most successful when the athlete feels that the clinician understands the central role that athletic competition serves in supporting her identity and self-esteem. The therapy plan might call for immediate reduction in or cessation of certain behaviors that the eating-disordered athlete is still strongly committed to as part of her overall training (e.g., exercising several hours a day or restricting caloric intake). In establishing a treatment contract the treatment team must help the athlete see clearly that behavior change that temporarily limits practice or training will in the long run lead to greater overall enjoyment of her athletic career.

When an athlete has been diagnosed with an eating disorder it is essential that the treatment team understand how eating-disordered behavior and attitudes are being reinforced by the athlete's performance goals. The onset of eating-disordered behavior such as restrictive eating or intense, prolonged exercise can be directly related to the athlete's performance expectations. Many athletes have discovered that these behaviors help them cope with certain aspects of everyday living, such dysphoric affect and intrapsychic and interpersonal conflict. These behaviors then become more and more entrenched as the athlete sees temporary improvements in her performance and repeatedly experiences temporary relief from the anxiety and depression that are part of everyday life. The long-term impact of such behavior, however, is quite debilitating, and it can be fatal. The disordered behavior and attitudes themselves must be treated as aggressively as possible.

Active approaches to helping patients manage and eliminate their symptoms include cognitive-behavioral, psychoeducational, self-management, and relapse-prevention strategies. Active interventions help patients to break down their eating disorder into discrete behavioral components and then to evaluate the functional value of each behavior. Many patients can make quick use of active symptom management strategies, but others cannot. Some patients require integration of these symptom-management approaches with psychodynamic psychotherapy. Patients with personality disorders or major depression are likely to make necessary behavior changes only within the context of an ongoing relationship with a psychotherapist. This is necessary so that the patient can understand and resolve the psychological problems that predispose her to develop the eating disorder and help to maintain it.

☐ AMBULATORY CARE

TIME-LIMITED PSYCHOEDUCATIONAL GROUP THERAPY

Psychoeducational group therapy is most useful for bulimics who are age 18 to 30, who have high motivation for change, who are at or near normal weight, and who do not have other significant diagnoses such as major depression or personality disorder.[13] Psychoeducational groups help patients to understand the cognitive, emotional, and interpersonal triggers of their symptoms. These groups also help members develop normal eating patterns and alternative strategies for coping with negative affect or conflict. Intervention strategies include self-monitoring, goal-setting, education about nutrition and the consequences of restrictive dieting, and challenging irrational beliefs about thinness and dieting.[16,17] Sharing experiences with other eating-disordered patients helps the individual overcome the shame that often accompanies an eating disorder. Group members are able to mobilize more quickly when they learn that they are not alone and that they are not "bad" or "weak" because they have these eating disorder symptoms. These groups work best for athletes when there is at least one other athlete in the group.

INDIVIDUAL PSYCHOTHERAPY

Individual psychotherapy is used to treat both the eating disorder symptoms[18,19] and the underlying psychological and emotional problems.[13] Patients who do not encounter significant problems in rapidly forming a working alliance with the therapist can make use of educational, behavioral, and cognitive techniques such as those mentioned above to reduce and rather quickly (1 to 4 mo) eliminate binge and purge behavior. Eliminating restrictive eating in low-weight bulimics and anorectics usually requires a longer, more dynamically-oriented course of individual therapy in which maladaptive patterns of self-regulation and attachment and separation are addressed. These patients often present with rigid defenses against experiencing anxiety that arises whenever they begin to develop intimacy. For bulimic patients, binges and purges are a way of regulating what they believe to be unacceptable impulses or feelings. That is, whenever these impulses or feelings arise, they turn to binge and purge behavior to generate an experience of tension build-up (binge) and tension release (purge). Without dynamic therapy these issues are likely to remain unresolved.

NUTRITIONAL COUNSELING

Anorexic and bulimic patients often base their eating and dieting habits on inaccurate information or incorrect assumptions about food, digestion, and weight gain or loss. For example, many patients believe that muscle tissue immediately turns into fat in the absence of a vigorous exercise regimen or that any fat that is consumed becomes a permanent part of the body. These false assumptions maintain and strengthen the unhealthy eating patterns. Counseling by a nutritionist or a well-informed nurse or therapist is an important component in the overall confrontation of the patient's illogical assumptions about food and weight. For example, patients can be given specific meal plans to follow. They can be guided in how often they weigh themselves as a protection against the day-to-day fluctuations of body weight, and they should be provided with a reasonable expectation of what their normal body weight should be (see Chapters 4 and 6).

MEDICAL MONITORING

Any patient who has not had a thorough medical examination within the past year should be advised to have one. Patients with very low weight, obese patients, patients who binge and purge multiple times a day, patients whose laxative abuse is severe or prolonged, and patients who have a medical illness such as diabetes that could interact with the eating disorder symptoms to create potentially life-threatening emergencies should be seen regularly by an internist familiar with eating disorders until the symptoms are significantly reduced. When deciding if a patient with severe symptoms needs hospitalization it is particularly important to assess medical risk (see Chapter 14).

PSYCHOPHARMACOLOGICAL TREATMENT

Some anorectic and bulimic patients are prone to major depressive episodes or panic attacks and chronic debilitating anxiety. Anti-anxiety or antidepressant medication can sometimes be useful, in two ways: first, the medication can reduce dysphoric affect and thereby reduce the athlete's need to rely on eating-disorder symptoms to manage them; and second, patients who are not overwhelmed with high levels of depression or anxiety can participate more effectively in the dynamic and cognitive-behavioral components of their treatment plan. The link between bulimia and major affective disorder remains unclear, but there is evidence to suggest that some bulimic patients develop bulimia secondary to the occurrence of affective disorder.[7] Biological symptoms of major depression suggest the strong possibility that pharmacological treatment of the eating disorder can be helpful.

FAMILY AND MARITAL THERAPY

Under certain conditions it is crucial to involve the identified patient's family in the treatment. Without such involvement, the family could unwittingly undermine the patient's progress if the identified patient's symptoms serve an adaptive function for the family as well, because the unassisted family system lacks the resources and support it needs to allow the patient to give up her symptoms. Some conditions that suggest the need for ongoing family sessions include (1) the patient lives with the family of origin, (2) the patient demonstrates little evidence of true emotional separation from the family, (3) there is another serious problem in the family (e.g., alcoholism or physical or sexual abuse), and (4) the patient requires hospitalization. Treatment goals include interventions that help the family to (1) reorganize dysfunctional relationships and structures, (2) better tolerate important affects, (3) encourage individuation, and (4) resolve conflicts between members.

A patient's spouse can facilitate both symptom management and emotional healing. Working with the marital couple can help each partner identify the intrapsychic and interpersonal experiences that trigger eating-disorder symptoms. Once these "triggers" are identified, alternative coping strategies can be developed with the couple working in partnership.

SELF-HELP AND OTHER SUPPORT GROUP MEETINGS

Support from the patient's therapist, spouse, or family members notwithstanding, ongoing support from others struggling with the same symptoms and underlying emotional issues can often facilitate recovery.

Group support helps patients process day-to-day stressors and increases their understanding of the links between feelings, attitudes, and their food-related behaviors. Not all patients can benefit from these groups, however. Patients with severe ego deficits might not find enough structure in peer-led, self-help groups and can disturb the supportive function of such groups for other patients.

HOSPITAL CARE

Under certain conditions, ambulatory care might be insufficient to get a patient started on the road to recovery. These conditions may include: (1) additional Axis I or Axis II diagnoses that preclude the patient from using the behavioral, cognitive, or relationship interventions offered in outpatient treatment, (2) medical complications from severe or prolonged eating-disorder symptoms that endanger the patient's life, and (3) evidence of self-injurious or suicidal behavior. When one or more of these conditions exist, more intensive interventions such as hospitalization or partial hospitalization (i.e., day or evening treatment programs) can be used. These interventions must then be followed up with one or more forms of the outpatient treatment mentioned above.

INPATIENT MILIEU. The primary goals of inpatient treatment are (1) to normalize patient's eating habits and weight, and (2) to lay the groundwork for ongoing recovery following discharge to outpatient treatment. The first goal is accomplished by having each patient move through a structured, well-monitored eating protocol according to which patients assume increasing responsibility for their nutritional needs. The second goal is accomplished by helping patients identify the self-destructive aspects of their symptomatic behaviors and by using the holding capacity of the milieu to reinforce self-care and to work through intensely negative transferences. The inpatient milieu can provide patients with the environment they need to learn the difference between acting out and working through their feelings. The holding capacity of the milieu disrupts the self-defeating cycle of acting out, followed by negative feedback (i.e., you are "bad" or "sick"), followed by more shame and self hate, followed by more acting out.

PARTIAL HOSPITALIZATION. Inpatient hospitalization is too restrictive for some patients and can interfere with the maintenance or development of ego strengths and coping behavior, yet psychotherapy once or twice a week is insufficient. Placement in a day or evening hospital program can sometimes be used as an alternative to inpatient hospitalization when the patient needs or wishes to continue working, going to school, or living at home during treatment. However, the powerful affects that are evoked when attempting to refeed some anorexic patients or when attempting to help a bulimic eliminate the use of laxatives can sometimes be too anxiety-provoking to manage even in such a program.

Placement in a partial hospital program can also be used as part of a discharge plan for hospitalized patients because they are most vulnerable to symptom relapse when they leave the structure of the inpatient milieu.

☐ CASE EXAMPLE

The following is a case example of a college athlete with bulimia nervosa and major depression. "Carey" was a 20-year-old college junior who became very depressed toward the end of the fall quarter. She was on a tuition scholarship for volleyball and had been on the varsity the last 2 years. She was 5'10" and ranged in weight from 150 to 165 lb. During the beginning of the winter quarter, she became so depressed that she attempted suicide by taking a large dosage of aspirin. She had significant difficulties falling and remaining asleep and could not concentrate on her schoolwork. She began isolating herself in her room until she decided to come home for the winter.

Carey was evaluated for her depression and eating difficulties. She weighed 165 lb at the time of the evaluation and wanted to lose 10 lb. She felt that she was very unattractive, especially when compared to her mother, who was thin and glamorous. The patient identified with her father, who was also depressed. Both father and daughter were passive, dysphoric, and introverted, whereas the mother was extremely extroverted.

There were three components to the treatment of this patient. First the patient was seen in individual psychotherapy twice weekly. She was also initiated on a trial of antidepressants. Individual therapy helped Carey examine core issues related to self-esteem and the difficulties she had in competing and identifying with her mother. Family therapy was also started to help begin some dialogue between mother and daughter, and to identify family issues that might have been impeding Carey's ability to separate from the family. It was particularly empowering for her to realize that she appreciated much more of what her mother had to offer than she had previously imagined.

Carey's bulimia was not severe and was largely driven by a desire to lose weight. She would diet for several days but then become frustrated and bored and go off the wagon. This led to self-criticism and decreased self-esteem. When she was able to recognize that her self-depreciation was, in part at least, due to competitive issues with her mother, she was able to reduce the pressure she put on herself to lose weight. Also, Carey found several articles about sociocultural pressures to be thin as reason enough to stop dieting. Instead, she resumed regular eating (i.e., 3 meals a day) and was able to initiate a reasonable aerobics regimen that enabled her to lose the weight she wanted without having to diet. She was able to return to school in the fall, where she continued in psychotherapy. She was also able to resume her participation in varsity volleyball.

While Carey did not have a particularly severe eating disorder, she is a good example of how complicated a clinical presentation these patients can have and of the number of treatment modalities that are sometimes necessary. Other patients are more completely organized around the eating symptoms and are able to talk of little else during the initial months of treatment. To the extent that Carey felt her weight reduction was critically important to her participation in volleyball, the eating symptoms could have been much more entrenched. Also, the family's ability to participate in treatment made the identification and resolution of competitive issues much more accessible.

In summary, though young women generally face sociocultural pressure to lose weight and reduce body fat, female athletes experience additional pressures due to the training regimens associated with various sporting events. This is particularly the case in sports such as gymnastics, swimming, and long-distance running. These pressures are increased when parents and coaches prioritize an athlete's performance over her well being. Greater awareness and sensitivity on the part of coaches and parents could significantly reduce the incidence of eating disorders among athletes.

Because eating disorders can present with a wide array of other difficulties such as depression and anxiety disorders, it is important that coaches and parents who notice an athlete having difficulty refer her to a practitioner or clinic with specialized training and experience in the treatment of eating disorders. Clinics that have both a broad professional base and a specialized program in eating disorders are recommended.

It is important that eating-disorder clinic staff offer information and skills training that can help patients regulate their eating. It is also important to look at the broader context in which the eating difficulties serve a function or role, such as the family. For some patients, eating-disorder symptoms can be resolved by eliminating the undue pressure to perform placed by their coach or parents. Other patients' symptoms reflect more serious affective and personality difficulties. It is important that coaches and parents do not try to make this determination on their own but defer to the expertise of clinicians with training in this area.

🞏 REFERENCES

1. American Psychiatric Association: Diagnostic and Statistical Manual of Mental Disorders. 3rd ed. Washington, DC, American Psychiatric Association, 1987.
2. Johnson, C., Tobin, D.L., and Enright, A.: Prevalence and clinical characteristics of borderline patients in an eating disordered population. J. Clin. Psychiatry, 50:9, 1989.
3. Johnson, C., Tobin, D.L., and Dennis, A.B.: Differences in treatment outcome between borderline and nonborderline bulimics at one year follow-up. Int. J. Eating Disorders, 9:617, 1990.
4. Pyle, R.L., Mitchell, J.E., and Eckert, E.D.: Bulimia: A report of 34 cases. J. Clin. Psychiatry, 42:60, 1981.
5. Gwirtsman, H.E., Roy-Byrne, P., Yager, J., and Gerner, R.H.: Neuroendocrine abnormalities in bulimia. Am. J. Psychiatry, 140:559, 1983.

6. Levin, A.P., and Hyler, S.E.: DSM III personality diagnosis in bulimia. Comp. Psychiatry, 27:47, 1986.
7. Hudson, J., Pope, H., Jonas, J., and Yurgelun-Todd, D.: Family history study of anorexia nervosa and bulimia. J. Psychiatry, 142:133, 1983.
8. Lee, N.F., Rush, A.J., and Mitchell, J.E.: Bulimia and depression. J. Affective Disorders, 9:231, 1985.
9. Rosen, J., and Leitenberg, H.: Bulimia nervosa: Treatment with exposure plus response prevention. Behav. Ther., 13:117, 1982.
10. Williamson, D.A., Kelly, M.L., and Davis, C.J., et al.: The psychophysiology of bulimia. Advan. Behav. Res. Ther., 7:163, 1985.
11. Johnson, C.: The initial consultation for patients with bulimia and anorexia nervosa. In Handbook of Psychotherapy for Anorexia Nervosa and Bulimia. Edited by D.M. Garner and P.E. Garfinkel. New York, Guilford Press, 1984, pp. 19–51.
12. Goodsitt, A.: Self-psychology and the treatment of anorexia nervosa. In Handbook of Psychotherapy for Anorexia Nervosa and Bulimia. Edited by D.M. Garner and P.E. Garfinkel. New York, Guilford Press, 1984, pp. 55–82.
13. Johnson, C., and Connors, M.: Bulimia Nervosa: A Biopsychosocial Perspective. New York, Basic Books, 1987.
14. Kohut, H.: The Analysis of the Self. New York, International Universities Press, 1971.
15. Minuchin, S., Rosman, B.L., and Baker, L.: Psychosomatic Families: Anorexia Nervosa in Context. Cambridge, MA, Harvard University Press, 1975.
16. Garner, D.M., Rockert, W., Olmstead, M.P., et al.: Psychoeducational principles in the treatment of bulimia and anorexia nervosa. In Handbook of Psychotherapy for Anorexia Nervosa and Bulimia. Edited by D.M. Garner and P.E. Garfinkel. New York, Guilford Press, 1984, pp. 513–572.
17. Johnson, C., Connors, C., and Tobin, D.L.: Symptom management of bulimia. J. Consult. Clin. Psychol., 55:668, 1987.
18. Garner, D.M., and Bemis, K.M.: Cognitive therapy for anorexia nervosa. In Handbook of Psychotherapy for Anorexia Nervosa and Bulimia. Edited by D.M. Garner and P.E. Garfinkel. New York, Guilford Press, 1984, pp. 107–146.
19. Fairburn, C.G.: Cognitive behavioral treatment for bulimia. In Handbook of Psychotherapy for Anorexia Nervosa and Bulimia. Edited by D.M. Garner and P.E. Garfinkel. New York, Guilford Press, 1984, pp. 160–192.

MANAGEMENT OF EATING PROBLEMS IN ATHLETIC SETTINGS

Randa Ryan

Only recently has the recognition and management of eating problems in athletes become an issue. This is true because relatively little work has been done to document the extent of the problem, to pinpoint risk factors, and to evaluate whether eating disorders in athletes are different from those in other populations. The chapters in this book help answer some of these questions and point to the conclusion that eating problems in athletes do exist and require intervention. If ignored, as coaches, parents, and teammates are prone to do, these problems do not go away. If left untreated, serious medical and psychological consequences can occur.

The purpose of this chapter is to describe the management of eating problems, through education, prevention, identification, and intervention. The work is based on (1) a review of the literature; (2) extensive conversation with coaches, athletes, and administrators; and (3) experience gained with hundreds of athletes from a variety of settings. The initial work was done in the Department of Intercollegiate Athletics for Women at the University of Texas at Austin. This athletic department was one of the first to establish an organized and coordinated program to deal with eating problems. The model used to assess and manage eating disorders at Texas is presented in this chapter.

☐ UNDERSTANDING AND IDENTIFYING THE PROBLEM

Understanding the problem is integral to its identification and developing the resources necessary for help. Though many factors are common to all levels and types of sport, each situation is unique. A division I university cross-country coach confronts a more complex athletic environment than a summer league track coach. A ballet instructor at a prestigious school needs a more thorough understanding than a physical education teacher working with elementary students. Yet each must learn the importance of identifying these problems and must develop means to educate their athletes. Understanding the nature of the problem as it exists in different athletic settings is integral to both the identification and management of eating disorders in athletes.

BARRIERS TO IDENTIFICATION

There are potential barriers to the identification of eating problems that are specific to sport. Awareness of these barriers is important. They include the following:

- Coaches avoid the issue because it seems overwhelming, too complicated, or because an athlete is training well and they are hesitant to interfere with success. Coaches also fear that they, in some way, have created or contributed to the problem; that their coaching style has pushed an athlete too far.
- Teammates are reluctant to seek help for their peers when they know something is wrong. They are uncertain about what can be done or how to help. Fellow athletes might also recognize behavior they see in themselves and therefore ignore the problem in teammates.
- Parents are not well informed and can inadvertently be part of the problem. Both the lack of knowledge and overzealous behavior pose difficult barriers to overcome.
- Athletic administrators find dealing with eating problems unpleasant and worry about legal issues and adverse publicity. They tend to look for ready answers or quick fixes to such problems.
- Even athletes who recognize the problem in themselves are still mired in secrecy, shame, and denial.

METHODS OF IDENTIFICATION

There is no single, accurate identification process for eating problems. Several different methods are described below, but it is the combination of these methods that proves most successful. By gathering information in a variety of ways, one can draw a more accurate representation of the problem.

The Use of Surveys and Questionnaires

Psychological measures are available to help identify individuals who might be at risk for or involved in an eating disorder. The Eating Attitudes Test (EAT),[1] the Eating Disorders Inventory (EDI),[2] and the revised Restraint Scale[3] are examples of this type of measure. These have been discussed in Chapter 9. For the majority of coaches, parents, support staff, and administrators, these questionnaires and surveys are not the answer. Expertise in the administration and interpretation of these tests is vital to their accuracy. Resources for these skills are limited in most athletic settings. Additionally, athletes are uncomfortable filling out such questionnaires. Many do not complete or answer the questionnaires correctly because of denial, fear of reprisal, or shame. Therefore other methods for identifying the problem need to be developed and used.

Observing the Population

Understanding the physical and psychological problems associated with eating disorders is an important tool in identifying the problem in an athletic setting. Though many behaviors are difficult to recognize, knowledge of the signs, symptoms, and behaviors associated with eating disorders is crucial information for people who work with athletes. This will help coaches, parents, support staff, and administrators recognize disordered behavior more effectively. Two examples underscore the role of observation. John Case is the tennis coach at a small junior high school. He knows that excessive concern about weight and distortion of body image are related to eating disorders. Alice, the newest player on the team, asks him about her appearance each day. Alice tells Coach Case that she is too fat and worries openly about how she looks in her uniform. He has tried to reassure Alice that her weight is within the normal range for girls her age, but she is not convinced. Her constant talk of dieting and how she looks distract and upset the other players on the team. After a match at a neighboring school, Alice leaves the table during the team meal. When her coach finds her, she tells him she is unwilling to eat with her teammates. Whether Alice's behavior reflects an eating disorder is not clear, but the signals are strong enough to indicate a problem; therefore the coach discusses Alice's behavior with her parents to determine whether intervention is necessary.

If ignored, Alice's problem could worsen. Because the coach is aware, he sees that Alice is at risk. Although this is an isolated incident, it reinforces Coach Case's commitment to educate his athletes and be alert for specific behavior. His knowledgeable observation is instrumental in identifying this young athlete's problem.

As a contrast, let's take Coach Smith, who has not been trained to deal with eating disorders. He is working with a nationally ranked college tennis team. Coach Smith is constantly talking with his athletes about being too fat. He tells them to lose weight, yet he does not guide them to do so in appropriate ways. When they perform poorly, Coach Smith relates it to their size. He weighs them twice a day but has never measured their body composition.

Coach Smith manipulates the women on this team psychologically. He rewards those with low weights by spending more time working on their games, joking with them after practice, and generally giving them more attention. The team environment clearly says, "Weigh less, get more." As a result, these athletes are part of a very unhealthy game. They are pitted against each other, not on the basis of athletic skills or a healthy rivalry focused on the team's goal of winning a national championship, but on what the scale tells them each day before workout. This is a serious problem waiting to happen. Only a disaster, or the presence of someone who recognizes the problem, will lead to a change.

A knowledgeable observer of this team, whether it is a member of the support staff or even an assistant coach, will provide the quickest recognition that something is wrong. This is a different and more difficult problem than the junior high situation in the previous example. Instead of one athlete in trouble, the team is at risk. The pressure is externally presented by the coach and internalized by the athletes. It has infiltrated the structure and dynamics of this team. Knowledgeable observance of this group in action would quickly identify a situation that is serious—one in which an extensive intervention process is necessary.

All individuals associated with sport should be knowledgeable about the signs and symptoms of eating disorders. Tables 9–1 and 9–2 in Chapter 9 are a good source for this information. Coaches should be particularly aware of the associations they make between body weight and performance to athletes. Both parents and coaches should pay attention when athletes isolate themselves from the team, feel uncomfortable about how they look, or exhibit unhealthy changes in eating behavior.

Talking with Athletes

In addition to observing individual athletes and team dynamics, working with athletes directly is a good way to recognize an eating disorder. Given the opportunity, in a secure and non-threatening environment, athletes are usually honest in expressing how they feel about themselves and about their self-image and self-esteem as they relate to body weight, appearance, and weight as a performance factor.

The accuracy of this information is affected by the security of the setting in which it is gathered. Many athletes, intimidated by coaches, administrators, or parents, are not truthful, telling only what they think the authority figure wants to hear. Again, fear of reprisal, shame, denial, and secrecy are significant barriers. Therefore, it is crucial to create a mechanism for athletes to express how they feel about these issues of self-image, appearance, and weight as a performance factor. Athletes are very aware of team norms, behaviors, and perceived pressure by the group. Many times they know whether the team or a particular individual is in trouble. As a result, some of the most reliable and useful information can come from the athletes themselves, if they feel secure enough to be honest.

This type of information can be collected in several ways. It can be collected by someone from within or outside the athletic setting, by individual or group interview, in person or in writing. A combination of these methods seems most effective because the variety of formats allows for differences in ability and style of communication.

INDIVIDUAL INTERVIEW. An individual from within the athletic environment has several advantages. Administrators, coaches, and support staff members have knowledge of the history, structure, and personalities in the setting. Athletes usually feel more comfortable with someone they know, and as a result they are more honest. It is important, however, that an individual from within the athletic environment not be biased about what creates the problem. Objectivity is essential when listening to athletes. Any hint of condemnation limits the utility of this information-gathering process.

It can also be helpful for the athletic program to acquire an individual from outside, an expert in the area, especially if no one from the department is qualified or confident to handle the process. Individuals experienced in eating disorders who also have an intimate understanding of the athletic environment are difficult to find, but both these skills are essential for such an individual to be effective. Athletes might find it difficult to be candid with someone they don't know, so the personal qualities of the individual are important.

Interviewing athletes individually allows them to speak about their thoughts and feelings without judgment from teammates or coaches. Some athletes feel secure in this type of situation, and are able to communicate about their sport, its relationship to self-worth, body weight as a performance factor, and self-image. Others find individual interviews uncomfortable and are unable to talk about pressures, feelings, and specific eating problems.

GROUP INTERVIEW. Talking to athletes in teams or by other categories provides a different kind of understanding. The dynamics of a team are often revealed in a group setting. Certain individuals are more comfortable when their feelings are reinforced by the group. They realize their feelings or responses are not strange or different if their teammates are expressing the same sentiments. A safe environment must be created for group interactions, and the athletes must believe there will not be negative repercussions.

WRITTEN INTERVIEW OR ANONYMOUS RESPONSE PROCESS. Allowing athletes to put their thoughts in a written interview or anonymous response process reaches those who want to contribute information but who are unable to do so verbally. This is unlike the questionnaire or survey mentioned earlier, which is scored to evaluate risk in an individual. A written interview could contain open-ended questions, or even be in a survey format, but it is gathered anonymously to generate a picture of the athletic population, not of a specific individual.

In using any of these methods, it is important that the athletes' responses to questions and conversations about body weight and performance be kept in perspective. If a group interview turns into "coach bashing," every effort must be made to determine the validity of the input. Athletes who struggle with tough or demanding coaches can misinterpret information about body size and performance. Again, this emphasizes the need for a skilled interviewer who is familiar with eating disorders and the demands of sport.

Combining Methods

Combining the process of talking with athletes about their *perceptions* of the situation, with observing athletes to identify eating-disordered *behavior* is the most useful method of determining the type and degree of problem that might exist in an athletic environment. An example illustrates the effectiveness of combining these techniques. A community swimming program has both boys and girls, ages 11 to 14. Jane Miller, the coach, has been working with this group for several years and knows the athletes well. This past season 3 of the girls started to undergo puberty. They were growing and maturing at a rapid pace. These girls began to isolate themselves from the rest of the team, both at practice and when they were on their own. They started wearing the same kind of suits and caps to workouts and would only swim well when they were in the same lane together.

Jane was experienced in working with young girls and was not alarmed by their current "group" approach to swim practice and the world. As time passed, though, the behavior became more noticeable and more unusual. Coach Miller observed group weigh-ins between the girls and strange eating rituals during team travel and meets. She had been talking to all the athletes on the team about their changing bodies, about self-image and feelings of being in sport. She knew she was not pressuring them about their weight and shape and its relationship to their performance.

During the next few weeks, Coach Miller had several special sessions with the girls after practice. She encouraged them to talk about their feelings, isolating themselves from the team, how they viewed their changing bodies, and the demands of their current level of swim training. She also contacted the parents to see if events at home or school were contributing to the situation. After working with them for several weeks, Jane was able to identify several factors that were creating difficult feelings for the girls. Most of the kids in school did not understand their commitment to swimming, and they made fun of their big shoulders and wet hair every morning. They were bigger than the other girls, and even the boys, which also made them feel different. One father teased his daughter about her ever-growing hands, feet, and muscles. Another's mother had put her on a diet, fearing that the quick growth was due to too much food. These factors, combined with the athlete's insecurities about their sudden growth and changes in their bodies, had caused them to withdraw and create safety within their group.

Coach Miller's observations of and sensitivities to the change in the athlete's behavior, combined with her willingness to talk to the girls at length about what they were thinking and feeling, were effective tools in helping to identify and confront the problem. Using these skills greatly decreased the time it took to recognize the problem as it developed, and the coach was able to work with her athletes and help get them on target.

☐ DEFINING STRATEGIES FOR INTERVENTION PROGRAMS

Defining the goal and strategies of intervention must be done with the specific athletic setting in mind. This permits consideration of the many factors that contribute to the development of eating disorders, with special attention to those that exist in a particular environment. Figure 22–1 shows the environment, social, and psychological factors that contribute to eating disorders as well as the factors that are specific to sport. This model can be used to help identify the potential contributing factors in any athletic setting.

Addressing these factors forms the core of the intervention strategy. This process is depicted graphically in Figure 22–2. These are the four steps in this process:

1. Within the specific athletic setting, identify and isolate the contributing factors.
2. Formulate goals concerning intervention and prevention.
3. After creating or acquiring resources to address these factors, create long-term strategies to alleviate the factors.
4. Develop educational resources about these factors.

Encouraging and allowing coaches, athletes, and support staff to participate in the creation of intervention strategies is critical to a well-rounded and balanced approach. Each group brings a unique and important perspective to this process. In addition, there is better understanding, support, and follow-through if all participants are involved in the intervention.

Figures 22–3 and 22–4 are examples of strategies developed for a division I collegiate level athletic program. The strategies for dealing with weight as a performance issue have been separated from the prevention and treatment of eating disorders, yet both protocols were developed and implemented concurrently because of the obvious relationship. In most athletic environments, the strategies might not be as complex.

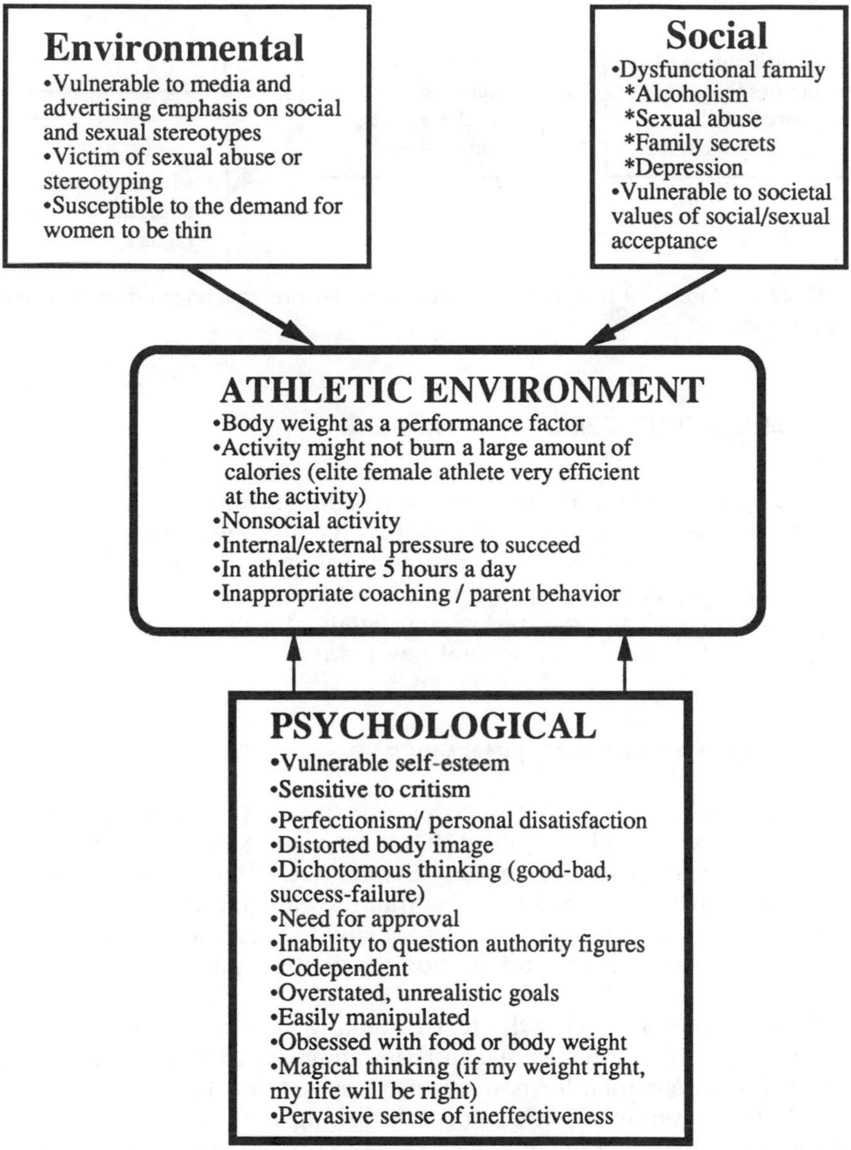

FIG. 22–1. Factors that can contribute to eating disorders in athletes. These include factors generally associated with risk of eating disorders and factors specific to the athletic population.

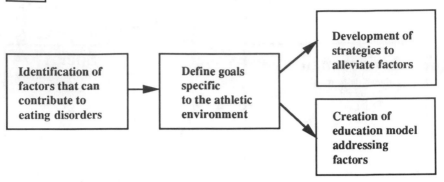

FIG. 22–2. Model for the process of developing an intervention strategy in an athletic setting.

◻ EDUCATION: REMOVING THE FEAR

Education is the central aspect of addressing and managing eating disorders in the athletic setting. It can involve a range of materials (e.g., booklets and videotapes) and professionals and speakers. Education should not be focused on just the athletes, but on the coaches, parents, and support staff as well. In designating an educational intervention, it is important to emphasize several key points.

POINTS FOR ATHLETES TO REMEMBER

It is important for athletes to recognize the characteristics that make individuals vulnerable to eating disorders. Those who bring the traits of perfectionism, compulsiveness, dichotomous thinking, and low self-esteem to their sport need to know that they are at increased risk. Athletes must be encouraged to take responsibility to educate not only themselves but their parents and friends about the signs, symptoms, and dangers of eating disorders.

It is also important that the fear of talking about eating disorders be removed and that athletes realize that eating disorders do not develop by talking about them or educating oneself about the risks. Fear also needs to be removed with respect to asking for help. Athletes must understand they will never reach their full athletic potential if they are involved in this type of behavior, because an eating disorder hinders performance. It is equally important to emphasize that getting help does not have to mean giving up sport. For some athletes, participation in athletics is part of the disorder, so they cannot continue, but many athletes have been able to get help for their disorder and return to competition.

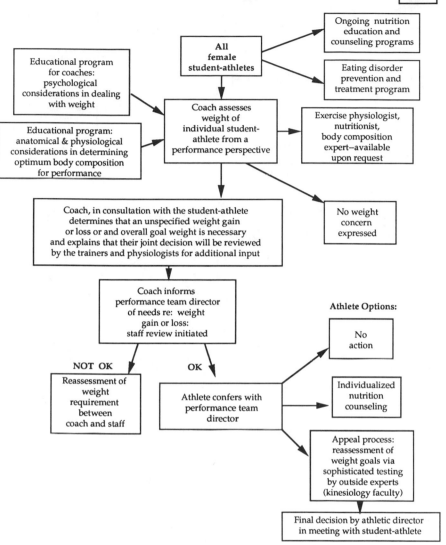

FIG. 22–3. Flow chart designed by Performance Team at the University of Texas at Austin to create a process for dealing with body weight as a performance factor.

POINTS FOR COACHES TO REMEMBER

It is critical for coaches to learn to distinguish the important variables that affect body weight as a performance factor and to identify athletes who might be prone to eating disorders. Coaches must also be responsible for educating themselves and for encouraging awareness in their athletes. Talking with athletes about eating disorders does not create or encourage the behavior. Coaches must not be afraid of the topic.

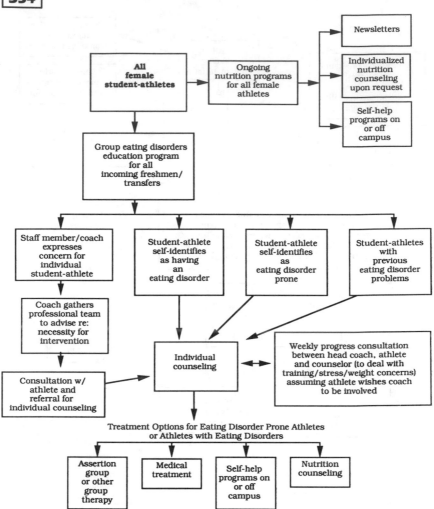

FIG. 22–4. Flow chart designed by performance team at the University of Texas at Austin to prevent eating disorders and provide services for those who suffer from them.

POINTS FOR PARENTS TO REMEMBER

For parents, helping their children to feel comfortable talking about their changing bodies is critical. Parents should learn not to make unrealistic demands on their children, especially in the areas of body type or sport performance. They must be aware of how much their words mean, especially when they are critical of body shape and size. As parents, they are in the best position to recognize change in their children's behavior. They also must take responsibility for educating themselves and their young athletes about eating disorders.

☐ SPECIFIC EDUCATIONAL TOOLS

Understanding what needs to be done is only part of the solution. Ensuring that everyone is aware of the potential problems that can arise in the athletic setting is of little help if athletes and coaches are not provided with—and use—the resources designed to effect change.

MEASUREMENT OF BODY COMPOSITION

When in training, athletes put on muscle. Muscle is denser than fat, it takes up less space, and it weighs more. Most female athletes increase their muscle mass and decrease their fat mass in the process of becoming trained. They feel leaner and their clothes are looser, yet the scale frequently reflects an increase in body weight. Though scientists are aware of what has happened, few athletes understand the differences between body weight and body composition. It is critical for athletes to be educated about the difference between the two measures and be provided with the resources to have their body composition evaluated as opposed to just having their body weighed. The measurement of body composition can be used to break the cycle of constantly weighing-in, which can give misleading feedback to an athlete. For example, it is not unusual for a female athlete to retain fluid. If she gains 3 lb of fluid in 1 day, and the scale is her only source of feedback, a quick gain like this can cause a real problem if she is sensitive about her weight.

When evaluating body composition, it is important for athletes to understand the measurement process, the potential error in the process, and the differences between various methods for assessing body fat. Detailed information on these matters is provided in Chapters 6 and 20. Using a good equation, obtaining measurements by the same individual each time, and reducing other potential sources of error are important. This information provides the athlete with a truer reflection of what occurs to the body through training. When coaches use body composition as a training tool, they must provide realistic goals for an athlete to reach. Setting an unrealistic body composition goal is just as harmful as setting a body weight goal that is too low. Body composition should be measured by an expert. If one is not available, it is worth paying an expert to train a staff member to do it correctly.

NUTRITION STRATEGIES

Accurate and usable nutrition information is integral to any athletic training program. Nutrition has become a necessary training aid in sport and is as important as good biomechanics or the sequencing of workouts. Yet providing sound nutritional information is only the beginning. If team functions still revolve around nutritionally poor meals, if travel and post competition eating are inappropriate, or if parents are not educated about good nutrition, athletes get conflicting messages. Athletes cannot be taught proper nutrition and be expected to use the information if good food is not available during training and travel. Stopping at a fast-food restaurant on the way home from a contest might spare the team's budget but sends the wrong message to athletes.

A sports nutritionist, someone who is knowledgeable about nutrition, sports training, and competition, is an important resource. Such a person can create education programs, evaluate training conditions, and be available for individual referral to athletes who need personal counseling. No athlete should be told to gain or lose weight without the provision of sound nutrition information from a knowledgeable professional. Details about nutrition counseling for the athlete are discussed in Chapter 19.

COUNSELORS, THERAPISTS, AND CLINICS

Each athletic setting should have a network of experienced support personnel. Included in this network should be a counselor and a therapist or clinic concerned with eating disorders. It is necessary to have individuals who can be relied on for information or referral if the need arises. It is especially important that athletes be made aware that they can see these individuals on their own. Athletes are more likely to get help if they can contact resource persons without disclosing their problems to others. Confidentiality in counseling and treatment is the critical issue here, and sometimes it can become difficult. If an athlete has chosen independently to get help, the issue does not usually arise, but if an athlete is required to seek counseling, then confidentiality must be addressed by the therapists, athlete, parent, and coach.

PEER GROUPS

Using peer groups to help facilitate education and intervention can also be an effective tool. Team leaders who are informed and are resourceful at responding to the needs of their teammates are an important resource and one that is easily developed. There are many ways to construct a network of team leaders. It can be as simple as making sure the team captain is knowledgeable about what to do if a teammate is in trouble. A weekly group meeting, scheduled and run by the athletes for the specific purpose of talking about these issues, is invaluable. Supporting other athletes and learning from those who know and understand them is a powerful process. A counselor can help athletes set up the group and be available to provide resources and input when necessary.

Creating peer groups does not mean putting young people in the role of providing intervention and counseling services. Team leaders should not be asked or expected to be responsible for confronting fellow teammates. But, athletes should know how to refer a teammate who needs help, making sure the right people know the person is in trouble.

☐ INDIVIDUAL ATHLETE INTERVENTION

Even when coaches are conscientious, athletes are educated, resource staff is available, and administrators are supportive, eating disorders will occur. Though upsetting to all who are aware of the situation, early intervention can greatly increase the chance of recovery and the potential of a return to sport. Once a problem has been identified, whether it results from difficulties of an entire team or an individual athlete, intervention is necessary.

THINGS TO REMEMBER

When approaching someone who is showing signs of an eating disorder, one should keep several things in mind:

- Be aware of the individual's eating-disordered patterns and behaviors, but do not attempt to interrupt or challenge the logic or significance of the behavior to the athlete.
- Take signs and symptoms seriously because the consequences can be fatal, but don't attempt to change the behavior yourself. The athlete will only resent it, and it could make the situation worse.
- Try not to give feedback about appearance and body size to an individual with an eating disorder, even if you think the change is positive.
- Approach an athlete about feelings of low self-esteem, depression, isolation, perfectionism, or other issues instead of specific eating behavior. Most people will only seek help on the basis of the way they feel, not because of their eating behavior.
- Do not think the problem will go away on its own, even if you do not see the behavior for some time. Get professional help as soon as possible.[4]

TYPES OF RESPONSES

Each situation involving an athlete and an eating disorder is different. Each time there is a range of responses from everyone involved. It is important to understand those responses and the effect they will have in the overall approach to the situation.

Potential Responses from the Athlete

RELIEF. Some athletes feel an overwhelming sense of relief when they realize that someone else knows. They are relieved they do not have to keep a secret any more. This is one of the easier responses to handle, because the athlete who responds this way is usually receptive to the concept of therapy.

ANGER. More often than not, athletes are angry that someone wants to change their behavior. This usually occurs with the athlete who denies having a problem. Anger is most common in athletes who are still performing well and have the positive impact of good performances to counterbalance how bad they might feel in other areas.

DENIAL. Denial is a classic response. It is difficult to handle because the athlete can be so convincing when he or she says that nothing is wrong. Again, do not approach the athlete about specific behavior but about how he or she is feeling.

DEFENSIVE. Athletes are strong, gifted people and are used to doing things themselves and "toughing out" difficult situations. Though they might be aware that something is wrong, it is common for the "get tough" attitude to take over and for athletes to want to fix the problem themselves.

SHAME. Shame is also a classic response. It is hard for anyone, especially for those who are public figures, to think that others know about their problems or failures in life.

Potential Responses from the Coach

DISAPPOINTMENT. Even the most sensitive coach will express disappointment. Like an injury, an eating disorder can seem unfair and overwhelming. Along with feeling concerned and interested in the athletic welfare, a coach might well feel that the athlete is lost to the team or the sport forever.

ANGER. As with anyone who has worked hard for a goal, coaches who have invested hours of time with a young person can become angry when confronted with a situation they feel is out of their control.

LACK OF INTEREST. Lack of interest is frustrating because it implies the coach knew about the problem and chose not to address the situation. This response is also likely in a coach who feels an athlete will never participate in sports again if help is provided. It is one of the more difficult responses to handle.

GUILT. Guilt can arise in two situations. Some coaches recognize that they put too much pressure on an athlete, including manipulation and exploitation, and that they must now face the results of their actions. Other coaches, who honestly worked hard with an athlete, might question themselves about how things went wrong, whether it was out of their control. Some coaches will feel that they should have known and successfully responded to an eating disorder even if they were not responsible for contributing to the situation.

SUPPORT. Good coaches will want to be a part of an athlete's recovery process and will help in any way possible. This might not be possible, but the attitude should be assessed for later work with the athlete and further education and understanding of the problem.

Potential Responses from Team Members

FEAR. Athletes carry a certain mystique about their abilities, feeling invincible against all odds. It is difficult for teammates to accept that one of their members has succumbed. It can generate thoughts such as "Could this happen to me?" There is also fear and concern about the teammate getting well.

GUILT. Team members can feel guilty, especially if they have been aware of the behavior. Expressions of guilt can be used as an opportunity to talk about how to handle these situations differently and how to get help for teammates in the future.

BLAME. Athletes, especially young ones, need to have a concrete reason for why things happen. This is difficult in situations such as these, and the coach, other teammates, or parents can receive the blame.

RELIEF. Athletes who have been aware of a teammate's behavior will be relieved if they know their teammate is getting help.

DISGUST. Some children will not understand and will show disgust for the athlete with an eating disorder.

DISAPPOINTMENT. Some athletes express disappointment and the feeling that their teammate has let them down.

SUPPORT. Eventually most team members want to be supportive to a fellow athlete's recovery. It is important that they understand as much as possible without violating the confidentiality of the stricken member.

☐ KEY ISSUES IN INTERVENTION

TYPE OF TREATMENT

The type of treatment to be implemented is the most important decision. The choice of inpatient care in a clinic or outpatient care directed by a trained therapist is dictated by considering the level and type of disorder the athlete is suffering from, the athlete's commitment to recovery, and physical state of health. Use an expert who is knowledgeable in the field of eating disorders to help with this decision.

CONFIDENTIALITY

Confidentiality can be a difficult problem in the sport setting. As mentioned in the previous section, if the athlete seeks help independently, it rarely becomes an issue. But if an athlete with an eating disorder has been confronted by a parent or coach, confidentiality must be addressed. Eating disorders can be life-threatening, and if they are added to the rigors of sport training without professional management, everyone is in a risky situation. When athletes are still denying that they have a problem, they might say they are getting help when in fact they are not. If an athlete agrees to get help, someone must be in a position to monitor that process. The ideal situation is for the athlete to sign a release with the therapist so that a parent, support staff member, or coach can monitor attendance. Most athletes will agree to this format if they are assured that their personal issues will not be discussed, only their attendance and progress in recovery. If a coach or parent is viewed as part of the problem, this procedure is more difficult to handle. Each situation is different and should be managed accordingly, but the therapist must be aware of the athlete's training demands should the decision be to continue to train, and the coach must be made aware of the athlete's treatment demands in order to facilitate the recovery process and not inadvertently add to the problem.

ROLE OF THE FAMILY

Family factors must be addressed, especially if the athlete is a minor. The family's level of emotional involvement and support of the athlete and their financial constraints and insurance resources must all be evaluated. The family's role depends on whether the athlete is a minor and, again, confidentiality factors. A licensed professional and the athletic administrator are the ones to make this decision along with the athlete.

TRAINING AND THE COACH

If the athlete and therapist chose an outpatient program, continued participation in training and competition must be addressed. Primary to the decision is the athlete's emotional and physical health status. If the decision is to continue training, then it leads to the next issue, whether the coach is to be aware of the athlete's treatment. This is not as difficult to resolve as it might seem. If the coach is part of the problem, it becomes obvious at this stage. The athlete and therapist will more than likely discontinue training or change the training to a different environment. If it is participation in sport or activity in general that is contributory, it will become necessary to discontinue training altogether or until the situation can be re-evaluated. When the coach is committed to being a part of the solution and dedicated to helping the athlete in any way possible, the coach can be included in the treatment process. This is ultimately important for medical reasons.

THE ATHLETE'S ATTITUDE ABOUT TREATMENT

The athlete's attitude toward treatment is also critical. If denial, resentment, and anger create barriers to treatment, it can be necessary to decide whether athletic participation will be allowed until treatment is sought. Again, each situation is unique, but if there is awareness of an eating-disordered athlete, and the athlete is still allowed to train without intervention, the athletic environment now supports the disorder. The environment is hindering effective treatment, and as a result, it is now a contributing factor to the athlete's problem.

☐ SUMMARY

Understanding the factors contributing to eating disorders is important. Awareness of those aspects of sport that may also contribute is primary to the management of these problems with athletes. In addition, there are barriers to intervening with eating problems in the sport environment. Most of these barriers are based on the lack of education and awareness of coaches, parents, and athletes. Some are based on the uniqueness of athletes and sport itself. Pressure to perform and fear of failure cause stress for those who compete. Improper management of athletic success can create social and emotional isolation. Athletes are gifted, physically strong people, who present a picture of indestructibility and are reluctant to admit they have problems or need help.[5] Some athletes are limited in their ability to interact with coaches, teammates, and peers because their time is primarily spent training. They might also limit their identity in other roles and as a result be lacking in needed social development. When athletes with eating disorders are training well, no one wants to interfere, even if they are exhibiting self-destructive behavior. When athletes with eating disorders are training poorly, everyone is afraid the additional stress of confronting a difficult problem will be too much.

Eating disorders in athletes are particularly difficult to deal with because body weight and composition are performance factors. Critical to the management of body composition is sound nutritional knowledge—a clear understanding of healthy eating habits and the physiology of training as it relates to muscle mass and body weight. An athlete's body is a tool used to perform. It is constantly measured, evaluated, timed, critiqued, and redesigned for improved performance. But unlike an ordinary tool, an athlete's body is an integral part of the athlete. The two cannot be separated. Too much measurement, too much critiquing, too much redesigning will set up even the most well-balanced of athletes for problems.

Educating coaches, parents, and athletes, recognizing problem behavior, and knowing what to do if any athlete is involved with problem eating are components of strong intervention strategies. Contributing factors should be identified, and resources need to be created to address these factors and to build long-term strategies. Athletes and coaches must be a part of this process to produce a balanced and accepted approach.

The intervention and management of eating disorders in the athletic setting is a new and difficult challenge. Eating disorders in sport take on a different meaning because of the athletic mystique. Many like to hear about the vulnerabilities of athletes because it makes them seem more human, more real. Others like to encourage the mystique and would not interfere with any behavior exhibited by an athlete, destructive or otherwise. But treating eating disorders and the similar issues of alcoholism and drug abuse must come before an athlete's sport performance. Extensive education, early recognition, and proper support services are the primary components in prevention. Eating disorders are serious, multifaceted situations. They are performance-limiting, they can be life-threatening, and they must be addressed.

☐ REFERENCES

1. Garner, D.M., and Garfinkel, P.E.: The eating attitudes test: An index of the symptoms of anorexia nervosa. Psychol. Med., 9:273, 1979.
2. Garner, D.M., Olmstead, M.P., and Polivy, J.: Development and validation of a multidimensional eating disorder inventory for anorexia nervosa and bulimia. Int. J. Eating Disorders, 2:15, 1983.
3. Stunkard, A.J.: Restrained eating: What it is and a new scale to measure it. *In* The body Weight Regulatory Systems: Normal and Disturbed Mechanisms. Edited by L.A. Cioffi. New York, Raven Press, 1981.
4. St. David's Eating Disorder Clinic: Materials for Eating Disorder Patients. Austin, Texas, St. David's Hospital, 1988.
5. Ryan, R., Lopiano, D., Tharinger, D., and Starke, K.: Mental Health of Female Athletes. University of Texas at Austin, Unpublished Manuscript, 1990.

INDEX